A Genealogy of Public Security

There are many histories of the police as a law-enforcement institution, but no genealogy of the police as a form of power. This book provides a genealogy of modern police by tracing the evolution of "police science" and of police institutions in Europe, from the ancien régime to the early 19th century. Drawing on the theoretical path outlined by Michel Foucault at the crossroads between historical sociology, critical legal theory, and critical criminology, it shows how the development of police power was an integral part of the birth of the modern state's governmental rationalities and how police institutions were conceived as political technologies for the government and social disciplining of populations. Understanding modern police not as an institution at the service of the judiciary and the law, but as a complex political technology for governing the economic and social processes typical of modern capitalist societies, this book shows how the police have played an active role in actually shaping order, rather than merely preserving it.

Giuseppe Campesi is Professor of Law and Society in the Department of Political Sciences of the Aldo Moro University of Bari.

A Genealogy
of Public Security

The Theory and History
of Modern Police Powers

Giuseppe Campesi

Routledge
Taylor & Francis Group
a GlassHouse Book

First published 2016
by Routledge
2 Park Square, Milton Park, Abingdon, Oxon, OX14 4RN

and by Routledge
711 Third Avenue, New York, NY 10017

a GlassHouse book

Routledge is an imprint of the Taylor & Francis Group, an informa business

Originally titled *Genealogia della pubblica sicurezza: Teoria e storia del moderno dispositivo poliziesco* (Verona: Ombre Corte, 2009), translated by Filippo Valente.

British Library Cataloguing in Publication Data
A catalogue record for this book is available from the British Library

Library of Congress Cataloging-in-Publication Data

Names: Campesi, Giuseppe, author.
Title: A genealogy of public security : the theory and history of modern police powers / Giuseppe Campesi.
Other titles: Genealogia della pubblica sicurezza. English
Description: Abingdon, Oxon ; New York, NY : Routledge, 2016. | Includes bibliographical references and index.
Identifiers: LCCN 2015046987| ISBN 9781138897793 (hbk) | ISBN 9781315709055 (ebk)
Subjects: LCSH: Police—History. | Public safety—History.
Classification: LCC HV7909 .C3613 2016 | DDC 363.2/301—dc23
LC record available at http://lccn.loc.gov/2015046987

ISBN: 978-1-138-89779-3 (hbk)
ISBN: 978-1-31570-905-5 (ebk)

Typeset in Baskerville by
Keystroke, Station Road, Codsall, Wolverhampton

MIX
Paper from
responsible sources
FSC
www.fsc.org FSC® C013604

Printed and bound by CPI Group (UK) Ltd, Croydon, CR0 4YY

Contents

Introduction

A few words of caution will be necessary by way of introduction to this work. In order to guide the reader's expectations and avert misunderstandings that can easily arise, I will briefly comment on the object and method of the investigation we are about to embark on. The idea of public security featured in the title of this work seems to clearly locate the investigation within a specific field of study. And, indeed, if we want to outline the genesis and characteristics of police powers (a major institutional part of the repressive apparatus), we should expect to be working within the tradition in police studies that is broadly criminological and analyzes the history of penal and social-control institutions. But that is only partly true. Certainly, as the title suggests, the investigation is devoted to the police, its institutional evolution, and the nature of its powers. However, I do not take the view that a history and analysis of police powers should be confined strictly within the methodological framework and theoretical constructs of police studies. In fact, it appears to me that much of the literature in this area proceeds from a narrow notion of police that cannot account for the wide range and complexity of functions the police apparatus (what Foucault called *dispositif*) has fulfilled over the course of the history of modern Western societies.

In the contemporary legal and political lexicon, the term *police* seems to refer strictly to the function of *ensuring the public order by preventing and punishing crime*, and so to the idea of the police as a subservient institution, serving to implement the functions exercised by penal institutions. However, the history and functions of the doctrinal and institutional complex that has developed around the concept-term *police* cannot be adequately analyzed exclusively by reference to an apparatus merely entrusted with preventing and punishing crime. This narrow notion of police cannot account for the experience that has unfolded in the shadow of that concept-term in the modern history of Western societies, nor can it account for the full range and complexity of the functions the police apparatus has served in the arc of time that has led to the birth of modern police institutions. Moreover, it can be argued that the narrow notion of police powers just described fits in perfectly with the classic repressive-conservative image of the functions of law and the state typically advanced by the whole of liberal political and legal philosophy, which—by conceiving the police as having no more than a repressive function,

and the institutional experience of the *Polizeistaat* as one of arbitrary repression—
has wound up misconstruing the real meaning those two notions have had in
the social, political, and institutional history of modern Europe (see Schiera
2003, 2004a).

Further testifying to the hegemonic force of the liberal legal-philosophical
worldview is the huge influence it has had on its keenest critics, who have found
themselves essentially reprising the basic theoretical assumptions of that intellectual
tradition. Indeed, much of the literature criticizing the functions of the penal
system replicates the timeworn image of law and the state merely as instruments
of repression, and in this way it ends up embracing the very conception it sets out
to criticize. This is the classic conception of the minimal or night-watchman state
that Marx already criticized in his essay "On the Jewish Question":

> Security is the highest social concept of civil society, the concept of *police*,
> expressing the fact that the whole of society exists only in order to guarantee
> to each of its members the preservation of his person, his rights, and his
> property.
>
> (Marx [1843] 1975, 163)

What seems to have a controlling influence, even in the most critical visions, is a
theoretical paradigm that can be traced back to liberal natural law theory, which
sees the state as an artificial society created to offset the natural asocial inclinations
of individuals and to enable them to survive in peace and security. In light of the
division of the social body into a civil sphere and a political one, the police is seen
on this theory as an institution that is extraneous to civil society, brought in from
the outside to perform some para-judicial and repressive functions aimed at
protecting and preserving a given political and legal order. That is precisely what
the notion of security does in the legal-philosophical lexicon: It expresses the
purely protective and preservatory or conservational character of the functions
served by modern political institutions.

The present investigation, by contrast, will attempt a theoretical account in which
the exercise of public power is not reduced to the enforcement of legal precepts and
the protection of private claims. The effort, in essence, will be to show how the
police has assumed a crucial role not so much in keeping and protecting order as in
producing order, a role reflected in the verb and gerund forms the term still retains
in English and French: *policing* and *policer* (Neocleous 2000a, 2–3). So, instead of
studying the police as an institution at the service of the law and of judicial power
in driving back crime, we will consider how, in the long transition from the medieval
social structure to the modern capitalist society, the police has taken on and
consolidated the role of a political technology serving to govern the population.

* * *

Police power has traditionally been conceived as essentially bound up with the
exercise of violence and as a coercive force that cannot be fully constrained by law.

In the celebrated image offered by Walter Benjamin, for example, police power melds together two forms of violence, a law-*making* violence and a law-*preserving* one:

> It is lawmaking, for its characteristic function is not the promulgation of laws but the assertion of legal claims for any decree, and law-preserving, because it is at the disposal of these ends. The assertion that the ends of police violence are always identical or even connected to those of general law is entirely untrue. Rather, the "law" of the police really marks the point at which the state, whether from impotence or because of the immanent connections within any legal system, can no longer guarantee through the legal system the empirical ends that it desires at any price to attain. Therefore the police intervene "for security reasons" in countless cases where no clear legal situation exists, when they are not merely, without the slightest relation to legal ends, accompanying the citizen as a brutal encumbrance through a life regulated by ordinances, or simply supervising him. Unlike law, which acknowledges in the "decision" determined by place and time a metaphysical category that gives it a claim to critical evaluation, a consideration of the police institution encounters nothing essential at all. Its power is formless, like its nowhere tangible, all-pervasive, ghostly presence in the life of civilized states.
>
> (Benjamin 1921, 243)

The ambiguous position of the police as an institution straddling legislative and judicial power is such that its force manifests itself directly as pure violence. It presents a latent, and within certain limits unsolvable, illegitimacy if judged by reference to the paradigm of the rule of law, for it tends to escape the legitimate monopoly over the use of force, a monopoly which in that paradigm crystallizes in the form of law and judicial judgment. The police can thus be said to exist in an ambiguous grey area between two forms of legitimate violence, "in a borderland between legislation and adjudication, enjoying the discretion of the former and the power of the other, all the while being untethered from the limitations and the sources of legitimacy of the one and the other" (Ferrajoli 1990, 799; my translation).

That is a view with a long history behind it in police studies, which has traditionally conceived police power as a power that, within certain limits, always operates outside the bounds of the law. On this view, the police does not just represent the state's repressive force, for in deploying that force the police always operates in a borderline area at the periphery of law and justice. This makes the police a power always existing in a sort of permanent state of exception, quintessentially embodying sovereign power, under which individuals always risk being reduced to a *bare life* (Agamben 1995). As suggested, however, it is reductive, if not misleading, to equate police power with repressive force alone. The police is an institution that has historically performed functions of much greater complexity. These are functions that can be considered as having emerged in connection with the problem of governing the social forces unleashed by capitalism at the dawn of the industrial civilization. The modern police was among the main political technologies enlisted in the effort to govern the social consequences of what Marx (1867, 785), with thinly veiled irony, referred to as the process of producing "free labourers." We therefore need to set aside the traditional image of the police as an *ancillary* repressive institution designed to aid the functioning of penal systems; with that done, we can revisit the birth of the police apparatus as a chapter in the story of the birth of the political technologies entrusted with governing the social upheavals that erupted with the development of modern capitalist society. The evolution of the police apparatus can in this sense be said to coincide with the evolution of what Michel Foucault called *governmentality* (Foucault 2004, 2008).

As is known, Foucault analyzed the emergence of the modern *ratio gubernatoria* proceeding from his reflection on reason of state. According to his reconstruction, the modern art of government developed out of the disquisitions on the *art of ruling* contained in handbooks for princes. What started out as discourses centred on the prince and the need to preserve his sovereignty gradually turned into a body of knowledge on the state's military and economic resources and on the means for preserving and increasing those resources. Foucault's reconstruction is consistent with the findings of the best institutional and social histories devoted to tracing out the birth of the modern sciences of the state and the development of modern military-bureaucratic apparatuses as devices of social discipline.[1] Indeed, as Max Weber (1922, 1087) and Gerard Oestreich (1980, 217) had previously observed, it was a renewed need to police society—regulating and disciplining the social spaces hollowed out by the progressive unravelling of the economic structures at the foundation of the medieval social formation—that caused the public apparatus to expand, while also setting in motion the birth of the modern art of governing.

Foucault took this reconstruction one step further by describing the accompanying emergence of modern liberalism as a force capable of at once criticizing and refashioning the modern art of governing. In fact, between the close of the course titled "Sécurité, territoire, population" and the first lectures of the following course, titled "Naissance de la biopolitique," Foucault developed an original analysis of the reason of liberal government as a complex politico-economic discourse set in contrast to the sciences of the state under the ancien régime (see Senellart 2003, 138; Dean 1999, 50). Foucault described the emergence of a new form of political rationality that certainly did reject the old pretence to total discipline of the life process—the kind of control the ancien-régime art of government was

---

1 The concept of social discipline refers to an institutional phenomenon that since the dawn of the modern age has accompanied the vast process that Weber and Elias describe showing how personality and the ethical sphere discipline themselves and redefine their structure over time. So, as much as social discipline affects simple social relations, these effects derive from its action in the public institutional sphere, and in this sense it cannot be fully assimilated to the concept of social control typical of the social sciences. See Härter 1996, 635ff.; Beuer 1986, 62ff.; Oestreich 1982. On the concept of social control, see Melossi 1990.

designed to achieve—but without trying to snuff it out entirely. Whereas the idea of social discipline proceeded from the assumption that political institutions were capable of controlling and directing processes in social life, liberal politico-economic thought proceeded from the assumption that we have no more than a limited ability to understand and direct the process of social production and reproduction.

The *ratio gubernatoria* described by Foucauldian genealogy therefore is not a monolithic kind of reason geared toward a total control of the social, economic, and vital space. This is reflected in the characteristic way in which two different basic types of *governmentality* can be singled out in Foucault's thought. Whereas eudaemonistic political philosophy takes the view that the ancien-régime art of governing should be designed to dominate and model the *bios*—living matter conceived as the complex of concretely manipulable biological and economic processes—liberal political philosophy turns this relation on its head, embracing the thought that politics should instead *yield* to the *bios*, allowing itself to be guided by the latter's autonomous dynamics: by its laws and irreducible nature (Esposito 2004, 3ff.).

It is around these two models of governmentality that in the pages that follow I will be attempting to outline a genealogy of the police apparatus. We will thus chart a course that from the end of the Middle Ages to the dawn of the modern age will unpack the way the institutional space and political technologies have evolved into the modern art of government. We will follow, in particular, the history of the tensions and conflicts that have shaped the evolution of Western institutional forms, beginning with the so-called judicial state of medieval politico-legal doctrine, continuing through the birth of the administrative monarchy of the modern reason of government, and finally moving on to the *Rechtsstaat* of politico-economic liberalism.

This reconstruction will make it possible to illustrate how the police apparatus has evolved within the frame of the complex dialectic that has forged the modern political technologies. But this dialectic should not be reduced to a simple succession from one political technology to the next, as if the medieval judicial state—centred on legal reason and the problem of the legitimacy and legality of political sovereignty—was first displaced by the administrative state of monarchical absolutism, based on the disciplines and programmes for regulating and directing socioeconomic life, and then by the *Rechtsstaat*, based on the modern reason of liberal government. It is certainly true that in the succession of the different institutional configurations through which historians tend to describe the different phases in the evolution of the modern Western state, there seems to be a certain prevalence of certain political technologies over others, along with the corresponding discourses. But if we dig deeper, moving beyond an analysis of what lies on the surface, we will be able to clearly appreciate how these same technologies could not have been forged if not by constantly playing off against one another. It is in fact impossible to understand how modern legal reason and the question of the legitimacy of political sovereignty should have ripened unless we take into account their constant dialectic with the nascent modern reason of government, which revolves entirely around the problem of disciplining the socioeconomic social processes set in motion by the development of capitalism. As mentioned, the whole premise behind the liberal art of government and modern economic reason was that socioeconomic processes needed to be allowed to unfold according to their natural dynamics, so it would have been inconceivable for that philosophy to take hold without first injecting the new economic sciences into the modern reason of government, and then enabling legal reason to come to full maturity with its discourse on the individual's natural freedom.

This movement is well reflected in the evolution of the notion of police. Indeed, this notion seems to have developed according to a dynamic involving three phases that can be viewed as corresponding to three moments in which the different political technologies took on their essential traits. A first phase in the evolution of the notion of police can be roughly located in the era of the so-called judicial state, when the notion of policing seemed to have been conservational, its point being to protect and maintain the good ancient order, an order that was still at once social and legal. Then came a second phase, stretching roughly across the era of so-called administrative monarchy, when the notion of policing seemed to suggest a more active function, the idea being to bring about the kind of order suited to the early manifestations of mercantile and manufacural capitalism. Lastly, there came a third phase, with the development of the so-called *Rechtsstaat*, when the term *police* seemed to refer to a security function, the idea being to protect against the social risks connected with the evolutional dynamic of modern industrial capitalism (Neocleous 2000a, 5–6).

Even though the evolution just outlined can be described in analytical detail, modern police power will always exhibit the traits and functions that are typical of the basic political technologies. The police, in short, will always retain a more strictly ancillary function dependent on legal technology and aimed at preventing and punishing breaches of the public order, just as it will always retain a support function in propping up the operation of disciplinary mechanisms, considering that the latter will never be able to operate without relying on the distinctive ability of police power to identify and target individual sources of danger. Even so, the essential functions of government of the population that the police apparatus assumed in the modern age were prevalently the ones necessary to govern the most disruptive social consequences of capitalist development, especially as concerns the question of the popular classes' poverty and living conditions in the nascent industrial agglomerations. The modern public-security apparatus thus crystallized in the 19th century as a social-police apparatus tasked with governing the externalities of the development model adopted by Western societies. Our genealogy of public security seeks to reconstruct the way this political technology unfolded out of classical liberalism so as to manage within tolerable limits the social danger and risk associated with the birth of modern industrial civilization.

* * *

It will, however, be useful to clarify from the outset what is meant here by *genealogy*. As is known, the genealogical method was developed by Michel Foucault so as to move beyond some of the more cumbersome structuralist constructs that saddled the earlier work he had more specifically devoted to the archaeology of the human sciences. Indeed, as he progressively shifted his attention from the formal structure of scientific discourse to the analytic of power, he took a second look at epistemic structures—namely, the conditions subject to which truth can be predicated of the discourse that is being produced (Foucault 1966)—and came to appreciate that as much as these structures may have acted as powerful controls in disciplining the way reality is perceived, they were not so powerful as to make discourse in itself an element capable of *constituting* social reality (Gutting 1989; Dreyfus and Rabinow 1983). The latter is still shaped by *action*, being the outcome of the concrete individual and social practices engaged in by humans moved by interests and passions: Social reality results from an interweaving of *discursive* and *nondiscursive* elements alike. So in order to understand the actual dynamic of power relations within society, Foucault undertook to enact an epistemological revolution proper, and instead of focusing exclusively on the formal structures of scientific discourse itself, he brought in a new element, studying the concrete material conditions under which this discourse was produced, while also taking into account the interests these kinds of discourse might have served (see Hacking 1986, 33).

This shift from archaeology to genealogy thus came about through an important insight that enabled Foucault to understand and highlight how pure linguistic phenomena morph into actual social practices capable of conditioning real life and exerting power, and in so doing he observed that this transformation is not just linguistic but takes place in the concrete institutional environment in which such discourses are produced and operate, with the whole constellation of interests that coalesce within the same environment. Testifying to this shift was a parallel shift in Foucault's vocabulary, with the concept of *episteme* (which had been central to the archaeology of human sciences) being substantially replaced by that of *dispositif* (apparatus), which was introduced in the 1970s and would take on an increasingly central role in Foucault's oeuvre (Dreyfus and Rabinow 1983, 121; Revel 2002, 25). Foucault made a varied use of the term *dispositif*, progressively widening its semantic field to the point of essentially defining it as a *réseau* or network that can be set up to join heterogeneous elements "consisting of discourses, institutions, architectural forms, regulatory decisions, laws, administrative measures, scientific statements, philosophical, moral and philanthropic propositions" (Foucault 1980, 194; cf. Foucault 1977a, 299). This *dispositif* or "apparatus is thus always inscribed in a play of power, but it is also always linked to certain coordinates of knowledge which issue from it but, to an equal degree, condition it" (Foucault 1980, 196; cf. Foucault 1977a, 300).

Genealogy can thus be described as a method for investigating the genesis, functioning, and nature of power *dispositifs* understood as complex webs that connect institutional practices with the forms of rationality (the discourses) that in these practices find their condition of possibility. In the same vein, our own genealogy of public security will try to work out the intricate web between practices and discourses that has shaped the police apparatus. The investigation will thus stitch together the lines that would otherwise separate the history of law and of modern political institutions, the history of politico-legal culture, and the sociology of law and of social control *tout court*, trying to tease out, in particular, how the modern police apparatus emerged from the complex interplay between, on the one hand, the conflicts that broke out with the evolution of modern political institutions and, on the other, the parallel theoretical dialectic that developed between the concept of *iurisdictio* and that of *politia*. Indeed, the social and political clashes occasioned by the birth of the autocratic institutions of the modern administrative monarchy—all of which historians of law and of institutions are very well familiar with—find an exact counterpart in the theoretical dialectic between the two concepts. Condensed in the semantic field of the concept of *iurisdictio*—with which medieval theorists of public law summed up the idea of political dominion—was a conception of power that would increasingly come into conflict with the more openly voluntaristic conception of law and politics that modern political and legal thought would gradually crystallize in the notion of *politia*. Running parallel to the political and institutional clash, then, was a theoretical clash between different conceptions of power, law, and politics that we have to reconstruct if we are to understand how the modern police science originated and developed alongside the birth and development of police institutions.

This genealogical journey across the history of institutions and of modern politico-legal culture seems indispensable to a proper understanding of the genesis and exact nature of the police apparatus. Our genealogy of public security, however, will not confine itself to reproducing the classical paradigms of the history of politico-legal ideas, for in tracing out the trajectory of the semantic evolution of the notion of police, we will be making constant reference to the institutional structure and concrete social conflicts that have unfolded in the background and have given shape to determinate politico-legal institutions. On the other hand, the reference made to the social clashes and conflicts that have accompanied the birth and development of modern politico-legal institutions should not be taken to suggest that we are attempting a materialist reading of the history of the police apparatus, for the different paradigms and notions that have given theoretical shape to those clashes will not be presented as mere ideologies, or as outgrowths of something deeper and more substantial that is working away in the background, but rather as autonomous epistemic structures that are relevant in their own right, themselves the object of a struggle and of attempts at appropriation.

By working through this dialectic between *iurisdictio* as the matrix of modern legal rationality and *politia* as the matrix of modern governmental rationality—a dialectic at once theoretical and institutional—we will be able to explain how the police apparatus has evolved into the basic tool for governing the population and managing social dangerousness. More to the point, we will be able, on that basis, to describe the trajectory of the theoretical and institutional evolution the police has gone through from the beginning of the modern age to that of the liberal society of the late 18th and early 19th centuries, when the formal and functional features of the police apparatus definitely crystallized into modern texts on public security.

In unravelling this line of evolution, we will take into account what can rightly be considered the three main institutional experiences and most significant traditions of modern legal and political culture in the West: the English, the French, and the German. Because these three matrixes have greatly influenced institutional development in Europe and beyond, in the areas that have come under Western hegemony, they will provide our necessary point of departure as we set out to construct a genealogy of public security. But this genealogy will last only through the end of the 19th century, with the birth of modern police institutions and modern texts on public security, not only because that development brings to a close the centuries-old theoretico-institutional evolution of the modern police apparatus, but also, and especially, because it ushers in a new model that seems too close to the dominant one still in effect.

Chapter 1

Iurisdictio and *politia* in the genealogy of the modern state

To trace out the birth of the modern police apparatus is to trace out the evolution of the modern art of governing and the set of powers and functions that have annealed around the institutional complex that is usually referred to as the modern state. Our journey across the history of modern political institutions should not, however, be understood as yet another history of the state alongside the many already in existence. The attempt will rather be to reconstruct a genealogy of the political technologies that have been forged in the process leading to the birth of the modern state, with all the tensions, conflicts, and clashes that process has triggered. On the one hand, these conflicts have found their locus in specific institutional places and governmental practices, while, on the other, they have often found expression in different forms of rationality, in different discourses on political power. It is this intricate dialectic of practices and discourses that I shall try to untangle, and the genealogy of modern political technologies that will be attempted here will thus be aimed at showing how out of that dialectic the modern police apparatus can be shown to have emerged.

In this chapter I will describe the emergence of the political structures that frame the institutional space within which the modern art of governing and the modern police apparatus developed. This institutional space is taken as an indispensable condition for the possibility of the theoretical and practical development of police powers, a development we will turn to in the following chapters.

As is known, the modern state developed in constant tension with the originally horizontal structure of power in the medieval political organization. This process involved a long and painful search for new operational modules on which basis to respond to the challenges that modernity laid before the nascent national monarchies. This dialectical tension came about when monarchical absolutism sought to centralize power, moving it away from the estates of the old *Ständestaat* (polity of the estates), and what emerged from this tension was the distinction between two structures and sets of operational modules. On the one hand is the judicial structure, which governed legal relationships of equality and was thus based on the formal horizontal structure of private law and on the discourse of modern legal reason; on the other hand is the administrative structure, which governed the asymmetric relationship between public interests and private interests, and was thus based on the formal vertical structure of public law and on the discourse of modern administrative reason.

And yet it is only by looking at the past through the lens of our modern conceptual categories that we can formalize the different political technologies that have emerged over the centuries in the dichotomy between, on the one hand, adjudication and private law and, on the other, administration and public law. These two conceptual categories have developed out of the history of conflicts that has led to the birth of modern political institutions, and therefore, as has often been done, it seems methodologically inappropriate to use them as a basis on which to revisit the history of the modern state. I agree with António Manuel Hespanha, in short, that even in constructing a history of law and of institutions capable of engaging with the sociology of law and helping to make its conceptual constructs less abstract, we need to take an approach that comes in radically from the *outside*, in such a way as to revitalize the legal-institutional models and dogmatic categories that give shape to those constructs, in essence reading the history of cultural forms *in context*, looking at the practical contexts in which those forms are embedded (Hespanha 1999, 63). It therefore seems best, in constructing a genealogy like the one just described, to draw on a vocabulary and a set of concepts rooted in an era when the distinction between private and public law, on the one hand, and adjudication and administration, on the other, was still in the making. That distinction will accordingly be rendered by speaking instead of the dialectic between *iurisdictio* and *politia*.

1.1. The polity of estates *(Ständestaat)*

It may seem a bit presumptuous to pretend that in the span of a few pages we might be able to even summarily discuss the forms of political organization that have characterized an entire millennium—the one that, at the risk of great super-ficial oversimplification, is customarily referred to as the Middle Ages. Indeed, it would be difficult, if not impossible, to identify any single dominant trait (however broad it may be) common to the different ways of organizing society so as to satisfy the political needs that persisted throughout this long stretch of history. For it is a plurality of organizational forms that we find in the Middle Ages, and indeed they are closely reflected in the complex landscape of ideologies (Tabacco 2000) and political languages (Black 1992) through which those forms of organization received a theoretical account. Even so, and not discounting all of the caveats just made, I am going to try to identify a few traits that might be said to mark out the medieval political experience. As Paolo Grossi has suggested, these traits make that experience a unique phenomenon which it would be a mistake to read with antiquarian interest as a bygone classical past; nor—from the opposite, forward-looking perspective—can it be read as propelled by a drive to reach the accomplished modernity of the present day (Grossi 1995, 11ff.). That uniqueness can be appreciated despite the fact that the image of the Roman Empire conti-nued to cast its majestic shadow even over the Late Middle Ages, when the political forms of modernity, based on the model of constitutional monarchy, were already beginning to form on the horizon.

The most evident characteristic trait of the medieval experience is that of the political void (ibid., 41), mainly to be understood as an absence of any form or entity capable of exercising a totalizing hegemony over the activity of producing and defending the orders under which different communities were organized. Indeed, medieval society was set up as a patchwork of legal particularisms completely detached from the events that shaped political power, a universe in which the normative structure of communities existed and was reproduced independently of the *voluntas* of sovereign power. In this sense, it is fair to describe that social reality as one in which the state was absent from politics (ibid.). Indeed, throughout the long course of medieval history, political power was very weak, a characteristic not in any way offset by the lasting influence of imperial political ideology. This weakness can be said to have emptied power of any grounding in public law, reducing political obligation of a sort of semiprivate agreement.

As is known, when the Roman political and administrative apparatus fell apart and no one was ensuring safety along the roads any longer, the empire's economic life went into an inexorable decline. As commerce languished and the Germanic peoples flooded in, plundering their way across the territory, the regions of the empire began to set up a new kind of social and economic organization no longer dependent on the city and based on a regional division of labour and on trade, but rather located in the countryside and based on local autarky and on manufacturing for consumption. An increasing role in this socioeconomic landscape came to be played by *villae*, large tracts of land where the local *potentiores* began to set up their own organization, providing not only a natural economy for the subsistence of the *oikos* (the "household" or estate) but also instruments of private protection and defence that in the incipient power vacuum were already prefiguring the political function that would later be served by the landed nobility. This is the picture that characterized the European economy and agrarian landscape at least until the 11th century, and in this context we can see how the possession of land—the estate—could have taken on an unprecedented political relevance. The distinctive traits of public law that established *imperium* over individuals seemed inevitably blended with the traits of private law that established *dominium* over things (Bussi 2002, 141; Poggi 1999, 40–42; Bellomo 1994a, 120; Van Caenegem 1988, 178).

Political domination—reduced to a simulacrum of the ancient Roman concept of *imperium*—thus began to be based on the possession of small plots of land, economically self-sufficient and easy to defend militarily. The political importance of possession typical of this sociopolitical structure fashioned lordly power into a form for managing and exercising political power very similar to what Max Weber called patrimonial power (Weber 1922, 221). Indeed, as is clear, in this sociopolitical context the distinction between public and private law tended to disappear, whereas lordly power, or what through our modern legal categories we would call sovereignty, took on the same legal attributes as property, in that it could be sold, donated, traded, and so on (Bussi 2002, 147). Lordship (the authority a lord would exercise through his patrimonial control of a landed estate) thus came to form the basis of a private kind of power over a territory, and as it became increasingly important to defend the territory from without and control it from within—a function over which the lord gained exclusive dominion—that power tended to take on the traits of the power that public law establishes over persons. When such landed power completed its evolution, it thus became a full power exercised over *land and person* (*Lande und Leute*), a typical manifestation of the royalism that would characterize the entire medieval experience, in such a way that individuals and the arrangements relative to their personal status would be pulled within the orbit of the legal arrangements of the *res* they pertain to (Grossi 1995, 73).

The sociopolitical structure of the landed gentry stood as the element that for a long time had to be reckoned with in any attempt to construct political organizations having any broader reach. One attempt to somehow overcome the rigidly localistic dimension of political power came with the "feudal constitution" (Hintze 1929, 50), through which the typical elements of Germanic political culture were grafted onto the lordly sociopolitical structure (see Mitteis 1948; Ganshof 1947; Bellomo 1994a). Indeed, as is known, throughout the feudal period, the control and defence of realms was organized through that complex system of personal bonds of mutual fealty, help, and protection between lord and vassal that, according to Bloch's description, made each person *another man's man* (Bloch 1948). The entire organization of the politico-military apparatus was structured on the basis of these semiprivate agreements between so-called *meliores terrae*. This associative contractual element typical of the feudal political organization would have a profound influence on medieval political culture, conferring on it some markedly anti-absolutistic traits. Indeed, far from being able to exercise any arbitrary power, a landholding lord was "bound to strictly observe the legal obligations incumbent on him in virtue of the feudal contract and of custom, and so even if the obligation was unilaterally imposed" (Bussi 2002, 165).

In a society like that of the Early Middle Ages—where central political authority was remote, travel was difficult and risky, and socioeconomic life had fallen behind the natural subsistence economy of small village communities—the need to control and govern vast landholdings under constant threat of invasion and war made it necessary to break up and allot administrative functions into autonomous spheres of competence. If a financially weak political authority was to keep vast realms under control, it inevitably had to divide and share power, and the feudal political system was the practical embodiment of this inevitable "systematic decentralization of power" (Weber 1922, 182).[1] As is known, this decentralized

---

1 It is, after all, out of this institutional phenomenon that we get some of the most characteristic aspects of what Damaška (1986, 25ff.) has described as the "horizontal configuration of authority." Indeed, as Weber pointed out, all these forms through which administrative functions are parcelled

power structure, based on personal bonds and on obligations to render services in kind, could be superseded only with the 11th-century rebirth of urban life.

The communes—these new socioeconomic entities that fit in perfectly within the frame of feudal economic relations by basing their prosperity on the uneven balance between city and countryside—did not initially seem interested in upsetting the feudal political order. Indeed, the cities and the mercantile classes that lived in them claimed a sphere of autonomy and self-government very much like that based on the privileges and *immunitas* of the nobility. But then the cities made their entry into politics as collective *potentes* acting next to the individual *potentes* that held sway in the Early Middle Ages, and that development inevitably accelerated the institutional evolution of European political organizations. Indeed, on the one hand, it was precisely within the city *communitas* that there slowly re-emerged notions bearing the distinct imprint of public law, very much like those that during the Early Middle Ages seemed to have vanished from European politico-legal culture; and, on the other hand, it was the cities' experience in self-government that provided the impetus for the creation and institutionalization of the assemblies within which the realm's different interests and social components could try to find common ground.

However, the new political constitution that Europe settled into in the late medieval period did not mark a radical turning point relative to what, with Hintze, was previously described as the feudal constitution. Indeed, the so-called *Ständestaat* (polity of estates) tended to replace a political organization based on person-to-person relationships with a form of organization within which relations between the sovereign and the *meliores et majores terrae* are already set up as relations among different institutions (Bobbio 1995, 106). The *Ständestaat* was thus already moving toward "a greater stabilization of populations and a closer definition of civil, legal, and political arrangements in different regional contexts" (Ortu 2001, 54; my translation). Its development signalled the dawn of the modern Western state, which precisely from this period would inherit one of its most characteristic institutions: the late medieval representative assembly. Indeed, these assemblies originated as organs through which to coordinate or reconcile the constellations of interests advanced by different social groups, or as tools for arriving at an agreed or concerted management of affairs in which all in the community had a common interest, or at least the affairs pertaining to the privileged sphere of some of the corporate bodies that composed the nascent proto-national political entities (in a transition from body corporate to body politic). It is precisely in recognition of the increasingly significant political role taken on by these social formations (estates or *Stände*) that the political organization of the Late Middle Ages is commonly referred to as a *Ständestaat* (see Schiera 2004b).

out have a tendency to loosen the bureaucratic mechanism, and in particular to weaken hierarchical subordination (Weber 1922, 69), thus favouring a marked decentralization of power.

The politico-institutional evolution of late medieval Europe thus revolved around the institutionalization of representative assemblies,[2] an institutionalization in which the convergent interests of sovereigns and the estates had an equal part. This convergence can be appreciated by pointing out two processes that proceeded in parallel. On the one hand, the ancient feudal obligation to provide one's own sovereign with *consilium et auxilium* gradually morphed into an obligation to pay duties or tributes, and in this way the financial question became the main source of conflict between the estates and the sovereign. As is known, this conflict was constantly being stoked by military engagements through which the monarchies themselves are thought to have been forged, as sovereigns firmed up their territorial boundaries, and within each of these territories a sense of national identity or consciousness accordingly emerged (Vives 1971, 227). And it was precisely to meet the growing financial needs of the monarchies that sovereigns in that period began to set up institutions through which to *contract* for extraordinary tributes to be paid by the estates. On the other hand, these same estates were in the long run capable of transforming these assemblies into the main instrument through which to protect their own interests against the expanding royal powers and to continually assert the ancient principle that the sovereign should be *self-sustaining* (Ortu 2001, 69ff.). As the assemblies took on an increasingly institutionalized form, they stepped into a more generic role defending the traditions and customs of the realm in the politico-legal framework that, depending on the occasion, would crystallize into what Werner Näf (1971, 53) described as *Herrschaftsvertrage* (seigneurial contracts), providing an early example of a law proper contracted between a sovereign and his or her subjects.[3] It was precisely through these seigneurial contracts that it became possible to gain an initial foothold from which to proceed in firming up, in the European political and constitutional consciousness, the idea of a solid core of fundamental laws that, being associated with the very existence of the body politic, stood above the sovereign's will (Ortu 2001, 71).

The ancient obligation to respect semiprivate agreements among *meliores et majores terrae* became institutionalized into an obligation to respect the prerogatives of the estates, whose sphere of legal autonomy was secured by the so-called fundamental laws of the kingdom. Owing in part to this progressive institutionalization of the essential political structures of the estate system, that political obligation itself increasingly went through a process of "juridification" that started out under the feudal system. It is out of these institutional matrixes that came the tendency

2 These included the Spanish *cortes*, the French *états généraux* (estates general), the parliaments of the Commonwealth, and the Reichstags of German-speaking Europe—all institutions which came out of the same matrix but which history would consign to different fates.
3 Historical examples are the Magna Carta of 1215, in England; the Golden Bull of 1356, in the Holy Roman Empire; the Salic Law of 1327, in France; and the *Privilegio General de Aragón* of 1283, in Spain. For a broad statement, see Bussi 2002, 178, and Ortu 2001, 59.

of medieval politico-legal culture to present the phenomenon of political power under the guise of the legal relation between sovereign and subject, with all of the rights and duties entailed by that relation. This tendency is well reflected in the prominent position that legal knowledge came to hold as a source of concepts and theoretical tools through which to engage in political reflection itself (Fumagalli and Brocchieri 2000, 57). Indeed, as Paolo Grossi has observed, "the legal dimension was so strong an central as to represent the authentic constitution of the medieval universe, an ontic dimension that preceded and stood atop the political dimension" (Grossi 1995, 35; my translation).

1.2. *Iurisdictio*

We can expand now on the two convergent processes previously mentioned by noting that, on the one hand, the emergent political institutions enabled the state to fashion itself into a unitary power, and this drove society to coalesce around its sovereign, but that, on the other hand, in grounding the lordship of the prince in the country, the same institutions asserted and institutionalized the prince's own constitutional limits. What emerges from the Late Middle Ages, then, is the full ambiguity of the figure of the sovereign. For, on the one hand, with increasing insistence, this figure was being sacralized and placed at the centre of the political life of the nascent national monarchies,[4] while, on the other, the sovereign's power was being limited by the concrete institutional functioning of the estate system. That institutional structure, in short, nurtured the process through which the political themes that ran through the Germanic conception of regality came to full theoretical fruition (Nelson 1988, 226; cf. David 1954; Ullmann 1975; Tabacco 2000; Miller 1956). These themes would serve as the historico-ideological basis for all subsequent constitutional and proto-liberal thought, and so as the basic source for all those who, in the anti-absolutistic reaction of the 16th and 17th centuries, made their case by invoking the kingdom's ancient constitution.

What this tradition sought to do in going back to ancient constitutionalism was to hold up against the incipient revolution the principle that the sovereign holds the status of lord *inter pares*, meaning that, as much as the sovereign played a prominent role, the person holding that position was still bound to respect the prerogatives of the *meliores* and the customs and traditions of the realm. The authentic foundation of power lay in the agreement between the sovereign and the people, an agreement symbolized by the oath of coronation, and which solemnly committed the *princeps* to defend the kingdom and uphold its legal traditions. "For the *esse* of the crown is to exercise justice and judgment and to maintain the peace" (Henry de Bracton, quoted in McIlwain 2007, 70; cf. Grossi 1995, 94–95). Indeed,

---

4 See Shennan 1974, 19ff., and Ortu 2001, 84–85. An essential reading here is Bloch 1961.

from this political tradition comes the idea of the king as *enforcer of justice and keeper of the peace*: He was entrusted with keeping the realm secure and with the purely judicial function of guaranteeing that the customs of the realm be observed, along with the rights and privileges enjoyed by his subjects (Shennan 1974, 25ff.). This was a conception aptly summed up as early as CE 600 in a celebrated formula by Isidore of Seville (*Etymologiae*, IX, 3), who offered an etymology of the noun *rex* and of the corresponding verb *regere* as a contraction of the phrase *recte agendo*, speculating that this idea developed into one of the conceits of medieval legal-political literature—namely, the dichotomy between the just king and the tyrant (Chevalier 1979, 175). This view of political power wound up finding its way as well into the *spaecula principis* of the time (so-called mirrors for princes), where the principles worked out in parallel in legal and political thought were gradually concreted into the rhetorical form of the ideal model of the just king in whom those principles are reflected (Senellart 2005, 46).

On the basis of that conception of power, the whole phenomenon of dominion and political power ended up being summarized in the concept of *iurisdictio*, a concept that, unlike what we are led to think on the basis of our own conceptual categories, did not refer to a mere judicial function. Indeed, *iurisdictio* expressed the most complete theoretical synthesis of political power: It was

> the power of the person (natural or legal) who held a position of autonomy relative to others invested with power, and of superiority over all subjects; it was not this or that power [. . .] but rather a composite of powers that no one is afraid to condense into a single person.
>
> (Grossi 1995, 131; my translation)

This concept found an exact embodiment in the institutional context of the Late Middle Ages, where the modern distinctions between the different powers of the state could not yet be accommodated, considering that within the framework of the ancient estate system it was not yet possible to conceive of the idea of an administrative and a legislative power set in opposition to a judicial power (Costa 1969, 95ff.).

Indeed, on the one hand, what we now associate with the idea of administration in the constitutional structure of the estate system, or corporate state, inevitably consisted in a practice where, as Max Weber underscored, "all 'administration' is negotiation, bargaining, and contracting about 'privileges,' the content of which must then be fixed" (Weber 1922, 844) so as to ensure that those interests are protected, and this practice wound up taking on the peculiar traits of a distinctively judicial and litigious activity. If the entire semantic field of political power was covered by the idea of judicature, understood as the power to decide justice, there could be no room in medieval doctrine for any conceptual autonomy of an administrative power proper. In the still embryonic conceptual sphere of medieval public law, *administratio* was the concrete exercise of *iurisdictio* (the administration of justice): It amounted simply to the management of the complex of coercive tools needed to enforce justice (Napoli 2003, 145–46).[5]

On the other hand, legislative activity proper could barely be distinguished from the pronouncements the sovereign issued in a *judicial capacity*, for medieval politico-legal doctrine could not yet make room for any voluntaristic element (Grossi 1995, 142). *Iurisdictio* certainly did express the vertical, asymmetrical relation of political subjection, but this was subjection to a sovereign who was not yet in a position to *make* law *(condere legem)*. In medieval thought, "law was a translation of a pre-existing order, more so than the creation or production of new relations without precedent" (Costa 1969, 138; my translation). *Iurisdictio* is defined as *potestas iuris dicendi et aequitates statuendae*, or the power to state what the law is and to enact justice, where that enactment is never the *conditio* of a *lex* but is always the statement of a *ius* that is already established in the order of things, an order of which the prince, qua *servus aequitatis*, is always the supreme interpreter (ibid., 139). The idea of enactment, then, did not yet refer to

> a *created* norm but rather to one that is *found*, reflected in the order of the world, in the mirror of the world eminently held by the emperor. *Iurisdictio* is a symbolic place where norms do not *modify* what is given in reality but rather *acquire* it.
>
> (Ibid., 143; my translation)

In order for voluntaristic elements to definitely emerge in the modern age, they had to carve out a space within the semantic sphere of the concept of judicature (judicial power). And so legal-philosophical thought could not have come up with the modern *ab legibus soluta potestas* (the idea of a power unbounded by law), or simply *potestas*—encapsulating the whole meaning of political power—unless it worked within the semantic universe of the old idea of *iurisdictio*.

Indeed, for a long time the king's imperative power—the embryo from which would come both legislative and administrative power, respectively understood as

---

5 The Middle Ages, then, seem to have lost the ancient semantic richness of Roman *administratio*. Indeed, in classic Roman law, the term referred to the activity of "arranging and using tools, men, things, and places in such a way as to achieve a specific practical objective" (Napoli 2003, 144; my translation), and this objective was not merely to preserve *iurisdictio* (as it would be in the Middle Ages) but was rather that of growth and betterment. *Administratio* was a task typically assigned to a *curator*, someone entrusted with administering private patrimonies. In the public sphere, *administratio* was instead a task entrusted to a magistrate vested with powers *pro curatio rei publicae* (as Cicero names them in *De officiis*), meaning the power to administer the public patrimony or common good. The only part of Roman *administratio* so described that seems to have survived in the Middle Ages is the idea of mere *administratio bonorum*, a function discharged by officials who held political powers, who could avail themselves of counsellors and aides, but who would always act as any paterfamilias in the administration of a lord's *oikos*. So, when *administratio* was not the administration of justice, it was a mere *oeconomica* administration—that is, the administration of a lord's personal patrimony or fiefdom (see Brunner 1968; Frigo 1985).

the power to *generally* and *specifically* intervene in the sphere of previously consolidated legal relations—was configured in the manner of the exceptional power of pardon that expressed the exercise of a superior distributive justice: It thus emerged as the very sublimation of the ancient concept of the *iurisdictio* exercised by the sovereign as a supreme judge (Mannori and Sordi 2001, 43ff.). The non-distinction between the powers of the state was, after all, well reflected in the central administration itself, considering the overlap between the functions of its institutional organs—namely, the *curia regis* and the representative assemblies—and the fact that there was no way to tell what the legal nature of their pronouncements was, or whether these were rulings or statutes, statements of law or modifications of law. At some point the sovereign's interventions began to present themselves as explicit changes introduced into the inherited legal framework, but for a long time they did so for the most part to create new procedures and means of judicial protection: They started out from the original *curia regis*, and on that basis they created an apparatus for the administration of justice.[6]

A decisive turn was taken between the 15th and 16th centuries as the nascent constitutional monarchies pressed forward with the centralization and institutionalization of judicial organs. Such institutionalization inevitably wound up formalizing and rationalizing legal materials, in a process that in turn drove a further development of legal systems and led to the birth of modern legal reason itself.[7] But since these developments took place at different times, they engendered a variety of "raw" intellectual materials drawing on which the secular authorities could proceed in fashioning legal systems in distinctive ways. It is at this historical crossroads that Western legal systems developed into their two main strands—namely, the common law and civil law systems—and even though they did take divergent paths proceeding from radically different cultural premises, they both sprang out of a common situation and both tended to push for greater and greater conceptual institutionalization and systematization.[8]

6 It was indeed by extending and developing the judicative mechanisms set up within an apparatus answerable to the crown that European sovereigns would, slowly but surely, begin to eat away at particularisms and at the residual powers of local town and seigneurial administrations, bringing about an initial harmonization of the legal and institutional framework within their realms. It is to that end that the fledgling monarchies devoted most of their rule-making: They mostly sought to reform *procedure* and the *legal order*, rather than to change the substantive law.

7 The process toward the rationalization of law is in fact closely bound up with the development of an apparatus of judicial administration, and in particular with the kinds of legal practitioners and culture produced by such an apparatus. In fact, as Max Weber (1922, 775) has observed, "formally elaborated law constituting a complex of maxims consciously applied in decisions has never come into existence without the decisive cooperation of trained specialists." However, there are any number of ways to rationalize law and develop its formal qualities, and the history of common law and civil law systems is indeed the history of two such ways. On the birth of Western legal tradition and reason, see Berman 1983, Stein 1984, and Van Caenegem 1987.

8 Indeed, although it is true that "right through the early Middle Ages and up to the mid-twelfth century English and Continental law belonged recognisably to one legal family, Germanic and

We should bear in mind, however, that the process of creating stable judicial organs and thus harmonizing the legal framework took a long time. Indeed, if we tried to "rewind" the development of modern national systems capable of reaching into every sphere of social life within a set territorial boundary, we might be able make out something that fits that description at the dawn of the modern age, but it would be vain to attempt to push that search any further back in time. Indeed, it was characteristic of the medieval legal order that within a single social space it accommodated distinct normative complexes administered by different judicial organs, all equally legitimate, and they overlapped on the basis of jurisdictional criteria that often became a subject of controversy.[9] It was precisely by setting up judicial institutions subject to monarchical control that the sovereigns of the emerging monarchies could begin to harmonize legal systems on a national basis. This led to the development of modern legal systems, on either side of the Channel, as "the common law of the king and of the king's courts gradually replaced most of the disparate features of tribal, local, and regional law within the territory" (Berman 1983, 406), and a crucial role in this process was indeed played by the creation of a relatively centralized apparatus for the administration of justice.

At the same time, however, because these high courts held the technico-legal knowledge needed to run the apparatus set up to administer justice, they also controlled the symbolic instruments for the legitimation of power. They always pretended to hold the sovereign to his role as *custodian* of the legal traditions, all the while carving out a hegemonic role for themselves in interpreting those traditions. In this sense, the whole of legal culture acted as an anti-absolutistic force in Europe, often to the point of neutralizing the most embarrassingly absolutistic

feudal in substance and procedure" (Van Caenegem 1987, 114), the rediscovery of the Roman legal tradition will, as is known, drive a deep wedge between the two legal cultures. On the one hand, in England the common law developed by gradually systematizing the ancient patchwork of local legal customs and traditions (see Pollock and Maitland 1898, Plucknett 1956, Van Caenegem 1973), while, on the other, on the Continent the complex of customs prevailing in the different territories would be remodelled through the predominant influence of the neo-Roman law developed on a European scale by jurists at the universities. The literature on this *ius commune* is boundless, but two useful introductions are Calasso 1951 and Bellomo 1994b.

9   There were in fact several legal spheres that vied for hegemony within the legal systems of the nascent monarchies. First, there was the sphere of canon law, administered across Europe under ecclesiastic jurisdiction. Second, there were feudal law and the *lex mercatoria* (or law merchant), both administered under special jurisdictions that, like the ecclesiastic institutions, covered the whole of Europe. And, lastly, below these jurisdictional spheres there existed jurisdictions with special privileges protecting the spheres of autonomy and self-government the sovereigns were bound to respect. These privileges were of two kinds: On the one hand were the political powers enjoyed by the landed nobility, who held the land under a feudal title that would typically carry the right to exercise jurisdiction within the fief or manor, and on the other were the charters and privileges granted by the sovereigns to the cities, which were comparable to the fiefdom in their ability to exercise autonomy and self-government. In general, see Berman 1983, 271ff.; Grossi, 1995, 223ff.; Hespanha 1999, 115ff.

passages of Justinian's *Corpus Iuris Civilis* (see Grossi 1995, 143–44; Pennington 1988, 426; 1993, 121; Cortese 1962, 152). The sovereign, in short, was never able to keep "his" judges, and much less "his" law, under control, at least not until the age of full modernity.

1.3. *Politia*

In the transition from the Late Middle Ages to the modern age, a series of changes began to build up that eventuated in what some historians consider to be a general crisis in Europe (Aston 1965). The development of mercantile capitalism disrupted the socioeconomic order and intensified the dynastic powers' struggle for hegemony on the Continent, on top of which came the discovery of new trade routes, with the attendant rivalry for control of those routes, as well as the religious wars and conflicts that often would act as flashpoints for deeper conflicts simmering in the background. This whole complex of factors plunged the estate system into a structural crisis that pitted its two constitutional components against each other in a show of strength that would deeply alter the essential makeup of that system. What also fuelled this breakup of the established political order was a process through which powers and prerogatives came to be concentrated in the figure of the prince. This process had already been underway in the late medieval period and peaked in the late 16th century, but along the way it resolved itself into the virtually permanent state of war and revolt that afflicted the whole of Europe from the late 12th to early 13th century.[10]

The social and political situation the main European powers came to find themselves in by virtue of the power politics they had set in motion caused the ancient revenue-raising system to irremediably fall into crisis, thus providing sovereigns with a pretext to exact exceptional tributes beyond the bounds of traditional limits (see Hartung and Mousnier 1955). Changes in the art and technology of war took place such that armies and fleets could be raised and maintained only by princes with free access to the country's economic resources, so it became increasingly clear that no sovereign aspiring to any position of prominence on the international chessboard could make much headway relying on his own resources alone. Modern warfare created fiscal needs that could no longer be met by the tributes contracted between the sovereign and the estates. This made the question of taxes the avenue through which the state-making process moved forward, subordinating all matters of internal politics to the need to bring in revenues (Mannori and Sordi 2001, 78; cf. Ardant 1975, 195).

---

10 This period of unrest took different forms at different times: It found an early expression in the religious wars in France; at later stages it took the form of the religious conflicts that set in motion the continent-wide conflict that spelled the end of the imperial institution; on other occasions it erupted in sudden bursts, as in the case of the revolutionary outbreaks of the early modern age; on other occasions still it debouched into a widespread and ongoing revolt, like the one that France found itself grappling with in its absolutist endeavours.

This need to increase the nation's revenue-raising capacity gave rise to policies, enacted at different times, that would have a deep social impact throughout the European continent. It was precisely in this regard that the ancient institutions for the administration of justice proved inadequate for the purpose, prompting the great powers of the time to seek new institutional arrangements. More to the point, the need to augment the financial resources the princes had been able to count on gave way to repeated attempts to reform the tax system, by creating revenue streams capable of securing larger and more stable sources of income (Bussi 2002, 223). This in turn put a strain on the dualistic structure of the estate system, a tension that was worked out in a process through which the central organs of government grew increasingly powerful, and in a sense autocratic, while the privileged estates found themselves being somewhat removed from the centre of power (Ortu 2001, 97).

In the Renaissance, as the dynasties and the principle of hereditary succession stabilized, the status of the sovereign became increasingly important, to the point where it would confer prestige on a political institution that by that time had gained continuity, with an ability to carry on independently of the monarch's physical survival.[11] The idea of the temporal stability of power had already set in motion the cultural process that gave rise to the impersonal concept of political sovereignty and in that way would make it possible to move past the understanding of power as embodied in a person and his or her patrimony. The same process also helped to limn in the popular mind a referent for the principle of *auctoritas* that the whole of absolutistic political doctrine went about setting on a new theoretical foundation (Shennan 1974, 93–116, 130–37; see, generally, Schiera 2004c and Anderson 1974).

In parallel, the need to increase the nation's revenue-raising capacity made it necessary to radically change the functions the political authorities claimed, giving institutions an unprecedented capacity to intervene in the nation's socioeconomic life. Authorities began to appreciate as well how *politically* important it was to have a growing national economy, and they accordingly sought to foster capitalistic development, however much with some wavering. So it was that sovereigns, in an effort to increase their ability to politically shape the nation's economic life, took the mercantile capitalism of the time under their stewardship, on the one hand protecting its economic interests,[12] and on the other taking over the levers of the nascent political economy by merging the self-governing bodies (such as corporations, guilds, and merchants' courts) with the law merchant *(lex mercatoria)* and

---

11 The essential source here is Kantorowicz 1957. See also Ortu 2001, 84–85.
12 This protection was afforded both from without and from within, for sovereigns would militarily secure the monopolized trade routes, while at the same time they would bring to bear their increasing capacity to both ensure a safe and uniform legal space for commercial dealings and govern the social bouleversement brought about by economic transformation. See Poggi 1999, 98–99; Dobb 1946, 117ff.; Braudel 1979a, 41ff.

commercial customs and trade usages that had been built up over the course of the Late Middle Ages.

The internationalism of the medieval age gave way to power politics, and among the fundamental tools the nascent national states deployed to compete was economic policy. On the basis of the cardinal principle that the power of a state is measured by the wealth of its subjects and the vibrancy of its economic activity, the economy was placed at the service of the state's institutions and of political power, and the state, conversely, placed itself at the service of the economy. This relation of mutual support found its perfect expression in the doctrine of mercantilism, which championed the state's absolutism in combination with private enterprise (Maffey 2004; cf. in general Schumpeter 1954, 155ff.; Braudel 1979b, 483ff.; Heckscher 1955; De Maddalena 1980; Spector 2003). This idea came into its own between the 16th and 17th centuries, under the politico-economic principle that the basis of the state's power lay precisely in the material wellbeing of its subjects.

The evolution of the political and institutional makeup, on the one hand, and of society and the economy, on the other, thus led political authority to take on an increasingly heavy and diverse load of tasks, functions, and prerogatives that were becoming increasingly difficult to fit within the classic categories of the medieval political and legal world. Indeed, precisely through the development just described, these categories came under a strong dialectical force that was injecting tension into them by virtue of the complex intellectual work that was progressively emptying out the older notion of *iurisdictio* while adding substance to a more openly voluntaristic and absolutistic notion of law and politics. Indeed, the royal magistrates no longer confined themselves to administering justice. Their role was progressively changing from that of merely presiding over an existing legal system to that of enacting a plan for governing society in view of certain objectives invested with public significance (Mannori and Sordi 2001, 53). They found themselves being entrusted with a whole range of new prerogatives which came into being with the developing capitalist modernity of the Western world, and which the public law of the Continental areas less constrained by the lexicon of Roman law was beginning to frame within the concept of *politia* (ibid.; cf. Oestreich 1971, 186–87; Heidenhamer 1986, 10).

Next to the ancient idea of *iurisdictio*, and increasingly in contraposition to it, there emerged the newer idea of *politia* as the sphere where sovereign political power is exercised. The ancient figure of the *king as dispenser of justice* could no longer be squared with a political reality increasingly shaped by the sovereign's repeated interference in social life, so much so that *politia* was by now stably relying on the prince as administrator and lawgiver (Stolleis 1998a, 557–58). The term can be traced back etymologically to the Aristotelian notion of *politeia* as rendered in the circa 1260 Latin translation of Aristotle's *Politics* by the Flemish scholar Guillaume de Moerbecke, and it would come into wide use throughout the modern age. This diffusion can be appreciated by considering how long the non-modern meaning of *politia* lasted (Mozzarelli 1988, 8), a process through which it entered the common stock of several languages (witness *policy*, *police*, and *Policey*), acting throughout the modern age as a counterpoise to the utter weakness of the other complex of nouns derived from the Greek *politeia* (*politia* in Latin)— namely, *politics*, *politique*, and *Politik*.

Although, as we will see, the idea of *politia* first came into being in response to the need to govern the mercantile centres, it was the grand project to socially discipline the modern state that developed its full practical and theoretical potential. Indeed, the scale of this project and the challenges it posed were such that the independent groups within the cities were no longer able to respond, so the project was initially entrusted to the old royal administration of justice, in whose remit, next to the older judicial activity aimed at settling *private* interests, there grew an activity aimed at satisfying collective *public* interests (Mannori and Sordi 2001, 55). In fact, it seemed only natural at first that, *ex consequentia eius iurisdictionis*, the ancient structure for the administration of justice should be invested with a broad regulatory power in those areas where no adequate response could be had by relying on the realm's ancient traditions, which had been forged to govern social relations in a mostly rural civilization, and which were therefore ill-equipped to deal with the modern challenges of a later age. This power was expressed in the frequent issuing of *edicts*, *bylaws*, and *arrêts de règlement* to more closely regulate areas which had recently been placed within the remit of the ancient magistracies, and even though a deep functional distinction had already set this power clearly apart from the ancient competence to issue judicial rulings, legal scholars were still finding it difficult to distinguish the two forms of authority.

Still, it was not long before structural tensions would crop up between the new functions the public authorities were taking on and the institutional makeup of the estate system. No sooner did the number of functions turned over to public bodies begin to multiply than it became apparent that the ancient apparatus of royal administration was not up to the task. Indeed, that apparatus was forged in a judicial culture devoted to the preservation of a pre-existing sociopolitical order, so it was not cut out to contribute to the programme the central authorities were developing to intervene in the socioeconomic life of the population. As much as the ancient prosecutorial nature of the procedural models of classic judicial administration gradually whittled down, such that procedures could to some extent be brought under the rules of public law,[13] some structural constraints remained in place, preventing the ancient administrative apparatus from working effectively as a channel through which to implement the sovereign's policies. In the first place, its operational modules were comparatively slow and costly:

---

13 Certainly, this process was more pronounced on the Continent—where *ex officio* inquisitorial procedure exerted a more direct and persistent influence—than it was in England, where the accusatorial tradition was more entrenched, such that only the mechanism for *initiating* a procedure, rather than the entire judicial apparatus, could be bent to the rules of public law. See, in general, Stein 1984.

They could be triggered only in response to a prior violation of law and so could not be used to prevent such violations. In the second place, and more importantly, there was the fact that, as we have seen, the whole apparatus for the administration of justice had been built up over the centuries to protect an existing legal order, and it tended to serve that function even against the sovereign's attempts at reform (ibid., 77).

So, as the central power increasingly took on new administrative functions, it led to the creation of new authoritative organs, forcing sovereigns to set up special authorities tasked with overseeing the public interest in matters increasingly detached from the jurisdiction of the ancient judicial magistracies. It is to the development of these special authorities that historiography ascribes the emergence of modern bureaucracy and administrative power (Mousnier 1972, 107ff.; Hintze 1929, 1ff.). Indeed, these initially came into being as temporary organs whose tasks would typically be confined to overseeing, supporting, and, if need be, carrying out the activities ordinarily entrusted to the ancient apparatus for the administration of justice. They were thus initially conceived to make ordinary judicial administration more efficient, especially relative to financial administration. In fact, it was not their creation that triggered conflicts with the ancient administration, but their gradual development into a stable apparatus under the sovereign's direct control (Ortu 2001, 99ff.).

Gradually, through the practice of issuing edicts (*ordonnances, Ordnungen,* proclamations) the princes managed to expand the subject-matter jurisdiction of the new special authorities, and thus their own rule-making power. As these efforts to more autocratically administer society advanced in a very concrete and *practical* way, so did the idea of a legislative power proper formulated on a *theoretical* level by the doctrine of absolutism. And such was the development of this idea that it wound up changing the very concept of law, which ceased to be conceived as the bundle of privileges and prerogatives recognized by and immune from sovereign enactment, and came to be regarded as the expression of a supreme will or *voluntas*. It was a two-pronged result that was set in motion by the development of these new magistracies and *police* legislation, for, on the one hand, this development lit the fuse to the powder keg that was all the tensions which had been building up within the political structure of the corporate state (setting off the profound institutional revolution from which would emerge the institutions of the modern state), while, on the other, it triggered the dialectic between the ancient *iurisdictio* and the modern *politia* from which would issue the modern police apparatus.

Before we can delve analytically into the nature of the modern police apparatus, we need to have an understanding, at least in outline, of the process that led to the genesis of modern politico-institutional arrangements in various parts of Europe. This is an indispensable premise, considering that, as we will see, it is this development that set into place the basic conditions for the existence of modern police. But the political institutions this development gave rise to were not uniform across Europe. Indeed, as much as it was a common set of problems that precipitated the crisis of the *Ständestaat*, the solutions devised in response to that crisis on the two sides of the Channel were radically different. This can be explained by pointing to the different socioeconomic conditions and degrees of capitalistic development in England and on the Continent: On the one hand, where the capitalist economy grew strong and developed on its own, the moderate absolutism that had sustained its early development was pushed more vigorously into a transition toward constitutional monarchy; on the other hand, where capitalism was moving more slowly, the same moderate absolutism morphed into the administrative monarchy that would serve as the seedbed for the birth of national economies capable of competing on a global scale.

1.3.1. The constitutional monarchy in England

At the dawn of the 16th century, the English political framework closely modelled the features of the limited monarchy of the late medieval period, for its central administration was based on the dualism between the sovereign and Parliament, while locally it was built on the centralized structure for the administration of justice. Since the age of the Norman conquest, this centralized structure managed to quash the autonomy of the nobles and the cities by superimposing on their courts an apparatus of royal judges ready to offer their judicial services in areas of particular interest to the Crown (Berman 1983, 450), and by the end of the 12th century the system of royal justice had thus essentially settled into a definite form. This system was based on the work done by two sorts of courts: On the one hand were the permanent central courts—namely, the Exchequer, the Court of Common Pleas, and the King's Bench—which developed through a process that increasingly specialized the functions of the *curia regis*; on the other were the so-called Courts of Assizes, entrusted with administering justice and important affairs at the *local* level, and staffed by itinerant professional judges called justices of the peace, who were secular functionaries the monarchy increasingly recruited from the lesser nobility of the countryside to engage them in the management of power (see, generally, Lyon 1960).

Reflected in this structure, as noted, is the classic organization of the estate system, and even England began to see the socioeconomic change that at the dawn of the modern age would set off a deep institutional change across the whole of Europe. Indeed, even in Tudor England monarchical power grew stronger, so much so that historians often speak of Tudor despotism to describe the period that began in the 16th century. It is true that, as Holdsworth observes, "England in the sixteenth century exhibits clearly enough two of the principal features of the continental scheme of government—the growth of the power of the king and his Council, and the beginning of a system of administrative law" (Holdsworth 1924, vol. 4, p. 60). However, despite the development of an aggressively interventionist monarchy, England's ancient constitution did not go through any major transformation. Indeed, as much as the Tudor reform went *against* Parliament, it was for the most part enacted *through* it (Adams 1963, 243; Taswell-Langmead 1960, 247; Polito 2005, 34). Certainly, the assembly was often at the mercy of the

Crown itself, the source of most political initiatives, which, as Holdsworth observes, were introduced under the Crown's supervision. It was, however, Parliament's close connection to the Crown that enabled it to survive, taking hold as one of the central institutions of the modern state (Holdsworth 1924, vol. 4, p. 88). The Tudors did in fact enact their reformist policies by relying on the unconditional support of the new aristocracy, which was drawn from those members of the great nobility of old who survived the decimation of the civil strife, as well as from the lesser nobility of the countryside, and which was being attracted to the court and increasingly involved in the activity of government. This was an aristocracy that, independently of its titles of nobility, shared governmental interests and responsibilities with royalty, and it was insistently being called on to participate in government. This shared experience solidified its membership as part of a social and political elite that became the basis of consent for the Crown (MacCaffrey 1965; Taswell-Langmead 1960, 248–49).

The Tudor monarchy therefore did not entail an immediate disbandment of England's 15th-century constitutional framework. Indeed, the most important reforms and the most robust interventions in socioeconomic life were by and large effected by *parliamentary* policy (Elton 1973, 68; von Friedeburg 1996, 582), and these policies generally gained the support of the socioeconomic elites represented in Parliament. In fact, the whole of the 16th century saw a large body of statutory enactments designed to respond to the needs arising out of a rapidly changing economy, and it was no longer possible to meet these needs by relying on the common law, which had been conceived in a stagnant reality stuck in the meshes of a subsistence economy. In a sense, there was no other option but to turn to Parliament and to statutory instruments if the radical reforms being introduced were to have any legitimacy, so much so that the task of applying the whole gamut of provisions dealing with social and economic matters fell to the administration of justice, and in particular to the justices of the peace. As a result of Parliament's assent—or, rather, of the substantial overlap between the Crown's interests and those of the new social and economic elites—the ancient legal framework fixed in the principles of the common law could be changed without bringing about an outright constitutional crisis. The ancient constitutional balance remained intact, at least initially, for in practice it continued to reflect the division between, on the one hand, matters to be treated by the sovereign in concert with other institutional organs and, on the other, *arcana imperii*, the so-called high policy within the exclusive competence of the Privy Council.[14]

---

14 Tanner 1951, 213. The development of the *curia regis* can be traced back to the 1487 establishment of the Star Chamber, and, contrary to what was thought at the time the chamber was abolished in 1641, even the chamber was not a violation of the ancient institutional order but was rather an office created *within* the Privy Council to handle matters of internal security, such as rebellion, sedition, and treason (ibid., 252ff.).

As much as the balance of the ancient constitution was never explicitly upset, the English monarchy did in the 16th century drift toward a "practical absolutism" (Adams 1963, 242) that made administration more autocratic by slowly expanding the scope of royal power (Ritter 1974, 80). Where the central organs of government were concerned, this development strained the relation between Parliament and the Privy Council. This strained relation can perhaps be explained by noting that as the reform expanded, Parliament became increasingly unwilling to serve in a subservient role as a mere okayer of the Crown's policies, often forcing monarchs to replace the assembly by wide recourse to regulations. Indeed, the Council retained the general power to issue proclamations and ordinances, which ranked below the common law administered by the royal courts and the statutes enacted by Parliament, and which would typically remain in effect only as long the sovereign who issued them held power (Holdsworth 1924, vol. 4, p. 100; Polito 2005, 36). Recourse to these kinds of provisions increased as Parliament's resistance made statutes an unsuitable instrument for governing England's social and economic life in the 16th and 17th centuries. And this expansion was in a sense validated by the 1539 act under which Parliament's statutes were made equivalent to the king's ordinances "concerning the advancement of the commonwealth of his realm and the good quiet of his people."[15] However, as much as this rule was set by an act of Parliament, the Tudor monarchs were financially strapped and their local administration was still scarcely bureaucratized, so it was only a limited use that they could make of that regulatory power, and they found themselves having to turn to Parliament, especially for the most innovative reforms in economic and social policy (von Friedeburg 1996, 583; Adams 1963, 253; Elton 1974a, 287). The regulatory power the Council was beginning to construct was instead used to carry out the political and economic policy set by the Parliament itself, especially to regulate detailed matters and force recalcitrant local powers to implement reforms.

It was precisely the need to effectively implement the increasingly numerous statutes and proclamations on social and economic policy that set administration on a path of greater autocracy. Indeed, the judges who ran the ancient judicial apparatus soon revealed themselves to be inadequate to meet the need for an effective interventionist policy by which to address the challenges posed by the capitalist development of English economic life. In addressing these problems, they used the methods they were familiar with, and administration was therefore carried out mainly by recourse to "judicial" instruments (Fisher and Lundgreen 1975, 478).

---

15 This act—giving the king's proclamations the force of law—was passed under Henry VIII and upheld throughout the 16th century. And although it did tilt the constitutional balance of the English monarchy, it faced many hurdles before passing. In fact, it significantly reduced the scope of the king's rule-making power, providing in particular that the ordinances issued by the King's Council could not contradict the common law or the statutes, and in this way it established a sort of hierarchy among the sources of law (see Holdsworth 1924, vol. 4, p. 102; Taswell-Langmead 1960, 562–63; Elton 1974b, 305).

Indeed, the Crown could scarcely exert any influence on its own judicial apparatus, which over the centuries had claimed a remarkable degree of independence.
Its judges did not see themselves as mere agents of the Crown but stuck to their
role as defenders of the laws and customs of the kingdom even in defiance of the
sovereign's will, often finding the reform provisions illegitimate (Fisher and
Lundgreen 1975, 478; von Friedeburg 1996, 588). It was indeed in this period, and
in connection with these needs, that a trend could be observed toward an expanding competence of the Privy Council and of the royal *justice retenue* (see Elton
1953).[16] This extended the Council's jurisdiction well beyond the scope of high
policy, and in particular it led to a deeper encroachment of so-called prerogative
courts on subject matter otherwise reserved to the judicial apparatus.[17] This might
sometimes happen by subjecting judicial decisions to review, other times by a
broad exercise of the justice retained by the king.

What held back the Tudors' reform policies, however, was in no small part the
reforms' slow and ineffective application at the local level. Local government, as
we know, depended on the royal organs of judicial administration, and in particular
on the justices of the peace. This framework was already sufficiently centralized,
so the sovereign could reasonably rely on it: "Though its units still retained much
of the mediaeval independence and initiative, though it was still a system of self-
government, it could be controlled, and, with some changes and additions, used
by the modern state" (Holdsworth 1924, vol. 4, p. 72). In taking on a central role
in local government, the justices had in essence turned to the legal models typical
of the ancient seigneurial and municipal courts, in such a way as to stably establish
the ancient medieval procedure based on disputative models and the jury (ibid.,
136). In the 16th century, however, the vast statutory enactments concerned with
social and political economic policy expanded the more strictly administrative
functions entrusted to the justices, and this office, along with its mode of operation,
therefore developed accordingly (ibid., 137).

Much of the local administrators' activity continued to be carried out in
accordance with the judicial forms set up by the common law and within the frame
of the quarter sessions. Here the justices of the peace followed all the formalities
typical of English common law procedure, with the hearing of witnesses and with

---

16 The notion of *justice retenue* ("justice retained," or reserved justice) refers to the king's residuary
prerogative of justice. It comes from the French politico-institutional tradition and is meant here to
sum up the process involving the creation of extraordinary magistracies that answer to the Crown
while gutting independent judicial organs, a process that goes hand in hand with the modern state's
shift toward absolutism.

17 The two organs through which jurisdiction was expanded were the Council Table, with competence
over matters more specifically tied to social and economic policy, and the Star Chamber, with
competence over the state's internal security, although a certain overlap must be noted between
these two areas of subject-matter jurisdiction, considering that in politically uneventful periods
the kingdom's ordinary internal affairs came within the purview of the Council Table as well
(see Tanner 1951, 250ff.; Polito 2005, 32).

juries entrusted with issuing verdicts (ibid., 142ff.). As the matters of public law entrusted to the justices took on an increasingly important role through the various statutes and ordinances that were being enacted, that typically adversarial procedure came to be particularly time-consuming and resource-heavy, and so it was that the justices of the peace started to gain greater and greater powers of independent initiative in the regular sessions. But the conferral of greater powers on the justices formed the basis of a much more important institutional development—namely, the birth of a complex of activities to be undertaken *out of session*. These activities were not subject to any fixed or particularly formal procedure, so much so that the assignment of work to the justices was handled by the King's Council by means of proclamations. Over time, however, the judges' work became organized. This process is described in Lambarde's classic treatise on the justices, where the distinction is drawn between activities the justices could carry out individually without any particular formality (Lambarde 1581, 80–190) and activities that instead had to be carried out by at least two justices sitting in what were beginning to be called petty sessions (ibid., 227–83). These special sessions also developed through the orders of the King's Council and through the distinction between the business the justices undertook in response to charges brought by a plaintiff and the business taken up by initiative of the justices themselves. This development was drawing a dividing line between strictly judicial activities and the broadly administrative activity assigned to the local courts (Holdsworth 1924, vol. 4, p. 148).

The real problem, then, lay elsewhere, in the need to change the kind of control exercised over that apparatus:

> What was most urgently needed was a change in the character of the control exercised by the central government. It must be a constant, a minute, and a regular control which should gradually enforce upon the units of the local government conformity to those newer and higher standards of government demanded by the modern state.
>
> (Ibid., 136)

This system was in large part envisioned by Thomas Cromwell and was perhaps the most significant contribution the King's Council made to the effort to modernize the English administrative apparatus. This apparatus was based on orders, advices, and exhortations, a complex of rules and directives aimed at closely regulating local administration and often collected and published in what were known as books of orders;[18] and it was also based on the inquiries conducted

---

18 The measures contained in the books of orders would usually be concerned with social, economic, and health policy and did not innovate on existing law. They were fully coherent with the social policies already in place, and in fact their main purpose was to support the practice of using the sovereign prerogative to publicize the sovereign's social policy, educate judges on its basic principles,

by special commissions entrusted with ensuring the efficiency of administrative activity at the local level, in keeping with the model that would become typical of the Continental experience.[19]

In short, the sovereign's increasingly direct intervention in the kingdom's socioeconomic life was shifting the ancient constitutional balance, extending royal power well beyond the sphere originally reserved for it in English political and legal theory. "These activities of the Council," Holdsworth observes, "tended to foster the continental idea that the crown and its servants were outside the ordinary law" (Holdsworth 1924, vol. 4, p. 85). It was in the turbulent waters of this institutional clash that the doctrine of pre-eminent power developed as a basis of royal policy, along with the companion idea that this power was needed to promote the state of the commonwealth. The need to govern the dynamic set in motion by the growth of the capitalist economy gave rise to problems that could not be adequately addressed on the basis of the ancient structure of the common law. This made it necessary to increasingly carve out exceptions to the kingdom's ancient legal traditions. In this way the king's prerogative began to expand beyond the scope of the high policy within which it was originally confined—beyond what, as we will see, was beginning to be generally referred to as *gubernaculum*: "In that period, to all appearances, *jurisdictio* was destined to be swallowed up entirely by *gubernaculum*" (McIlwain 2007, 85).

The Tudor era put several pressures on the English constitutional setup, but without channelling institutional development toward a clearer and definitive solution (Holdsworth 1924, vol. 6, p. 5). After all, as we have seen, the policy pursued throughout the 16th century was not aimed at superseding the ancient constitutional design but rather at bringing back and progressively formalizing the institutions that underpinned the limited monarchy—namely, Parliament and the ancient structure for the local administration of justice. Only with the Stuart crisis and the fiscal crisis of the first decades of the 17th centuries was there an actual

and oversee its application (Slack 1980, 3). The practice of collecting the most important statutes, often also including the relative ordinances and memorandums, had already begun in the 16th century, becoming firmly established in the latter half of the century. As direct expressions of royal power, the provisions collected in these books would often fail to find a receptive audience among the local judges to whom they were specifically addressed (ibid., 18–19).

19 Von Friedeburg 1996, 593; Elton 1973, 164; Holdsworth 1924, vol. 4, p. 68. The institutional developments of Tudor England clearly signalled the trend line that English institutions would be following, increasingly creating special courts to support the organs of judicial administration. This trend can be clearly appreciated in the reform projects introduced by Thomas Cromwell. Consider, for example, that his original reform projects envisioned a commission tasked with overseeing the execution of social reforms and the poor laws (Elton 1973, 139), and even more significant in this regard was his proposal to create new administrative officials to be named Conservators of the Common Weal and entrusted with applying the vast body of economic legislation. These proposals anticipated the idea of the special authorities that would be characteristic of Continental absolute monarchy, and that (as conceived by Cromwell) would enjoy broad discretionary powers to intervene in any matter pertaining to the common weal (Tanner 1951, 141).

attempt to resolutely expand royal power beyond its traditional boundaries. The attempt was made to exercise royal legislative and fiscal power without parliamentary oversight or approval, to legitimize the power to make arrests without the courts' judicial authority, and to claim for sovereign bodies the power to oversee the judicial apparatus. This set the Crown against Parliament and the judicial apparatus, and it is through that conflict that England evolved what would become the definitive form of its modern institutional framework (Taswell-Langmead 1960, 344ff.; Holdsworth 1924, vol. 4, p. 165ff.). In fact, that struggle came to a head with the Glorious Revolution of 1688, which made it possible to solve a political crisis that hinged on the question of the institutional balance between *jurisdictio* and *gubernaculum*, as well as on the related question of the limits of sovereign power, and it is significant that in the effort to work out this question in the context of that crisis two intellectual traditions grew to maturity: on the one hand, English absolutistic thought; on the other, modern liberal constitutionalism (McIlwain 2007, 115ff.; Eccleshall 1978).

We cannot here trace out in any detail the phases of a constitutional clash out of which came what is widely considered to be the first liberal revolution of the modern West. Indeed, what matters here is what can be observed by stepping back and looking at the big picture, which importantly reveals that out of the clashes among the English constitutional organs there emerged a new social elite with an incipient force of its own. This class had already gained a strong economic footing, and it developed the political consciousness that came with that newfound position, so much so that it sought to itself take the helm of the kingdom's political life. It never would have suffered the paternal care of an absolute monarch. So, while the bureaucratic bloating that got underway in the Tudor era set the conditions for the state to drain financial resources in huge quantities and encroach on many areas of social life, England's new social and economic elite put its political and cultural resources to use in a bid to take over this huge machinery and run it itself, in light of its own framing of its interests so as to model the political institutions accordingly.

The revolution dealt a final blow to any notion of eudaemonistic absolute monarchy in England, nipping in the bud the development of an administrative apparatus under the king's control. Once the jurisdiction of the special courts and the Privy Council was reduced, the constitutional design that came out of the revolution was going to stand on two pillars: Parliament—the true sovereign body, which would meet regularly, rather than when discretionarily summoned by the king—and the 1689 Bill of Rights, which set the new basic law of the kingdom and served as the basis for the administration of justice. From this point on, terms such as *gubernaculum* and *policy* could only conjure up the idea of tyranny and arbitrary government in England (Mannori and Sordi 2001, 81–82), and the task of leading the nation through the challenges of modernity would thus be entrusted to the body best suited to represent the interests of the country. England led the way in ridding itself of mercantilist policies, and in the 18th century it was already embracing a proto-industrial free-market capitalism. It came to realize early on that it would have been better off without an *economic police*,[20] considering that it could rely on the judicial administration inherited from the past in managing both the sphere of free economic transactions and the residual functions of *social police*, meaning the activity of governing, or "disciplining," the poor and the labour market, a sphere of activity that, as we will see, would take on an increasingly important role with the development of an industrial and urban society.

1.3.2. The monarchie administrative in France

As in England, the constitutional monarchy in France relied on a centralized political structure. France, too, managed to create a complex structure for the royal administration of justice marked by two key features: It was closely modelled after the image of the king as *enforcer of justice*, an idea inherited from medieval political thought, and it exercised a wide variety of functions by relying on modern judicial categories (see, in general, Carbasse and Leyte 2004, 142–52; Olivier-Martin 1951, 513; Sueur 2001a, 163). However, the abiding image of the sovereign as the wellspring of justice *(fontaine de justice)* would soon come into conflict with the changes the kingdom's political structure would see in the transition from the Middle Ages to the modern age. The idea of a king confined to the mere role of preserving the inherited legal order became difficult, if not impossible, to reconcile with the actual practice of kings, who with greater and greater assertiveness would innovate by promoting social and political reform. This process brought into being a sphere of political activity that today we would recognize as legislative and administrative power.

The royal judicial organs played a decisive role in moving past the ancient feudal political structure, this by providing a blueprint for a monarchy that could already be considered to some extent national. Indeed, in the 16th century, by progressively expanding the areas within the remit of royal *justice déléguée* and making it increasingly burdensome for its officers to administer seigneurial and municipal justice, the king managed to almost entirely gut the so-called *justice concédé*, meaning the whole complex of judicial functions exercised through a feudal title or through a privilege granted to a municipality (Sueur 2001a, 163ff.; Olivier-Martin 1951, 513ff.; Barbiche 2001, 46). The royal administration of justice—whose competence, as mentioned, was wide-reaching and even included rule-making powers— was structured on two levels. On the one hand were the lower courts, staffed by *prévôts* and *baillis*:[21] These were honorary judgeships assigned to a nobility that

---

20 Today's equivalent would be economic policy, but I am using the term *police* to underscore both its derivation, or genealogy, and its connection with the French *police economique*. For a similar use and a brief account of that genealogy, see Dubber 2004, 107.

21 *Prévôts* emerged in the Middle Ages as sole members of single-judge courts of first instance, but they could also review and hear on appeal cases previously tried in seigneurial courts. They had broad jurisdiction covering all subject matters outside the scope of a *bailliage*. With the single exception

lacked the required judicial training and so tended to sell these offices to so-called lieutenants—that is, officials entrusted with proxy powers exercised in place of another.[22] On the other hand were the higher courts, or *parlements*, prominent among which was the *parlement* in Paris (see, generally, Sueur 2001a, 195–221; Olivier-Martin 1951, 528–52; and "Parlements," in Marion 1969, 422–24).

The *parlements* were a direct issue of the medieval *curia regis*, out of which they evolved by a process of specification. The function they served accordingly came out of that particular hybrid of strictly judicial powers with politico-administrative powers that, as mentioned, was typical of all regular courts in the ancien régime, so it would be an oversimplification to describe that function as straightforwardly judicial. Indeed, in addition to serving as the highest courts of appeal and the single courts of first instance for certain classes of cases, the *parlements* served an important political function by more or less effectively playing a part in the stewardship of the public good. The *parlements* could in the first place exercise a general power to issue *arrêts*, and far from being only a judicial means of settling a controversy, these could also take the form of *arrêts de règlement*, true regulations of general scope (Sueur 2001a, 144, 145; Olivier-Martin 1951, 539). Even more significantly, however, the *parlements* were entrusted with recording ordinances and royal provisions, and in this they exercised a deep form of control over the nascent legislative function (Sueur 2001a, 81ff.; Olivier-Martin 1951, 541ff.).

The power to express "remonstrances" and "advisory opinions" started out life as a support tool that the royal courts provided for the king. In this way the royal courts helped to establish the king's political centrality to the detriment of the feudal powers (Olivier-Martin 1951, 543; Sueur 2001a, 86), supporting in particular the birth of a regular rule-making power that the king exercised by issuing letters patent empowering the same courts to record rules and carry out writs of execution.[23] However, as the French kings took to making increasingly autocratic claims, that power of the royal courts developed into authentic claims to exercise legal and political control over the king's activities, which purported to trace its roots to the proto-liberal doctrine of limited monarchy. So the *parlements*—relying on the celebrated theory that constructed them as the only heirs of the

of the Paris *prévôt* to the Châtelet—an office that continued to play a central role and gained great prestige (see "Chatelet," Marion 1969, 88)—the provostship would gradually lose ground to the other lower court, that of the bailie (see, generally, Sueur 2001a, 186–95; Olivier-Martin 1951, 552–56; "Bailli" and "Prévôt," in Marion 1969, 31 and 453).

22 See "Lieutenant," in Marion 1969, 335. Lieutenants emerged with the widening use of learned Roman law and Roman canon law, and since the nobility who held these offices was generally unqualified, the lieutenantship, too, became available for purchase. Beginning in the 16th century, it was stably formalized under some royal decrees that definitively entrusted the administration of justice to civil and criminal lieutenants, generally doctors of laws acting on behalf of the officeholders.

23 Letters patent could take the form of an *ordonnance* or an *edit*, depending on how general the provision to be enforced was (see Olivier-Martin 1951, 350; Sueur 2001b, 67; "Ordonnances," in Marion 1969, 409).

estates general, by that time already defunct—sought to style themselves as defenders of the ancient freedoms of the French, and they accordingly more or less energetically resisted all the attempts that, at least from the mid-16th century, were being made to limit their power to hear challenges and record royal decrees. These attempts were being made by extensive recourse to normative acts of so-called full or extraordinary power, meaning the whole complex of provisions issued outside the scope of judicial oversight exercised by other bodies (see, in general, Sueur 2001b, 73–75; Olivier-Martin 1951, 348–51).

This institutional structure covered a wide range of competences, and so next to traditional *justice* there grew a more general *police* function. This function was still loosely defined, but the kings were beginning to pay more and more attention to it, pretending a more effective action that the regular courts, with their persistent structural limits, were unable to fulfill. Indeed, historians have often noted that the judicial offices through which the monarchy in Renaissance France administered the kingdom were still merely patrimonial and essentially prebureaucratic. These offices were being held by a new class, a true *noblesse de robe* that managed to limit monarchical claims to power so far as to prompt some historians to speak of a new feudality (see Mousnier 1945, 19; cf. Pagés 1972, 227ff.). So it would not yet be accurate to speak of absolutism at the beginning of the reign of Louis XIII. As much as the French monarchy had already begun to do away with the greater nobility, it was still finding itself forced to construct its administrative apparatus by selling its offices, whether by reason of its inherent financial weakness or by reason of the traditional patrimonial conceptions of power. In the 16th century and the first half of the 17th century, it was still in point of fact a limited monarchy whose operation rested on the venality or sale of offices (Pagés 1972, 523; cf. Fisher and Lundgreen 1975, 496). An apparatus so constructed did, however, give rise to further problems, mostly having to do with its inability to meet standards of efficiency. Its officials and personnel, in other words, were drenched in a legalistic culture primarily geared toward guaranteeing the protection of the law, so it proved difficult to repurpose the apparatus into a tool with which to develop and carry out specific policy-driven programmes (Mannori and Sordi 2001, 98) for enacting the social and economic reforms needed to make tax collection more efficient and to increase the tax-paying capacity of all subjects.

So when France came out of the religious wars, it was only partway a modern state. The king did not have full control of his administrative apparatus, nor was there yet a capitalistic bourgeoisie devoted to commerce and manufacture; so, too, the economy was still largely based on agriculture and on rents (return on land), while the upward mobility of the new classes depended for the most part on income derived from the holding of public offices (this has been widely documented by Gary Pagés [1972] and Roland Mousnier [1945]). It was inevitable that, at the height of the struggle for European hegemony against the Habsburgs, monarchs such as Henry IV and Louis XIII, and to an even greater extent Louis XVI and ministers such as Sully, Colbert, Mazarin, and Richelieu, should have felt it necessary to fully overhaul the state's overall structure, so as to weed out the inefficiencies of the ancient administration of justice, by keeping at bay the traditional powers' ever-renewing effort to undercut the royal prerogative and the obstacle they posed to the development of economic policies through which to secure the material resources necessary to sustain the political ambitions of a European power such as France. The need to exert greater control over the apparatus for the administration of justice thus fuelled attempts to increasingly disempower the ancient class of functionaries.

The royal assignments of judicial functions were not considered definitive. As *haut justicier*, the king could always "retain" these functions, exercising them himself or entrusting such exercise to organs closer to him in that capacity. It was precisely the expansion of the so-called *justice retenue* (retained justice) that brought about the transition from judicial administration to the so-called administrative monarchy, and indeed that was the institutional phenomenon that most distinguished French political absolutism (Sueur 2001b, 246ff.; Olivier-Martin 1951, 518ff.; Haruel et al. 2006, 495ff.). Well into the modern age, the main body of the French administration's functionary corps was entirely made up of commissarial personnel, whose offices in fact became considerably stable. Examples were councillors of state, the secretary of state, the comptroller general of finances, the attorneys general of the *parlements*, and especially the officials who ran the peripheral administration, meaning the intendants and the general police lieutenants—a cohort of royal servants who did not have the status of regular judges and so were more malleable and willing to effectively execute the sovereign will (Sueur 2001b, 316).

A central role among the new royal functionaries was that of the intendant,[24] whose full title was *intendant de justice, police et finances, commissaire départi pour l'exécution des ordres de sa majesté* (intendant of justice, police, and finances, commissaire dispatched to execute his majesty's orders). These were created as offices for extraordinary commissaires, but in the space of 150 years, between the 17th and 18th centuries, they grew into one of the most important organs of France's modern administrative monarchy. And although the commissarial office of intendant did become progressively stable, the functions attributed to it never settled into a fully crystallized form. Indeed, the *lettres de commission* through which it would always be set up could be revoked *ad libitum*, and the office itself would vary considerably from province to province, for, as its full name suggests, it covered the vast functional space comprising justice, police, and finance (Mousnier 1972, 108). Even though the intendancy kept expanding its powers, its role was still being regarded as that of keeping watch over the regular courts. The intendants were the watchdogs sent out to check on the state's administration, large swaths of which were still entrusted to the old judicial apparatus (Mannori and Sordi 2001, 117;

---

24 The literature on the birth of this institutional figure has by now grown to vast proportions, but for an overview the reader can refer to Sueur 2001a, 347ff.; "Intendants," in Marion 1969, 293ff.; Haruel et al. 2006, 497ff.; Barbiche 2001, 383ff.; and Petracchi 1971.

cf. Fisher and Lundgreen 1975, 500). Even so, they increasingly cut out for themselves a range of specific and exclusive police powers, reserving for themselves the task of broadly intervening in all matters pertaining to the public interest and welfare. This covered the broad area known as *police du bon ordre* (with the function of protecting the security of goods and people, ensuring public health, and managing social welfare), and the even broader area encompassing economic and financial police, where the intendant acted as an essential tool for conveying information and carrying into execution the economic dirigisme conducted by the comptroller general of finances (Sueur 2001b, 357).

The citizen equivalent to the intendant, particularly as concerns the exercise of the important functions connected with the police, was *lieutenant général de police*—another functionary that was key to the development of France's modern administrative monarchy. This office—created under a reform introduced with an edict of 1667 and extended in 1669 to all the main cities across the kingdom—was designed to settle the constant conflicts of jurisdiction among the magistracies in Paris, and in particular among the civil and criminal lieutenant and the *prévôt* to the *Chatelet*.[25] This crucial institutional reform was the outcome of a council for general police reform summoned by Colbert which took place from October 1666 to February 1667, and which discussed all the findings of the inspections carried out by the state's councillors to ascertain the state of administration in Paris (Olivier-Martin 1948, 102; de Chassaigne [1906] 1975, 40). The new magistrate would have separated the regular judicial powers from police activity, embodying the institutional figure of the first authentically modern administrative functionary, bundling together a vast range of powers.

The creation of these new functionaries was not, however, intended to fully replace the ancient administration of justice. The idea was instead to support that administration in carrying out the daily tasks it was responsible for under the functions entrusted to it. But since the old structure proved inadequate to the tasks at hand and put up resistance, while the new magistracies were invasive in fulfilling their own functions, a conflictive crescendo of mutual interferences ensued. The clash revolved in particular around the complex of functions relative to the *police générale*. These functions had begun to emerge as the regular magistracies' sphere of competence, where the *parlements* themselves often exercised broad regulatory powers (Sueur 2001a, 146; Olivier-Martin 1951, 539), and with greater and greater insistence the king was now trying to manage the same functions autocratically through a mounting series of normative provisions—called *ordonnances sans addresse ni sceau* and *arrêts du conseil du roi*—whose execution was being directly

---

25 This was a dispute that engaged all of the city's highest authorities in an attempt to settle the question of whether the police function was to be deemed part of *criminal* justice, and thus entrusted to the criminal lieutenant, or of *civil* justice, and thus entrusted to the civil lieutenant. This question we will have to come back to, considering how central it turned out to be in explaining the distinctive traits the police apparatus would take on. A broad account can be found in Delamare 1705, pp. 114ff., and Olivier-Martin 1948, 97ff.

entrusted to the new magistracies. This crisis was already watering down the ancient notion of *iurisdictio* and was being fully played out in the dialectic and the conflicts that flared up between the two institutional complexes, both trying to better redraw their respective areas of competence.

Stoking up this conflict was a personnel which had hitherto viewed itself as the authentic representative of the monarchy, and which now saw its prerogatives being encroached upon. What followed was a whole series of attempts to define the different spheres of competence at issue, and hence the theoretical distinction between *iurisdictio* and *politia*. What made it difficult to trace out such a distinction was that, with the important exception of the general police lieutenancy, the king's organs of autocratic administration were not conceived as essentially different from the ordinary magistracies, and so in practical terms they lacked any definite functional distinction. By the same token, as the *conseil* set out to expand its range of activity—in effect emptying the *parlements* of their independence by shifting areas of jurisdiction to the king's *justice retenue* and depriving them of regulatory powers—the *parlements* could only put up a response betraying the frustration of an institution that saw its ancient constitutional centrality disappear in favour of organs with a sphere of competence whose contours could not be drawn in any clear-cut way.

What in any event emerges from these conflicts, considering how long-drawn-out they were, is that France never managed to stabilize and legitimize the institutions of its administrative monarchy to the extent that can be observed elsewhere in Europe, as in the German area, where that process even made it possible to set on a scientific foundation the government techniques put into practice by the new politico-administrative institutions. The intendancies and police lieutenancies in France never achieved the degree of legitimacy needed for the birth of an authentic police science modelled on the one developed to support the military-administrative complex in Prussia. So shapeshifting was the scope of their competence, and so indiscernible were the features that should have set them apart from the ancient apparatus for the administration of justice, that they lacked the foundation on which to give start to a systematic study of police administration.

1.3.3. The Polizeistaat *in the German territories*

The German lands never reached a level of politico-administrative integration comparable to that reached even in the 15th century by the English and French monarchies. Once all the ancient universalistic aspirations were compromised, even the Holy Roman Empire's internal political unity broke up. The imperial reforms of the 15th and 16th centuries did proclaim a universal and perpetual peace in an attempt to reconstruct a political unity under a framework regulating the relation among principalities, thus enabling them to form into an association. These reforms, as is known, were based on three institutional pillars: the Empire, the Imperial Diet (Reichstag), and the Imperial Chamber, the Empire's highest court (De Benedictis 2001, 39ff.). But all the way to the end, this political framework retained a functional design essentially aimed at settling conflicts among the various constitutional components. The constitution of the Reich thus exemplified to perfection the *Ständestaat*, the corporate state or polity of estates based on a *Reichsfundamentalgesetze* (a basic law) and on the political role of the Reichstag, which gave the Empire the form of a limited monarchy proper (Bussi 1957, 29ff., 171–72).

By this time the Reich was reduced to a mere territorial lordship, and the only thing separating the emperor from his peer electors was the rank of an office cast in the Germanic mould of shared power, rather than in the Roman mould of absolute power (Bader 1972, 261). In this scheme of things, the Reich's supreme political power would inevitably take the form of a compact the Kaiser and the *Stände* vowed to stand by (Bussi 1959, 87, 177). In this way, the Imperial Diet assumed the makings of an institutional complex entrusted with protecting and preserving privileges and prerogatives, without leaving any room for the development of autocratic organs of political and administrative stewardship. It was, after all, as an outgrowth of this situation that the imperial supreme courts should have favoured an increasing juridification of political life, framing that activity within the terms of the Empire's constitutional law. And all these developments in turn favoured a rereading of the main political and institutional conflicts of the time through the lens of the classical notion of *iurisdictio* (Stolleis 1998a, 196–207).

Setting a definitive seal on a breakup of imperial power that had been in the making throughout the 17th century was the Thirty Years' War, which under the Peace of Westphalia accorded to the territorial *Stände* the right to form their own alliances, thus establishing the principle that conferred sovereignty on the territorial principalities (Bockenforde 1974, 357; Bussi 1959, 253ff.; Stolleis 1998a, 335–43). This treaty, which did much to shape European history, rose to the rank of fundamental law of the Empire, thus playing a decisive role in reframing the German lands' constitutional design. Indeed, on the one hand it definitely gutted the Reich, reducing it to a federal body deprived of any political or administrative independence, and on the other the territorial princes received recognition as sovereign entities, to the detriment of the lesser nobility and the autonomous municipal bodies. However, in making the territorial principalities the main vehicles of political and institutional development, the interests behind international politics rallied together with the greater nimbleness that the territorial institutions demonstrated in working out solutions to the main problems arising in connection with the question of the modern state's constitution (Schiera 1968, 196; cf. Fisher and Lundgreen 1975, 499).

If we are to trace out the trajectory the German area followed in developing modern political institutions, we will therefore have to look at what happened in the territorial states, trying in particular to determine which of these states in the 18th century, and even more in the 19th, would play a prominent role on a par with the other great European powers of the time. The most significant experience in that regard is undoubtedly that of Prussia. Indeed, although the Prussian model of the Hohenzollerns did have some distinctive traits, it fit into the frame of a European-wide political and institutional development and served as a blueprint for the institutional solutions that throughout the German area were being probed in response to the challenges posed by the political and economic development of modern Europe.

The Hohenzollerns of Brandenburg built their powerful empire out of the complex territorial composition that had been taking shape in the early decades of the 17th century, in which context they gained control of Pomerania, Prussia, the Duchy of Cleves, and the Counties of Mark and Ravensberg. So constituted, the principality stretched across a territory that was second only to the Habsburg domains, but even though these territories played a role of great economic and strategic importance, they were still fragmented and lacked political unity (Carsten 1954, 176). The principality was thus still made up of lordly estates that only the autocracy of the Hohenzollerns could bring to any politico-administrative unity. But it was a long time before this unity could take its station in the diplomatic language of the period.[26] This situation emerged out of the political and social evolution that shaped the different territories comprising the realm of Brandenburg-Prussia, hamstrung by the chronic weakness of the territorial princes and the political centrality of the estates, which over the centuries had secured the place of the *ius indigenatum (Indiginatsrecht)* as the effective law on which basis to assign the most important offices (Carsten 1954, 92–93; Dorwart 1953, 3). This politico-institutional model left the majority of the political and administrative tasks and responsibilities in the hands of the lords and the landed nobility, and thus was established the political and social dominion of the *Landstände* (Carsten 1954, 174).

Like all the principalities across the German lands at the dawn of the modern age, Prussia had a political constitution roughly modelled on that of the Holy Roman Empire, and hence built around the territorial estates' prerogatives, which were rooted in custom and which crystallized into privileges secured through the agreements formed with the *Landesherr*, that is, the territorial lord (Bussi 1971, 182). Political life therefore revolved around the activity of the territorial diet *(Landtag)* and the territorial government (the *curia regis* or *Regierung*), in which the territorial estates widely participated in view of their traditional function in providing *auxilium et consilium* to the prince, thus supporting the prince in fulfilling the most important political functions (ibid., 202). In parallel, and in keeping with institutional development throughout late medieval Europe, the *curia regis* became the source from which issued the *Hofgericht*, literally a judge in the king's court, an office entrusted with strictly judicial functions, out of which in turn came the *Kammerricht* (Dorwart 1953, 55). Starting from the 15th century, this court gradually rose to the rank of court of last resort within the principality; all around it, however,

---

26 Indeed, the Prussian chancery referred to the *States and Provinces of Her Royal Majesty*, a phrase that stuck around for quite some time, considering that as late as 1794 the *allgemeines Landrecht* was being imposed not on Prussia but on the Prussian states (Rosenberg 1958, 27; Carsten 1954, 184–85).

there emerged a series of other *Hofgerichten*, lordly supreme courts over which the court of the Elector of Brandenburg could barely exercise any jurisdictional authority (ibid., 57). On the other hand, this latter court—which, too, was created out of the *curia regis*—acted at the same time as a *Landesgerichte*, a territorial court woven into the fabric of the broader institutional structure of the Empire's apparatus for the administration of justice, and it thus fell within the jurisdiction of the Imperial Chamber, the Empire's highest court (Hubatsch 1973, 211; Dorwart 1953, 60–61).

As much as there existed organs like the *Geheime Justizrat*—an expression of the king's reserved justice, exercised in areas of special interest to the state and available only to persons with special privileges (Dorwart 1953, 62)—the Prussian administration of justice still relied on a largely inefficient structure. It was based on the work of different courts reflecting the particularistic interests of the different territories and lacked a single high court with territorial jurisdiction across the entire realm, so it could not answer the needs stemming from the plexus of reform policies the House of Hohenzollern required to transform its vast holdings into a modern state. If this composite *Territorialstaat* was to become an organic political unit, it would need to effect a set of administrative reforms aimed at diluting the role of the political institutions beholden to the different territorial estates that made up the realm. This was precisely the policy pursued by Frederick William, Elector of Brandenburg, who in a few decades set the foundation on which to remake Prussia into a modern state, doing away with the ancient polity of estates. But this revolution was brought about by envisaging for the ancient landed aristocracy a role in the new administrative structure, and so without depriving it of its social and political weight.

The decisive turnaround came in the wake of the Thirty Years' War, when the king's increasing fiscal needs injected strong tensions into the realm's political structure. It was against this backdrop that the territorial prince Frederick William of Brandenburg set out to reorganize the principality on the model of French political absolutism (Rosenberg 1958, 34; Carsten 1954, 253). This transformation was set in motion in the second half of the 17th century, when the prince continued the drawn-out wartime practice of attempting to institutionalize the first violations of the ancient constitutional framework. The decisive blow to the ancient political structure came when the prince managed to gain three political monopolies, with the exclusive power to make decisions in military matters, to maintain a standing army, and to introduce extraordinary taxes. The idea was to rest the violation of the ancient constitutional framework on a sort of state of war and permanent necessity that would justify the creeping administrative revolution. On the basis of those premises, the Hohenzollerns began to systematically trump the prerogatives of the central governing bodies, thus setting in place the building blocks of personal government by the prince (Oestreich 1972, 125–60).

The ambitious plan to create a great power starting from the composite territorial state that in the mid-17th century was still Brandenburg-Prussia was going to require a vast reform programme whose first step would, of course, be to reorganize the highest council, in which an increasingly important role had come to be played by the so-called *Kammer*, where the sovereign addressed the most important business (Dorwart 1953, 9). Over time this internal advisory body earned a place next to the two central governing bodies already in existence, the *Regierung* and the *Landtag*. Both were controlled by the realm's different sociopolitical components, and both lost influence next to the emergent *Kammer*. This was the first step toward the development of an autocratic politics by the princes of Brandenburg-Prussia. But even more important in giving concrete form to this development was the effort to reform the local administrative bodies across the territory by laying on top of the ancient structure for the administration of justice a network of military commissaries fashioned after that of the French intendants (Rosenberg 1958, 39).

At the heart of the administrative reforms were the commissarial positions previously created as early as the first decades of the 17th century and thereafter gradually institutionalized over the course of the Thirty Years' War. Particularly important were the district commissaries *(Kreiskommissaren)*, who were charged with managing and supplying the troops quartered in the different districts *(Kreis)*, and whose original function was to collect an extraordinary tax to fund military expenses (Dorwart 1953, 130). However, although the creation of an apparatus for military administration was initially conceived as a tool for setting up a standing army with which to defend the realm, it did much more than that. It also served as the main tool for raising revenues independently of the control exercised by the territorial estates (ibid., 129). With the need to expand the tax base and manage revenues to satisfy the growing military administration came the need to develop a broad programme of political, economic, and social reforms (ibid.), and the two needs were inextricably bound up. Military and fiscal reform were at one with mercantilist policy between the 17th and 18th centuries in Prussia, where that highly centralized bureaucratic-military structure was also functional to a planned fiscal exploitation and to a policy geared toward stimulating economic growth and increasing the realm's revenue-raising capacity.

At the core of that policy lay two institutional figures that reported directly to the *Kriegskommissar* stationed in each of the provinces. The first of these figures was the *Steuerate*, the city fiscal commissary—with broad authority in matters of *economic police*, as well as over the administration of the cities within his district—and the other was the *Landrate*, the fiscal commissary entrusted with analogous police functions in the rural areas. These magistracies were the two cornerstones of the reform made to Prussia's administrative structure, even though the differences between them ran deep. Indeed, the *Steuerate* was an official appointed directly by the king, and so was a typical expression of the Hohenzollerns' political autocracy, modelled on that of the intendants and lieutenants who staffed the French police, while the *Landrate*, based on the model of the English justices, was instead an expression of the local political elite, for this was an officer elected by the territorial estates in concert with the central authority, and was also the main manifestation of the compromise struck between the sovereigns and the ancient landed aristocracy (ibid., 150–52).

The administrative reform initiated by the Great Elector was brought to completion by Frederick William I, who gave definitive form to a police state firmly structured around the supreme figure of the sovereign (ibid., 30). It was indeed under his reign that Prussia definitely settled into place as a state based on a solid military-bureaucratic apparatus (a development by reason of which the king earned the epithet *Soldatenköning*, or Soldier King). He provided the basic framework for an efficient apparatus capable of enacting the vast social, political, and economic policy needed to create the complex of human and material resources necessary in giving birth to a great power. This comprehensive administrative systematization was realized in the decade from 1713 to 1723, one of Prussia's most intense reform periods, along with that of the reign of the Great Elector between the 18th and 19th centuries (ibid., 34).

It was in this period that a strongly centralized administrative apparatus built around the sovereign council took on its basic contours. Indeed, the ancient *curia regis*—initially organized into departments with territorial authority, reflecting the ancient federative idea of the state as an association of independent territories— was progressively structured around the principle of subject-matter jurisdiction, and three main departments wound up being created on that basis: the *Justizstaatsrat*, competent to address legal issues and spiritual affairs; the *Cabinetsministerium*, built out of the original *Kammer*, the sovereign's privy council, with competence over foreign policy; and the *Generaldirektorium*, with competence over all matters pertaining to the police, as well as over economic and financial questions and for military affairs (ibid., 33). This last department, created in January 1723 by merging the military and fiscal departments, which had hitherto been formally separated, became the institutional centrepiece of the entire administrative apparatus revolving around the commissarial officials.[27] This new structure for administering the prince's personnel, with all its outstretching ramification, became the institutional basis for *Policey* throughout the 18th century (Schiera 1968, 203). Indeed, the authority vested in this commissarial apparatus extended its scope well beyond fiscal and military matters to include the whole of social and economic policy under Prussian absolutism, thus playing a decisive role in transforming and modernizing the realm. Under the helm of the new magistracies entrusted with ensuring *gute Polizei* (or good governance) for the realm, unfarmed rural areas were repopulated and colonized, and a mercantilist policy was pursued to favour commerce and the development of manufacturing. Prussia's entire social structure was transformed.

---

27 In this scheme, the lower ranks—answerable to the local and provincial officials, the police inspectors *(Polizeireuter)* and the gendarmes *(Ausreiter)*—would be filled by military personnel (Dorwart 1953, 171).

This structure retained its shape throughout the 18th century, until the general administrative reform introduced by Heinrich Friedrich Karl von Stein between the 18th and 19th centuries. The administrative structure inherited from Frederick the Great, the first of the enlightened despots, was by this time sufficiently consolidated, and for this reason he could confine his effort to rationalizing the *Generaldirektorium*, and focus instead on the administration of justice in an attempt to modernize it. The 18th-century reforms certainly came in response to a need for greater oversight by the sovereign, even in the sphere of the ancient *iurisdictio*,[28] but they also reflected a need to be even sharper in drawing the institutional boundaries between what had by then been developing as two sectors proper of the state's apparatus. On the one hand was the sphere of the ancient *iurisdictio*, embodied in the apparatus for the administration of justice; on the other was the sphere of the modern *Polizei*, embodied in the apparatus for commissarial administration.

The birth of the commissarial offices was not without conflict. Although, as illustrated, it came about within the frame of a compromise with the ancient sociopolitical elite, the effort to draw a sharper distinction between the spheres of competence reserved to the magistracies within the ancient judicial apparatus, on the one hand, and to the new magistracies, on the other, became the object of numerous institutional clashes, and, as we will see, it also spawned a copious doctrinal literature in the theory of public law. The attempt to set out an accepted criterion for allocating competences—a task that naturally made it necessary to more clearly distinguish *iurisdictio* from *Polizei*—began as early as the first decades of the 18th century, when the special jurisdiction was established for the sovereign's autocratic organs in all areas pertaining to *militaria, politiam et statum oeconomicum* (Dorwart 1953, 68–69). Although a concrete sphere of competence was identified outlining the scope of society's general police and government, where the commissarial organs would enjoy a good deal of autonomy, the overall solution did not manage to settle all controversies. The dividing line between the two administrative compartments was still in many respects blurry, especially when it came to the interpretation of the increasingly numerous *Polizeiordnungen* (police ordinances), and the conflicts persisted throughout the 18th century.

Not until the mid-18th century was some degree of balance found, under the reforms instituted by Samuel von Cocceji, who sought to settle the matter in the 1748 *Codex Fredericianus Marchicus* through a clause setting forth the competencies of the judicial organs. Cocceji was trying to unambiguously separate the judicial sphere from the executive sphere, if need be even subjecting the autocratic organs to judicial review (Rosenberg 1958 133; Mannori and Sordi 2001, 172–73),

---

28 The minister responsible for reforming the judicial apparatus was Samuel von Cocceji, and his main objective was indeed to make the legal system more uniform and the courts more efficient (Hubatsch 1973, 212; Rosenberg 1958, 123. On the work of this great reformer of Prussian enlightened absolutism, see also Tarello 1976, 223ff.

following a line of development that was already heading in the direction of a progressive juridification of the *Polizei*. Although he succeeded in his effort to draw sharper boundaries between different spheres, he was unsuccessful in his attempt to judicialize the administrative apparatus by subjecting it to the scrutiny of the regular administration of justice. Indeed, the autocratic administration by and large retained the broad, loosely judicial powers it had previously enjoyed over all controversies arising out of its own discharge of police functions, a scheme that worked to the disadvantage of the judicial bodies proper by eating into their sphere of competence (Hubatsch 1973, 214).

The upshot of institutional development in Prussia was to enable *Polizei* to reach a high degree of theoretical and practical maturity, all the while bringing into sharper focus its contraposition to the sphere of the ancient *iurisdictio*. The same development also brought into being the first proper example of modern professional bureaucracy in Weber's sense. It was indeed in the 18th century that there began to emerge the modern civil servant, one whose title to office is based on no more than dispassionate competence. This professionalization was favoured by the need to increase the finances required by a rising nation such as Prussia, a need that induced sovereigns to foster the development of a systematic, scientific interest in a study of the questions pertaining to the state's financial administration, and hence a study of a general police for society. And from this interest would emerge cameralism and police science as authentic forerunners of the modern administrative sciences.

Chapter 2

The theoretical roots of modern police power

Having described in outline the politico-institutional environment that secured the essential historical condition for the development of modern police powers, we can now attempt to trace out their theoretical genealogy. As I have tried to illustrate, it was with the birth of the modern administrative monarchy that a more overtly voluntaristic and absolutistic conception of law could find a concrete institutional embodiment, giving shape to that complex of sovereign powers that, as we saw, concretized into new apparatuses and into the nascent police legislations. It is only natural, then, if in tracing out the theoretical genealogy of the modern notion of police, we should go back to the original matrixes of political absolutism, and in particular to the construct of the modern prince as legislator and administrator, a construct that emerges next to the medieval idea of the *king as enforcer of justice*, in some respects displacing this latter idea.

As mentioned, the term *police* established itself in the European legal lexicon via the translation of Aristotle's *Politics*, which along with his *Nicomachean Ethics* and the pseudo-Aristotelian *Economics* formed the textual basis for the teaching of the *practical* disciplines in the liberal arts schools of medieval universities. The Aristotelian model long stood as something of a paradigm for political reflection, so much so that, as is known, the division of practical disciplines into ethics, economics, and politics—a tripartition introduced in Latin culture by Boethius—was taken up across the board in medieval Scholasticism, when it became the foundation of university curricula throughout Europe (especially in central Europe: see Maier 1962, 59–116), and for a long time thereafter it retained its basic makeup. It is to this intellectual tradition that we need to trace the semantic development of the modern notion of police.

The sense in which the classic authors understood the notion of *politeia* is well known. At least since Aristotle, the term designates the overall order of the city *(polis)*, the set of rules and formulas under which everyone can live with everyone else (Mozzarelli 1988, 9). Aristotle's *Politics* presents a view of political institutions as natural, in that they respond to principles rooted in the biological order. Like any other natural being, the *polis* is a compound of elemental components set in a certain balance. These components are the individual members of the *polis*, and the balance that obtains among them is the outcome of their tendency to associate in increasingly complex forms of communitarian existence in view of their need to satisfy their primary needs. The *polis* is thus a natural organism held together by its components' tendency to seek a sociopolitical balance enabling them not only to live or survive *(zen)* but to live well *(euzen)*.[1]

For the classic Latin writers, the concept of political order was instead expressed by the term *res publica*, which accordingly upstaged *politia* in the lexicon of political science. Not so in the Middle Ages, when the fall of the Roman Empire set political philosophy on a quest for a principle of universal order on which basis to refound the political community. And this was precisely the thrust of the reflection that political thinkers developed around the notion of *politia* when in the Middle Ages they rediscovered Aristotle's *Politics*. In the late-medieval translation of that book, the Aristotelian expression *politike koinonia*, understood as a synonym of *polis*, was rendered as *communicatio civilis sive politica*—hence the marked tendency of the time to use *politia* both as a noun, expressing the idea of a political community, and as a modifier, expressing the idea of a *well-ordered* political community. The term *politia* thus became imbued with values that turned the Aristotelian conception into a moral paradigm of life in society, and so also into an ideal frame within which to situate all the concrete forms the social order can take (Mozzarelli 1988, 11).

Through the Scholastic filter, the Aristotelian notion of *politia* thus made its way into the various vulgate tongues, taking on highly conservative overtones, encapsulating the idea of what it meant for a political community to be in *good order*. And what this idea pushed into the foreground was the need to maintain a proper balance among the different components of the community, in keeping with the theoretical centrality the notion of order took on throughout medieval thought and culture (Grossi 1995, 81; Duby 1978). In this frame of thought, *politia* was the activity of protecting the realm's legal and social order, and in that sense it could hardly be distinguished from the competing notion of *iurisdictio*. *Politia* still expressed the broad subjection of politics to law that would not be overturned until the birth of the institutions of political absolutism.

Political absolutism made wide use of Aristotelian themes and the Aristotelian lexicon without making the clean theoretical break with that tradition which would come only with natural law theory.[2] Indeed, as Norberto Bobbio (1980, 510) has

1 So central is the organicistic metaphor in Aristotle's political science that in the famous Book V of *Politics*, on the varieties of political constitutions and their degeneration, the argument is made that political organisms become corrupted when a component within the organism grows or is transformed in such a way as to alter its perfect symmetry with the other components (Vasoli 1992, 55).
2 In the canonical historiographical reconstruction, the intellectual break that came with the birth of modern philosophical rationalism is traced out, making the assumption of a close connection between Aristotelianism and Scholasticism, but the Aristotelian influence persisted even beyond the crisis of Scholasticism, as can be appreciated by considering how widespread Aristotle's works continued to be among humanists, and how these scholars continued to debate and rethink their translation (Riedel 1975, 110ff.; see, generally, Schmitt 1983). This is especially true of his political works, so much so that the suggestion has been made that this intellectual tradition made it past the

commented, it is Hobbes that lays Aristotle's authority to rest. However, as much as the legal and political thought of monarchical absolutism did draw widely on the themes and lexicon of Aristotelian political thought, it did make two significant changes to that frame of thought, for on the one hand it broke with the tripartition of the practical sciences, and on the other it replaced the medieval emphasis on conservation with a modern, openly voluntaristic emphasis on changing the legal and social order. Particularly significant in this regard, as we will see, is the semantic trajectory of the notion of police, for although this concept will propel a typically Aristotelian notion fully into the modern age, it will at the same time use that notion to definitely eclipse the conception of politics predicated on the supremacy of law and morals, along with idea of the sovereign as guarantor of the natural equilibrium of the political organism.

The evolution of the notion of police thus came by way of the key theoretical innovations of modern political absolutism, especially its revival of themes in public law and the development of the modern arts of government. For a long time, however, legal knowledge and politico-administrative knowledge will exist as a theoretical tangle whose strands it will not be possible to disentangle until a science of public law, on the one hand, and an economic science, on the other, come into their own as independent disciplines. The semantic development of the notion of police aptly captures the intellectual evolution that throughout the modern age unfolded through the mutual feedback between legal sciences, on the one hand—engaged in an effort to rethink the few materials that Roman law devoted directly to the question of *sovereignty*—and modern political and administrative knowledge, on the other, which on the foundation of legal knowledge built its own theoretical edifice by developing the idea of *government*.

In a nutshell, the police apparatus was created around two fundamental intellectual processes running in parallel to each other. On the one hand was a process of progressive *Verwissenscaftlichung* (Stolleis 1998a, 83–84) in the study of public law, or *ius publicum*, which was advancing as a knowledge of the legal relations involving the *public person*—the more so as the mounting institutionalization of modern political apparatuses increasingly awakened the consciousness of a sovereign public sphere. On the other hand was the theoretical foundation of politico-administrative knowledge as a guide to sovereign action within the widening spaces that were being opened by the doctrine of *ius publicum*. This knowledge was largely informed by the themes of political neo-Aristotelianism and by the debate on reason of state and *prudentia civilis*.

The police idea was thus forged from an alloy of *prudentia iuris (publici)* and *prudentia civilis*, or, otherwise stated, of legal knowledge and politico-administrative

transformative threshold of the 16th century without much damage (Riedel 1975, 116). The themes, concepts, and lexicon of Aristotle's political thought thus made it into the modern age, and in fact when we turn to reason of state, we will see that this debate takes up Aristotelian themes and sometimes borrows its lexicon (see Nuzzo 1995, 40; Skinner 1978, 23ff.).

knowledge. It came into being and developed within the framework of the reasoning that politico-legal culture was devoting to the two basic notions of sovereignty and government, and in a sense it wound up encapsulating the main advances made in thinking about those two notions. Before we can analyze the semantic and conceptual nuances the concept of police took on in the different cultural traditions, we will need to explore its theoretical roots, however brief that exploration may be.

2.1. Sovereignty

As mentioned, throughout the Middle Ages, it was the legal dimension that prevailed over the political dimension. Sovereign power is insistently described as limited by an obligation of compliance with a binding and all but immutable legal framework—a legal universe that lacks any internal distinction and does not carve out any particular legal space for the public person. This conception of the politico-legal universe began to fall into crisis, however, with the practical development of absolutism, a development that compelled political and legal science to find a foundation on which to legitimize the sovereign's continuing and increasingly insistent interventions in political and social life. It was out of this need that there emerged some of the essential concepts of modern politico-legal discourse, meaning the complex of reflections made in thrashing out the relation between politics and law. A body of thought developed in the dual debate devoted, on the one hand, to the nature of the highest *potestas* and, on the other, to the essential traits of legal norms and the question whether the sovereign can introduce exceptions to such norms. This in turn prompted a reflection on the concepts of *necessitas, utilitas publica,* and *iusta causa* as devices through which to justify and at the same time keep in check the incipient absolutistic tendencies of political authorities. Through these politico-legal concepts, the framework of ancient constitutionalism came under strains that ultimately caused it to fall apart, and the stage was thus set for the development of the modern notion of sovereignty. These seminal concepts, as is known, originated out of the classic Roman sources available to political and legal thinkers in the Middle Ages (Post 1964, 253; Gaudemet 1951, 465), and they formed the concrete theoretical foundation on which basis to advance the scholarly treatment of *quaestiones iuris publici* (Stolleis 1998a, 80–87).

The first thinkers to sketch out a properly modern theory of sovereignty and of the relation between sovereign power and the law were the canonists, with the glosses they made to the papal decrees. The canonists were, in particular, the first to introduce voluntaristic elements into a legal and political doctrine that for a long time had proceeded from a concept of law as the expression of a changeless universal reason (Pennington 1993, 45). The debate was framed around the issue of *dispensatio*, the supreme authority's power to introduce general or personal exceptions to the obligation to follow the law (Cortese 1962, 100ff.). This issue raised much broader questions on the nature of supreme power, and its theoretical development would go through the basic notion of *plenitudo potestatis*.

This notion had a role to play in the development of the theories on papal monarchy, when it was used to refer to the pope's supreme power. But the scholar who gave it theoretical depth was the canonist Henricus de Segusio, known as Hostiensis, who introduced a distinction that would become central to the whole of subsequent legal and political thinking: the distinction between *potestas absoluta* and *potestas ordinata* (Pennington 1988, 435; 1993, 75).[3] Hostiensis argued that the pope, acting within his *potestas ordinata*, was bound to respect the legal framework in force, but since in that framework he enjoyed a *potestas absoluta*, he could consider himself relieved of that obligation. The idea of a *potestas absoluta* thus served to justify a general power to exempt himself from the obligation to respect positive law, but it could not be used in an absolute sense to also justify the violation of higher-order precepts and norms. In this regard, Hostiensis also introduced two further notions that would be pivotal in subsequent political and legal theory: the notion of *iusta causa*, serving as a justificatory principle, and the notion of *utilitas publica*, serving as a criterion by which to guide the sovereign's action in exercising his *potestas absoluta*. These two notions echoed those of *ratio* and *necessitas* that theologians were developing in treating the pope's power of self-dispensation from compliance with norms, and they would find their way into the legal principles of *causa necessaria* and *ratio publicae utilitatis* (Cortese 1962, 105; Post 1964, 264). The canonists' conceptual toolkit thus marked a fundamental stage in the later development of modern legal and political thought and of the modern notion of sovereignty.

> If a sovereign's will was the source of law and not restricted by the strictures of reason and morality, and if, under certain circumstances, a monarch could promulgate and act contrary to standards of justice and the precepts of reason—even though in the Middle Ages these acts were always justified because of the common good or because of great necessity—all the necessary elements were in place for what later would be called "reason of state."
>
> (Pennington 1988, 436)

These stepping stones to the development of an explicitly absolutistic theory were met with resistance by the medieval doctrine of politics and law, which for a long time, as noted, remained eminently constitutional in its outlook. We can see why the jurists were initially reluctant to unambiguously affirm the legitimacy of a political power not bound by the legal framework if we consider that the legal

---

3 This distinction, grounded in theological doctrine, first appeared in Book Three of Hostiensis's *Lectura in Decretales Gregorii IX*, where it was used to comment on two decretals issued by Pope Innocent III (*Proposuit* X 3.8.4 and *Magnae devotionis* X 3.34.7). In that context, the distinction was introduced to more accurately spell out the idea of papal monarchy, and in particular the idea that the pope could dispense himself from the obligation to comply with canon law (Pennington 1993, 54ff.).

corpus they were working with was rather contradictory,[4] and that on this basis they were expected to interpret a legal universe where legislative activity was still scarce and much of the law was still customary. However, as much as medieval legal thought would inevitably be prodded by Ulpian into espousing the view that the sovereign could not be held responsible under the law, it did in various ways seek to limit that *ab solutio* doctrine by conceding, in line with the *Digna vox*, that the prince could elect to voluntarily submit to the rule of law. Over time this argument came to be interpreted in a legalistic way, the more so as strict adherence to the letter of the Justinianian texts, and with them of Ulpian's formula, gave way to a looser reading (Cortese 1962, 148ff.). This push in favour of upholding constitutional principles was further supported by a trend where the idea of natural law inherited from the classic sources took on broader significance as an expression of reason and equity. In this way that idea, originally a doctrinal construct framed within strict categorial boundaries, morphed into a broad and malleable principle of *ius aequissimum* carrying an equitable force that could even be brought to bear on positive law (ibid., 47).

It should not come as a surprise that, within that theoretical frame, the question of the power to act outside the law, either as a matter of general principle or on a case-by-case basis, began to revolve around the notion of *iusta causa* understood as a foundation of rationality and legitimacy. Indeed, civilists began to recognize the legitimacy of partial exceptions by going back to notions worked out by the canonists, and initially they endorsed the validity of exceptions to higher-order norms only *in casibus specialibus* but not *in sua corpori universitate* or only in the concrete application of law that on its merits could be found to be always good and just (ibid., 120). All this prudence of the glossators in accepting derogations of law by political power was, however, turned around by Azo of Bologna, who pointed the way for subsequent commentators. His *Summa codicis* contained an early reference to *iusta causa* as a basis for disregarding a higher-order law, and an even more explicit statement to that effect would later appear in his *Lectura codicis*, identifying *publica utilitas* as the model criterion of *iusta causa*.[5]

---

4 As much as historians may tend to see Justinian's *Corpus Iuris Civilis* as the main source of modern political absolutism, these texts also contained some essentially constitutional notions that served as a foothold in all attempts to limit sovereign power. Be that as it may, the few texts explicitly devoted to setting out the relation between political power and the law ultimately rested on Ulpian's two definitions in the *Digest*—namely, *quod principis placuit legis habet vigorem* (Dig. I.4.I) and *priceps legibus solutus est* (Dig. I.3.31)—both typical expressions of an imperial conception of power. But in this regard Justinian's *Codex* also contains a text in which political sovereignty seems more closely bound up with an obligation to respect the law. This is the so-called *Digna vox*, a 429 constitution by Theodosius II and Valentinian II that reads: "Digna vox maiestate regnatis legis alligatum se principem profiteri. Adeo de auctoritate iuris nostra pendet auctoritas. Et re vera maius imperio est submittere legibus principatum. Et oracolo presentis edicti nobis dicere non patimur iudicamus" (Cod. I.14.4). This is described by Pennington (1993, 78) as the most important constitutional text of the Middle Ages.

5 "Iura naturalia dicuntur immutabilia [. . .] et obtinet haec regula, nisi iusta causa interveniat" (*Summa Codicis*, I, Si contra ius vel utilitatem publicam, 2); "iura naturalia dicuntur immutabilia

Later legal scholarship developed this theme by following the glossators and using the concept of *iusta causa* to support the view that even natural law and higher-order norms are subject to derogation. As has been commented, "the seed planted in the time of Azo of Bologna was beginning to bloom under the sedulous care of the first glossators" (ibid., 123; my translation). The concept of *iusta causa*, or *causa necessaria*, had already found itself at the centre of the controversy over the prince's exceptional powers, so much so that political scientists tended to frame those powers within legal concepts such as that of *necessitas* (Post 1964, 290–300; Saint-Bonnet 2001, 118–38). These uses of *iusta causa* and *ratio necessitatis* therefore tended to also call into play the broader question of the definition of political power, a concept framed by recourse to those of *plenitudo potestatis* and *absoluta potestas* worked out by the canonists (Cortese 1962, 162).

Despite these early attempts to bring the notion of *potestas absoluta* into legal and political thought, such a distinctly voluntaristic concept still remained extraneous to medieval political culture. The very notion of *potestas absoluta* that was taking shape in legal thought was received by political Aristotelianism through a partial distortion of Aristotle's *Politics* in the Latin translation of 1260. Indeed, this translation laid the groundwork for a distinction between a *regimen politicum*, where the sovereign is at the same time governor and governed, and a *regimen regale*, where the sovereign by contrast seems fully untethered to the legal order that governs the political community (Senellart 2005, 194ff.). The jurists, for their part, were much more reluctant to resort to a notion of that sort, with its absolutistic potential, so much so that they tended to favour an essentially legalistic reading of the Roman sources that were most compromised by a voluntaristic conception of political power. Even when the idea of a *potestas absoluta* not bound by the constitutional framework or by higher-order norms passed muster, it would always be subject to criteria of *iusta causa, ratio necessitatis*, and *utilitas publica*. The exercise of such lawless powers *sine causa* inevitably fell within the rubric of tyranny (Pennington 1993, 117–18; Cortese 1962, 165).

Resistance to legal notions that foreshadowed the making of a political power *ab legibus solutus* was even stronger among jurists working in the tradition of customary law. But even here, notions carrying the potential to tilt the development of political thought in the direction of absolutism were beginning to emerge despite the ability of constitutional visions to hold their ground.

As is known, English legal and political thought in the 13th century leaned heavily in favour of constitutionalism, as did its highest exponent, Henry de Bracton. In the opinion of many, most notably Pollock and Maitland (1898, 160ff.), what made it possible for this legalistic stance to take hold was a total lack of Roman themes in English legal and political thought, and in particular in that of Bracton. But this idea needs to be toned down in several respects, and not just in the sense that it is superficial to read Roman sources as mere statements

[. . .] nisi iusta causa interveniat, vel pubblica utilitatis" (*Lectura codicis*, gl. Quae generali in Cod. 1,22,6). See, generally, Cortese 1962, 121; Post 1964, 278–79.

of absolutism. Indeed, as has been compellingly argued by now, it is doubtful that Bracton did not actually come under the influence of Roman law. Quite the contrary, his study of the Roman foundations of law deeply informs his *De Legibus et Consuetudinibus Angliae* (see Plucknett 1958; David 1954, 246ff.; Post 1964, 165ff.; Schulz 1945, 176; Tierney 1963, 295). In any event, as much as Bracton's work contains many Romanist motifs, one can agree with Pennington that Bracton did have only a passing familiarity with the work that was being done on the Continent in treating the relation between sovereign power and the law, so much so that he ignored many of the newly minted notions in that regard, especially that of *plenitudo potestatis* (Pennington 1993, 93).[6] Bracton's strong endorsement of constitutionalism is most likely owed to the historical and political context, in that, unlike what had been happening on the Continent, England in Bracton's time had already gone through several constitutional crises that placed the question of the relation between sovereign power and law at the centre of political and legal thought, making any reference to *plenitudo potestatis* entirely idle (ibid., 92).

In this sense, as is often remarked, perhaps no one better than Bracton exemplifies the medieval conception of law and sovereign authority as *iurisdictio*. The law consists of a set of time-tested and hence unchangeable customs which the sovereign simply *finds* in existence, and which he is tasked with preserving and defending, whereas a sovereign who should willingly ignore the law's guidance is thereby considered a tyrant, if not the devil's servant (Miller 1956, 276; Carlyle and Carlyle 1950, 37). According to McIlwain's classic interpretation, however, Bracton's conception of limited sovereignty also opens up a space in which the *princeps* can manoeuvre with greater freedom. As previously suggested, Bracton did not here rely on the notion of *plenitudo potestatis*, nor did he look to the distinction between *potestas absoluta* and *potestas ordinata* which the canonists had developed and the civilists were beginning to embrace. He instead drew a fully analogous distinction between two spheres of political activity, one pertaining to classic *iurisdictio*, the other to what is called *gubernaculum*, where "no one, not even a judge, can question a specifically royal act so as to bring its legitimacy into doubt" (McIlwain 2007, 71). This reading is based on a passage that to many—including Tierney (1963, 306) and Miller (1956, 274)—has seemed insufficient to support the view that Bracton was explicitly taking up the Continental theories on *potestas absoluta*.[7] But even if we reject McIlwain's exegesis, we still have to recognize that

---

6 Cortese, for his part, comments that although Bracton did make original contributions to the study of law, that originality should not be overstated, for it is mostly owed to the forcefulness of his views. The sources he relied on gave him greater leeway, enabling him to bypass the problem of abstract supreme *auctoritas*, which alone entailed a full espousal of the concept of *plenitudo potestatis*, and which in his time had to obligatorily be connected with the idealized figure of the emperor (Cortese 1962, 154, n. 19).

7 The passage in question reads: "Habet enim omnia iura in manu sua quae ad coronam et laicalem pertinent potestatem et materialem gladium qui pertinet ad regni gubernaculum. Habet etiam iustitiam et iudicium quae sunt iurisdictionis, ut ex iurisdictione sua sicut dei minister et vicarius tributa unicuique quod suum fuerit. Habet etiam ea quae sunt pacis [. . .] Habet etiam coertionem

this basic distinction—between a *regular* sphere of political action, where sovereign action runs up against all the limits imposed by the legal orders, and an *exceptional* sphere in which sovereign action is not subject to the law—appears to be reflected in Bracton's reference to *gubernaculum* as a supreme and unexceptionable power to use force and wage war. On the other hand, as Tierney (1963, 309) himself concedes, it is also true that a similar distinction was taking shape in the practical exercise of sovereign functions. And although this distinction was being framed through the Thomist dichotomy between *dominium politium* and *dominium regale*, in later centuries it would come back in an even more explicit form in English political thought through the work of Sir John Fortescue and his *De laudibus legum Angliae*.

Inevitably less thorough than Bracton in setting out the relation between the sovereign and the law was the contemporary jurist Philippe de Beaumanoir,[8] even though the imprint of Roman legal science was on the whole stronger on his work than it was on Bracton's treatise. Indeed, Beaumanoir seems to have already taken up some of the ideas on the sovereign's *potestas absoluta* (Miller 1956, 266), and in particular the concept of *necessitas* or *ratio necessitatis* and that of *utilitas publica*, both previously developed at length by the canonists and civilists (Dunbabin 1988, 487). Indeed, unlike Bracton's sovereign, Beaumanoir's was less bound by the inherited legal framework. However, in ascribing an absolute exceptional power to the prince, Beaumanoir tended to confine the exercise of such power to a range of very specific cases, while subjecting it to institutional limits and to general policy guidelines: "Before the king can enact new statutes," Beaumanoir comments, "he must make sure he does so with cause [*resnable cause*] and for the common benefit [*commun pourfit*] and with the great council, and especially that they are not contrary to God or to good mores" (Beaumanoir 1900, chap. XLIX, "Des establissemens et des necessités," par. 1515, p. 264; my translation).[9] We can see, then, that with Beaumanoir French legal language and culture acquires the absolutistic motifs that legal scholars previously developed under the labels of *ratio necessitatis* and *utilitas publica*, rendered as *resnable cause* and *commun pourfit*, respectively (Miller 1956, 278).

---

ut delinquentes puniate et coercet. Item habet in protestate sua ut leges et constitutiones et assissas in regno suo provisas et approbatas et iuratas, ipse in propria persona sua observet et a subditis suis facies observari. Nihil enim prodest iura condere, nisi sit qui iura tueatur. Habet igitur rex huiusmodi iura sive iurisdictionis in manu sua" (*De Legibus*, 55b, II, 166). And indeed Bracton's reference to the "material sword" *(materialem gladium)* has been argued to be too generic to support the argument in question, for it could simply be meant to evoke the idea of the supreme coercive force associated with the exercise of the traditional *iurisdictio* conferred on the civil powers as distinct from the *spiritualis gladius* conferred on ecclesiastical authorities (Tierney 1963, 307).

8 Beaumanoir's main work was the *Coutumes de Beauvaisis*, conceived as a *balliage*, or systematic collection and organization of customs, in a small area in the kingdom of France known as Clermont en Beauvaisis. The work's design and purpose therefore explain why questions of legal and political theory are treated only tangentially in it.

9 The French original: "Tout soit il ainsi que li rois puist fere nouveaus establissemens, il doit mout prendre garde qu'il les face par resnable cause et pour le commun pourfit et par grant conseil, et especiaument qu'il ne soient pas fet contre Dieu ne contre bonnes meurs."

Legislative power was conceived by him as an exceptional power arising out of necessity (Saint-Bonnet 2001, 158–61); however, even under the constraint of these legal notions, what was beginning to emerge on the horizon was, here too, the idea of an absolute power not bound by law *(legibus solutus)*—an idea that would figure centrally in the new conceptions of political absolutism.

* * *

What I have tried to describe in this brief detour is the slow process through which legal scholarship wound up in a sense normalizing the state of exception, to the point where the powers conferred on the sovereign on specific occasions—and subject to the legal constraints encapsulated in notions such as *causa, necessitas,* and *utilitas publica*—became a distinguishing element of the modern conception of sovereignty. Once these became entrenched, the stage was set for a theoretical space in which to nurture and consolidate the idea of absolute power *(absoluta potestas)* that would form the theoretical foundation for modern politico-legal absolutism.

This politico-legal absolutism can be traced back to numerous early formulations that in various ways foretokened its coming, but its most mature expression undoubtedly came with Jean Bodin. Indeed, there are two readings of his thought: one that tends to underscore its novel elements, and in particular the modernity of a voluntaristic conception of law whose production is at this point monopolized by a public authority; and another that instead tends to underscore the traditional elements in connection with the idea that absolute power is bounded by the laws of God and of nature. We will not be concerning ourselves here with such interpretive controversies, which would have us also take into account the view of those who have reread the *Six Books of the Commonwealth* in light of the theoretico-conceptual legacy that Bodin inherited from the civilists and from medieval legal thought at large. But for all the range of interpretations, it would be odd to downplay Bodin's full modernity and the revolutionary import of his work, which can be recognized in the way he treated notions such as those of *necessitas* and *utilitas publica*. Indeed, as much as he took up a traditional theme extensively debated throughout the whole of previous politico-legal thought, he wound up expanding these notions to the point of nearly draining them of all legal significance, depriving them of any ability to put a check on supreme sovereign powers (Saint-Bonnet 2001, 190–99).

Bodin, as is known, proceeded from the view that "the principal mark of sovereign majesty and absolute power" lies in "the right to impose laws" (Bodin [1576] 1955, 32). He thus seems to be spelling out in bold letters the idea of an absolute legislative power, but he does not go so far as to decouple that power from the sovereign's obligation to respect the basic laws:

> If we insist [. . .] that absolute power means exemption from all law whatsoever, there is no prince in the world who can be regarded as sovereign, since all the princes of the earth are subject to the laws of God and of nature, and even to certain human laws common to all nations.

> (Bodin [1576] 1955, 28)

Given that the prince is bound by the laws of God and of nature and by the law of peoples, he cannot "without just and reasonable cause" (Bodin [1576] 1992, 39) encroach on the private sphere of his subjects, particularly by infringing their property rights. So again we run into this idea of *causa* that we found across the whole field of previous legal thought. In Bodin, however, the sovereign stands as the absolute interpreter of *cause juste et raisonnable*: "If the need is urgent, the prince ought not to wait for the Estates to meet or for the consent of the people, since its welfare depends on the foresight and diligence of a wise prince" (Bodin [1576] 1992, 21). It therefore falls within the remit of princely prudence to make judgments about the state of necessity, and hence about whether there may be good reason to violate the basic laws. Princely prudence is thus the highest interpreter of the collective interest, a role it can play as keeper of the basic principles of natural law: "Natural reason instructs us that the public good must be preferred to the particular, and that subjects should give up not only their mutual antagonisms and animosities, but also their possessions, for the safety of the Commonwealth" (Bodin [1576] 1955, 34). To be sure, Bodin can in this sense be described as the first theorist of sovereignty understood as the absolute power to make decisions in a state of exception (Schmitt 1922). But through his reference to the "foresight and diligence of a wise prince" *(la prévoyance, et diligence d'un sage Prince)* he also clearly highlights how the spaces that politico-legal knowledge recognized for politics were such as to bring about the need to set sovereign action on a rational foundation. This was the enterprise that was being taken up by the doctrine of reason of state and in the reflections that were being devoted to *prudentia civilis*—the two main manifestations of the nascent *ratio gubernatoria*.

2.2. Government

The *ratio gubernatoria* did not come about and develop, except incidentally, as a body of thought concerned to define the nature of political authority and ground its legitimacy. Unlike politico-legal thought, this kind of discourse tends to take the sphere of sovereign prerogatives as a given, turning instead to the question of identifying the proper way to exercise political power. In a sense, then, the modern *ratio gubernatoria* could not fully develop until the legitimacy of political power had already been established and the conditions were in place for the concrete, material development of political power. Its roots lie in the treatises on princes and on *prudentia regnativa*, which more than laying out constitutional schemes for the realm would tend to sketch out an image of the ideal prince in which rulers might see a reflection of themselves—hence the name *spaecula principis*, or mirrors for princes (Skinner 1978, 118; Senellart 2005, 47; Tuck 1993, 33). However, it is only when the rhetorical tropes of this literature were superseded that we can see the birth of a proper *ratio gubernatoria*, when the image of the just king as the addressee of a moral and legal disquisition on how to rule wisely became a familiar staple, giving way to increasingly elaborate constructions on the general conditions that a kingdom needed to have in place in order to thrive and a prince needed to observe in governing that kingdom. And, as is known, what eclipsed the genre of the medieval *spaecula principis* was the growing body of literature on reason of state.

Two fundamental moments in this development of political thought were the work of Machiavelli and the anti-Machiavellian debate it sparked. Another was the development of Taciteanism and neo-Stoicism, which emerged out of the practical philosophy that was being taught at universities and out of the political thought that was taking shape in that same milieu. These reflections on the *ratio status* and *arcana imperii*, with their marked tendency to consider political questions on an empirical basis, set in train the process through which the doctrine of politics would develop into a fully fledged science (Stolleis 1998b, 44). The figure of the prince remained central, as was called for by the rhetorical style of the time, but next to it there emerged the *territory* as a domain which, unlike that of the exclusively legal concept of the medieval *regnum*, set the exercise of power within a geographically bounded area (Senellart 2005, 53). What was underway, in essence, was a gradual shift from ethics to statistics: from a menu of princely virtues and prudence to a proper science of statecraft.

The notion of reason of state, as is known, traces back to a work that Giovanni della Casa wrote in 1547 under the title *Orazione a Carlo V imperatore intorno alla restituzione della città di Piacenza* (Oration addressed to Emperor Charles V on the return of the city of Piacenza: Della Casa 1733). As early as 1521–23, however, the idea of the "reason and practices of States" (Guicciardini [1520] 1994, 159) comes up in Francesco Guicciardini's *Dialogue on the Government of Florence*, which first introduced that notion in the political debate of the period (De Mattei 1979, 10ff.; Tuck 1993, 39). The expression *reason of state* is commonly taken to refer to a way of thinking about and wielding political power, and in particular the unlimited political power, free of legal constraints, associated with the birth of modern political absolutism (Tuck 1993, 6; Viroli 1992, 67–82; Stolleis 1998c, 14). Although the expression does not figure in the classic legal and political lexicon, it can be considered a translation of earlier expressions such as *ratio reipublicae* and *ratio status rei publicae*, or even *ratio necessitatis*, which in the legal and political debate of the period, as we have seen, came into use precisely for the purpose of constructing spaces for political action not subject to legal constraints. In a short time the expression established itself widely, becoming the key notion around which revolved the legal and political debate across Europe. And the reasons for that quick uptake can be traced to its roots, enabling it to capture the gist of some concepts in wide use, which made the political and intellectual environment of the time particularly receptive to it (De Mattei 1979, 24ff.; Tenenti 1992, 12–13).

The idea of reason of state is thus commonly associated with three core elements—that is, with (i) the emergence of modern political institutions, (ii) the creation of a sphere in which political powers can act outside the law; and, finally, (iii) the idea of the political as an independent sphere of action in which sovereign authority is in the first place concerned with preserving its own political pre-eminence. However, this is in a sense a biased understanding of reason of state filtered through the lens of the critics who took exception to its *bad* use, and which then went through the liberal criticism of political absolutism. This understanding not only glosses over the fact that even among those who criticized reason of state, and even in the heart of liberal constitutions themselves, a sphere has always been recognized for exceptional or lawless action (Lazzeri and Reynié 1992, 10; Saint-Bonnet 2001, 285–376), but it also winds up depriving the notion of reason of state of its theoretical richness, by coupling it with the question of the relation between legitimate power and arbitrary action, between law and politics, or the conflict between the governed and the governors. Indeed, as will be argued, this notion provided the original matrix for an entirely new conception of political rationality:

> The government of reason of state would rely on a body of knowledge that was slowly becoming more formalized, as well as on a modern theory of the political that finally anchored itself to the tightly packed content of a science of administration and a science of its effects on society whose core lies in mercantilism, cameralism, statistical science, and police theories.
>
> (Lazzeri and Reynié 1992, 11; my translation)

So, just as the development of the notion of reason of state provided the theoretical backing for the voluntarism and subjectivism that accompanied the birth of political absolutism, that same notion also provided the original matrix for the modern rationalism of statesmanship, for modern statistics understood as a science or knowledge of the state.

2.2.1. The Machiavellian break

According to an established view, it is essentially to Machiavelli that we owe the invention of modern reason of state, meaning politics as a sphere of thought and action kept specifically apart from the sphere of law and morality (see Croce 1994; Meinecke 1957; Stolleis 1998b, 33–35; Stolleis 1994, 23; Skinner 1978, 134). One scholar who has done important research on the origin of the expression is Rodolfo De Mattei, who in analyzing Guicciardini's *Dialogue on the Government of Florence* has vividly illustrated that its reference to the "reason and practices of States" (Guicciardini [1520] 1994, 159) is essentially Machiavellian. Indeed, as De Mattei argues, in this famous dialogue on the killing of prisoners of war,

> the essence of reason of state already finds a sufficiently clear statement. At issue is that political interest which as such, for Machiavelli, trumps any other consideration, uncompromisingly rejects anything less than full satisfaction, and authorizes violations of the moral law (cruelty) that are undoubtedly contrary to God's precepts.
>
> (De Mattei 1979, 5; my translation)

The notion that Machiavelli essentially founded the independence of politics has not, however, received unanimous consent. It is in particular Gaines Post who, in a well-known study on the politico-legal terms *ratio publiacae utilitatis, ratio necessitatis,* and *ratio status rei publicae,* has argued that this political rationality has been with us since the Middle Ages, and indeed that it may even go back to a timeless past, at least when taken as a set of principles that legitimize our placing the public interest above private interests, resorting to extraordinary means when necessary, and bending moral rules for the sake of higher moral ends (Post 1964, 253).

These views capture a kernel of truth. Indeed, on the one hand, it is true that we cannot credit Machiavelli with singlehandedly conjuring into existence the idea of a sphere of political action unmoored from the sphere of legality, since, as mentioned, the political traced its deeper origin to the debate on the state of exception and of necessity that for centuries had been engaging writers on law. Then, too, as Foucault has compellingly argued, Machiavelli was still in several respects working within the tradition of mirrors for princes. The reason he was laying out, then, was the reason of princes, not reason of state (Senellart 1992, 21; Vasoli 1994, 50). On the other hand, we cannot downplay the novelty of the modern political rationality which came into being precisely with the debate sparked by Machiavelli's work, even if this debate inevitably overcame the limitations of that work. In short, although it was Machiavelli who "broke the mirror for princes," it was the literature which developed around the issues he brought into focus and in opposition to his themes, in an effort to piece that mirror back together, that laid the foundation for a political theory and practice in which the ancient political conceit of the ideal ruler could no longer be accommodated (Zarka 1994a, 104).

To be sure, Machiavelli's *Prince* falls neatly into the literary genre of the mirrors for princes, whose rhetorical style and pedagogical aim it follows. But even though it is not yet a treatise on the government of the state—for it is essentially designed as a handbook for sovereigns and bears the stamp of that genre—it does, on a *theoretical* level, make a radical break with that same tradition (Senellart 2005, 213; Stolleis 1998c, 15). Indeed, ahead of anyone else Machiavelli lucidly underscored the role of brute force in politics, shifting the focus from a need to preserve basic freedoms and uphold justice (two concerns that continued to underlie mirrors for princes between the 14th and 15th centuries) to a need for the prince to protect the realm (Skinner 1978, 125). At the core of Machiavelli's interests, then, was the question of how to maintain the integrity of the state. As noted, however, he was referring not to the state *per se* but to the "state of the prince"—that is, to a personal status or domain over a territory that the prince was expected to defend and preserve (Senellart 2005, 212). Politics thus consisted in the set of principles of rational action that would make it possible to preserve one's dominion within the frame of a sort of state of permanent necessity (Saint-Bonnet 2001, 183–89). To this end, under the shocking title of Chapter XVIII, "How Rulers Should Keep Their Promises," Machiavelli did not hesitate to claim that the sovereign is justified in resorting to violent means or to subterfuge, even in explicit violation of the laws and agreements the sovereign had himself pledged to uphold.[10]

Politics was explicitly severed from morality and law. It was also deliberately severed from the rhetoric of the common welfare and the public interest, so much so that it wound up being reduced to the means enabling the prince to protect himself from his own people (Senellart 2005, 20–21; Stolleis 1998c, 15; D'Addio 1970, 2). Therein lies Machiavelli's deep break with the previous literature. This break was most evident in his conviction that there was no such thing as a universal model of virtue and morality that could be held up for the prince to follow, but that he must be able to gauge his action to the varying circumstances and to the moment in view of what is expedient and effective.[11] However, in reducing the art of government to military technique and the use of political power for the sole purpose of enabling the prince to keep control of the territories he has acquired, Machiavelli still in a sense found himself stuck in the ancient patrimonial conception of political power (Senellart 1992, 24). Even though, as discussed, the concept of the state was already coming into its own, the focus of Machiavelli's analysis was still on the prince and on the "fragile link" (Foucault 2004, 92) by which he was connected with his principality:

> For Machiavelli, the Prince exists in a relationship of singularity and externality, of transcendence, to his principality. Machiavelli's Prince receives his principality either through inheritance, or by acquisition, or by conquest; in any case, he is not a part of it, but external to it.
>
> (Ibid., 91)

10 In fact, even though the prince can, and indeed must, ordinarily govern according to the laws, when the occasion calls for it he must at once be able to resort to all the tricks of the trade. Writes Machiavelli in this regard: "You must know there are two ways of contesting, the one by the law, the other by force; the first method is proper to men, the second to beasts; but because the first is frequently not sufficient, it is necessary to have recourse to the second. Therefore it is necessary for a prince to understand how to avail himself of the beast and the man" (Machiavelli [1532] 1988, 61). As Machiavelli sees the matter, then, it is not always possible to govern by law. The more critical the circumstance, the more unabated must be the means deployed in dealing with it. That does not, however, make military and coercive force the only option available to the prince in such circumstances, for he can also resort to stratagems and subterfuge: "A prince, therefore, being compelled knowingly to adopt the beast, ought to choose the fox and the lion; because the lion cannot defend himself against snares and the fox cannot defend himself against wolves. Therefore, it is necessary to be a fox to discover the snares and a lion to terrify the wolves. Those who rely simply on the lion do not understand what they are about" (ibid.).
11 Writes Machiavelli in this regard: "And you have to understand this, that a prince, especially a new one, cannot observe all those things for which men are esteemed, being often forced, in order to maintain the state, to act contrary to fidelity, friendship, humanity, and religion. Therefore it is necessary for him to have a mind ready to turn itself accordingly as the winds and variations of fortune force it, yet, as I have said above, not to diverge from the good if he can avoid doing so, but, if compelled, then to know how to set about it" (Machiavelli [1532] 1988, 62).

It was by virtue of this fragile relation between the prince and his principality that the Machiavellian art of government became the art by which the prince could maintain and consolidate his personal dominion, for

> inasmuch as it is an external relationship, it is fragile and constantly under threat. It is threatened from outside, by the Prince's enemies who want to take, or re-conquer, his principality, and it is also threatened internally, for there is no a priori or immediate reason for the Prince's subjects to accept his rule.
>
> (Ibid., 91–92)

Machiavellian politics essentially came down to the art of warding off the threats, both internal and external, that might unsettle a still fragile and unstable political sovereignty, in a way that would later be further developed by one of Machiavelli's main apologists, Gabriel Naudé, in whose *Considérations politiques sur les coups d'État* (Naudé [1639] 1723) we no longer find even a single reference to the justice of political action, and everything is judged by how expedient or effective it is in protecting political dominion (Saint-Bonnet 2001, 219–25). As librarian to political men of the stature of Cardinals Mazarin and Richelieu, Naudé drove to extremes the idea of political reason under a state of exception, defining reason of state as "excessus juris communis propter bonum commune" (departing from common law in the interests of the common good: Naudé [1639] 1723, 77). Such reason of state was conceived by Naudé as a theory of the coup d'état (Zarka 1994b, 154)—that is, as extraordinary action, precisely the *excessus juris communis* that was thought to be indispensable for the safety and security of the state. "Coups d'état," says Naudé, "could be brought under the same definition we gave to maxims and to reason of state, *ut sint excessus juris communis propter bonum commune*" (Naudé [1639] 1723, 77; my translation).[12] Just as in Machiavelli the art of governing required the prince to set aside the classic virtues described throughout the literature proposing to give counsel to the prince, so in Naudé reason of state was "something that breaches the laws, or at any rate does not submit to the laws" (Foucault 2004, 262). Reason of state was now couched in a language that lived outside the boundaries of legal reason and could no longer be framed within the ancient legal notions of *causa* and *necessitas*: It was now political reason proper, a reason of expedience. As Naudé put it, "natural, universal, noble, and philosophical justice [*justice*] sometimes falls outside the boundaries of custom and proves inconvenient for the practice of the world." Therefore, "it will often be necessary to avail oneself of the artificial, the particular, the political [*politique*], designed and tailored to the needs of polities [*Polices*] and states" (Naudé [1639] 1723, 438; my translation).[13] The reference

---

12 The French original: "Coups d'Etat, qui peuvent marcher sous la même définition que nous avons déja donnée aux Maximes & à la raison d'Etat, *ut sint excessus juris communis propter bonum commune*."

13 The French original: "Mais d'autant que cette justice naturelle, universelle, noble & Philosophique, est quelquefois hors d'usage & incommode dans la pratique du monde [. . .]. Il faudra bien souvent

made to coups d'état was precisely a reference to an overly political action, to the sphere of *arcana imperii* (the principles of power, or statecraft), where the criterion of effective and useful action precedes and trumps all efforts to set it on a rational foundation of legitimacy.

2.2.2. The genesis of the modern ratio gubernatoria

Few books could lay claim to fame quite like Machiavelli's *Prince*. At once celebrated and reviled, it enjoyed the privilege of making it into the *index librorum prohibitorum*, even though its early editions had been to some extent sanitized, gaining papal approval in Rome, where they were published (Procacci 1995, 5ff.). We will not be concerned here with the question of whether or not the book's notoriety was actually justified in light of its substance, but either way, such was the shrewdness of its more conspicuous claims that, like matches in the tinderbox that were the religious wars and the political clashes triggered by the surging political absolutism, they set off a witch-hunt (De Mattei 1970, 40; Mastellone 1970, 48; Senellart 1992, 26–27).[14] An extensive anti-Machiavellian debate developed around *The Prince*, and even though it sometimes would break out into simple political squabbling—ultimately reducing the name *Machiavelli* and the idea of Machiavellianism to a rhetorical device, an accusation ready to be hurled at one's opponents—on other occasions the debate was driven by higher theoretical aims, aspiring to bring the sphere of politics back under the control of law and morality. This latter aim can be detected in particular behind the reference to *true* reason of state that Della Casa made in his *Orazione* in contraposition to that reason which is "wrongful and false and dissolute, and willing to engage in theft and evildoing, and to which the name *reason of state* has been attached" (Della Casa 1733, 7; my translation).[15] It was precisely this debate on true or authentic reason of state that made it possible to move beyond the problem of the *prince* by reframing the question into that of governing the *state* (Senellart 1992, 24). So, far from merely attacking Machiavelli—more often than not taking issue with the

se servir de l'artificielle, particuliere, politique, faite & rapportée au besoin & à la necessité des Polices & Etats."

14 Critics seized in particular on Chapter XVIII, insistently going back to the metaphor of the lion and the fox as evidence of Machiavelli's wickedness (Stolleis 1998c, 21ff.). What *The Prince* bespoke, however, was not the dark wickedness its critics would often see in it, but a clear-sighted pragmatism that can be appreciated in Machiavelli's wide recourse to traditional notions like that of necessity (Senellart 2005, 227). After all, his critics sought to use those very notions of *causa* and *necessitas* to instead *limit* the absolutistic potential packed into reason of state (Stolleis 1998c, 23), and even those who, as we will see, sought to ground reason of state in the ancient texts of political thought found it impossible to steer clear of Machiavellian themes, so much so that through Tacitus or Aristotle they would often unavowedly wind up endorsing Machiavelli's political realism (De Mattei 1979, 49).

15 The Italian original: "due Ragioni, l'una torta, e falsa, e dissoluta, e disposta a rubare, e a mal fare; ed a questa han posto nome di Ragion di Stato."

vulgarized accounts of so-called Machiavellianism—this literature was beginning to set the foundation for a constructive development of its themes.

The foundation on which to rest a *ratio gubernatoria* proper was laid by revisiting the debate on reason of state in light of the theoretical models inherited from antiquity. This work began with the first sympathetic efforts to reread Machiavelli himself in light of Aristotle (Firpo 1970, 24; Procacci 1995, 63ff.), but it came into full bloom with the search for higher theoretical matrixes to which to trace the expression *reason of state* (De Mattei 1979, 40ff.). This search led in particular to an effort to revisit reason of state through Tacitean notions like that of *arcana imperii* or the Aristotelian notion of *politia*, and it played a decisive role in putting the debate on a stronger theoretical footing. Indeed, the debate on true reason of state initiated by Della Casa reached theoretical maturity by taking on the question of *prudentia civilis*, which had become a core component of the practical sciences curriculum taught at university. The academic reflections on *politia* and *prudentia civilis* were thus worked into the debate on *ratio status*, and in this way the intellectual vogue of the time gained theoretical authority (De Mattei 1979, 144; Stolleis 1998a, 249). The question of princely prudence had already begun to be framed as that of the practical knowledge needed for all things political (Nuzzo 1995, 50; Borrelli 1995, 188), so the debate was moving away from its focus on the political wisdom needed to manage the state of exception for the purpose of protecting the prince's hold on power, and in symbiosis with Aristotelian themes it began to evolve into a true *ratio gubernatoria* understood as an economic and administrative science aimed at increasing the power of the state.

The ancient literature on the art of governing was turning from a discourse on reason *of* state to one concerned with reasoning *about* the state—that is, with providing the prince with the knowledge needed to augment not his own power but the strength and resources of the state. In essence, political thought was becoming less and less concerned with the question of the prince and how to preserve his tenuous political sovereignty, and increasingly it was taking into account the complex totality made up of different *elements* (the prince, the territory, the people) and different *relations* (not only those of domination but also those needed to maintain balance and sustain trade and the movement of goods and people), as well as different *interests*, such as those in power, security, prosperity, and welfare (Senellart 1992, 37). Political reflection, in other words, was turning to a new object of study, the state, understood neither as a politico-legal entity, in the manner of the legists, nor, in the manner of Machiavelli and his epigones, as the prince's personal dominion—always unstable and under threat. The state was no longer conceived as a multitude of individuals held together by a legal unity and subject to the dominion of a single political decision-maker, and it began to take on the guise of a stable political entity organized around an economic, social, political, and military structure (Zarka 1994a, 103).

Two authors are particularly illustrative in that regard: Giovanni Botero and Justus Lipsius. Owing to the wide resonance of their works, they can be credited with having provided a proper theoretical foundation for reason of state as a science of government, over against reason of state as the political reason of the state of emergency, a conception whose foundation, as discussed, is instead owed to Machiavelli and Naudé.

2.2.3. Prudentia civilis

The art of government could already be appreciated to be making clear strides in the work of the Piedmontese abbot Giovanni Botero, the first thinker to have used the well-known expression *reason of state* in the title of a work, enabling it to gain firm lodgement in the European political lexicon.[16] Botero's 1589 *Ragion di Stato* went through numerous editions and was translated into all major European languages—evidence of its influence as a seminal work in political thought, so much so that it brought fame to its author as the fountainhead of a whole school of thought (De Mattei 1979, 51). All that aside, the work perhaps stands as the most typical example of how the anti-Machiavellian debate started out from a strongly critical stance—taking exception to what in the premise Botero described as a "barbarous mode of government" (Botero [1589] 1956, xiii)—and proceeded on that basis to lay the groundwork for the modern *ratio gubernatoria*.

Botero famously defined the state as "stable rule over a people" (ibid., 3) and reason of state as "knowledge of the means by which such a dominion may be founded, preserved and extended" (ibid.). These definitions seem to hark back to Machiavelli, at least in the sense of taking for granted the independence of politics understood as the art of exercising and maintaining dominion (Bonnet 2003, 319; De Mattei 1979, 63–64). Nor was this peculiar to Botero, considering that, as mentioned, the entire debate that came in the wake of *The Prince* in various ways more or less tacitly picked up Machiavelli's legacy through the use of Tacitean themes and hiding behind the facade of a nominal anti-Machiavellianism. The truly innovative aspect of Botero's work had to do with his strategy of looking for *ordinary* means for exercising and maintaining political dominion (Bonnet 2003, 321), for in this way he took the first step in moving away from both the political focus essential to Machiavelli and the legal focus essential to Bodin. Botero, in substance, effected the transition from the political to the economic (Senellart 1992, 32) that was beginning to bring to the forefront of political reflection the question of wealth and the industry of men as a tool of political power. "Nothing," Botero thought, "is of greater importance for increasing the power of a state and gaining for it more inhabitants and wealth of every kind" (Botero [1589] 1956, 150–51).

---

16 Equivalent expressions established themselves in every language except maybe German, where the term *Staatsräson* struggled to win acceptance, at least initially (Stolleis 1998b, 36). Indeed, the title of Botero's 1589 treatise, *Della ragion di Stato*, was translated by resorting instead to Aristotelian notions more familiar to the political culture of central Europe. The German edition came out in 1589 under the title *Gründlicher Bericht von Anordnung guter Policeyen und Regiments* (Fundamental report on the arrangement of good policies and political regiments).

The people were still conceived by Bodin and Machiavelli as subject to the sovereign's political power, but with Botero they began to take on a life of their own as a population, with its economic and social processes and its relations with the environment. The centrality of the population as a factor of political power emerged clearly in *Delle cause della grandezza e magnificenza delle città* (On the causes of the greatness and magnificence of cities), a short treatise published as an appendix to the more famous *Ragion di Stato*. The thesis, which would become a *topos* of subsequent political and economic thought, was that the puissance *(possanza)* of cities was owed not to the *extensive* greatness of their political dominion but on their *intensive* greatness (Descendre 2003, 314)—that is, on the density of their populations:

> A city is said to be an assembly of people, a congregation drawn together to the end they may thereby the better live at their ease in wealth and plenty. And the greatness of a city is said to be, not the largeness of the site or the circuit of the walls, but the multitude and number of the inhabitants and their power.
> (Botero [1589] 1956, 227)

The notion of a city's "muscle" or puissance was not just about its population. It was also a measure of the economic prosperity deriving from its economic activity, in turn dependent on its numbers, customs, and industriousness in relation to its accommodation *(commodità)*—that is, to its "ground plan," the territorial layout of its political dominion. The state over which the sovereign had to exercise his dominion was thus beginning to be associated with the web of relations among the life of the population, economic output, and the territory (Zarka 1994b, 109); its strength was thus made to derive from a complex set of factors that by this time encompassed much more than military power. Not incidentally, in granularly describing the tools with which to ensure the protection and security of political dominium, Botero expressed himself in the plural, rather than in the singular, thus pivoting the discussion toward an analysis of the *forces* in which the *puissance* of states was concreted (Descendre 2003, 316). And, as mentioned, these forces importantly included not only military power but also the *people*, the fundamental element from which all other forces were made to depend:

> We now come to the true strength of a ruler, which consists in his people: for upon them depend all his other resources. The ruler who has plenty of men will have plenty of everything which the ingenuity and industry of man can provide, as we shall discover as we proceed. We shall accordingly use the terms "people" and "strength" indiscriminately.
> (Botero (1589) 1956, 143, 144)

The focal point of Botero's reflection was thus the state, a complex entity that by this time upstaged the ancient discussion of the prince's personal virtues. This was an entity which in a sense existed even independently of its prince, and which the prince needed to be able to preserve, ensuring the spontaneous internal equilibrium that enables the political domain to survive like any other natural entity (Suppa 1992, 68–69).[17] The principle that the elements that make up a state must all be in balance seems to hark back to the idea of order as a general factor of discipline and obedience which sometimes crops up in Botero, but that preservative ability did not turn exclusively on the sovereign's political and military virtues. To be sure, the figure of the prince does not entirely disappear, nor does the reference made to the virtues that make political dominion acceptable to all subjects, but what was beginning to come into the foreground was the more general idea of *prudentia civilis* understood as a knowledge of the practicalities that enable the prince to effectively govern not only his own affairs as prince but also those of the state, or the things and people the state is composed of (Borrelli 1995, 96; Zarka 1994b, 117):

> It is more important for a prince than for anyone else to know many things, for his knowledge may be useful and profitable to all his subjects. In particular it is useful, and indeed essential, that he should have a wide knowledge of all that pertains to human feelings and behaviour, such as are expounded fully in the works of moral philosophers, and to the methods of government described by political writers. From moral philosophy he learns of the passions that are common to all men, and political science teaches him rules of good government by which he may temper or encourage these passions and the effects which they have upon his subjects.
>
> (Botero [1589] 1956, 34)

In Botero, the prince's prudence is thus refashioned into the mastery of the mechanics of the interests and passions that go into human conduct. It is crucial for the prince to master not only the art of war and the *arcana imperii* but also the promotion of industry as an essential condition of the strength and internal stability of states.

> For a people who are secure from foreign or civil wars, who have no fear of being assailed in their homes by violence or deceit, and who can have cheaply the food they need, cannot but be contented and will not trouble themselves with other matters.
>
> (Botero [1589] 1956, 73)

If the prince is to achieve this state of affairs, he must understand not only the material structure of the state but also the social structure of the population, so as

---

17 Writes Botero in this regard: "Clearly it is a great task to preserve a state, because human affairs wax and wane as if by a law of nature, like the moon to which they are subject. Thus to keep them stable when they have become great and to maintain them so that they do not decline and fall is an almost superhuman undertaking" (Botero [1589] 1956, 5–6).

to gauge his political action to the changing dynamics of the interests by which the different sectors of the population are moved (Bonnet 2003, 325).

The question of *prudentia civilis* was magisterially developed as well by Justus Lipsius (Stolleis 1998a, 138ff.), whose 1589 *Politicorum sive Civilis doctrinae libri sex* (Six books on politics or civil doctrine)—perhaps the most important example of Protestant political neo-Aristotelianism—was widely read and translated across Europe, so much so as to join Botero's *Della ragion di Stato* as a classic of political literature (Stolleis 1998a, 140–49; 1998d, 201ff.; Senellart 1994, 111; Oestreich 1982, 39; Tuck 1993, 45). As professor of law and history at Leiden University from 1578, Lipsius gained fame for the erudite philological work he did on the texts of Tacitus, out of which developed the current of political thought known as Taciteanism, which coupled the study of the *arcana imperii* with that of the *ratio status* that was already dominant in the European political debate (Stolleis 1998b, 41–43; Tuck 1993, 39–45). It is Oestreich who deserves credit for reviving the interest that Lipsius's political and moral thought deserves after the long oblivion it fell into. The main purpose of the *Politicorum* was to bring into politics the themes of self-discipline that Lipsius had himself previously developed in his 1583 two-book treatise of moral philosophy *De Constantia in publicis malis* (On constancy in times of public evil) (Oestreich 1982, 13; Senellart 1994, 116; Tuck 1993, 52). Not incidentally, the *Politicorum* starts off with an explicit reference to the earlier *De Constantia*: "Just as in the two books on constancy our concern was with priming different *peoples* for patience and obedience, so in this work our concern will be with showing how *princes* need to govern" (Lipsius [1589] 1998; my translation, italics added). The discipline of one's self and that of others are thus connected from the outset as the bedrock of Lipsius's *prudentia civilis*.

The *Politicorum* can be broken down into three main parts: one devoted to the state as a moral institution (ibid., 1–138), another to the state as a command institution aimed at ensuring civil and social peace (ibid., 139–417), and a final one devoted to military questions in connection with the power of the state (ibid., 418–584). Just as in Botero's work, here we can observe a shift away from the classics of legal and political thought of the time. Indeed, Lipsius did not concern himself with the legal foundation of sovereignty, as Bodin did, but neither did he reduce politics to the mere question of power and its preservation in a state of exception, as Machiavelli and Naudé did. To be sure, Lipsius, with a keen interest in military matters and the question of reform of the army, did not refrain from invoking a sort of political reason of the state of exception, so much so that he brought the *prudentia mixta* into play to argue for a qualified acceptance of Machiavellian themes. But it would be reductive if his contribution to political doctrine were to be filtered only through the view he put forward as a participant in the debate on the legitimacy of extraordinary political measures (Senellart 2005, 126; Tuck 1993, 56–57). Indeed, the importance the *Politicorum* attributes to reforming the army and creating standing armies *(miles perpetuus)* was already drifting toward a broader interest in the problem of administrative and social reform, laying the groundwork for a theoretical foundation on which to rest the idea of the disciplinary function allotted to the bureaucratic institutions of the modern state apparatus (Oestreich 1982, 71; Tuck 1993, 61). The aim of political activity, in Lipsius's view, was to set up and reinforce that impersonal institution which was already morphing into the modern state, centred around the military-bureaucratic apparatus entrusted with ensuring the *social disciplining* needed to maintain an orderly civil life (Senellart 2005, 232–34).

However, this *social disciplining* function was not something that public institutions could fulfil only by means of military force. It was Lipsius's view that these institutions were endowed with *auctoritas*, which, unlike the brute force exerted on the unruly, is brought to bear on those who in some measure accept the dominion they are subject to. *Auctoritas* can in this sense be said to imply a certain relation between the prince and his people. It is made to depend on three factors: on the form of the command, which needs to be severe, constant, and concentrated in the prince's hands; on the power of the command, which is mainly a function of the wealth and strength of the weapons available to the sovereign; and on the customs of the sovereign himself, which in large part account for the opinion in which he is held by the people, an opinion that, according to Lipsius, is *precipua vis imperii*. But what in Lipsius comes to play an even more important role as a fundamental political concept is that of *discipline*, which is broken down into *exercitium, ordo, coercio et exempla* (regimen, order, coercion, and example) as guiding principles in light of which to reform the military-bureaucratic apparatus (Oestreich 1982, 51–53).

With Botero and Lipsius, in short, we have in embryo the theoretical blueprint for what would become the modern art of government, an art understood as the political ability to channel individual impulsions toward the pursuit of a set of shared political goals, which Lipsius identified as those of *commoditas, securitas*, and *salus*. Plentitude, security, and health were conceived as political ends attainable by drawing in part on an improving ability to have a hold on the social sphere—an ability that runs parallel to the birth and development of modern military and bureaucratic institutions, which in turn were a crucial vehicle in bringing about the profound socioeconomic revolution that would overtake modern Europe.

Chapter 3

Police science

In the formative period that led to the emergence of the modern state, treatises on the governmental arts tended to converge with politico-legal treatises on sovereign power, in that they both posited the aim of the public good and the welfare of the political community as broad justifications for sovereign power. As can be appreciated, however, where the *utilitas publica* was still a strictly legal concept, serving to limit a political power that dangerously perceived itself as entitled to act outside the frame of the law, the *bonum commune* existed as a distinctly political concept, one that paved the way for a mature development of reflection on the art of government, the art of steering the ship of state in view of the public good. Even so, the debate still could not pick apart the legal and the outright political elements that, as we saw, had thus far been intertwined, so much so that the two survived as one even after Bodin's well-known distinction between state and government (Bodin [1576] 1986, vol. II, II, 1, p. 7). Indeed, reflections on the foundation for the legitimacy of sovereign power, condensed by Bodin in the concept of *souveraineté*, continued to be run together with the discourse on the concrete administration of political domains, a discourse that, as we saw, came into form in dealing with the question of *ratio status* and *prudentia civilis*. This confusion was undoubtedly nurtured by much of the writing on reason of state, with its tendency to frame the debate in terms of the foundation of sovereign power and the legal limits it was subject to, so much so that the very notion of *ratio status* found itself increasingly enmeshed in an attempt to juridify that status by invoking the classic notion of *ratio necessitatis* or the idea of a special public right, a *ius politico* or *ius politiae* subject to the exclusive prerogative of supreme authority (Stolleis 1998a, 311–12; De Mattei 1979, 260). On the other hand, once political sovereignty established itself *de jure* and the power of absolute monarchs was legitimated, there also developed in parallel an interest in figuring out how such acquired *summa potestas* could be reinforced *de facto* through a sound governing or sound policing of public affairs (Napoli 2003, 40).

This ambiguity would be clearly reflected in the two-pronged discourse that developed in connection with the police apparatus, which from the outset was theorized both as *ius politiae*—a politico-legal construct pertaining to the sovereign prerogative—and as good government, or *good police*, where the effort was to develop a *ratio* aimed at guiding the king in exercising sovereign powers. However, it was this very notion of good police that would set in motion the development that would lead to the modern *ratio gubernatoria*, the endpoint of the gradual transition from the idea of a government of *men*—an idea deeply rooted in the concern with territorial sovereignty and the people typical of all prior politico-legal thought—to the idea of a government of *things and affairs*, an idea that took shape with the constant appeal to the modern sciences of the state as a technique for administering the complex of material and human resources constituted by the territory and the population.

Once the discourse on reason of state had been set into the theoretical frame of practical philosophy and of *prudentia civilis*, it went well beyond the simple assertion of the principle that *necessitas non habet legem* (necessity has no law). Reflection on the art of government no longer confined itself to a concern with preserving the state. It stepped into modernity by turning to the question of the state's power understood in part as the thriving of commerce and manufacturing. European political thought was thus beginning to grasp the importance of social and economic policy, and in view of the population's material and moral welfare, the Machiavellian reason of state was turning into statecraft proper. The sphere of politics broadly construed—or "high" politics, concerned with the survival of the political organism—thus began to distinguish itself from the more circumscribed sphere of internal police, or "low" politics, but without yet resolving itself into a mere guarantee of peace, security, and order (Schmitt 1932, 11). Indeed, the theoretico-conceptual development of modern police found its main breeding ground in the mercantilist policies driven by the aim of increasing material wealth, which policies marked the turning point when an economic science proper began to develop, by freeing itself from the Scholastic scheme of the practical sciences, still focused on the *oikos* (economics as the management of the household). It was from this circumscribed dimension of the *oikos* that the art of government proceeded in reframing its consideration of economic affairs in view of the tasks the modern state was now assigning to it. Under the pull of the art of government, the sphere of the *oeconomia*—encompassing all considerations relative to commerce and manufacturing—was sucked into the sphere of *politia*, the province of disciplines concerned with the question of authority (Schiera 1968, 283ff.; Napoli 2003, 54–55). It was precisely through this twofold process of *politicization* of economics and *economization* of politics that there began to develop a systematic interest in *economic police* and, more broadly, in police *tout court*.

It is no accident, then, that all across Europe the very first manifestations of the concept of police, at the dawn of the modern age, should have been tied to the sphere of local government, and in particular to the government of the cities. Indeed, in these early uses, the concept referred to the complex of principles and disciplines that were essential to the economic life that was developing in the mercantile centres of the Late Middle Ages. These principles and disciplines arose in response to the need to govern a complex of socioeconomic activities that had now become something entirely different from the natural subsistence economies that characterized the agrarian landscape across Europe. Through these activities the cities became a springboard for an authentic revolution in political technologies and the birth of what Max Weber ([1922]1978, 1219) called "urban economic policy" *(Stadtwirtschaftspolitik)*. Indeed, urban centres in the Late Middle Ages found themselves facing a series of problems ranging from the regulation of markets and productive activities to the health hazard attendant on the ever-present risk of an epidemic outbreak, and they also had to figure out how to cope with the constant influx of people from the countryside—hapless drifters who were thought to skirt the duty to contribute to the economic life of the city and were thus regarded as posing a constant threat to order and security. It was therefore in the cities that a new and ever-increasing social intervention sector first developed with the creation of designated public authorities (Oestreich 1980; Napoli 2003; Schiera 1968; Sbriccoli 1986).[1]

In the Late Middle Ages, therefore, it was already clear what fell within the scope of police, broadly understood as the government of society. Throughout the ancien régime, this new area of public activity took the territory, the economy, and the population as its object. However, as much as these police activities were already clearly defined in practical terms, they still lacked a solid theoretical foundation. On the one hand, they already entailed for the authorities a set of functions different from that of simply protecting the established order, but, on the other hand, they still found themselves tethered to the more traditional, Aristotelian concept of police, based on the view that *politeia* or *politia* boiled down to the undifferentiated task of maintaining the social order on which hinges the survival of the *polis* itself. Although the problems addressed by the urban institutions were already distinctly modern, they presented themselves on too small a scale to prompt the development of an innovative theoretical framework within which to frame the concept of police beyond a concern with the practical exigencies of the occasion. Because monarchical power did not significantly overhaul the older tradition of city government, but only expanded the old urban economic and social policy on a national scale, it was only with the development of political absolutism, when the royal authorities took on this new set of functions, that the conditions were set for the concept of police to fully develop in a dynamic way. What emerged out of this concept was, with increasing clarity, the view of the sovereign as having a personal part in the management of public affairs, a development that overturned the medieval conception of power: "Police now became the transitive process designated by the verb *policer* (to police), otherwise referred to as governing or propping up" (Napoli 2003, 30; my translation).

Throughout the Renaissance period, however, the term *police* continued to be ambiguous, and even when there began to emerge the first suggestions of something like a sovereign interest in intervening in socioeconomic life in a more

---

1 On the urban setting as the origin of police, see also Foucault (2004, 334), who refers to it as the "condition of existence of urban life."

systematic way, it became difficult to distinguish the ancient *iurisdictio* and the modern *politia*. It was only slowly, and in an entirely haphazard manner, that the idea began to take shape of a general police function requiring royal officials to address the affairs of the community through forms other than the ones traditionally used to resolve legal disputes. This conceptual confusion had its counterpart in a parallel institutional confusion. Indeed, as we saw, at the dawn of the modern age, the general police functions that sovereign authority took on in addressing social issues at large would often continue to be framed within the institutional complex set up under the old judicial administration. As long as police functions remained institutionally unspecified, it would prove impossible for the idea of police to attract anything more than a mere *practical*, piecemeal interest in working out the problems that public authorities were beginning to confront in the face of capitalistic development. Indeed, it was a laborious process that led from the original idea of good government or good police as the simple function of protecting the established order of the community (in a sense still closely tied to the medieval *iurisdictio*) to the more modern idea of police as stewardship of the *res publica*, or the public good as a whole (Napoli 2003, 25; Oestreich 1980, 215; Schiera 1968, 272; Maier 1966, 189).

Be that as it may, at the beginning of the 17th century the concept of *policy/police*—along with its Continental analogues, the French *police* and the German *Policey*—could still be observed to bear strong parallels to its institutional counterparts, meaning the complex of regulatory and administrative activities undertaken by local authorities at first and national ones later, more or less independently of each other, for the purpose of governing the territory, public spaces, markets, manufacturing, and the population. Indeed, the semantic evolution of the three concepts began to break up along institutional lines of divergent development. This meant that, on the one hand, on the Continent, the concept found a fuller theoretical grounding—in fact, with the full development of the institutions needed to run the administrative monarchy, it became the object of a police science proper—while, on the other hand, in the Anglosphere, with the defeat of absolutistic projects, it essentially withered away.

3.1. Police and policy: the English tradition

The history of police in England has always been described as the evolution of a specific tool designed to prevent and punish crime. Indeed, the term *police* is ordinarily understood by historians as a synonym of *constabulary*, referring to that part of the social organization which is specifically entrusted with maintaining public order or with preventing and punishing crime (Chapman 1971, 51; Neocleous 2000a, 10). The restrictive sense in which the term *police* is understood by English-speaking historians is all the more surprising if we consider how in *A History of Police in England*, at the beginning of the 20th century, an entire discussion is devoted to "commercial police and policy under the Tudors" (Melville Lee 1901, chap. V). Under that rubric, Melville Lee grouped the social and institutional developments that even England went through between the 16th and 17th centuries, noting that "as trade increased and as the skilled workman became a recognized power in the state, the police horizon widened, new interests needed protection, new laws and regulations had to be made and enforced" (ibid., 86). This new complex of disciplines and regulations gave rise to a *commercial police* proper, which would later be flanked by what can be described as a *social police*, which under a pervasive "grandmotherly domestic policy [. . .] told people what they were to eat, how they were to dress, and the number of hours they must labour" (ibid., 95–96).

In England, too, the need for reform brought about by economic development came from the cities, but since at that time, at the dawn of the 16th century, the Tudor monarchy was already sufficiently centralized and comparatively modernized, it could soon step in to guide and regulate social and economic life in the kingdom. This huge and precocious practical development of police activity in England did not come without a corresponding theoretical development in the governmental arts. At that time, however, legal and political discourse in the English language had not yet found a place for the terms of Aristotelian origin *police* and *policy*.[2] An early use of the term can be found in the title given to one of the first English treatises devoted to economic questions, the *Libelle of Englyshe Polycye* (1436–38), of unknown authorship, containing what is perhaps the first knowledgeable account of the tools the sovereign ought to use in governing the dynamic of economic processes that shape the life of the nation (Ferguson 1965, 22, 104). At any rate, it was only in the early 16th century that the terms *pollycy*, *pollycye*, and *policie*—which would later become *police* and *policy*—began to enter the common store of the language, when public documents increasingly addressed the need to preserve *good pollicie* or *pollycye and common weal* (Polito 2005, 8).

The term *police* entered Modern English directly from the medieval political tradition, which in England was embodied in John Fortescue's *De laudibus legum Angliæ* (*Commendation of the Laws of England*, first published posthumously circa 1543), with its distinction of Aristotelian descent between *dominium politicum* and *dominium regale* (Fortescue [1775] 1825, chap. XIII, p. 222)[3] and the close link established in this work between the form of government and the welfare of the body politic. Fortescue in fact undertook to lay out the ideal political structure, which he identified in the mixed government typical of the limited monarchies, capable of preserving the natural balance of the social organism (Garizzo 1987, 696). In a sense, the whole of political thought in the Tudor era worked up to this

---

2 To wit, in the 1538 translation of Aristotle's *Politics*, the terms *politeia* and *polis* were rendered as *policy* and *commonwealth*, respectively (see Neocleous 2000a, 11; Von Friedeburg 1996, 579).

3 The distinction was introduced in connection with the mixed constitution of England and Scotland: "So the kingdom of *England* [. . .] became a mixt kind of government, compounded of the *regal* and *political*. So *Scotland*, which was formerly in subjection to *England*, in the nature of a dutchy, became a government partly *regal*, partly *political*" (Fortescue [1775] 1825, chap. XIII, p. 39; italics in the original).

peculiar mash-up of medieval constitutionalism and political Aristotelianism, as is evidenced by the importance that over the 16th century would be ascribed to the question of mixed government and limited monarchy and the metaphor of the body politic (Ferguson 1965, 116).[4]

These themes were developed in particular in the extensive debate on social and political questions that took place throughout the 16th century. It was indeed in this period that there came into focus the question of the king's council and of the need to support sovereign prudence with the virtues that only the moral sciences and a knowledge of *littarae humaniores* could afford (Guy 1993, 16; Polito 2005, 53; Ferguson 1965, 162; Zeeveld 1948). This debate certainly reflected the discussions that were taking place on the Continent, but while these discussions would come together under the broad umbrella of treatises on *ratio status*, in England the debate began to show the signs of a prescient modernity. The great Tudor reforms owe a lot to the counsel the king was receiving from the humanists at court who on theoretical grounds were developing the concepts of *pollycye* and the *common weal*.[5] The idea of the commonwealth was beginning to crop up as well in the preambles to royal statutes under the formula of the *advancement of the common weal of this Realm of England,* and its use was also spreading in regulations concerned with social and economic matters (Jones 2000, 25), and in this process it was moving closer to the Aristotelian idea of a balanced state of affairs within the social organism, a balance the king was responsible for preserving and guaranteeing. The confusion between the two concepts of policy and the commonwealth was especially apparent in the work of Thomas Starkey, whose *Dialogue between Pole and Lupset* made frequent use

4 The medieval conceit of the polity as an organism found its highest embodiment at the dawn of the modern age in Edmund Dudley and his work *The Tree of Commonwealth* (Dudley [1509–10] 1948), where the idea of the political body was expressed through the metaphor of the tree. But perhaps no rendition of the organicistic metaphor was more influential on later English social and political thought than the one found in the 1521 English translation of Christine de Pisan's *Le livre du corps de policie* (1404–07), which came out under the title *The Booke Whiche Is Called the Body of Polycye* and stated the idea as follows: "For lyke as ye body of a man is dyffectyfe and dyfflourmed when he lacketh ony of his membres. In lyke wyse the body of Polycye maye not be parfyte ne entyre if these estates that we haue spoken of here tofore be not well Joyned and assembled all in one/so that euery of them may helpe other/and echone of them to excercyse that offyce that they be called to" (De Pisan 1521, part 3, chap. 1, p. xlviii)—a formula that only a few years later would be repeated almost verbatim by the English political theorist and humanist Thomas Starkey.

5 This latter concept emerged in particular as the late medieval equivalent of the Latin *res publica*, and in the modern age it wound up being used to refer to the state, an idea that was still struggling to emerge. But the *res publica* could never quite be equated with the commonwealth, which was expressly concerned with the common good and so invited the reflections on good governance that humanistic literature was beginning to articulate. The commonwealth certainly did capture the idea of the political community, but even more importantly it also expressed the duty of rulers to maintain a proper balance within that community. The theoretical development of the concept of the commonwealth therefore proceeded in parallel with the interest that political thinkers took in the practical problem of governing the state, the political body as a whole, an entity that was beginning to transcend the prince, even while incorporating the prince at the top of the pyramid (Jones 2000, 20, 21).

of the term *pollycy*, referring on some occasions to the collectivity as a whole and on others to the governance of that collectivity, on the assumption that the prince's responsibilities include both ensuring proper policy *(pollycy)* and the administration of commonwealth *(commyn wele)* (Starkey [1535] 1983, 118).

This has been called the movement of the commonwealthmen, and there is some question about that description (see Elton 1979),[6] but, regardless, it is within this vast intellectual and political landscape that the two terms of Aristotelian lineage *police* and *policy* were first set on a firm theoretical footing. The movement was made up of thinkers, reformers, and politicians who in the face of the socioeconomic problems of Tudor England superseded the old *specula principum* genre by framing the questions at hand in a way that ushered in the modern treatise on the art of governing (Ferguson 1965, 142). Indeed, although they saw themselves as councillors to the king working within the tradition of that traditional genre, they took the more modern outlook of physicians treating the body politic (Skinner 1978, 221; Ferguson 1965, 203). Central to these humanists' concerns, in other words, was the typical question of the practical sciences in the Aristotelian fashion—that is, the question of good governance, which was now beginning to be framed in broader terms: not as the moral problem of the prince's self-government or as the economic problem of household government, but as the problem of governing the *common* or *public weal* and maintaining a proper balance within the *body of polycye* (Guy 1993, 17; Polito 2005, 54; Jones 2000, 33; Ferguson 1965, 164).

The season of humanist political and social philosophy in England is conventionally made to begin even before Thomas Cromwell's era, when conditions were ripe for intellectual production, and if there is a single moment of inception in that regard, it is marked by Thomas More's 1516 *Utopia*. This was undoubtedly the first work in which the question of the nation's welfare and prosperity as the aim of sovereign activity is systematically treated at length (Garizzo 1987, 701; Ferguson 1965, 139). But it was also the work that set the model for social and political philosophy in the Tudor era, and More himself sought to adhere to that model as a statesman (Jones 2000, 45). But for all that, the first and most influential champion of political humanism in England is thought to be Thomas Elyot (Ferguson 1965, 171). A man of state closely associated with the humanist circle that formed around More, Elyot wrote *The Book Named the Governor* (1531), a treatise addressed to anyone who might find themselves in a position to govern themselves or others as heads of households or as public officials (Polito 2005, 59).[7] In this work the governor was

---

6 It was Pollard (1900) who came up with this name, which was subsequently revived by Tawney in his classic *Religion and the Rise of Capitalism* (1923), after which it became a staple of the best political historiography (cf. Skinner 1978, 216).

7 "It is to be noted," writes Elyot ([1531] 1907, bk. III, chap. VIII), "that to hym that is a gouernoure of a publike weale belongeth a double gouernaunce, that is to saye, an interior or inwarde gouernaunce, and an exterior or outwarde gouernaunce. The firste is of his affects and passions,

for the first time clearly depicted as a physician of the political body called on to diagnose the ills of the social body and make sure that none of its components should grow disproportionately, in such a way as to alter the natural balance that ensures the collective wellbeing (Guy 1993, 20):

> Semblably, the uniuersall state of a contray or citie may be well likened to the body of man. Wherfore the gouernours, in the stede of phisitions attending on their cure, ought to knowe the causes of the decaye of their publike weale, whiche is the helthe of their countraye or cytie, and thanne with expedition to procede to ther mooste spedy and sure remedy.
>
> (Elyot [1531] 1907, bk. III, chap. XXVI)

The organicistic metaphor and the idea of the governor and his councillors as physicians of the political body are invoked as well by Thomas Starkey (Ferguson 1965, 172; Garizzo 1987, 720–25). In his *Dialogue between Pole and Lupset*, which he began working on in 1529 and completed between 1532 and 1535, the state is even described through an elaborate metaphor which for each component of the political body identifies an analogue in living organisms.[8] The political body thrives when everyone diligently carries out his tasks, and it is in particular in this regard that Starkey deploys the idea of police and princely prudence as tools with which to achieve the perfect commonweal. When the multitude of the people and the political body *(polytike body)* are healthy, beautiful, and strong, there is true commonwealth *(commyn wele)*, the most prosperous and perfect state that in any country, city, or town by policy *(pollycy)* and wisdom may be established and set.[9] Starkey offers what is perhaps the best synthesis of political Aristotelianism and rhetoric on the subject of limited monarchy. The idea of police/policy was indeed still closely bound up with that of justice, and the sovereign is explicitly called on to preserve and protect the *good policy* of the realm from corruption (Guy 1993, 19; Jones 2000, 35). Starkey ([1535] 1878, 48) argues that "from the pryncys and rularys of the state commyth al lawys, ordur and pollycy, al justyce, vertue, and honesty, to the rest of thys polytyke body." Indeed good police/policy and true

---

which do inhabite within his soule, and be subiectes to reason. The seconde is of children, his seruanuntes, and other subiectes to his autoritie." Elyot wrote the book hoping to ingratiate himself with the court, and in particular with Thomas Cromwell, after he had lost favour with his previous protégé, Thomas Wolsey. For this reason, the book was also intended as a tool providing theoretical support for the king's incipient attitude of active engagement in the kingdom's social and political life.

8 Thus, the heart corresponds to the ruler, the head to the officials appointed by the ruler, the hands to the craftsmen and the warriors, and the feet to the farmers.

9 The original text: "when fyrst the multytude of pepul and polytyke body ys helthy, beutyful, and strong, [. . .] ther ys the veray and true commyn wele; ther ys the most prosperouse and perfayt state, that in any cuntrey, cyte, or towne, by pollycy and wysdom, may be stablyschyd and set" (Starkey [1535] 1878, 56).

commonwealth are achieved only when all the parts of the whole, like the limbs of a single body, are knit together in perfect love and unity, everyone performing his office and duty in such a manner that whatever status, office, or degree they have, they each fulfil their duty with all diligence and to the best of their ability, and without envy or malice toward others who are doing the same.[10]

Statesmen in this period were the practical counterpoint to the wide humanistic debate on the commonwealth. In their government action they developed a vast social and economic policy programme whose early manifestations can be found in the work of Thomas Wolsey, and especially in the incipient phenomenon of the enclosures and its aftermath, the gradual movement of people away from the English countryside (Jones 2000, 42–43). The best historiography, however, sees in Cromwell the author of the first authentically systematic social and economic reform programme. To be sure, he was not the first official to have devoted himself to the practical advancement of the commonwealth in the Tudor era, but the design and sheer scale of his reform project certainly marks him out as a pioneer (Elton 1973, 111ff.; Jones 2000, 51). Besides framing social and economic policy within a coherent model, his programme also provided for the institution of the new public officials advocated by Starkey, the *conservatorys of the common wele* responsible for overseeing the social and economic policy activity entrusted to the officials of the ancient judicial administration (Jones 2000, 52; Ferguson 1965, 331; Elton 1974c, 246).

The issues of social and political reform were further developed in the 1540s and 1550s, when they became the focus of renewed humanistic interest (Ferguson 1965, 140). Spearheading this *commonwealth* movement in this period was Edward Seymour, Duke of Somerset, lord protector to Edward VI (Garizzo 1987, 737; Jones 2000, 56). In important respects, however, the discussion continued along traditional lines, driven by a concern to criticize those whose ambition led them to upset the proper balance of the social organism (Garizzo 1987, 738; Ferguson 1965, 286). Once more, the focus of such criticism was, of course, the large land-holders' "insatiable greediness" (Jones 2000, 59), which in the royal proclamation announcing the inquiry on enclosures was identified as the root cause that lay waste to the English countryside (Garizzo 1987, 740). On the whole, the social policy developed under the tenures of Wolsey, Cromwell, and Somerset can be constructed as a desperate attempt to cope with the most disruptive consequences of the emerging capitalistic economy, an attempt supported by the idea of having to maintain the ancient equilibrium of the political body, with its social hierarchies,

---

10 The full simile in its original statement: "For lyke as in mannys mynd ther only ys quyetnes and hye felycyte, wher as in a gud body al the affectys wyth reson dow agre, so in a cuntrey, cyty, or towne, ther ys perfayt cyuylyte, ther ys the true commyn wele, where as al the partys, as membrys of one body, be knyt togyddur in perfayt loue and vnyte; euery one dowyng hys offyce and duty, aftur such maner that, what so euer state, offyce, or degre, any man be of, the duty therto perteynyng wyth al dylygence he besyly fulfyl, and wythout enuy or malyce to other accomplysch the same" (Starkey [1535] 1878, 54–55).

threatened by the oncoming social and economic revolution (Jones 2000, 64–65). In light of that background, it was inevitable that the notion of police should have retained the strongly conservational meaning we saw Starkey impart to it by using it as a vehicle for the view that sovereign activity ought to be aimed at maintaining a proper balance among the different parts that make up the social body. This was a view that made that notion still very close to that of *iurisdictio*.

In a sense, the semantic trajectory of the terms *police* and *policy* in Tudor England reflected the constitutional balance that had been reached and the consequent lack of absolutistic terms in the politico-legal discourse of the time.[11] Reflection on sovereign power still revolved around the classic medieval distinctions between powers belonging to the sovereign's *natural* body and those belonging to his *political* body, or again between ordinary and absolute powers.[12] Although that classic distinction did serve to underscore that there could be no exercise of political power outside the frame of public law, it could not yet serve as a criterion by which to specify what the powers conferred on that body politic consisted in, except through a generic reference to policy and government, nor did it clarify whether the king was only the head of a political body fleshed out by the nation meeting in joint session or whether he alone was recognized as having authority to interpret and represent public needs, or the commonwealth (Holdsworth 1924, 204). Here writers on law confined themselves to identifying some powers they called *inseparables*, in that they could be exercised solely by the king in person and could not be alienated from him, and these were the powers through which the king would set what came to be called *high policy*.

Despite the deep political and social transformation England went through in the 17th century, its institutions developed in a way peaceful enough that a political theory like the Thomas Smith's, cast in the medieval mould of limited monarchy, could still aptly capture the spirit of the age. Indeed, his 1565 *De Republica Anglorum*, subtitled *The Maner of Gouernement or Policie of the Realme of Englande*, could uncontroversially reprise the Aristotelian motif of the balance that needs to exist among the different components of the body politic and argue for the constitutional supremacy of the *king in parliament* that was typical of the medieval ideal of the

11 In fact, the only use of the imperial language of absolute *potestas* in Tudor England came on the occasion of its clash with Rome and was in this sense limited. It was functional to claiming the sovereign's independence from external and concurrent powers, and it was mostly to this end that English political and legal thought in the 16th century deployed the notion of *absolutio* (Guy 1993, 35ff.; Daly 1978, 228).

12 The dominant political doctrine of the time was aptly captured, for example, by the crown lawyers in the *Duchy of Lancaster* case of 1562: "The king has in him two bodies, viz. a body natural, and a body politic. His body natural (if it be considered in itself) is a body mortal, subject to all infirmties that come by nature or accident, to the imbecillity of infancy or old age, and to the like defects that happen to the natural bodies of other people. But his body politic is a body that cannot be seen or handled consisting of policy and government, and constituted for the direction of the people, and the management of the public weal" (Holdsworth 1924, 202).

mixed constitution (Jones 2000, 94; Daly 1978, 230). This work, penned by a high-ranking government official, not only offered the best statement of Tudor political thought but also showed "the manner in which mediaeval institutions had been adapted, with the minimum of change, to suit a modern state" (Holdsworth 1924, 209).

The discourse on the need to maintain an equilibrium within the body politic and to uphold justice and fairness continued into the Elizabethan age, but even in that context ideas began to emerge with the express intent of reforming economic and social policy (Jones 2000, 66; Ferguson 1965, 315). Paradoxically, among those who were putting these ideas forward was Thomas Smith, the author who (as just noted) summed up a political theory infused with Aristotelian themes and medieval constitutionalism. The view was now taking shape that there needed to be direct government measures explicitly aimed at supporting and stimulating economic life across the realm. Also gaining ground in this phase was the mercantilist view that on the wealth of the nation depended its power and might, and this development provided an initial theoretical grounding for classic humanistic reflection on the social and economic problems of Tudor England (Jones 2000, 67; Ferguson 1965, 300).

A case in point was the *Discourse of the Commonweal of This Realm of England*, a work written around 1549, published in 1583, and now unanimously attributed to Thomas Smith. The *Discourse* was among the first European treatises to attempt a systematic theoretical treatment of socioeconomic issues (Wood 1998, 140), described by Jones (2000, 57) as an "original and forward-looking analysis of the rationale of governmental action on economic and social issues." Indeed, although Smith viewed his work as one of practical philosophy—for it sought to determine how a city or realm ought to be ordered and governed, and so was concerned with the question of the "policy or good government of a commonweal" (Dewar 1969, 12)—his treatment of policy explicitly drew the *oikonomia* within the sphere of politics, thus breaking the classic Scholastic partitions, and in this respect Smith's *Discourse* can be said to have pioneered the development of modern rationality in government.

Smith agreed with many contemporaries that the ills of his time could be put down to human nature—in that humans were essentially driven to act individualistically out of self-interest—but, unlike his contemporaries, he did not content himself with simply hurling moral condemnations at the spirit of the time and the desire to climb the social ladder. He rather set out to find by what means such individual self-interest could be turned to profit and made to work for the benefit of the community. He thought that greed and profit-seeking were in fact moral forces, and therefore that the government should not be trying to suppress them but rather to channel them appropriately. Instead of curtailing action through the fear of punishment, the government should encourage action by creating expectations of profit (ibid., 60). Through a well-designed system of incentives and disincentives, the very individualism that lies at the root of the ills of society can be harnessed as a source of public profit (Ferguson 1965, 306). In this sense, the wisest policy should not just consist in prohibiting people from engaging in bad behaviour but in spurring them to pursue their wellbeing. As Smith puts it:

> We must understand also, that all things that should be done in a Commonwealth, be not to be forced or to be constrained by the straight penalties of the law; but some so, and some either by allurement, and rewards rather.
>
> (Dewar 1969, 58)

Already condensed in this project was an economic policy proper (Wood 1998, 147; Ferguson 1965, 282).

In framing his discussion on the welfare of the nation, Smith refrained from invoking the idea of the good old order to be preserved, sensing that the path of interdiction and prohibition was not just ineffective in promoting the nation's wealth and wellbeing but could even be counterproductive in that regard. What Smith limned, in other words, was a clear idea of social policy and regulation, an idea that had a new role to play when entrusted to governmental agencies equipped with a full panoply of tools and political technologies. By knowledgeably intervening in the realm's socioeconomic life, the government could make sure that the atomistic nature of the economic process should work out to the benefit of the public. For the first time a case was being made for the ideal of an individualistic anthropology, for the notion that if the pursuit of personal profit was properly channelled and guided, it could advance the welfare of the entire community. Smith laid out a systematic economic policy based on the use of legislative and administrative tools capable of acting as incentives and disincentives designed to favour a proper socioeconomic balance (Ferguson 1965, 280; Garizzo 1987, 748).

So the ideal of the common good, hitherto couched in the language of good policy and the commonweal embraced by humanists and men of government, was now taking on new life as a basis on which to justify a more aggressive intervention by the sovereign. As the head of the political body, the king now saw himself being invested with a direct responsibility for steering the social and economic life of the realm (Kelley 1996, 75; Jones 2000, 91). As we know, the development of the governmental arts, practical and theoretical alike, was altering the ancient constitutional balance between what English political and legal thinkers referred to as *iurisdictio* and *gubernaculum*. This, of course, carried consequences for political and legal theory. Indeed, the increasingly insistent recourse to the notions of policy and the commonweal as bases on which to legitimize intervention in social and economic life tended to overlay the parallel distinction between the features of the sovereign prerogative (Jones 2000, 118ff.; Garizzo 1987, 697). Political and legal theory, in other words, was working to reshape the ancient dichotomy between regal and political power (in Fortescue's terminology), for next to the idea of the king's competence over high policy—in matters pertaining to the security and survival of the political community, an area in which his authority was unchallenged and unconstrained by law—the idea was being fleshed out that this absolute sovereign prerogative also covered the vast area comprising the regular government of economic affairs that Tudor politics had progressively extended over (Holdsworth 1924, 207). Even in England, therefore, these developments, and in particular the theoretical advancement and consolidation of an explicitly absolutistic discourse on the prerogative of the English kings, were setting the stage on which the concepts of *police* and *policy* could flourish, expanding their semantic range and finding a firm theoretical footing.

As is known, when the institutional tensions that built up in the Tudor era reached their breaking point, the effect was twofold: On the one hand came the Stuart ascension to the throne, and on the other the deep fiscal crisis that afflicted the English monarchy in the early 17th century. While the Tudors had managed to maintain a balance among the state's different institutions, the new Stuart sovereigns tried to tilt that balance in favour of the monarchy itself by systematically constructing a constitutional arrangement in the fashion of an administrative monarchy. The institutional clash was thus triggered by the Stuarts' practical efforts to stretch their prerogative beyond the limits of the previous constitutional arrangement. This they did by claiming powers not conferred on them under that arrangement, and in particular the power to legislate, levy taxes, and oversee the activity of the ordinary courts. These attempts gave rise to many legal cases and parliamentary debates over the course of which the key concepts involved in the main constitutional issues pressed themselves into the public mind and into the political debate of the time.

The challenge the Stuart sovereigns mounted against the competing powers of the state was explicit and direct. The main theoretical tool of absolutist encroachment, a tool first put to use by James I,[13] consisted in an argument for expanding the sovereign prerogative. The Stuart doctrine proceeded from the classic assumption that the sovereign prerogative was amenable to a distinction between absolute and ordinary power; the former power they tended to unduly extend on the premise that the power the sovereign exercised in tending to the wellbeing of his subjects had the makings of a *patria potestas* (Garizzo 1980, 168; Levy Peck 1996, 86–87; Jones 2000, 123).[14] This idea of the sovereign's power as essentially patriarchal permeated the whole of absolutistic culture in the first half of the 17th century and was crystallized by Robert Filmer in his *Patriarcha, or the Natural Power of Kings*. It was written between 1628 and 1632 in response to the parliamentarians' growing claims—culminating in the 1628 Petition of Right presented to King Charles I—and in it Filmer reasserted the theses that James I had previously expounded in his own political thinking (Levy Peck 1996, 104).

---

13 When he was still James VI of Scotland, he had already written two noteworthy treatises on the nature of sovereign power—*The Trve Lawe of Free Monarchies* (1598) and *Basilikon Doron* (1599)—encapsulating the conception of power he would put into practice over the course of the troubled political life that England would go through in the first decades of the 17th century (Daly 1978, 232; Holdsworth 1924, 21; Levy Peck 1996).

14 "Kings are also compared to Fathers of families; for a King is truly *parens patriae*, the politic father of his people" (James I, speech to Parliament, March 21, 1610, quoted in Kenyon 1986, 12).

Filmer proceeded from the Aristotelian idea of political society as an extension of the natural society consisting of the family. Even in Thomas Smith, however, these Aristotelian themes had already been decidedly superseded by the injection of *oikonomia* into *politia* and by the systematic use that was already being made of the metaphor of the domestic economy as a heuristic device with which to understand the economy of the realm and to substantiate the idea of the sovereign as a *paterfamilias* entrusted with ensuring the wellbeing of his extended family.

The Aristotelian themes had by this time been woven deeply into the absolutistic politico-legal language rooted in European thought, and thus wedded they became widespread with Bodin, whose *Les Six livres de la République*, of 1576, had been translated in 1606 under the title *The Six Bookes of a Common-Weale*. The natural foundation of sovereign power extended the royal prerogative and the natural duties of the patriarch beyond the limits established under the precarious constitutional balance that had been struck in the Tudor era. The king was regarded as the supreme interpreter and protector of the common good, and in that capacity he definitely stood above the law: "the prerogative of a king is to be above all laws, for the good only of them that are under the laws, and to defend the peoples' liberties" (Filmer [1680] 1991, 44; cf., generally, Levy Peck 1996, 108–09; Garizzo 1980, 198; Daly 1978, 244–45; Schochet 1975; and Sommerville 1994).

The most propitious outcome to have arisen from the spread of such a political culture imbued with eudaemonistic motifs lay in the discussions occasioned by the big constitutional controversies of the time, and in particular by a series of legal cases that became *causes célèbres*, often crowned by heated parliamentary debates. These clashes among constitutional organs were invariably triggered by the king's attempts to broaden his royal prerogative, especially in economic and fiscal policy, and particularly famous was the incident involving John Bates, a merchant with the Levant Company who refused to pay the import duties imposed by James I. The legal case that followed came to be known as Bates's Case or the Case of Impositions (1606). It played an especially important role in shaping English constitutional history, and it matters to us here because it also highlights the role that political absolutism might have had in bringing to maturity the semantic and theoretical potential inherent in the concept of *police* or *policy*.

The judges who wrote the opinion siding with the royal prerogative blocked out in outline a political theory proper that is worth looking at in its entirety:

> The King's power is double, ordinary and absolute, and they have several laws and ends. That of the ordinary is for the profit of particular subjects, for the execution of civil justice, the determining of *meum*; and this is exercised by equity and justice in ordinary courts, and by the Civilians is nominated *jus privatum*, and with us Common Law: and these laws cannot be changed without Parliament, and although that their form and course may be changed and interrupted, yet they can never be changed in substance. The absolute power of the King is not that which is converted or executed to private use, to the benefit of any particular person, but is only that which is applied to the

general benefit of the people and is *salus populi*; as the people is the body and the King the head; and this power is [not] guided by the rules which direct only at the Common Law, and is most properly named policy and government.

(Bates's case 1606, quoted in Kenyon 1986, 62)

What appears evident in this passage is that the judges who argued for the royal prerogative, working from the ancient distinction between *iurisdictio* and *gubernaculum*, were quite close to offering a theoretical statement of the sphere of public action that throughout the Tudor era progressively accreted with new and different political and economic policy functions, a sphere the judges quite appropriately described as policy and government. However, this area of the sovereign prerogative was still scarcely defined. It was no longer regulated by common law (and so by the pure legal rationality that shapes the action of the ordinary administration of justice), while the idea of a rationality at the basis of government was still struggling to emerge. Indeed, the passage went on to say that

as the constitution of this body varieth with the time, so varieth this absolute law according to the wisdom of the King for the common good; and these being general rules and true as they are, all things done within these rules are lawful.

(Ibid., 63)

The judges who wrote the opinion thus only made a passing reference to the prince's "wisdom" (which, as discussed, is a classic theme in the literature on the governmental arts), and this, it seems, was the only criterion they could identify as a basis for governing sovereign action geared toward the general welfare of the realm. They could not further elaborate on the concept of policy by giving it any theoretical depth.[15]

At the centre of the constitutional conflict was the question of the king's claim that he should be able to independently manage the kingdom's economic and fiscal policy, a question that became the object of a bitter constitutional clash when

---

15 In a famous essay on judicial power, Francis Bacon drew a similar distinction between an ordinary sphere of judicial activity, pertaining to relations under private law, and an "extraordinary" sphere entrusted to the government: "it is an happy thing in a state when kings and states do often consult with judges; and again when judges do often consult with the king and state: the one, when there is matter of law intervenient in business of state; the other, when there is some consideration of state intervenient in matter of law. For many times the things deduced to judgment may be *meum and tuum* [mine and thine], when the reason and consequence thereof may trench to point of estate: I call matter of estate, not only the parts of sovereignty, but whatsoever introduceth any great alteration or dangerous precedent; or concerneth manifestly any great portion of people. And let no man weakly conceive that just laws and true policy have any antipathy; for they are like the spirits and sinews, that one moves with the other. Let judges also remember, that Solomon's throne was supported by lions on both sides: let them be lions, but yet lions under the throne; being circumspect that they do not check or oppose any points of sovereignty" (Bacon [1601] 1825, 184–85).

in 1626 Charles I, in deep financial straits, overstepped the limits of that power by forcing his subjects to subscribe to forced loans. This in turn led to a debate on the thorny question of detainment under executive warrant by special command of the king. The issue first came up in Darnel's Case (or Case of the Five Knights) and then became the object of the more famous parliamentary debates that followed (Holdsworth 1924, vol. 6, p. 32; Taswell-Langmead 1960, 410ff.), but in 1591 the judges of the Common Bench had already brought the issue to the King's Bench in protest against the practice of arbitrary arrest *per speciale mandatum regis* (ibid., 347; Holdsworth 1924, vol. 6, pp. 32–33). The text of this remonstrance became the basis for adjudicating the cases involving the discretionary imprisonments of the early 17th century. The issue of their legitimacy was not fully clarified in the 1591 remonstrance, for although the judges seemed to assert the right to assess the reasons behind such imprisonment, they did not clarify whether persons could lawfully be committed to prison simply by virtue of a royal command.

The occasion to go back to the thorny issue came with the writ of habeas corpus filed by Darnel and the other detainees held by royal committal for their refusal to pay the extraordinary taxes requested by the royal agents (Holdsworth 1924, vol. 6, p. 34; Taswell-Langmead 1960, 410–11). The counsel for the detainees argued that the writs of arrest were in violation of the common law and the Magna Carta, and the attorney general, Sir Robert Heath, replied that the king's prerogative rights in fact stood on a par with the common law. They were exercised *per legem terrae*—that is, by due process of law—and so were a sufficient cause of arrest (Holdsworth 1924, vol. 6, p. 35). Any act the king or the Privy Council might take in defence of the state and exercising the royal prerogative was an act taken by force of law, and the same applied to an arrest by special command of the king. It was deemed a legitimate cause of imprisonment no less than all the other causes recognized by the common law.

The question came up again when Charles I summoned a parliament in 1627 to raise the money he needed for his campaigns, at which point the House of Commons set up a Committee of Grievances to address issues relating to "the liberty of the subject in person and estate," which, of course, included the vexed issue of "illegal exactions under the name of loans" (Taswell-Langmead 1960, 412). In the ensuing debate the Commons drew up the famous Petition of Right of 1628, through which some of the fundamental principles of modern legal and political thought were passed into law. The Lords tried to slip in a saving clause stating that the petition was being presented "not only with a care of preserving our own liberties, but with due regard to leave entire that *sovereign power* wherewith your Majesty is trusted for the protection, safety, and happiness of your people" (Taswell-Langmead 1960, 412–13; italics in the original), testifying to the difficulty involved in striking the right balance between the primacy of the law and the primacy of the king's discretionary power (Holdsworth 1924, vol. 6, p. 37). The Commons refused to consider this or any other amendment to the Petition of Right, clearly signalling its intention to tilt the scales of the constitutional balance in favour of the common law and Parliament.

The Stuart era marked the beginning of a long phase of intellectual evolution as a result of which an individualistic and liberal culture came up against a persistent tendency to justify sovereign intervention in the social and economic sphere on the basis of the ancient eudaemonistic ideology of the commonweal. The escalating clashes with the king and the interests of the political and economic elite marked the birth of a new social and political philosophy asserting that the sole and essential task of the authorities was to guarantee the conditions for free citizens to exercise their individual rights. This development inevitably affected the notion of the commonwealth (Jones 2000, 139). Indeed, serious doubts began to be raised in the 17th century, not only about the legitimacy of sovereign intervention in defence of the commonwealth, but also about the notion of the commonwealth itself as a basis on which to legitimize a social and economic policy program (ibid., 203). The commonwealth was no longer simply set in contrast to private interests but, on the contrary, was said to lie in the ability of each individual to pursue his or her personal interests.

This semantic transition was already underway in Sir Edward Coke's *Grievances of the Commonwealth* (1621–28), offering one of the first explicit defences of individual freedoms against the increasingly aggressive interventionist policies of the crown and the ministers (Jones 2000, 143). Coke is unanimously considered the father of the modern common law tradition, to which he devoted his famous thirteen-volume *Law Reports* and the equally famous *Institutes of the Lawes of England* (Santoro 1999, 20ff.; Hill 1965, 225–26). In addition to producing invaluable work as a jurist, he also distinguished himself as Lord Chief Justice of England and Wales and as a member of Parliament, in which roles he defended the constitutional primacy of the common law courts over the prerogative courts. The common law had revealed itself to be inadequate as a basis on which to regulate the complex life of a rapidly changing society such as England had been since the Tudor era, and it had fallen to the royal statutes and decrees and to the prerogative courts to make up for the inadequacy of England's ancient customary law. Coke's work was fundamental in renewing a legal order that at the dawn of the modern age seemed inevitably bound to be supplanted by a law issued directly by the sovereign (Hill 1965, 227). As we have seen, this renewal was geared toward enabling ancient English law to respond to the needs of the ascending social and political philosophy, while protecting civil life from encroachment by sovereign action (Wagner 1935; Hill 1965, 234). Through his frontal attack on the sovereign prerogative, Coke was setting the stage to proceed on two fronts at once: On the one hand, he sought to make the common law more respectful of individual freedoms and attuned to the needs of a society increasingly based on trade and commerce (Hill 1965, 256–57), while at the same he was priming the common law for constitutional supremacy over the sovereign's power, this by seizing on the myth of the ancient constitution of the realm and on the idea that embodied in the common law was the ancient legal wisdom the English people had built up over centuries of practice (Hill 1965, 257; Santoro 1999, 24; the essential reading here is, of course, Pocock 1987; but see also, generally, Weston 1995).

Legal and political thought in 17th-century England was thus embracing the idea of individual freedom and the correlative idea of the limits that needed to be placed on sovereign power. These ideas could be championed by looking to either of the two main paradigms then available—that of the common lawyers or the liberal conception of it developed in the latter part of the century by John Locke— but in either case the outcome was always anti-absolutistic (Santoro 1999, 34; Costa 1999, 197). And even after the Restoration, the political forces sympathetic to the sovereign prerogative found it impracticable to go back to the patriarchal and eudaemonistic themes that had formed the theoretical basis of absolutism in the first half of the century. As much as sovereign power was still absolute and not amenable to any challenge, it could no longer claim a right to extend its reach into the private sphere with a view to pursuing the common good; in fact, it was now styling itself as a guarantor of individual rights (Daly 1978, 239). And it is perhaps significant that even in those thinkers who were making the case for an unlimited political power, such as Hobbes, there was no longer any thought that the leviathan should be responsible for pursuing the social and economic welfare of its subjects. Even Hobbes in the end made reference only to security as the basis of political power, in which respect his outlook can be likened to the liberal political philosophy that would later be expounded by such a one as Locke (Jones 2000, 172).

As the merchant and entrepreneurial classes began to gain a consciousness of their emergent role, the ancient ideology of medieval constitutionalism increasingly came to be reframed in individualistic terms (Appleby 1978, 204–05; Macpherson 1962), but what was especially taking hold was the idea of the market as an organic entity that, unlike the body politic envisioned by the theorists of the Tudor era, did not depend on the sovereign's stewardship in order to survive and prosper. This key idea of the market was already beginning to take shape in the early 17th century in works such as Thomas Mun's *England's Treasure by Forraign Trade* (written in 1623 and published in 1664), where it was conceptualized as a *commercial flux*—not an artefact or an institution, the creation of a central authority, but a natural, impersonal entity emerging out of the single moves of individual agents in search of personal gain (Appleby 1978, 44). In this way there emerged for the first time the idea of a sphere of civil life in which sovereign action could not intervene without disrupting the natural dynamics that drove the course of events. The natural flux of commerce identified by the economists of the early 17th century implied the idea that some human relations are underpinned by a uniformity and coherence of virtue in which they could be investigated as independent phenomena. To identify such relations was also to claim for society a whole sphere of autonomy in activities that had hitherto been subject to the control of the prince (ibid., 53).

So on top of the political charge the liberal political thinkers were leading against sovereign power, the economic thinkers were mounting a scientific challenge, calling into question not only the legitimacy of that power but also its effectiveness. And in this way they were making a further ideological lever available to the individualistic political philosophy that was gaining ground. Individualistic economic behaviour could now be legitimized not only on the basis of the time-tested precepts of the realm's ancient constitution or the principles of natural law but also on the basis of the golden rule that the common good and the wealth of the nation depended on the free dynamics of personal egoisms: "What could increase the commonwealth if not private wealth?" the merchant Edward Misselden rhetorically asked in his 1623 book *The Circle of Commerce* (Jones 2000, 139).

The demise of political absolutism in England spelled the end of the theoretical and institutional spaces needed for the concept of police to develop. The political crises of the 17th century, coupled with the increasing inability of sovereign power to lay out a systematic program to manage the realm's socioeconomic life, instead made it possible to develop the first form of economic liberalism proper (Holdsworth 1924, vol. 6, pp. 303ff.; Jones 2000, 244). It was in this scenario, long perceived as in certain respects anomalous, that some prescient economic writers could conceive the idea that economic life was governed by its own dynamics and principles. The development of English institutions, in other words, prevented police from evolving into a broad domestic policy carried out by centralized bureaucratic apparatuses (precisely what the Privy Council and the prerogative courts were beginning to turn into). More generally, that institutional development prevented the concept of police from expressing the very idea of the nation's political organization, an idea that was instead beginning to be referred to by the term *constitution* (Heidenhamer 1986, 12). The idea of the constitution wound up squeezing out that of police, along with the correlative idea of a duty to preserve the nation's *good police* and *common wealth* entrusted to the sovereign, and at the same time it ended up restricting the idea of *police* to that of the *police as a security apparatus*, which, as we will see, would become distinctive of liberal thought in the modern age. In this respect, we can also understand why English-speaking historiography never quite picked up on the semantic wealth of the Continental concept of police or the complexity of the Continental experience of the *état de police* or *Polizeistaat*. Indeed, the literal translation of the term as *police state* has given rise to a huge historiographical misunderstanding, leading to the conclusion that the whole experience of the administrative monarchy could essentially be reduced to an expression of the police as pure repressive power, and hence to the idea of an exercise of the state's coercive powers not held in check by the law (Chapman 1971, 52ff.).[16]

16 It is significant in this regard that a historian of institutions should have found it necessary to introduce a new term in the hope of taking down the language barriers erected over the course of two centuries of divergent conceptual evolution, and in place of the standard *police state* as a translation of *état de police* and *Polizeistaat*, he suggested the rather infelicitous *policy state* (Dyson 1980, 118).

3.2. *Police*: the French tradition

In France, it is the figure of police lieutenant for the city of Paris that has long attracted the attention of historians, in certain respects obscuring the broader social and institutional meaning the notion of police has had between the Middle Ages and the modern age (Rigaudière 1996, 98).[17] In reality, even before the birth of the lieutenant, the French *police* was already forming into shape in its various aspects—as a notion, a function, a complex of norms, and a ground and officer corps—thus beginning to outline for public authorities a sphere of intervention distinct from the classic judicial sphere.

It was especially in the urban centres of the Late Middle Ages that there first emerged the governance problems that a dynamically changing society was thrusting upon the authorities; and in fact the cities, with their charters and magistracies, were developing a social and economic idea of police closely resembling the embodiment it would take in the modern age (Mestre 1985).[18] More generally, however, all the regular magistracies increasingly took on new functions, not only the traditional ones tied to the administration of justice but also a general police function empowering them to manage all matters pertaining to material and moral life across the territories within their competence (ibid., 66). As Delamare himself concedes, even in the 16th century it seems quite clear that the jurisdiction conferred on various city officials and magistracies entailed a general power to "maintain peace, the purity of customs, abundance in the supply of food, and good faith in commerce" (Delamare 1705, 34; my translation). This police competence still entailed broad regulatory powers that only with the development of a sovereign prerogative over legislation would progressively be pared down to a mere supplementary function (Sueur 2001b, 61).[19]

However, even if police agents and functions were already taking on their essential traits, the notion of *police* in this period still lacked theoretical distinctness. It rarely figured alone in the regulatory provisions, and rather formed part of the

---

17 It has been commented, for example, that "the history of police is primarily the history of the police in Paris. Indeed, over the course of more than a century the capital was the only city in France to have a coherent police administration. Such was the General Police Lieutenancy" (Euloge 1985, 11; my translation).

18 The Paris *prévôt*, for example, exercised broad regulatory powers, as is clearly attested by the *Livre des métiers* (a collection of ordinances completed in 1344) and the later *Livres des couleurs* (a collection of ordinances on social and economic matters) (Olivier-Martin 1948, 90–92). These powers would usually be renewed *pour le bon gouvernement & estat de la police dicelle ville* under the sovereign edicts entrusting broadly regulatory and administrative functions to the *prévôt* and the magistracies in Paris (Delamare 1705, 114). And, of course, these powers and collections (the so-called books of trades and métiers) were not distinctive to the capital alone (Olivier-Martin 1948, 68–71).

19 It was in particular the *parlements* that for a long time had been entrusted with an important regulatory police function; and so central was this competence that initially the royal provisions simply collected and systematized the regulations that the higher courts issued in concert with the city magistrates in carrying out their local police functions (Sueur 2001b, 146; cf. Olivier-Martin 1951, 539; 1948, 58–59).

broader judicial functions that the public law of the time entrusted to authorities charged with keeping good order. Until the modern age, the term *police* still referred to the broad sphere of activity concerned with ensuring an orderly society, an activity for which the officials entrusted with the administration of justice were no more responsible than city organs and trade corporations (Rigaudière 1996, 100ff.). Throughout the Renaissance period, then, there was a close connection between *justice* and *police*. This connection was constantly reiterated whenever the king would grant the municipalities a power of taxation or renew that grant, and it was also implicit in the general authority the king would confer on his magistrates in their function of tending to the common good. The same connection was also expressed by Claude De Seyssel, for whom *police* and *justice* came together to make up the traits of the limited sovereign as a figure responsible only for respecting and protecting the judicial customs of the realm. Indeed, in his *La monarchie de France* De Seyssel identified *police* as one of the *freins* (or checks on power) through which to limit abuse of power, and in this sense the idea of *police* took on a meaning equivalent to that of the fundamental laws and of the "good order and harmony existing among all classes within the realm" (De Seyssel [1515] 1961, 127; my translation). As can clearly be appreciated, this understanding of *police* harked back to the Aristotelian conception of the hierarchical structure and class organization of society which the king was responsible for preserving and respecting (Skinner 1978, X).

Not until the modern age would the meaning of the concept-term *police* begin to change. On the one hand was a slow process under which the functions ascribed to *police* authorities would become increasingly specified (although, as discussed, this process would remain for the most part incomplete); on the other hand was the likewise slow process that brought to the surface such elements of *police* law as would make it possible to better discern the notion and single out its different aspects (Durand 1996, 171). These developments would also make it possible to mark out a theoretical space specific to *police*, thus releasing it from the ancient bond that still kept it fastened to *justice*, while at the same time definitively linking it to a modern idea of power as the expression of the highest lawmaking and administrative authority.

This evolution got its start, in particular, when the science of public law began to set some of its building blocks in place, such as the concept of *commun purfit* (the French rendition of the Roman *utilitas publica*) and that of *nécessité*. It was indeed thanks to the effort of modern political and legal science to work out these concepts that there first emerged in embryo the idea of a *ius publicum*, or *ius politiae*, understood as a sphere of the legal order in which the public interest trumps private interest (Mestre 1985, 98; Olivier-Martin 1949, 51). This latter idea established a firmer and firmer footing, starting from the 16th century as the sovereign organs multiplied their regulatory initiatives and, even more importantly, extended their recourse to interventions of general scope. As has been remarked by Olivier-Martin (1951, 351), what the king did through his decrees was essentially to promote the common good, a function that went beyond that of protecting private rights. Indeed, the ground covered by state intervention tended to exclude anything to do with *in rem* and *in personam* rights, and likewise excluded, as a rule, was criminal law. The growing body of provisions issued by the king dealt with areas of civil and social life not regulated by the common civil law applied by the ordinary judicial courts, tending instead to be addressed at two broad regulatory areas: on the one hand the establishment and management of the politico-administrative powers necessary to promote the general interest, on the other the body of rules put in place to maintain the realm's moral and material order. Both of these areas came under the umbrella notion of *police générale* (Sueur 2001b, 63; Olivier-Martin 1949, 94).

The growth of this vast legislative activity thus provided a seedbed for the flourishing of a theoretical framework within which to specify the king's legislative and administrative power (as distinguished from the judicial view of power and the centrality of the common civil law). This flourishing came about precisely in the slipstream of the concept of *police*. Indeed, the term began to find systematic use in the various royal decrees under the designation of *police et bon gouvernement*, or again that of *conduite et police de la chose publique de nostre royaume* (the conduct and police of the public good of our realm), ultimately becoming a key concept in the princely chancellery and in the earliest politico-legal treatises on sovereign power, beginning with Jean Bodin's *République*.

In the *République* the term *police* is used in three senses. Its *prima facie* sense is that of the good order that every sovereign is responsible for keeping, and on this understanding it can be assimilated to the Aristotelian *politia*.[20] More often, however, the term *police* seems to refer to the conduct of the public good, or commonwealth. As a theorist propounding an organicistic view of the state, Bodin saw in family units the building blocks of the body politic and thus rejected the Scholastic distinction between *oeconomia* and *politeia*, finding the jurisconsults at fault because, as he saw it, they "divorced economy or household management from police or disciplinary power" (Bodin [1576] 1955, 6), where they should instead have "unified into a single science their treatment of the laws and ordinances pertaining to police, corporative bodies, and families" (Bodin [1576] 1986, vol. 1, bk. 1, chap. 2, p. 40; my translation).[21] The well-ordered republic *(la république bien ordonnée)* is the fruit of the good government carried out by the sovereign, whom Bodin unequivocally entrusts with *police* powers, on the model of the economic government entrusted to the head of the household, or *paterfamilias*. "Thus the well-ordered family is a true image of the commonwealth, and domestic comparable with sovereign authority. It follows that the household is the model of right order in the commonwealth" (Bodin [1576] 1955, 6–7). An important part

20 It should be noted, however, that when Bodin is thinking about this meaning of the term *police*, he usually prefers to go with the term *justice* (see Stuardi 1988, 16).
21 The French original: "Mais les jurisconsultes, et législateurs, que nous devons suivre, ont traité les lois et ordonnances de la police, des collèges, et des familles en une même science."

of this scheme are the intermediate bodies, since Bodin sees them as playing an essential practical role in maintaining a well-ordered political community. Indeed, to these bodies are entrusted the *police* functions that need to be carried out within their territorial jurisdictions, and since the political community's good order depends in large part on the internal harmony among its individual components, equally essential to that end is the *police* entrusted to bodies corporate (Stuardi 1988, 21). As much as *police* is in this sense an attempt to meld *oeconomia* and *politeia*, it is not understood as a governmental activity aimed at forging social order. Bodin's criticism of the social order envisioned by the practical sciences under Scholasticism is functional to his aim of grounding absolute sovereign power, while his use of *police* seems still tied to the idea of protecting the ancient good order of the corporate or estate society, whose harmony, on the conception we saw earlier with De Seyssel ([1515] 1961, 127), falls under the responsibility of the sovereign, entrusted with keeping everything in its proper place in view of the whole.

In yet another sense Bodin uses *police* in reference to concrete the governing activity entrusted to royal officials. We have already seen that, in the *République*, the stewardship of the commonwealth is the sole responsibility of the king, whose main power is "to give law to all in general and each in particular" (Bodin [1576] 1955, 43), but the king can delegate the execution of his provisions to officials he appoints and who carry out functions in a number of areas, which in addition to *justice, finance*, and *guerre* (war) also include *police*. However, we are not told what this *police* function concretely consists in, except that—in line with a tradition which, as discussed, traces back to the Late Middle Ages—Bodin ascribes that function to royal officials at large. The best that we can find is an occasional but summary list of functions ascribed to these officials, a list that, in addition to justice, finance, and war, includes the task of providing for the "fortification and upkeep of public places," ensuring the supply of victuals and other necessities, guaranteeing "the city's health and hygiene," and finally tending to the "streets, waterways, forests, ports, and roadways" (Bodin [1576] 1986, vol. III, p. 88; my translation).

In essence, in the *République*, when *police* does not blend into *justice* and the mere task of maintaining the good ancient order and harmony among bodies, it tends to be assimilated to legislative and regulatory power, and so to sovereignty itself as *la plus grand puissance de commander*. Of course, this higher power of command rests exclusively with the king, but the king can delegate more specific regulatory powers to his officials so that they may interpret the king's *ordonnances* and adapt them to the case at hand (Stuardi 1988, 32–33). In a similar vein, Charles Loyseau, in his 1608 *Traité des seigneuries*, described *police* as a rule-making power set up on two levels of hierarchy, with a general power of the king to issue ordinances (decrees) and a concrete edictal power of the single magistrates, and he accordingly distinguished between *police générale* and *police particulière* (Durand 1996, 198; Boulet-Sautel 1980, 48). Already expressed in this latter power, however, is a more explicitly active idea of the functions of public authority, whose objective is not so much to protect the established order as to work for the *accroissement de l'état*, the buildup of the state (Loyseau 1608, sec. 92). To this end the magistrates set forth a *ius politiae* proper for all royal officials, defining this capacity as

> the power to establish particular rules for all the citizens within the magistrate's own district and territory, a power which exceeds that of a simple judge, who only has the power to adjudicate between plaintiff and defendant and lacks the power to issue rules unless a case is brought to the court by a defendant or a hearing is held for a plaintiff; the particular rules of the magistrate, by contrast, apply to an entire population, and the power to issue them resembles and carries the advantages of that of the prince more than that of the judge, considering that these rules are like laws, or like particular decrees, and for this reason they are properly called edicts.
>
> (Ibid., sec. 3; my translation)

It was in this direction—that is, toward a framing of *police* as a rule-making power—that the whole of legal and political theory would subsequently move. *Police* had now been identified as a key concept referring to the vast power to intervene in social life. As such it would develop starting from the 16th century, and it was through this activity that there came into being the primordial outline of a public law proper in France, a law whose essential traits would definitively be encapsulated in theoretical form by Jean Domat. As much as Domat started out from the notion of *police* used by his predecessors, he wound up completely juridifying it, fashioning *police* into a specific police law that, along with the fundamental political laws and the rules for the establishment of public offices, formed part of the broader notion of public law (Mestre 1985, 163). Similarly, in *Institutions du droit français* (Institutions of French law), Claude Fleury ([1692] 1858) offered the following definition of *police* (which along with justice, war, and finance was by then considered part of public law): He defined it as the set of "rules that concern what is most necessary to the life and commerce of men, which rules are particular, considering that they vary greatly from place to place and cannot be easily be grouped under any general law" (ibid., vol. 1, p. 91; my translation). This definition revolved around the particular means that characterize the police function. Indeed, as an instrument of policing (from the French *policer*), this body of rules could not be compared to a body of laws; the legitimacy of this rule-making activity could not be grounded in the sovereign will *(voluntas)* but instead depended on its ability to satisfy principles of convenience and effectiveness. Because policing was tailored to each specific case, its legitimacy could only be judged by a means-ends criterion. Police rules had to be crafted in view of the specifics of each situation. Unlike the law—which tended to exist as an expression of *auctoritas*, as the symbolic concretion of a legitimate *imperium*—police rules were keyed to the minute exigencies of workaday life (Napoli 2003, 59; Boulet-Sautel 1980, 50).

Throughout this phase, the theoretical evolution of the concept of *police* thus proceeded in tandem with the development of the politico-legal concept of sovereignty and the concrete rise of a normative and regulatory power that was largely extraneous to the study of the law of the realm and to the jurisdiction of the regular courts, and so it ultimately wound up converging with the evolution of concepts and doctrines broadly classifiable as pertaining to public law (Legendre 1966, 12). In parallel to this development, as the institutions of the administrative monarchy gradually solidified, the need to govern the clash between different apparatuses prompted several attempts to define *justice* and *police* as two distinct areas. These attempts began to be made as soon as the institutional figure of the intendant began to take shape, at which point the king on several occasions reiterated his intention to claim for himself and for the officials of the nascent autocratic administration the power to run all affairs relating to *raison d'état* (Mestre 1985, 191), but it was only in 1667 that a satisfactory result was achieved, when the office of police lieutenant was instituted in Paris.

As previously mentioned, this royal official was essentially the answer found to the problem of defining the exact scope of the *police* power conferred on the Parisian *prévôt* and his lieutenants: "Considering that police is mixed up between civil and criminal," Delamare wrote, "the civil lieutenant and the criminal lieutenant found themselves contending over what subject matter belonged to their own tribunal" (Delamare 1705, 116; my translation). This *querelle* did not find an effective solution until 1666, when the council was summoned that would bring into being the general police lieutenant. It was indeed only through that institutional design that *police* found a preliminary theoretical framework. As Delamare wrote, sketching out a crucial distinction,

> what we call *police* is in effect concerned with nothing else if not serving the prince and maintaining the public order; policing is incompatible with the niceties and minutiae of litigation, it being closer to the functions of government than to those of the courthouse.
>
> (Ibid., 127; my translation)

This distinction between judicial and police functions was sketched out in the very edict through which this special office was established. The distinction served as a justificatory basis for the same office, and it painted the image of a power that in pursuing its ends does not have to confine itself to settling controversies between private citizens and upholding the law.

The edict set out the competences of the lieutenant in detail, but even more importantly it clearly summed up for the first time what were believed to be the specific tasks assigned to *police*. Here is a key part of the preamble, which, having stressed the need to effect a major overhaul of *justice* and *police*, offered the following clarification:

> Considering that the functions of justice and police are often at odds, and that between them they cover too much ground to be properly exercised by a single magistrate in Paris, we have resolved to split them up, calculating, on the one

hand, that since the administration of litigative and distributive justice requires a presence on the ground at multiple places at once, as well as a constant focus—both to regulate the affairs that individuals engage in and to exercise the oversight that needs to be had over those individuals—a single and complete magistrate is needed for that function, and calculating, on the other hand, that police likewise requires a magistrate specifically designated to it, in view of the fact that this function consists in ensuring peace for the public and for all individuals, in clearing the city from those who can be expected to disturb the peace, in providing for abundance, and in having everyone live according to their station and duty.

(Delamare 1705, 131; my translation)

According to what Bielfeld (1760, 7) reports, the first president of the Parisian *parlement*, Achille Du Harlay, conferred the office of general police lieutenant on the Marquis D'Argenson by uttering the following words: "Le Roi, monsieur, vous demande sûreté, netteté, bon-marché" (The King, Sir, requests security, clarity, and abundance and an affordable market).

The progressive institutionalization of magistracies and police functions made it necessary not only to legitimize the sphere of sovereign power, a task that fell into the hands of the budding science of public law, but also to develop an array of concrete techniques for administering the commonwealth and governing the realm's social and economic life. Institutional development, in other words, had brought about a new need for *bonne police*, and with it an opportunity for the practical sciences to frame that notion within a theory, developing around it a modern administrative science concerned with the set of governing techniques that were becoming increasingly formalized. It was in particular in the 18th century that, with increasing urgency, the need was being felt to set on a stronger theoretical basis what some were even describing as a "science of government" (De Curban 1761–64).

This aspiration, however, would be frustrated by the entrenched interests that had formed in the universities in France around the study of public law and the practical sciences.[22] In fact, theoretical developments in the 18th century, later described as the apogee of *police* in France, at best produced a rough sketch of something like a police science within the frame of compilatory or casuistic works. Paradigmatic in this regard was the empirical approach taken in the monumental

---

22   The training of future royal officials tended to focus on the classic disciplines of Roman law, and the king—very much aware of the need to update that training—made several attempts to endow chairs in French public law starting in 1679. But this effort to reform the curriculum met resistance from jurists tied to the apparatus for the old administration of justice, for they were afraid that the changes sought to be introduced would enable public law to overshadow private law, thus acting as yet another backdoor through which their sphere of competence would be curtailed in favour of the organs of royal autocracy (Mestre 1985, 169–70; Sueur 2001b, 148).

Traité de la police, written by the commissaire of the Châtelet Nicolas Delamare.[23] This was essentially a sourcebook written by a practitioner for others engaged in the practice of the law, and it gave rise to a literary genre proper,[24] testifying to the need to impart a systematic order to that vast hodgepodge of legal provisions on which rested the monarchy's nascent social and economic policy. This need was expressly pointed out by Delamare himself, who in the introduction to his treatise remarked that the subject of *police* is

> scattered over such a great amount of texts [. . .], and is furthermore so randomly interspersed among so many other subjects, and commingled with them, that it takes a painstakingly laborious effort just to pull it out and tease it apart from all that does not belong with it.
>
> (Delamare 1705, unnumbered preface; my translation)

The exigencies of daily practice thus made it necessary to compile a "code of police laws" (ibid.), that is, a collection of legal provisions—*ordonnances*, *arrêts*, and *règlements*—concerning police. It was actually typical of the period to worry over the state of this panoply of police regulations broadly understood—still insufficiently rationalized, to the point of potentially undermining the functionaries' ability to effectively carry out their duties—so much so that we find the same concern expressed almost verbatim even in the introduction to Edme de La Poix de Frémeville's 1758 *Dictionnaire*.[25]

---

23 Delamare was born in 1639 into the high bourgeoisie *de robe*, and it was in 1673 that he received his appointment as *commissaire au Châtelet*. In devoting himself to *police* matters, he undertook a massive study of public law which would form the substance of his treatise on police, an initiative encouraged by some of his superiors, who supported him by facilitating his access to all the legal sources held at the supreme court in Paris and elsewhere. Through this work Delamare gained a reputation as "the official police historiographer" (Olivier-Martin 1948, 9; my translation; cf. Bondois 1935). The work ultimately came out in four volumes, the first one comprising as many books devoted to (a) police in general, its magistrates, and its officials; (b) religion; (c) customs; and (d) public health; the second and third volumes instead addressing the question of victuals; and the fourth that of roadway mobility. But this was not the original plan for the work, which was intended to run to six volumes, addressing the questions of security in the cities and on the thoroughfares, the liberal arts and sciences, commerce, the mechanical arts, servants, domestic workers, manual workers, and paupers. In 1684, the king granted Delamare an annuity so that he could bring the work to completion, but despite this perquisite, the enterprise proved such a financial burden that, even with the publication of the first volume (in 1705) and the second one (in 1710), he could not recover the expenditures. In 1713, he resigned from all public offices and thus managed to put out the third volume (1719). In the last phase of his life he relied on the help of a young lawyer, Anne Leeler du Brillet, who in 1723, after Delamare's death, completed the fourth volume. The fifth and sixth ones, as mentioned, never saw the light of day.

24 Other works cast in this same compilatory mould that came out in the 18th century treating the subject of *police* on the model of Delamare's *Traité* were De Frémeville 1758, Du Chense 1757, and Des Essarts 1786–91.

25 De Frémeville compiled his dictionary drawing inspiration from Delamare, looking to offer a useful practical guideline for police officials stationed in the rural areas, where Delamare's *Traité* was

But although Delamare's *Traité* started out as a compilation of legal provisions, it morphed into something else. It is Demalare himself who points this out to us:

> In the regulations I was going through I discovered so much wisdom, such an orderly arrangement, and such a perfect relation among all the parts of police that I thought I could reduce it to an art or discipline by tracing it back to its principles.
>
> (Delamare 1705, unnumbered preface; my translation)

So as Delamare proceeded to analyze all the subject areas relating to police *law*, he attempted to set out the essential features of a police *science*. This attempt at a theoretical foundation naturally began with a definition of *police* in which he sought to pin down its nature by highlighting its functional contrast to *justice*. Indeed, Delamare stated he saw a perfectly marked "division" between "two types of functions" in virtue of "their ends" and "their exercise," one being "concerned with the affairs and interests of individuals, the other having no other aim except to serve the king and the public good" (ibid.). With the *function* of police defined, however, there still remained the problem of clarifying the nature of its specific *object*, that public good which so often cropped up in the discourse of the politico-legal sciences. This latter clarification was provided by recourse to the eudaemonistic criteria typical of political absolutism. Indeed, for Delamare, the core aim of police was to "shepherd man to the highest happiness," the most perfect welfare and wholesomeness, which in turn he saw as dependent on three types of good: "the good of the soul, the good of the body, and what is referred to as the good of one's fortunes" (ibid.).

In addressing the distinctive object of police science, then, Delamare designed his *Traité* around this preliminary distinction among three main areas within which he thought all police provisions could be made to fall. More to the point, police tends to the "welfare of the soul" by regulating religious life and the life of customs; to the "welfare of the body" by regulating public health and managing foodstuffs and resources, as well as housing and security, and ensuring tranquillity and the good upkeep of public spaces; and to "fortunes" by exercising oversight over productive and commercial activities. In more general terms, the threefold police function was (i) to make life "good and wholesome," in the sense of bringing it

---

perceived as a work primarily addressed to lieutenants operating in the cities. De Frémeville, too, lamented the fact that police law was "scattered across such a vast number of books, and is mixed in with so many other subjects, and in such a haphazard way, that it is impossible to make the distinctions necessary to apply its provisions and put them into practice" (De Frémeville 1758, p. VI). So strong was the emphasis the French tradition laid on the need to collect and rationalize police laws that even works entirely conceived in the compilatory fashion introduced by Delamare came to be referred to as codes, a case in point being Du Chesne's (1757) previously mentioned *Code de la police*.

into line with religious and moral precepts and proper custom; (ii) to "preserve" life, in the strictly biological sense of keeping people in good physical health; and (iii) to make life "comfortable" and "pleasant" by providing for all the amenities of transportation, facilitating commerce, and supporting the arts. Delamare concluded:

> It therefore stands to reason that whatever condition man might find himself in, and whatever part he may take, police will constantly keep watch over his preservation and secure all the goods it can, for the good of both his body and soul, and for his good fortunes.
>
> (Ibid.)

So what was emerging with increasing force in France at the end of the 17th century was the need to more clearly draw the boundary between *justice* and *police*, a boundary whose exact definition, as discussed, had become the object of an institutional clash. And if any work can be singled out as the best response to that problem, it is Delamare's. But Delamare, despite his stated intention to dig out the underlying *principles* of *police*, was unsystematic in treating all the subjects that fell within that large container, and so its distinction from *justice* can at best be gleaned, almost en passant, from his remark that police—this important part of the activity carried out by sovereign organs—"consists rather in government than in litigative adjudication" (ibid., unnumbered preface), or again we have to glean the distinction from a memorandum by La Maire where it is remarked that *police* "consists in administration properly so called" (La Maire 1878, 9; my translation).[26]

The insistence with which the new magistracies sought to expand into *police générale* triggered a reaction on the part of the ancient magistracies, but this cannot be analyzed as simply a "turf war" between institutions. In contention were two competing views of the functions of the state. Ranged on one side of the field were the *parlements* and the ancient ordinary courts, which struggled to wean themselves from the classic judicial conception of the king as mere defender of the legal traditions and of the realm's good order of times past, and in whose hands the already modern concept of *police* was thus beaten into shape according to the ancient conservative tradition of *iurisdictio*. On the other side were the commissaires of the intendancy and the police lieutenants, who were already looking at their function as that of functionaries serving an administrative monarchy which no longer confined its action to that of preserving a pre-existing order but also took on the task of shaping society according to its political interests, thus giving the concept of *police* an active, fully modern inflection.

---

26 La Maire wrote this memo in response to a request that Maria Theresa of Austria sent to the police lieutenancy in Paris inquiring about Parisian police. The lieutenant in charge, De Sartine, in office from 1750 to 1774, instructed the *commissaire au Châtelet* Jean-Baptiste-Charles la Maire to write a report to be sent to Austria. It was completed around 1770 and was published only eight years later under the editorship of Augustin Louis Gazier.

Although France's institutional development had irreparably compromised the ancient judicial conception of power, there had yet to come a theoretical account of *police* strong enough to make a modern police science out of it. Indeed, it would take a *practical* development for the idea of an administrative function to finally come into its own, along with a corresponding science. That would be the French Revolution and the institutional design brought into existence under Napoleon. With the revolution, the ancient state based on a system of justice was transfigured into the idea of a state based on the rule of law. On the one hand, this change brought to a flashpoint the tensions and conflicts that had been building up around the bodies the monarchy sought to institutionalize and the functions it sought to claim for itself, while at the same time it offered an opportunity to bring greater theoretical clarity to the distinction between justice and administration. This was a distinction that institutional development in the Napoleonic age would definitively concretize into different apparatuses: a judicial one and an administrative one. Only with the administrative science of the 19th century would there be that theoretical development which between the 17th and 18th centuries French *police* had not yet seen. Indeed, *police* had remained an activity entirely focused on the exigencies of everyday practice, so it could not offer itself as an organic synthesis of the political universe that instead had developed around *Policey*. But with the theoretical advances of the 19th century, the rationality of government would again be brought to bear on legal discourse. And the same advances would irreversibly box ancient *police* into the casing of the modern science of public law.

3.3. *Policey*: the German tradition

The concept of police in the German area followed a similar path as that of *police* in France—that is, it developed out of the experience of the mercantile cities of the Late Middle Ages, with the attendant need to govern the territory, production, and the population. The term emerged in Germany in the latter half of the 15th century. This is attested by numerous city charters, such as the famous one that established the city of Nuremberg, which under an imperial grant of 1464 acquired a general authority to administer its own internal affairs—a competence to establish a government and police over all things: *Polletzey und regirung in allen Sachen ordnen, setzen und fürnehmen*—and the same is evidenced by lordly edicts containing early references to the need to "provide for good order and police" *(loblichen polliceien und guten ordnunge versehen)* (von Unruh 1983a, 389; cf. Knemeyer 1978; Schulze 1988).

It is true that city and lordly courts, as early as the 15th century, were granting statutory provisions containing references to *Polletzey*, *Pollucy*, *Pollicei*, and *Pollicey*, but it was only with the legislative activity of the imperial chancellery, followed by that of the territorial chancelleries, that the term developed into its distinctive meaning. Indeed, what enabled the term to come into widespread use was the development of a more stable political framework throughout central Europe, especially with the 1495 proclamation of perpetual peace *(Ewiger Landfriede)*, under which the territorial princes acquired supreme jurisdiction to maintain peace and ensure security. This imperial enactment thus formed the legal basis for the rebirth of a centralized public power, in which context the term was being used precisely to express this idea of a judicial power broadly understood, endowing princes with a general competence to keep peace within their territories; and so, at least in this initial phase, the term designated something like an art of adjudication and justice (von Unruh 1983a, 391).

It was thus the crystallization of imperial institutions in the early modern age that helped the term develop into this meaning, which is the meaning it carried when it entered the politico-legal language of the territories, expressing the idea of the public functions as a whole (ibid., 392). The term was used by the imperial chancellery to designate the overall authoritative power to guarantee *ordnung und pollucy* (though there is scarcely any mention of its use in any official text until 1521), in which context it would have been specifically used where an imperial edict of Charles V originally written in French needed to be sent in a German translation to the territorial diets, and the edict would thus refer to the imperial *pollices*. The term would later be used for the incipient legislative activity that began to shape the political life of the Holy Roman Empire and its territories, particularly in the form of the monumental *Reichpolizeiordnungen* (imperial police ordinances) enacted starting in the 16th century, and thus it became a term of art in the practice of the chancelleries (ibid., 392).[27]

However, *Policey* continued to go back to the Aristotelian tradition as remodelled by Christian medieval philosophy, in which the term took on some strong moral and political overtones: *Politeia* or *politia* came to designate the orderly condition needed for a polity to thrive, "the governing harmony between the prince and the estates" (Stolleis 1998a, 521), and by extension it referred to the complex of means and rules needed for such good order to be maintained (von Unruh 1983a, 390; Schulze 1988, 73). The subject of good administration or good police—*bona administratio* or *bona politia*, typically expressed by way of the modifier *polizeyn*—thus fell into the grip of a strong conservative conception, where it meant that the sovereign was entrusted with maintaining a well-ordered community.[28]

---

27 Its earliest attestation appears in a 1530 project of the Diet of Augsburg proposing to institute a legislative commission *über die Polecey und über die Reformation des kaiserlichen Cammergerichts* (on police and the reformation of the imperial courts), and in this project the term encompassed all the different aspects relating to the lives of subjects. In another acceptation, however, contemporary imperial language was using the term *Politzey* as a German equivalent of the French *politique* (von Unruh 1983a, 393). Although several provisions issued between 1495 and 1529 dealt with issues that at the time would have been regarded as pertaining to police, the first official use of the corresponding term appeared in a provision of the 1530 project providing for a reform commission to be set up: The project was titled *Ordnung und Reformation guter Polizey im Heiligen Römischer Reich* (Order and reformation of good policy in the Holy Roman Empire), and it addressed a range of questions concerning the empire's social and economic life. The 1530 *Reichpolizeiordnungen* essentially provided the regulatory blueprint for those that followed.

28 A typical expression of this Aristotelian and conservative conception of police in the German area was Oldendorp 1530, on which see Maier 1966, 106ff., and Stolleis 1998a, 522.

In any event, this initial practical and conceptual development of the police apparatus which came with *Reichspolizeiordnungen*, and which also affected the territorial principalities, meant that police activity and subject matter needed to be clarified (von Unruh 1983a, 395), and in this process police fell almost entirely within the competence of the territorial authorities. The concept slowly transitioned toward encapsulating an active sovereign authority over the entire domain of the state's internal administration. This sovereign power came both in the form of orders and regulations dealing with *particular* situations and in the form of broad legislative enactments such as the *Landespolizeiordnungen* (territorial police ordinances) which, couched in the language of the imperial chancellery, began to invoke the idea of *gute Ordnung und Policey*, or good order and police (von Unruh 1983a, 395; Stolleis 1998a, 558–59). Until the mid-17th century, these ordinances were still mainly restorative, being designed to correct departures from *gute Policey*, but over time they became tools of social reform proper, and instead of referring to a good ancient order to be restored and protected from decadence, their preambles—under the formula *Förderung des gemeinen Nutzen*—began to point out the need to "promote the common good" (Raeff 1983, 50). It is precisely to the gradual expansion of this broadly legislative and administrative activity of the territorial principalities that we have to ascribe the full theoretical and practical development of the concept of *Policey* (Schiera 1968, 269ff.; Maier 1966, 93ff.).

The notion of *Policey* explains how the territorial state in the German area actually came into being by developing out of the imperial structure. So, unlike the development in France, *Policey* did not simply consist of a complex of functions that, in fits and starts, only tended to be ascribed to institutional offices within an already well-established political framework, but rather pointed to the emergence of a sovereign political power proper, capable of overturning the empire's ancient institutional framework. It was perhaps precisely in view of the need to rearrange the political makeup of the German territorial states that institutional development was accompanied by a process through which, unlike anywhere else in Continental Europe, the concept of *Policey* became the linchpin of a theoretical construction that guided the development of all political thought in the German area (Maier 1966, 94), and, in fact, "the concept, at the height of its evolution, can be said to have captured the essence of the modern German state" (Schiera 1968, 263).

Policey thus came to mean the whole sphere of internal policy over which princely authority was consolidating its dominion, and in particular its role in regulating social life, a role it managed to carve out for itself in addressing problems the old institutions could no longer effectively respond to. We have followed the institutional development through which the territorial princes managed to assert their role as undisputed protagonists in the political life of the territorial states, and in particular we have traced out the birth of the commissarial apparatus that progressively disempowered the old apparatus for the administration of justice. This apparatus was increasingly being expected to apply and make effective the vast police legislation that over the same arc of time was being developed. The princes' newly constructed role of political ascendancy crucially expressed itself in the aforementioned *Landespolizeiordnungen*, the concrete manifestation of the *ius politiae* through which the science of public law in the German area captured the idea of a sovereign *potestas* concentrated in the hands of the territorial prince. Indeed, just as public law emerged in opposition to the ancient *ius commune* of Roman lineage, a parallel division developed between the new administrative structure headed by the prince and the old structure of judicial administration.

The *ius politiae* was thus the key politico-legal concept through which the territorial princes gradually managed to deprive the institutions of the ancient judicial state, and in particular the *Reichskammergericht* (the Imperial Chamber Court) and the *Landesgerichten* (the territorial courts), of the sovereign *potestas* they had been building. The princes, in other words, gained the power to infringe and reshape the realm's legal traditions settled by *ius commune* and *iura propria*. They could break tradition by *specific* intervention—administratively introducing particularistic provisions enforced by military power—and they could change tradition by *general* intervention, that is, by rewriting the *Landespolizeiordnungen*, or territorial police ordinances (von Unruh 1983a, 398). In this sense, this state that frees itself from any subjection to justice is referred to in Germany as a *Polizeistaat*, for the police power acquired by the prince evolves into a state power that will not tolerate any resistance or opposition (Bussi 2002, 256).

This idea of a sovereign *ius politiae* is key to absolutist legal and political thought in Germany, especially in its theoretically most mature versions from Martin Luther to modern natural law. However, in establishing a legal foundation for the legitimacy of sovereign power, this body of thought was very far from theorizing the arbitrary power so cherished by liberal political historiography. The German natural law tradition always looked to natural and divine law as a constraint on sovereign power, and this was in agreement with absolutist theory (which, as is known, invoked that constraint without fail in its every expression). Moreover, this tradition held a distinctive view of the constraints the prince was bound by in exercising his *ius politiae*, a view that probably sprang from the strong eudaemonistic inspiration found in German natural law theory, at least in its Wolffian strand. On this view, the sovereign could also be held responsible for a *culpa in omittendo*, that is, for failing to provide for the common good of the nation (ibid., 294–95).[29] This eudaemonistic view of sovereign duties came up as early as with Pufendorf, when he turned to the question of the foundation of authority as the linchpin of individual happiness, but it was properly developed by Christian Wolff, who made happiness the natural foundation of social life; and this became a favourite ideological tool for the growing paternalism of the German territorial princes.

29 On the eudaemonistic motifs present in German natural law theory, see Tarello 1976, 144–50. On the schools that followed the teaching of Christian Wolff and Christian Thomasius, see Bobbio 1980, 496.

Happiness became so central to Wolff's conception that he made its pursuit an obligation of every individual, in the sense that everyone is bound to submit to the paternal issuances of established authority, thus fulfilling their obligation to strive for moral and material perfection. Indeed, according to the general principle of Wolff's eudaemonistic philosophy, every man is obligated to pursue happiness and avoid unhappiness: "Quoniam homo obligatur ad felicitatem consequendam et infelicitatem fugiendam, seu operam dare tenetur ut sit felix, sibi autem cavere debet ne sit infelix" (Wolff, 1764, vol. I, 2, § 281). From this principle derive all other particular duties: to preserve one's body (ibid., § 349), eat appropriately and secure a livelihood (ibid., § 383), keep healthy (ibid., § 413), keep a proper wardrobe (ibid., § 430, 461), maintain a household (ibid., § 462), and live a comfortable life (ibid., § 466, 468). In Wolff's ideal society, finally, idleness is banned: "hominibus laborandum est" (ibid). The need to help and encourage individuals in their pursuit of personal happiness, moral and material alike, also entails a duty of the state to procure general welfare and happiness. To this end the state must be enabled to reach into every sphere of human life so as to regulate its every aspect and thus realize the universal principle of happiness.

Although it may be too much to characterize Wolff as the ideologue of German absolutism, for he confined himself to picking up and systematizing motifs that were already present throughout German natural law theory, there is no doubt that he is, par excellence, the philosopher of the *Polizeistaat*:

> It would not, in reality, have been possible to envisage any more rational foundation on which to rest the obligation to submit to the prince's interventionist measures, mainly enacted through the *Polizeiverordnungen* with the support of the advancing power of the bureaucratic machine.
>
> (Schiera 1968, 244; my translation)

All German natural lawyers theorized the need for the prince to enjoy full powers in ensuring the general welfare of society, and thus was provided the most powerful intellectual weapon of the absolutism embraced by the princes, who in pursuing the welfare of the country could easily break free of the constraint of the legal traditions by invoking their *ius politiae*. In this sense, the ideal *pactuum* by which society is created legitimated sovereign power and thus wound up ascribing to the authorities the task of providing for and increasing the welfare of the state *(salus rei pubblicae)*. The idea that the function of the prince is merely conservative—an idea that marked the whole of medieval and Renaissance thinking devoted to limited monarchy and that elsewhere was already morphing into modern liberal thought—was now being superseded for the first time not only in the actual practice of government but also at the highest levels of philosophical speculation. The sovereign was now being explicitly called to action: He was expected to positively intervene in the realm's social and economic life, having a right—and even a duty—to do everything the public interest required.

It was a constant and abiding influence that eudaemonistic philosophy, and Wolff's in particular, exerted throughout the German area.[30] But this influence extended well beyond the discourse of politico-legal knowledge. Indeed, the theme of welfare was central to the entire Aristotelian tradition of the practical sciences, a tradition which never lost vitality in the Continental area, and which in fact was now poised to flourish anew in combination with the investigations that legal and political philosophy was turning to. Out of this symbiosis of eudaemonistic and Aristotelian themes would emerge modern *police science* understood as a practical discipline concerned with administering and governing the public good (Maier 1966, 172). However, this merger of discursive spheres around the notion of welfare revolutionized the ancient Aristotelian tradition, reshaping the ancient motif of good order into the doctrine that called for an active pursuit of the welfare of society as the key notion on which the modern *Polizeistaat* would be built (Stolleis 1998a, 526).

In the conception propounded by the eudaemonistic theorists, the *ius politiae* rose to the status of a philosophical principle, serving as the foundation and justification of sovereign political power, and yet even as it grew into this role it remained conceptually unspecified. Only with the development of the copious literature on the technico-administrative aspects of *gute Policey* could this specification be achieved. The development of a police science did not arouse much interest at the law schools except in connection with the issue of the legal foundations of the *ius politiae* understood as a criterion by which to legitimize the gradual expansion of sovereign powers. The real impetus for the development of a governmental science instead came from the need to deal with all the practicalities involved in the effort to rationalize the administrative apparatus, an effort in turn driven by the development of Prussian political absolutism, which required a cadre of functionaries trained in the politico-economic disciplines centrally involved in the activity of the new administrative organs (ibid., 566). Indeed, the treatment of policy and the economy had hitherto proceeded largely within the Scholastic paradigm of the practical sciences, a rigid paradigm that could not keep up with the development of *prudentia civilis*, a unique combination of economic and political Aristotelianism. In this context there emerged a need for this line of investigation to be instituted as an academic discipline, which never reached any deep level of philosophico-political speculation but did for the first time place a systematic emphasis on the state's operation, on the set of concrete government activities aimed at pursuing the welfare of the community.

---

30 Eudaemonistic themes ran all through the Continental absolutist tradition, and in this connection they can also be found in those passages in the *Traité* where Delamare fashions authority in the image of the paternal figure, described as "that which the tutor is to the pupil, which medicine is to the sick, the captain to the ship, the magistrate to the citizen" (Delamare 1705, 238; my translation). But only in Germany did these themes reach the highest levels of theoretical refinement.

It was through the effort of the Hohenzollerns, especially at the urging of Frederick William I, that in 1723 in Halle the first chair was endowed in *Oekonomie-Polizei und Kameralwissenschaft* (economic police and cameral science), followed in 1727 by another one like it in Frankfurt an der Oder. As a derivation and development of the practical sciences, the new course was placed within the philosophy curriculum, signalling the distance that had come to separate the legal disciplines from the nascent administrative sciences (ibid., 570). This was the institutional landscape within which this discipline carved its own niche and specialty, for it would soon set aside the question of the aims and legitimacy of the state so as to focus exclusively on that of the merely technical and practical knowledge needed to exercise power. And this was indeed the whole point of cameralistics as a general science of administration, or *allgemeine Haushaltungwissenschaft*, as Daniel Gottfried Schreber called it, analogizing in its very name the economic administration of the state to the government of a household (or *Haushaltung*). This showed how persistent the Aristotelian political and legal lexicon was in a discipline that set itself the task of investigating

> what the ills and shortcomings of a state are in relation to its wealth and power and in connection with the tools needed to that end; the discipline is concerned with the state of health or with the illness of the body of the state and its parts, and in this sense it can be defined as a pathology or therapy of the state.
>
> (Schreber 1764, 97–98; my translation)

The first of the official cameralists was Simon Peter Gasser, a professor of law who held the chair in Halle and served as a functionary in the Prussian administration (see Schiera 1968, 349, for a fuller biographical account). He wrote the first textbook on the cameral sciences, titled *Einleitung zu den ökonomischen, politischen und Cameral-Wissenschaften* (Outline of economic, political, and cameral sciences: Gasser 1729), which is mostly focused on the economic and financial aspect, devoting little, if any, attention to *Policey*. Gasser's approach to the subject was based on the premise that students had to learn the basics of the economic and fiscal disciplines, a complex of fiscal administration and the management of commerce and industry. This approach reflected an abiding attitude that tended to view the cameral sciences in light of the need to develop industry and commerce, thus also growing the revenues of the state. That was the underlying attitude of early official cameralism, reflecting the initial phase, costly and difficult, in the construction of the absolute state (Schiera 1968, 349). In this early phase, fiscal policy tended to outweigh *Policey* at large, for it was necessary to first consolidate the apparatus of princely administration and secure a solid financial basis. Only then could the scope of princely intervention be expanded.

The second chair in cameral science established by the Hohenzollerns was held by Justus Christoph Dithmar, who taught history and natural law theory (a fuller bibliography in Schiera 1968, 361) and wrote a book that would go on to achieve great success: *Einleitung in die ökonomischen-, Policey- und Cameral- Wissenschaften* (Outline of economic, police, and cameral sciences: Dithmar 1745). With Dithmar, the discipline reached a higher level of theoretical systematization, for the first time gaining a general part defining its different subject areas. Dithmar proceeded from a definition of economic science *(ökonomische Wissenschaft)*, literally understood as a science of home economics and an art of housekeeping writ large *(Hauswirtschaft- und Haushaltungskunst)*, which he defined as a science that "teaches us how welfare and wealth can be obtained through legitimate economic activities, in town and country alike, for the pursuit of general happiness" (ibid., 14; my translation). He next turned to the complex of sciences concerned in the vast menu of police ordinances, so as to provide an outline of police science *(Polizeiwissenschaft)*, understood as a discipline that "teaches us how to keep the state's internal and external system in good order and sound condition in view of general happiness" (ibid.). This police science provides the principles the highest authority needs to look to in carrying out its task of making sure that

> its subjects, in the greatest possible number, will lead a life in awe of God—Christian, righteous, honorable, and healthy—to which end their commitment must be sought, as must the superfluous—relying on a thriving economic activity, agrarian and urban alike, to provide a supply of this-worldly goods—and it must also be ensured that the country is in sound condition.
>
> (Ibid., 18)

Dithmar's exposition closed with a definition of cameral science *(cameral-Wissenschaft)* as a discipline that

> teaches how the state's revenues can be increased by the good use of demesnes and regalities, in addition to relying on obligatory contributions owed by subjects and on other common lands, and how such revenues must be used to ensure the sound maintenance of the community.
>
> (Ibid., 19)

That an interconnection obtained among these three areas was quite clear to Dithmar, who observed that "they are so closely bound up that the economic system cannot stand without good police, while the cameral system must permanently rely on both as its sources" (ibid.).

It was Dithmar, then, who set in motion the process of systematization and unification of the cameral and economic sciences. He did so in particular by framing in theoretical terms the contents of *Policey* as the object of a *Polizeiwissenschaft* proper, defining the former as the "sound order and constitution of persons and of the affairs of a state" and the latter as a discipline that teaches how to bring such order into being and maintain it "for the purpose of realizing the happiness of every individual and of the community as a whole" (ibid., 153). Economics and cameral science are thus pulled into the sphere of *Policey* as a tool of government having the twofold purpose of increasing commerce and industry while multiplying the capacity of every subject within the state to contribute to the latter's revenues. The theoretical systematization begun by Dithmar would be completed by Georg Heinrich Zincke, first in his *Grundriss einer Einleitung zu deren cameral Wissenschaften* (Introduction to the cameral sciences) of 1742 (Zincke 1742), and then in the more monumental *Cameralisten Bibliothek* (The cameralist's library: Zincke 1751–52). In this latter work Zincke provided a theoretico-systematic foundation of the cameral sciences, setting out some fundamental principles. His clear point of departure was the eudaemonistic principle on which everyone has a specific right and duty to pursue their moral and material happiness, and citizens confer on the state the authority to be helped and guided in this enterprise (ibid., 21). To this end the state needs to have at its disposal the means necessary to intervene in all spheres of life on which such happiness depends. Cameral science is understood by Zincke as

> a theoretical and practical science aimed at identifying, improving, and fostering good police laws and institutions on the basis of the nature and state of a country's economic conditions, as well as at grounding, maintaining, increasing, and administering the satisfaction of a country's needs and its tranquility and wealth, and through that means the public patrimony necessary to the state and the prince, to this end proceeding according to wisdom, intelligence, justice, and skill, with a view to the good of the state and its governance, following special rules and maxims deriving from the complex of rights and duties ascribed to a prince.
>
> (Ibid., 45–46; my translation)

So, even though cameral science was unitary, it was made up of three parts: economics, police science, and cameralism proper. *Policey* was characterized in particular as a science aimed at affording a decent life for a multitude of people, to this end also seeing to the correct allocation of material resources. It was therefore principally conceived as *economic police*—that is, a science for increasing and properly distributing wealth—its primary purpose being to ensure that "everyone can have, acquire, maintain, and properly use comfort, an easy life, and wealth for themselves in proportion to the common good" (ibid., 61). The institutional complex tasked with these functions is subject to the prince's directive authority, and through this apparatus "all the assets of the state and the people are subordinated to the prince for the purpose of pursuing the common good or, more to the point, the security, peace, and tranquillity of all" (ibid., 66).

By a constant reference to natural law theory and the concept of happiness—which in the *Cameralisten Bibliothek* is primarily understood in a material, economic sense—Zincke raised his discourse to the level of a politico-administrative doctrine of the police state, the practical side of Wolff's eudaemonistic philosophy. In this way, this doctrine reached its highest theoretical development, following a path that from the second half of the 18th century onward would see it break up into three independent disciplines: economic science, police science, and the cameral sciences proper, or finance. The process got underway as early as with Joachim Georg Darjes, a jurist and philosopher in whose work cameralism was developed especially as an economic science, setting out its basic principles (Schiera 1968, 425ff.), but only with Johan Heinrich Gottlob von Justi did cameralism come into its own, in a conception where the primary interest is in *Polizeiwissenschaft* (police science).[31]

Even Justi was deeply influenced by the eudaemonistic philosophy of German natural law theory, and so he, too, rested his entire conception on the notion of collective happiness (Maier 1966, 220; Schiera 1968, 440; Bussi 2002, 300). But, as noted, he is at the same time considered the father of modern *Polizeiwissenschaft*, the discipline devoted to providing the tools for the practical realization of the community's material and moral welfare. It is fair to say, then, that Justi offered the best synthesis of natural law theory and political Aristotelianism, the trait that, as suggested, was distinctive to German politico-administrative thought in the early modern age.

Indeed, in *Die Natur und das Wesen der Staaten* (The nature and essence of states), the work in which Justi most closely focused on policy and law, he took up the classic contractarian themes on the formation of the state, or *Staats-Gesellschaft* (von Justi 1760, sec. 23). In accord with the storyline envisioned by natural law theory, Justi locates the birth and foundation of the state in the act by which individuals, exercising their natural freedom, decide to relinquish their self-interested pursuits within civil society (the *bürgerliche Gesellschaft*) so as to merge those interests into a single collective will (ibid.). This general *Gesammtwillen* harnesses the collective forces of the people into a single force set in motion by the supreme power.

31 Justi was born around 1720 in Brücken, Prussia, and studied law in Jena and Wittenberg. He taught Germanic eloquence at the Theresianum Knights Academy in Vienna, and then he also taught *Kameralistik*, a subject introduced in Austria following the example set in the reign of Prussia. A few years later he was in Göttingen, serving as *Polizeikommissar* and teaching *Staatsökonomie und Naturwissenschaft* (political economy and the science of nature), but his career as a bureaucrat and teacher was cut short when he took aim at the realm's monetary policy, advancing some criticisms that even led to his imprisonment in 1762. He subsequently won his way back into the favour of Frederick the Great and was appointed Prussian Inspector of Mines, Glass, and Steel Works. Yet he still died in prison, in 1771, having been convicted of fraud against the state. Justi wrote many works on economics and cameral and police science and is considered the father of *Staatswissenschaften* (sciences of the state), to which he devoted an introduction in his treatise of political economy (von Justi [1755] 1963), proposing a project to reform the curriculum in sciences of the state designed to train future public functionaries. In addition to this work on matters strictly connected with the economy, Justi published many others, prominent among which are his treatises on police principles (von Justi 1756); manufacturing and factories (von Justi 1758–61); and the system of finance (von Justi 1766); his collection of works on politics, the art of war, cameral science, and finance (von Justi [1761–64] 1970); and finally a specifically political treatise on the nature and essence of states (von Justi 1760). On Justi, see Maier 1966, 220ff.; Stolleis 1998a, 574ff.; Schiera 1968, 440ff.; and Bussi 1971, 20ff.

How exactly this public power, or *Gesammtkraft*, may be used and by whom is a matter governed by the political constitution enshrined in the basic laws of the state *(Grundgesetze des Staates)*. In these basic laws lies the very source of the sovereign's power, and so there is no discretion that he can exercise over them (ibid., sec. 46), so much so that the relation they frame between the sovereign and his subjects is contractual, such that even supreme power can be revoked if exercised in violation of these basic laws (ibid., sec. 47), whose ultimate justification lies in the law of nature. If the prince should act contrary to these basic laws, and hence contrary to the welfare of the people, he can be considered a tyrant or even an enemy, as Justi says in his "Kurzer systematischer Grundriss aller oeconomischen und Cameralwissenschaften" (Short systematic blueprint for the economic and cameral sciences), the most important essay in his collection of political and financial writings (von Justi [1761–64] 1970, vol. 1, p. 544).

However, the aims for which the sovereign can put this *Gesammtkraft* to use are construed by Justi as having a quite broad range. Indeed, they do not just cover internal and external security but also extend to *allgemeine Glückseligkeit*, that is, the general welfare or happiness:

> The aim of the state is that of general happiness, and the welfare of the prince *(Regent)* is inextricably bound up with that of his subjects. Both are consequently bound to give of their own to the happiness of the state, an aim with respect to which they both have obligations.
>
> (Ibid., 511; my translation)

According to the definition Justi provides in his "Kurzer," the *allgemeine Glückseligkeit* is a twofold concept requiring, on the one hand, "that everyone in the state have the security needed to enjoy his wealth or income and live free from any prepotency" and, on the other,

> that the country find itself in a situation enabling everyone to live comfortably according to his station and abilities, while also bearing the expenses necessary to govern the state happily, contributing to its revenues but without thereby having to be forced into penury for the sake of its necessary maintenance.
>
> (Ibid., 513)

The general happiness therefore implies a dual duty for the prince: On the one hand is the more specific duty to ensure the security of the state; on the other hand is the broader duty to provide for the wealth and prosperity of the population (Bussi 1971, 69).

These, then, are the politico-legal foundations of Justi's *Polizeiwissenschaft*, which clearly needs to be understood as a tool in the service of the *allgemeine Glückseligkeit*, that is, as a tool of *Wohlfahrths Polizei*, or *welfare police*, whose foundations are set out in his 1756 *Grundsatze der Policey-Wissenschaft* (Principles of police science). In this well-known work he sought to provide a theoretical foundation on which to rest police science, while at the same time distinguishing it from other related disciplines, an enterprise that, as Justi comments, had hitherto been attempted only in France with Delamare's 1705 *Traité de la police*, "which contains a good deal of useful insights, except that they are not brought into any relation with one another and its principles are not grounded in the nature of the thing being treated" (von Justi 1756, unnumbered preface; my translation).

In the same preface Justi claims, with respect to police science, "to be the first to have equipped it with a system grounded in the nature of the thing itself, and to have treated it independently of all the other sciences that pertain to it" (ibid.). The main problem, he goes on to say, "is to accurately distinguish between *Policen* (police) and *Staatskunst* (politics, or statecraft), a distinction that has often appeared to recede from view" (ibid.). As he explains, these subject areas

> in effect each have their own limits and boundaries. Politics is aimed at the internal and external security of the republic, and its main business is to be informed about the conduct, action, and aims of foreign powers, so as to anticipate their undertakings, as well as to establish a good order among subjects and know the feelings they harbour in relation to one another and in relation to the government, so as to stifle any factions or seditions that may arise and take the measures necessary to prevent them. Police, by contrast, is exclusively aimed at ensuring the welfare of the state through the wisdom of its rules and to augment its power as far as possible. To this end it keeps watch over crops, provides inhabitants with the things necessary to secure the necessities of life, and establishes a good order among them; and to the extent that in this last regard it, too, is concerned with the internal security of the state, thus acting as a tool of politics, it only deals with those offences that do not jeopardize the constitution or the maintenance of the state.
>
> (Ibid.)

Once police is distinguished from politics, it needs to also be distinguished from the cameral and financial sciences *(cameral- oder finanz- Wissenschaft)*, even if the latter have their "foundation" in police itself, considering that it is the task of police "to assess the extent to which it is possible to increase taxes without undermining the public interest" (ibid.). More than having a direct role in financial affairs, "police is concerned with increasing and preserving the state's revenues through the wisdom of its rules" (ibid.). And it needs to be further distinguished from both the economic sciences (with which, in Justi's view, it tends to be confused by Zincke) and the moral sciences and from the law of nature (the object of Wolff's investigation).

Thus isolated, police science can be studied as a freestanding discipline, however much it is inextricably bound up with its sister disciplines, and this investigation cannot but proceed from an effort to exactly pin down the meaning of the term *police*. Having pointed out the Greek roots of the term and its connection with the *polis*, or city-state, Justi defines the term as it was commonly understood at the time, distinguishing in particular two current acceptations of it, a broader one and a narrower one:

> In the narrower sense, the term refers to the internal rules which govern territorial institutions, and in virtue of which the overall resources of the state can be consolidated and incremented, its strengths can be put to the best use, and, most importantly, the happiness of the community can be promoted, and in this sense police covers areas including commerce, science, the economy of the cities and the state, and the management of mines and forestlands. To the extent that the government decides to entrust police with the general welfare of the state, [. . .] the term in the second, broader sense will encompass everything that can contribute to the welfare of the citizens, and especially to the maintenance of order and discipline, by establishing rules that tend to make their lives comfortable and to afford them the things they need to earn a livelihood.
>
> (Ibid., 4)

Having defined the *concept* of police, Justi proceeds to more accurately set out its basic principles and functions. He does so by working from his general definitions to extract derivational postulates, and on this basis he divides the work into three books meant to encompass "the entire theory of this science" (ibid., 14). The aim of realizing the "welfare of society" proper to each state cannot be achieved unless public resources are administered wisely under the guidance of the very cameral and economic sciences *(die ökonomischen- und Cameralwissenschaften)* whose task it is to set out the principles by which to design and carry out sound police. Indeed, whereas politics *(Staatskunst)* is in the first place concerned with "asserting and increasing the power of the state," police is aimed at "increasing and preserving public wealth" (ibid., 5), an aim entailing powers of broad scope. As a science, it is therefore devoted to the purpose of "regulating all things that relate to the present state of society *(des Staats)*, preserving that state, improving it, and making sure that everything works together in bringing about the welfare of the members of society" (ibid., 6–7). Police therefore entails a universal power to interfere in the economic and social life of the nation so as to "preserve and increase [. . .] the state's internal power," and such power and prosperity "is inherent not just in the general republic and in each of its members but also in the skills and talents of all those who belong to it" (ibid.).

This power of interference functions as a general principle from which three spheres of police competence can be extracted by deduction. So, to begin with, "considering that the power of the state lies in the real estate belonging to the republic and to its members [. . .], it follows that the state's territory must be carefully tended to" (ibid., 7). The strength of the state further depends "on work and on the number of inhabitants in the country" (ibid., 8); indeed, since only through work is it possible to "make part of the territory suitable to serve as a homestead for its inhabitants and to provide them with what they need to make a living and build cities affording a safe and comfortable shelter," it is necessary for police not only to see to the administration of public space but also to "increase the number of inhabitants" (ibid., 8–9). But this is only the first of the spheres in which police is called on to intervene, for

> the power of the state also lies in the goods belonging to the individuals who make it up, and since they are the fruit of human labour and industry, which depends on real estate, it can clearly be appreciated that one of the ways to increase the wealth of the state is to multiply their number.
>
> (Ibid.)

On the fruits of the earth and on industry rest "the inhabitants' livelihood and comfort, and hence the welfare of society" (ibid., 9), for which reason it is essential to favour both production and the exchange of wealth. There is, finally, the third sphere of civil life in which police is asked to intervene: that of disciplining individual behaviour. As Justi goes on to explain,

> among the things that contribute to the power of a state are industry and the talents of the state's different members. It therefore follows that if such power is to be maintained, increased, and put in the service of the public welfare, the subjects must be obligated to acquire the skills and knowledge necessary for the different jobs they may be put to, and among them the order and discipline must be maintained that will make for the general good of society.
>
> (Ibid., 10–11)

As a systematic study of legislative techniques for the exercise of the *ius promovendi salutem pubblicam* attributed to the prince, *Polizeiwissenschaft* thus implies the development of a broad activity by which to steer the country's social and economic life so as to "establish the closest consonance between the welfare of families, which together make up the state, and the common good" (von Justi 1760, 466; my translation). It is no accident that Justi's work offers the first systematic attempt to set out the nature of police legislation, an attempt that foreshadows some of the key conceptual distinctions of modern legal science. In this regard he proceeds from the basic distinction between political laws and civil laws, the former pertaining to the institutional structure of the state, or what we would now call constitutional law, the latter instead regulating relations among individuals, a sphere in which he also includes "the criminal laws, in that these tend to guarantee the security of all subjects and protect their freedom from wrongdoers" (ibid., 322). The body of police law *(Polizeiverordnungen)* is in turn understood by Justi as having three specific senses. In one sense, it is the set of laws aimed at "increasing the state's internal power and common patrimony, so as to make that power and patrimony efficient and coherent with the good of all," and so this would fall into the category of the realm's *economic police*. In another sense, police law comprises the set of provisions "aimed at maintaining the order and discipline needed to sustain civil life, enable living conditions to flourish, and make the welfare of individual families consistent with that of all" (ibid., 468), and so its function in this sense is that of the realm's *discipline* or *social police*. And, in the third sense, police law comprises the "set of city ordinances concerned with sanitation, decorum, and order, as well as with weights and measures and with the need to keep residents safe" (ibid.), and so these rules fall into the specific category of *Stadtpolicey*, or *police of public spaces*.

Out of this attempt to define police rule there emerged, however still inchoately, the idea of a form of political rationality neatly distinguished from ancient *iurisdictio*. Indeed, whereas law and justice in the era of the *ius commune* acted as a negative command protecting entrenched privileges and prerogatives, *Policey* established itself as a form of politico-administrative rationality, and so as a power of social direction and production set against the strictly conservative and protective function of legal rationality. Justi's attempt at definition thus bears on the fundamental question of the distinction between the two spheres of public power ushered in by administrative development, and so on the question of how to define the scope of *Policey* that princely power wanted to wrench from the administration of justice. As discussed, throughout the process that drove the development of administrative monarchy, the effort to distinguish police subject matter—and in particular the nature of police rule as distinct from civil law— answered a need that went well beyond a scientific interest in achieving theoretical clarity, for it was concerned to reshape the constitutional configuration of the state's powers. This explains the copious literature that came out in the German area addressing the distinction between *politia* and *iurisdictio* (see, for example, Rechemberg 1739; Schreiber 1739; Daries 1763; Hommel 1770; von Hohenthal 1774), and a recurrent theme in this literature is the basic distinction that, as mentioned, had been anticipated in France: the distinction between subject matter that—pertaining to relations among private persons, thus entailing the need to afford protection from injuries in the private sphere—falls within the province of *iurisdictio* (be it civil or criminal), and subject matter that, pertaining to the pursuit of the nation's happiness construed as the moral and material welfare of the population, falls within the province of *Policey* as an activity intended to stimulate economic life, ensure discipline, and enable social reform.

This distinction between the complex of activities pertaining to the administration of justice and the complex pertaining to princely administration under the *Generaldirektorium* had yet to lead to any definitive specification of law that would set the powers of princely administration apart from those of the ordinary courts, and this situation of uncertainty triggered a series of institutional conflicts and theoretical controversies over the *ius politiae* very much like those that had been taking place in France almost at the same time. In the German area, however, the preparatory theoretical solution to the dialectic between *iurisdictio* and *politia* would soon lead to a viable institutional solution that in several respects anticipated the French institutional experience of the 19th century. Indeed, if there is any inaugural moment of modern administrative power, it would have to be when Frederick the Great of Prussia entrusted his program of enlightened reformism to Samuel von Cocceji, who in designing that program introduced a stable criterion by which to distinguish between ordinary justice and police, thereby also opening the institutional space for the full theoretical development of *Polizeiwissenschaft*.

Chapter 4

Police powers and social disciplining

As we have seen, the development of the state's administrative machinery in the transition from the Middle Ages to the modern age made it possible to steer and regulate economic life with greater control and accuracy. The effect on civil authority was twofold, at once qualitative and quantitative, for just as the state's sphere of intervention increased exponentially, an equally transformative process affected the nature of the functions attributed to it. And that is precisely the transformation I have attempted to trace out following modern governmental reason in its constant conflict with legal reason, the conflict between *politia* and *iurisdictio*. We have tried to account for this dialectic following the institutional and cultural developments that unfolded between the 16th and 18th centuries in relation to the concept of police. What we need to do now is specify the nature of this police apparatus brought into being by modern governmental reason. We will begin by singling out the areas of police intervention and will then specify what appears to have been the inherent nature of the police apparatus in the modern age.

We have looked at the process that slowly but definitively shifted the centre of political reflection in such a way as to overturn the paradigm of the ancient treatises on sovereign prudence and the governmental arts. The end of govern-mental activity was no longer to ensure a prudent application of time-honoured orders but to maintain and increase the state's power or, as Giovanni Botero called it, the state's *possanza* (puissance). A new complex entity found its way to the centre of political reflection, an entity made of constituent elements, driven by independent aims, and equipped with an economic, social, and military structure. Police thus emerged as a new and further level of governmental action next to the classic areas of justice, finance, and war: It emerged as a complex formed by different kinds of knowledge and institutional means suited to growing the wealth and resources of the state.

In a sense it was an enlightened political aim that the police apparatus set for itself. Indeed, promoting the prosperity of the state entailed the ability to intervene in, direct, and regulate any human activity that might help toward that objective, even if only indirectly. The state was thus expected to attend to every matter that could advance the overall political objective that Justus Lipsius had summed up in four key concepts: *salus, commoditas, scuritas,* and *disciplina.* This was a principle of interference that went well beyond the simple need to ensure the subjects' physical survival, taking on responsibility for an entire population's moral and material life. "So what police thus embraces" in the modern age, Foucault (2004, 421) suggests, "is basically an immense domain that we could say goes from living to more than just living." Its interest in the life of the population is aimed not simply at securing conditions of security but also at ensuring a *happy* existence. Police is concerned not only with the population's mere existence—or "being"—but also with its material and moral *well*being. As Delamare put it, police was concerned with the soul, body, and fortunes of the population, something that Johann Heinrich Gottlob von Justi described as the closer consonance between the welfare of the single families and the common good. Indeed, central to the discussion that was developing around the question of police were concepts such as commonwealth, *Wohl,* and *bienêtre*—all typical expressions of the eudaemonistic philosophy that inspired the nascent sciences of the state.

The political objective of welfare thus justified the authorities in intervening broadly in the civil life of the nation. To appreciate how broad the range of police intervention could be, we need only take a quick overview of the subject matters that came under the regulation of various police statutes, *ordonnances,* and *Ordnungen* and the powers attributed to intendants, lieutenants, justices, and commissaires. These areas of intervention were indeed extraordinarily disparate, spanning across all areas of a nation's social and economic life. As Delamare commented, police could be "encompassed in its entirety [. . .] within eleven subject areas: religion, the discipline imposed by custom, health, foodstuffs, public security and peace, the liberal arts and sciences, commerce, manufacturing and the mechanical arts, domestic workers, manual labourers, and the poor" (Delamare 1705, 4; my translation).

In France, for example, the intendant was responsible for broadly intervening in all affairs pertaining to the public interest and welfare, that is, in anything having to do with the *police du bon ordre,* encompassing the security of people and property, public health, and poor relief. The responsibilities ascribed to the intendant additionally included a sort of administrative oversight over municipal bodies, as well as functions pertaining to the regulation of economic activity. The intendant was made into an essential informational and executory tool for the economic dirigisme carried out by the comptroller general of finances, to this end overseeing arts and crafts guilds and manufacturers' guilds, intervening in labour disputes, ensuring that the city was well supplied, and carrying out grain policy. Also ascribed to the intendant were broad powers to set rural and farm policy, with the task of favouring the development of the agricultural economy, as well as a general power to police ground and river transportation and to make urban-planning decisions (Sueur 2001b, 357; Marion 1969, 293ff.). Similar powers were ascribed to urban police lieutenants in Paris, as can be gathered from a list contained in an edict of 1667 that mentioned the following areas of competence: state prisons and the Bastille, bookstores, theatrical performances, postal oversight, hospitals, provisioning, the execution of royal orders, and oversight over arts and crafts guilds, as well as manufacturing establishments, commerce, lotteries, Jews, room renters, public security, hygiene, and the cleanliness and upkeep of places. As can be appreciated, these competences ran the whole gamut of subject areas, and they came with regulatory, inspectorial, and sanctionative powers to be exercised by summary procedure (Delamare 1705, 131; Marion 1969, 412).

To a greater or lesser degree of accuracy, the picture just outlined can also be said to describe magistracies in England and in the German area. In England, statutes and proclamations were used to broadly regulate a vast inventory of matters, a process that, as discussed, prompted a parallel evolution involving justices of the peace and their operating modules, for in fulfilling the functions they were insistently being entrusted with by royal provision, the office of the justice took on the traits of the institutions and procedures typically associated with Continental administrative monarchy.[1] In the German area, the broad *Landraten* and *Steuerarten* powers were aptly summed up in the *Instruktion* that regulated the *Generaldirektorium*, the central organ entrusted with overseeing the activity of the commissarial magistracies. The provision was enacted in 1722 and became a manifesto of economic and social policy in 18th-century Prussia, conveying a good idea of the scope of intervention reserved exclusively for the autocratic organs of government (text reprinted in von Schmoller 1894–1935, vol. 3, n. 280, pp. 575–651). The functions of the General Directorate included military administration (Arts. 4, 5, and 6) and the realm's general defence of internal and external security (Art. 7); the levying of taxes and excises (Arts. 8 and 9); oversight over domestic and foreign trade in agricultural and manufactural goods (Art. 10); general authority over productive, agricultural, and manufactural activities, whose development it was charged with promoting (Arts. 11 and 12); and general authority over the administration of fallow lands and over the construction and administration of new cities (Art. 15). Also, the same *Instruktion* empowered provincial organs to set grain prices; establish taxes on necessities, bread, and meat; and manage civil security, and fire prevention in particular, by inspecting the upkeep of public places (Art. 16). And, finally, the sovereign would have direct authority over some industries, such as salt-works and breweries, as well as over the management of publicly owned material and natural resources, forestlands, and mines (Arts. 18–27).

It is an apparently disorderly and incoherent picture that emerges from this summary list of subject matters reserved for the different magistracies. Police deals

---

1 The justices of the peace were entrusted with broad administrative powers to regulate industrial and commercial activity and manufacturing, setting the price of grain and other foodstuffs, and generally exercising oversight over productive activities, the marketplaces and commercial activities, weights and measures, and the holders of commercial monopolies and privileges. They also had the power to supervise poor relief, the construction of new buildings and urban planning, sumptuary legislation, apparel, and the leisurely pursuits and customs of everyday life (Holdsworth 1924, vol. 4, 297ff.; Lambarde 1581, 190–226).

with disparate matters ranging from foreign trade to sumptuary laws. But if we read between the lines, we will see that three broad areas can be made out, the same ones which we saw crystallizing in the late medieval cities, and which are now being taken up by sovereign policy and applied nationally across the entire territory of the nascent state. These broad police areas are those that cover the territory, the economy, and the population. Let us take them up in turn.

4.1. Territory

Police in the first place took on the general function of regulating living spaces. As discussed, it was precisely by extending the *ius politiae* that the sovereign managed to stake out a sovereign space at once territorial and legal, thus encroaching *horizontally*, as it were, on the local, feudal powers of tradition. But the encroachment of police disciplines also cut *vertically* into the purview and territories of the ancient legal order, eating into the jurisdictions that claimed exclusive competence in different areas and spaces of civil life. By a complex set of regulatory enactments pertaining to the care and maintenance of the territory, the police apparatus involved the authorities in an enterprise aimed at constituting public spaces by working within the sphere of political sovereignty more or less controversially recognized for each authority (Rigaudière 1996, 136–37). With the invention of public space came the ambition to exercise a dominion over territory that is not just politico-legal but also straightforwardly geographic. This dominion consists in the capacity to intervene in and manipulate space not just by drawing boundaries that may have to be defended and fortified (the physical marker of political sovereignty) but also by approaching the entire territory as a natural environment in which the population's biological and social existence unfolds. Police addressed the territory as a space of circulation that formed the basis for the security and swiftness of communications and commerce; for the reproduction of life as a form of existence reliant on trade; for the territory as a reservoir of material resources, rivers, forests, and mines needed for production in economic life; and finally for the territory as a more or less wholesome vital space to be reclaimed, sanitized, secured, and made fit to sustain the life of all populations.

This topic of the *police of the territory* took up much attention in all classics of police science. Justi, for example, addressed this topic in his 1756 *Grundsätze der Policey-Wissenschaft*, devoting to it the first section of the first book, where it is referred to as the "external care of the territory." Delamare and La Maire devoted an equally extensive investigation to this topic, however much less systematically, scattering its treatment across the different headings that came under the rubric of ground mobility police (La Maire 1878, 15–16; Delamare 1738) and security police (La Maire 1878, 16–17, 49–53). The classics of police science are all in agreement in stressing that the territory and its material resources need to be managed "in such a way as to make for a suitable environment in which the inhabitants may find their abode and the basic necessities of life" (von Justi 1756, 19; my translation). The territory is construed as one of the primary areas of sovereign action, and this capacity for intervention requires the deepest knowledge of "the nature and qualities" (ibid., 23) of the nation. To exercise dominion over one's territory is thus to know the territory in its every facet, but this knowledge should not be keyed exclusively to the task of securing political domination by an appropriate allocation of military and strategic resources. Already we can see this knowledge turning into an economic geography proper, where the effort is to paint a full and detailed picture of a nation's economic and social potential.

> To this end the sovereign must have his lands surveyed and mapped, not only indicating the names of the cities, towns, and hamlets but also providing annotations that mark out the areas suited to planting forests and vineyards and can sustain work [. . .], grazing, and the like.
>
> (Ibid., 25)

But in the overall economy of this sort of political technology for organizing and managing the territory, it was urban space that would always take pride of place. Indeed, as a sort of originary vital space, the city offered itself as the primary locus in which to exercise a power designed to manage the population and its different aspects relating to biological and social life. That is because for the first time, in the densely populated space that makes up the city, humans appear in a new light: No longer are they merely seen as legal persons subject to sovereign power, and hence as subjects whose essential trait lies in their obligation to obey the supreme *voluntas*, but as living beings bound by complex relations to one another and to the environment. And so "with this technical problem posed by the town [. . .] we see the sudden emergence of the problem of the 'naturalness' of the human species within an artificial milieu" (Foucault 2004, 37). Simply by living, humans come into contact with others like them and with the environment, consisting of the natural space formed by the complex of social, economic, and biological relations that characterize the life of a population. In this sense humans are not inert in relation to the dynamics of vital processes, and in fact they condition such processes by channelling their development and shaping their potential for expansion.

The problem, then, becomes that of the equilibriums and rules that need to be respected in organizing an artificial environment best suited to fostering the development of the population's vital and social process. Writes Justi in this regard:

> A city is formed by the set of families and individuals who gather in a common space under police surveillance, so as to live in society and more easily practice the trades and professions they have embraced. A city so understood is a moral body that, in the manner of the arteries of a human body, facilitates the circulation of the species and maintains a union among the different members the state is made up of.
>
> (von Justi 1756, 30; my translation)

The city thus guarantees circulation and exchange. It is the place where life is reproduced and regenerates, conveying its beneficial effects throughout the nation: "The bigger the cities are and the more they thrive, the more the countryside does well and flourishes" (ibid., 31). But it is not size in absolute terms that accounts for the cities' ability to thrive and spread wealth to the whole nation:

> There are rules to be observed in this regard which cannot possibly be disregarded. When cities grow too big, they harm agriculture and cause it to be neglected; and when a multitude of cities bear no relation at all to the products the country provides, they wind up being cities in name only, failing to achieve the aims for which they are established.
>
> (Ibid.)

There is, then, a balance to be observed between the size of a city, its population, and the health of the nation's economic prosperity. The right proportion needs to be maintained among all the parts that make up the body of the state, and this applies in particular to the city as the storehouse of all the nation's social forces:

> The size of a city and the number of its inhabitants need to be gauged to the nature and quality of the country's internal product and to the foreign commerce the city can engage in [. . .] and this is something the government can never devote too much attention to when the question comes up of establishing a new city.
>
> (Ibid., 32)

The relations that hold between the material, artificially produced space (the containant) and the natural dynamics of the population's biological and social life (the contents) thus become the main object of this *police of the territory*, or *Stadtpolizey*, as Justi occasionally elects to call it. The establishment and government of a city require that attention be paid to the physical place in which the city is to rise,[2] and in this regard account needs to be taken of the city's own vocation or calling, considering whether it is best suited to devote itself to commerce or to manufacture, or to act as the seat of government or be home to a university, or again to serve as a military garrison. But more generally, the authorities need to see to it that the very structure of the city is organized and "laid out in such a way as to ensure that goods can circulate with the necessary ease, that air can flow freely through it, and that no noxious vapours are given off" (ibid., 45). What all these desiderata imply is a diverse combination of disciplines offering the knowledge needed to organize a public space capable of making daily activities easier and more

---

2 A city is to be established "in a space where air and water are safe, far from marshlands, and close to the sea and to rivers, where the environs are fertile" (von Justi 1756, 34).

comfortable,[3] but there also needs to be a specific area of expertise that grows out of police science but ultimately develops into an independent discipline, and that is urban planning (Cavalletti 2005, 20ff.). The urban space thus becomes the locus around which revolves a form of rationality that nonetheless retains its connection to the political need in response to which it originally emerged and continues to have its reason for being. This is the need to govern the complex of social, economic, and biological processes that unfold within the city, and to do so ensuring an appropriate level of security. Hence the need for a rationality on which basis to design an artificial vital space capable of fostering various economic activities, all the while minimizing the risks incident to urbanism, notably epidemics, crime, and civil unrest (Foucault 1982).

However, this discipline developed to deal with public spaces and the territory winds up organizing not only the environment but also the population's living time, in effect *manipulating* that time by breaking it down into working time, "exchange time," and leisure time. This manipulation combines with the discipline that regulates the essential activities of social and economic life. It combines with a process through which the population's material life is properly speaking organized. This whole organizational endeavour is based in the first place on *economic police*—that is, on the complex set of regulations that deal with agricultural and manufactural production, on the one hand, and the circulation of goods and money, on the other. But even more importantly—in relation to the more general disciplinatory effects of regulating production and work, including working hours, the workplace, and the manner of working—this whole process rests on the third key area of police activity, the area concerned with disciplining bodies and souls, namely, the *police of the population*.

4.2. Economy

The complex of disciplines pertaining to the regulation of economic life perfectly encapsulates the essential traits of what is commonly referred to as mercantilism. It is in the definitive crisis of the feudal economy and the rise of powerful and competitive nation-states that we are to locate this body of thought devoted to economic questions. Mercantilism cannot, however, be regarded as a fully fledged economic theory.[4] It was rather the complex of political-economic measures favoured by the main European states in the transition toward the modern age.

---

3 The same goes for the transportation network, whose "discipline is most essential in favouring commerce" (von Justi 1756, 46), as well as for the management of fountains and aqueducts (ibid., 49), the cleaning and proper illumination of public spaces" (ibid., 50–51), the discipline concerned with the use of public spaces and the distribution of different productive and commercial activities according to their characteristics (ibid., 52), and the establishment of criteria for the construction of buildings (ibid., 55ff.).

4 The expression *mercantile system* was, after all, introduced by Adam Smith to refer to the protectionist economic policies of the European states in the 17th and 18th centuries.

Strictly speaking, none of the writers of the time who dealt with economic questions developed techniques and methods that might make a science proper out of their economic thinking. None of them can be considered economic scientists proper, in that none attempted to validate their claims empirically. The vast majority of them were councillors, administrators, and essayists who addressed practical problems of political economy, and these problems were those of the nascent nation-state (Schumpeter 1954, 155ff; De Maddalena 1980, 639, 638; Braudel 1979b, 483). Mercantilism was not so much a body of economic theories as it was a system of political power based on the premise that the wealth of a nation depended on the growth of its domestic economy as measured by its ability to maintain a trade surplus. In this respect, the mercantilist authors can all be considered disciples of Machiavelli (De Maddalena 1980, 640), in that they all adapted to the economic sphere the objectives that reason of state pursued in the political sphere. Indeed, central to their thinking in every case was the practical objective of consolidating the power and wealth of the state.

So mercantilism is best described not as an economic theory but as a philosophy of statesmanship, a philosophy whose central tenets can be seen at work in the economic policies enacted in England under the Tudors, in France under the financial guidance of Jean-Baptiste Colbert, and in Prussia under Frederick the Great (see, generally, Cole 1938; Cunningham 1920–22; Dorwart 1953). Mercantilist thinking thus presents itself as a loosely bound set of remarks, observations, recommendations, and proposals that cannot be distilled into any single or unitary theoretical account. Although it is certainly possible to tease out recurrent motifs, what gets them to "hang together" is not any theoretical consonance but a shared set of approaches and solutions to the practical problems that come up in governing economic life. The classics in this current of thought include works such as Antoine de Montchrestien's 1615 *Traité d'économie politique*, Thomas Mun's 1664 *England's Treasure by Forraign Trade*, and Josiah Child's 1690 *A New Discourse of Trade*, but for a proper statement of the mercantilist philosophy we have to look to the treatises of police science, since in these works the question of government is addressed head on. Nowhere did this philosophy of government reach greater heights than in the works of Justi, for as much as these works in a sense come onto the scene as the last great achievement of an already dying political culture, they also offer the most effective encapsulation that the *economic police* of the ancien régime ever received.[5] And for a systematic account of the essential features of ancien-régime economic science, we can do no better than to follow the outline that Justi gives us in the second book of his 1756 *Grundsätze der Policey-Wissenschaft*.

Of course, in the context of an economy that for the most part was still rural, as is the case with the European economy under the ancien régime, police agencies

5 On the economic thought of the so-called cameralists beyond Schumpeter's work (1954), see Small 1909.

could not neglect agricultural activity: "The rural economy," Justi remarked, "deserves the full attention that police can devote to it, for it produces not only raw materials but also the grain that people need to live" (von Justi 1756, 82; my translation). Europe's agricultural landscape was perhaps the one that persisted the longest without change in resisting the economic transformation brought on by the modern age. Thus, even with the rise of the capitalistic logic, it proved a challenge to counteract such distinctive traits of the rural economy as its lordly structure, the ancient peasant freedoms, local autarky, and an economic management conceived more in a spirit of subsistence and self-sufficiency than in one of productive reinvestment. In the division of labour that took shape between western and eastern Europe at the dawn of the modern age, the territories east of the Elbe actually slid back into a process of refeudalization that tied the peasants even more firmly to their lands. Changes were nonetheless in the offing, and in some cases, as with the enclosures in England, they forced their way in with disruptive force, upsetting the ancient social arrangements and highlighting the need to call on political authorities to govern the consequences of the incipient economic revolution (see in particular Braudel 1979b, 217ff.).

In either case, sovereign policy found itself facing the peasant reaction to a significant deterioration in living conditions, whether this regression was owed to the so-called second serfdom of eastern Europe or to the birth of capitalist agriculture in western Europe. This reaction would occasionally burst into open rebellion, but day to day it could be observed in the phenomenon of collective peasant desertion and vagrancy. It was in response to these pressing problems that the agricultural policy of the ancien régime was conceived, with a view to curbing as much as possible the flight away from the countryside (to which end a number of devices were used that included lowering the property taxes levied on landholdings): "As far as possible peasants need to be deterred from devoting themselves to livelihoods other than farming, barring them from any trade other than that of selling their produce" (von Justi 1756, 85).

At the same time, farming provided the raw materials needed for the main manufacturing activities, especially in the textile sector, which formed the core of production in the preindustrial era.[6] An ironclad correlation was therefore established between a growing manufacturing sector and a prosperous rural economy. Police was concerned in particular with the conditions to which the productive process was subject and with the quality of production itself, regulating every aspect of manufacturing activity down to its smallest detail.

Such police legislation was modelled on the regulations developed in the cities of the Late Middle Ages. The municipal regime for controlling production was

---

6 "The second source of wealth for the state is manufacturing: It is the factories that work the raw materials which come from the rural economy and which enable it to be productive" (von Justi 1756, 100).

indeed taken up and extended in later centuries by the nascent state institutions, which established a bipartition of productive activities. On the one hand were the so-called "free" trades, which did not require an apprenticeship, and these came under the control of local police authorities (typically municipal ones), which set the regulations and oversaw their application; on the other hand were the trades organized into guilds and corporations, which tended to prevail over the free trades, and which required an apprenticeship with a final examination administered by tradesmen and police authorities, and subject as well to the payment of entry fees, often very steep ones. The rules of the trade were set in the guild charters, normally approved by sovereign courts or by police authorities.[7]

Not everything fell within the corporative system. It was not just the free trades that escaped its regulation and that of police authorities, but also the countless niche crafts and the cottage industry based in the countryside, and even more so the trades practised under grants of individual privilege (Olivier-Martin 1951, 622ff.), as opposed to grants that confer privileges on everyone in a given trade. *Economic police* in the ancien régime made wide use of such monopoly patents, as they were known in England (Holdsworth 1924, vol. 4, p. 343), for the purpose of promoting new industries. Privileges could thus be granted to private citizens, and these would often be foreigners attracted from abroad by advantages guaranteed by statute, or they could be individuals entrusted with setting up a complex of productive activities under the direct supervision of public authorities. This, as is known, was the industrial policy pursued by Colbert's *manufactures royales*, subject to the *inspecteurs des manufactures*, who reported directly to the comptroller general of finances.

---

7 In France, this whole trend can be observed in the practice of reviving the old *livre des métiers*, or book of trades. These books collected the rules in force in a group of cities or across a certain territory, and the enforcement of these rules was a task now shared between the corporations and the local police authorities. Later on the inspectors responsible for these activities would be appointed by the general council of trades, with the approval of police authorities, who in any event retained a power of general oversight over corporations (Olivier-Martin 1951, 620). In the late 16th century, the sovereign authorities in France actively promoted the creation of guilds by issuing two edicts that even taxed the monopolies granted to the trades, and Colbert finally tried to further expand the system of so-called *métiers jurés* as a way of bringing in more revenues. Similarly, in England an attempt was made to guarantee the quality of products and the competence of producers by giving countrywide scope to ancient charters governing the arts and trades when they came up for renewal. So throughout the first half of the 16th century, statutory rules were enacted regulating apprenticeships in various trades and the practice of the trades themselves. But it was only in 1562–63, with the Statute of Apprenticeship, that a general regulatory framework extending across the entire realm was established, and it was modelled after the statutes in force in London. Even here the application of these rules was entrusted to municipal authorities and to the ancient guilds, which received new charters under public law (Holdsworth 1924, vol. 4, pp. 341ff.). In the German area, finally, the regulation of production rested in large measure on the existing corporative system, explicitly so under the imperial ordinances of 1530, 1548, and 1660, which provided the general framework on which basis the local authorities would regulate apprenticeships and the powers of guilds in detail (Raeff 1983, 103).

Police thus took over all aspects of manufacturing, and in particular it was entrusted with making certain that the complex of productive activities could ensure "not only enough manufactured products to satisfy the needs of all inhabitants, but also a surplus of such products, so as to maintain a positive trade balance with foreign countries" (von Justi 1756, 110; my translation). Political authority thus took it upon itself to protect the nascent manufacturing industry, in some cases even intervening as an economic player. This protectionist policy, however, was not aimed at stimulating the manufacturing activity as a source of economic growth in its own right, for in preindustrial capitalism it was commercial activity that continued to act as the main driver of economic growth—a fact reflected in all the classics of mercantilism, which treated manufacturing in view of its ability to affect commerce and the balance of trade (Braudel 1979b, 486). "The success of such manufacturing establishments," Justi, for example, wrote, "depends above all on the circulation of goods both within the country and without" (von Justi 1756, 111).

Economic activity and police regulation in the ancien régime thus continued to revolve around commercial activity, which lay at the core of mercantilism, and which in Book Two of Justi's 1756 *Grundsätze* forms the subject of an entire chapter, the tenth, titled "Bon denen Commercien und Gewerben" (On commerce and trade). Indeed, the discussion opens with a statement clearly spelling out the mercantilist approach to ancien-régime *economic police*:

> Since the wealth of the state is measured by the quantity of staples it stockpiles and the quantity of goods it manufactures, one can easily appreciate that commerce is its mainstay, and that as such it deserves the government's specific attention.
>
> (Ibid., 130; my translation)

In very large part, this chapter covered the ground that Justi had already covered in his 1755 *Staatswirtschaft* (Small 1909, 376). Indeed, it treated police tasks in relation to commercial activities by distinguishing between domestic commerce—referred to as *Gewerb* (the trade and exchange involved in business transactions)—and foreign commerce. Even though the former contributes less directly to the wealth of the nation, "considering that produce and manufactured products do not go outside the national boundaries, for they only change hands, amounting to no more than a simple trade or exchange," it still "forms the basis of the kind done with foreign countries" (von Justi 1756, 130; my translation). And it also contributes essentially to the crucial function of providing the means necessary to satisfy the population's basic needs: "The government must therefore seek to amass the greatest quantity of goods, facilitating their circulation within the realm" (ibid., 131). This was the end to which fiscal and protectionist policies all across Europe were put to, for which reason they were designed to ensure a *fair price* for goods and a *good market* for basic necessities and to prevent food shortages by using all means by which to forcibly keep the market well supplied.

Among the principal areas of *economic police* in the ancien régime, exemplifying its distinctive traits, was indeed the policy on farm products, and grain in particular. Grain was, after all, the mainstay of the popular diet, and it also served as the basis on which to calculate what economists today would call the cost of labour. Historically, the policies for regulating markets had always included rules designed to avoid scarcity and favour abundance. These rules were set forth in statutes and in the police regulations issued by city authorities. This ancient practical knowledge that formed the basis of the cities' political economy was borrowed by the sovereigns, who did nothing but reiterate even more solemnly the essential duty to replenish the market and censure the practice of stocking up on crops for the purpose of speculating. The main priority of sovereign policy was to favour the production of basic necessities, while prohibiting the rural economy from diverting its efforts toward other activities that might yield greater profits. As a rule, sovereign authorities therefore prohibited the exportation of goods, permitting it only when the market was abundantly supplied, and the internal circulation of goods likewise came under direct sovereign control. At the same time, farmers were obligated to sell all their produce on the market and not accumulate crops, and any excess product had to be traded. Of course, commerce was practised under the direct control of police authorities, which favoured the practice of bargaining at standard prices based on price lists. With the average price of grain thus set, it was possible also to control the price of baking goods and productive activity in general, preventing the cost of labour from rising out of proportion (Olivier-Martin 1948, 172ff.).

According to the mercantilist philosophy of government, what really contributed to a nation's prosperity, enabling it to accumulate wealth by selling all "excess inventory" abroad, was trade with foreign countries. For a snapshot of the core tenets of this classic mercantilist doctrine we can turn to Justi:

> The more a country produces those things which are necessary to life, the happier it will be; the fewer the commodities it imports from abroad, the richer it will be, the more so the more it provides its neighbours with excess commodities; the basis of commerce thus lies in a nation's ability to export more commodities than it imports, thus keeping the balance of trade in its own favour.
>
> (von Justi 1756, 136; my translation)

The commercial activity that on this conception forms the basis for wealth of the state must in principle be free, but "this freedom must have some limits," for "it is necessary that the markets engage in commerce in such a way as to serve the public good" (ibid., 137). Encapsulated in these remarks are some core tenets of the commercial policy that to a greater or lesser extent held sway in the major European countries, even though, as is known, the paragon of excellence in this regard was the commercial policy that informed the Navigation Acts enacted between the 16th and 17th centuries. Even if these protectionist policies were being praised by contemporaries for their positive effects—and we can see this, for example, in Child's 1690 (1693) *New Discourse of Trade*—the whole mercantilist conception was beginning to draw criticism from those who observed its negative impact on local manufacturing, which by this time had developed to such an extent as to require some deregulation of commerce. As Child pointed out in response to such objections, the point of the Navigation Acts was not to increase the nation's wealth per se but to increase as well its power and its ability to control the seas through a mighty merchant fleet:

> My answer is, That I cannot deny but this may be true, if the present profit of the generality be barely and slightly considered; but this Kingdom being an Island, the defence whereof hath always been our shipping and seamen, it seems to me absolutely necessary that profit and power ought jointly to be considered.
>
> (Child 1693, 114–15)

The *economic police* of the ancien régime thus highlights the nexus that mercantilist philosophy established between the economy and the state's power, including its military power. A nation's economic prosperity and commercial power thus bear directly on its external security. If any of the main economic players on the European and world stage should grow richer, the other players necessarily had to lose out, becoming poorer and weaker. The economy as seen through a mercantilist lens was a zero-sum game—in effect an extension of the political and military clash, now carried out through the economic means of customs barriers and protectionist policies (Foucault 2008, 52–53; Braudel 1979a, 33). But more generally a connection was thought to exist among the economy, order, and a state's internal security. This connection became immediately apparent in the policy regulating farm products,[8] but it played an equally important role in *social police* and *labour police*, both meant to ensure that the popular classes were well disciplined.

4.3. Population

Mercantilist economic thought allotted a particularly important role to the problem of the population, considering its number, its attitude to work, and in general its moral and material wellbeing (Perrot 1992, 143ff.; Schumpeter 1954, 215ff.; De Maddalena 1980, 665ff.). For an entire 200-year period spanning from the 16th to 18th centuries, the problem of population was in large part a problem of underpopulation. To be sure, it was an age marked by what Fernand Braudel

---

8 Wrote Justi: "It very frequently happens that when it comes to the indispensable means of subsistence, the population lapses into discontent and turns edgy if left in the lurch to face the plunder of private interest" (von Justi [1761–64] 1970, vol. 1, pp. 522–23; my translation).

(1979c, 52ff.) called the "ancient biological regime," and it was also a chapter in European history punctuated by political crises and wars that in some cases deprived entire regions of their populations, but the discourse advanced by populationists was still framed around loose notions and conjecture. In the economic thinking of the time, the population and its growth were understood as the source of a nation's wealth, so much so that the two might well have been equated. This was because, as we have seen, the nation's wealth was thought to be inextricably bound up with its military power. When Europe took on a new shape structured by competition among the great powers, the population therefore almost naturally became the measure of the economic and military power that each state could deploy.

In this way populationism became a sort of commonplace in treatises devoted to economic questions and the sciences of the state, and that discourse was thus carried over into the classics of police science. Justi, for example, was unequivocal in claiming that "we must adhere to the fundamental principle that there can be no such thing as too many inhabitants, whatever reason one might allege to the contrary" (von Justi 1756, 56ff.; my translation). The populationist objective guided the activity of police authorities, who were thus entrusted with

> rooting out the vices and excesses that lead to illness and death, to which end they must rely on regulations and on means of indirect persuasion designed in such a way that the subjects they are addressed to do not feel that their freedoms are under attack.
>
> (Ibid., 56ff.)

Indeed, police had to see to it that all subjects maintained their physical health and productive capacity. They were only partly in charge of themselves. Collectively, they formed the biological basis of the strength and prosperity of the state, and were thus expected to manage their own lives as if they were managing part of a public trust.[9] The health of the population thus stands out as a primary concern of the state, which entrusts police with doing the best job it can to fend off all threats to such health. In fact, as Justi comments, "it is part of wise government not only to prevent whatever tends to depopulate the country, but also to avert or at least mitigate all calamities by which men are afflicted" (ibid., 77).

It was not just the *physical* health of the population, its biological survival, that Justi was referring to, however important that was. He was also thinking of the vices and excesses that cause disease and death, and this idea encompassed

---

9 In his *Kurzer systematischer Grundriss aller oeconomischen und Cameralwissenschaften*, Justi drew a distinction between the subjects' *immediate* duties—falling within the general duty to obey the sovereign—and their *mediated* duties, meaning those duties which all subjects "owe *immediately* to themselves, but which are *mediately* also duties owed to the state and the prince, since any neglect of such duties will turn subjects into useless members of the body social, making them incapable of contributing to the happiness of the state" (von Justi [1761–64] 1970, vol. 1, p. 553; my translation).

the nation's *moral* decay no less than its physical decay. Discipline and health were thus inextricably bound up. And the connection was even more explicit in Des Essarts, whose entry for *Peuple* in his *Dictionnaire universel de police* began by spelling out the connection between discipline and the wellbeing of the population: "Since it is on the wellbeing of the population that the nation's wellbeing depends," police authority is bound to offer "constant protection" to the former, for it is "by protecting the population that it can be made to love its duties" (Des Essarts 1786–91, 60; my translation). Physical wellbeing therefore entails moral wellbeing, discipline, and a cognizance of one's own duties. Indeed,

> among the sources of the vices and crimes by which the population is afflicted, few are more baleful than ignorance of its duties; to instruct the population about its duties is to give it the greatest service, to care for it, to act as its benefactor.
>
> (Ibid., 61)

Police, in essence, is entrusted with the all-important task of enlightening the people and providing them with the means necessary to avoid all the evil which does not stem from nature, and for which they accordingly only have themselves and their own lifestyle to blame.

There were two avenues in particular that experts on police science pointed out as means by which to achieve this aim. One was to reinforce religious sentiments. It is religion, Justi thought, "that puts subjects in the condition to fulfil their duties with the greatest exactitude" (von Justi 1756, 192; my translation). To this end, the police must control the subjects' beliefs, and this control must be *direct*, keeping a watchful eye over the practice of cults so as to make sure that "no evil doctrine insinuates itself into the deep core of the state" (ibid., 195). But even more importantly, police is tasked with regulating working and leisure time. It needs to

> regulate national holidays, since these days of festivity have an effect on the work done by the people and on the economic order, but the number of days devoted to such occasions should not be excessive, lest the population should be distracted from its occupations.
>
> (Ibid., 199)

The concern here was, of course, to make sure that social and physical energies should not go to waste, owing to lifestyles and consumption patterns that were not suited to the popular classes, and to reduce as far as possible all public events, traditions, and popular festivals that would be particularly counterproductive, undermining the general productivity of the population. The police sought to blot out the popular practices, beliefs, and superstitions that were least favourable to the mercantile civilization the authorities were building, and this meant reshaping the overall makeup of popular culture. The effort was to control the potential for disorder and insubordination incident to the typical events of popular culture—a social-reform project explicitly aimed at achieving the economic output and performance sought by the state (Raeff 1983, 87).

In the second place it was necessary to enable subjects to develop and maintain "the skills and talents needed for them to be useful to society" (von Justi 1756, 190; my translation), to this end banishing idleness and aversion to work, since

> nothing can be more harmful to the state than idleness. The aim the republic sets out is for all of its members to jointly work toward the common good, and this will not be possible if agriculture, manufacturing, and commerce are neglected. A nation will not be able to flourish if its population should shirk work for leisureliness and shiftless idleness.
>
> (Ibid., 236)

Apart from being contrary to the basic duties of the citizen, idleness leads to demoralization: "Since the human spirit is by nature active, it cannot dwell in a state of inaction; unless it applies itself to something good, some evil pursuit will inevitably seize hold of it" (Des Essarts 1786–91, 346; my translation). And as we have seen, in the eyes of those who propounded this police science, the moral degeneration of the population almost inevitably leads to its physical degeneration, sapping the biological body of the nation: "Idleness is the source of many diseases, for in addition to making the humours heavier and the solid tissues flabbier, it enervates the body and hastens ageing" (ibid.).

Two broad areas of law were developed in this regard for the purpose of maintaining the people's productivity and their willingness to work. One was *labour police* and the other was *pauper police*. These two areas were complementary, supporting each other in governing the population. For this reason, I have chosen to treat *labour police* under the heading *police of the population* rather than under the apparently more appropriate *economic police*. To be sure, *labour police* had an important economic role to play, governing crucial aspects of productive activity, but, as I will argue, the majority of its provisions were designed to work in concert with poor relief in governing a segment of the population that, in the transition from the feudal society to the mercantile society, was always being tossed about between marginalization and socioeconomic integration.

Except for the large-scale royal manufacturing plants and the cottage industry that was emerging under the initiative of large merchants looking to wrestle free of the control that guilds and corporations were wielding over production, the productive structure of the ancien régime was still largely based on small workshops that rarely would employ more than a dozen workers. Labour was broken up into myriad different classes of work that reflected the corporative structure of the larger economy. Naturally, some of the most skilled workers were members of some guild who worked under a master craftsman but who would often come up against all the obstacles the organization put on the way to the title of master, thus never advancing beyond the status of apprentice. Beyond this rather small social class were those who found themselves having to sell their work to the satisfaction of different workshops, operating either independently or under the domestic system (Braudel 1979b, 259ff.; Castel 1995, 141ff.). The vast majority of those in the workforce therefore offered their labour or plied their trade outside the corporative system. This was a segment of the labour force made up of people who in police texts were referred to by the label *ouvrier* or *manouvrier* (labourer or workman), encompassing an army of porters, enterprisers, day labourers, in-home workers, and independent labourers of all sorts who every day would have to figure out where and how to sell their labour and services.

The condition of apprentices was essentially equated with that of in-home workers; they lived in a condition of quasi-servitude, being subject to the "household authority of masters" that the *parlement* in Paris invoked in 1776 as a way to fight back the first attempts to eliminate the corporative system at the initiative of Anne-Robert-Jacques Turgot (Kaplan 1979, 23). The first instrument of labour discipline and police were thus the guilds, or corporations. As the Parisian *parlement* itself remarked in that regard, "what police would be sweeter than the *jurandes*?" (ibid., 26). These corporations under the ancien régime thus acted as police authorities proper empowered to govern their members, leaving it to the state authorities to cover the shortfalls of this socio-professional structure. In fact, the discipline imposed by corporations could go well beyond the task of regulating productive activity, laying down meticulous rules for their members to follow in every area of their lives, including their habits, dress, free time, housing, and religious practices, and even the company they kept. Police authorities confined themselves to homologizing the charters of corporations and collecting tips on individual cases of members failing to hew to the rule of discipline. In the effective metaphor conceived by the Parisian *parlement*, the corporations were links forming a "chain with which to keep good order," making it possible to "enforce police on a mass of more than 100,000 individuals." To take down the corporative system was to break this chain, replacing "good order" with "confusion," inordinately stoking the mobility of the popular classes (Flammermont 1888, 308–24).

This disciplinary system for controlling work was structured around a few fundamental rules that with little variation governed across the whole of Europe. The core subject areas these rules addressed were apprenticeships and the process for gaining the title of master tradesman, but just as crucial were the rules designed to ensure a proper *labour police*. The most important of these rules set forth the obligation to serve at one's trade at the fair price set by police authorities jointly with the representatives of the different corporations. Next to that was the prohibition against forming workmen's associations. And finally was the rule prohibiting workers from leaving their masters without authorization. A worker wishing to leave a workshop needed to show cause and obtain a written release from his master, failing which that worker would have an arrest warrant served on him as a fugitive. The obligation to have a written release was codified in the statutes of apprenticeship enacted in Tudor England, as well as in Prussia's imperial ordinances of 1530 and 1548 (Holdsworth 1924, vol. 4, pp. 380; Raeff 1983, 104), and what congealed around this obligation was nothing short of a system for locking individuals into a socio-professional disciplinary structure. The practice of requesting the release certificate had been in use for some time, and it was formalized even in France, though only in 1749, and the same goes for the practice of completing the certificate with details about the characteristics, discipline, moral conduct, and professional skills of the worker in question (de Frémeville 1758, 239; Kaplan 1979, 49).

As a group, uncertified workmen were a variegated lot comprising wage workers, day labourers, and in-home workers. This was a social universe that the development of modern industry would use to advantage in working around the constraints of the corporative system. At the same time, however, this segment of society still raised many concerns among police authorities, who perceived its members as prone to vagrancy and as work-averse. The task of governing this segment of the population was entrusted to the complex apparatus of pauper police. In the Middle Ages, the question of pauperism did not rise to the level where it could attract the interest of the central authorities. Relief for the poor and the disadvantaged essentially depended on the role one played in one's community, and if the community could not take on that burden, then the Church would step in, using its tithe funds in support of the destitute. Poor relief was thus an incoherent system incapable of distinguishing between different kinds of recipients—an indiscriminate relief system that nonetheless was effective enough in coping with a problem that until the end of the Middle Ages was not yet acute (Mollat 1978). But as the mercantile and manufacturing economy began to displace the ancient subsistence economy, the traditional order of European society began to break down, and the ancient social welfare system would soon follow, bringing out all of its shortcomings. When the problem of pauperism erupted, it was felt destabilizing to distribute alms indiscriminately, and authorities all across Europe were thus prompted to call for a new social policy (Castel 1995, 54; Geremek 1994, 123).

In the transition from feudal society to the modern capitalist society, the rule-making aimed at reforming social welfare and the management of pauperism became so central as to become the most salient trait of police regulation, both quantitatively and qualitatively. This engendered what is known as the great confinement,[10] a development around which a vast literature has grown up that interprets the reform of social welfare in a variety of ways: now as the outgrowth of a new work ethic that developed out of the Reformation, now as a process owed to the central role that concepts such as temperance and discipline played in the humanistic culture that was spreading throughout Europe, now as a typical

10 As is known, the process that reformed social welfare and brought about the spread of secured hospital establishments has been defined by Michel Foucault (1988, 38) as the "great confinement." In this process, scholars working from a variety of perspectives have located the birth of modern prisons (see Melossi and Pavarini 1982).

expression of a mercantilist government philosophy aimed at multiplying the nation's social forces by bringing out the productive potential in every individual.[11] I will not here be going into the merits of these interpretations, except to note that they are not mutually exclusive. What does matter to us is to have a broad outline as a foothold on which to proceed in illustrating the essential features of pauper police in modern Europe.

The first innovations in poor relief came from the cities of the Late Middle Ages, which updated the old system of indiscriminate social welfare by introducing a distinction that would be central to pauper police in the centuries to come. This was the threefold distinction among the poor who lacked the ability to work, those who did have that ability but chose not to work, and the idle drifters. A differential treatment was thus accorded to individuals depending on which side of that distinction they fell on. Under different city ordinances, permissions could accordingly be granted for the disabled poor to ask for and receive charity, and parishes were entrusted with collecting and distributing the money, but at the same time it became an obligation for the able-bodied to work, and a complex of corporal and shaming punishments were introduced targeting those who shirked work and were thus deemed slothful and vagrant. What especially alarmed municipal authorities in this phase was the unchecked inflow of people toward densely populated centres. It was against this background that there began to spread provisions banishing migrants from the city and forcing them to return to their native towns, as well as stationing armed guards at city gates. But above all the reform process brought another key change to social welfare: the cardinal principle that each community was responsible for its own poor (Castel 1995, 51).

It is thus fair to say that, at the beginning of the 16th century, some of the essential traits had already been set that would later shape the pauper police enacted by state authorities. The reforms introduced by the municipal authorities were built around the ancient system of private charity, thus creating an administrative function for parishes, now entrusted with managing public welfare under the supervision of local secular authorities. This reformed system served as a blueprint for the national policies that would be developed later on in the century. England did so with a statute of 1535, France with the 1566 *ordonnance du Moulins*, and the German area with an imperial ordinance of 1548—all giving shape to a welfare machinery entirely modelled on the experience of the late medieval cities (Paultre [1906] 1975, 107ff.; Slack 1988, 117ff.; Dorwart 1971, 96). The reforms thus firmed up a set of principles that had been in the making in the previous

---

11 As mentioned, the body of literature devoted to this topic is quite large, so I will only offer a few instructive sources. An overview is provided in the previously mentioned Castel 1995 and Geremek 1994, but the reader can also refer to Lis and Soly 1979, Dean 1992, 215–51, and Dean 1991. On the English context, see Pound 1971 and Slack 1988 and Fideler 1998, 194–222; on the French context, see Paultre (1906) 1975 and Gutton 1971; and on the German context, see Sachsse and Tennstedt 1980, Dorwart 1971, and Harrington 1999.

decades: the duty to share in the effort to help the poor became a legally enforce-able obligation; under the supervision of local police authorities, parishes consolidated their public function of assessing the extent of the problem and collecting and managing the money the citizenry pay into the fund set aside to help the poor; and, finally, the welfare system settled definitely into shape on the basis of the threefold distinction among those unable to work, those who did have that ability but chose not to use it, and the idle vagrants.

But the reforms of the mid-16th century had not yet translated into a general system for confining the poor. Welfare for the able-bodied came in the form of forced labour, and in particular through the public-works system, requiring individuals to find and report to a master. This system, too, was based on the fundamental distinction between the poor as such and the poor whose condition was attributed to idleness or vagrancy, and those in this latter category were treated more punitively, for they were either deprived of compensation for their forced labour or subjected to the ancient system of shaming punishments. These punishments, however, counted for little, as the apparatus for forcing the poor into labour was yet to be perfected. Under the reforms of the mid-16th century, police authorities and parishes were responsible for putting the able-bodied poor to work, but this principle was not accompanied by any provision stating how such persons should be forced into labour. Apart from the manpower needed for public works, there were no provisions obligating workshops to take the poor into their employ regardless of economic conditions, and so even when there was no actual demand in the economy for any additional labour. The system thus proved largely ineffective at least until an institutional machinery was developed for confining the destitute in workhouses and general hospitals.[12]

In short, the reforms of the 16th and 17th centuries put in place a new system of restrictive welfare based on a few core principles: The able-bodied poor should have no access to social welfare except through confinement and forced labour; welfare was reserved for the disabled poor, who were occasionally allowed to panhandle; the poor out-of-towners were to be expelled from the city, under the

---

12 The trailblazer in this development was England, where some cities set up institutions of their own for the purpose of housing the poor while putting them to work, in this way complying with the statutes enacted in 1535. In 1557, for example, London established a hospital for the poor at Bridewell, a royal palace no longer in use; a similar institution was created in 1571 in Norwich, and so on in other cities. An act of 1575–76 brought these institutions under the scope of national legislation, making them the cornerstone of English pauper police. It was thus established that similar workhouses had to be set up across the kingdom and entrusted to the municipal authorities and local parishes under the oversight of bishops and justices of the peace (Holdsworth 1924, vol. 4, pp. 396ff.; Slack 1988, 118ff.). A similar development took place in France, though almost a century later, when in 1656, having commissioned an extensive study and entered into a lengthy consultation, the main authorities in Paris issued a royal edict—the *Édit du Roi, Portant établissement de l'Hôpital-Général, pour le renfermement des pauvres mendians de la ville & fauxbourgs de Paris*—establishing an institution for the confinement of the poor, an institution that under an edict of 1662 would then be extended across the realm (Paultre [1906] 1975, 207ff.).

principle that each community was responsible only for its own poor; and vagrancy was to be severely repressed. In subsequent decades the reform's repressive tenor was only exacerbated, in an attempt to make up for the shortfalls of a system that was chronically inept at dealing with the problem of managing poverty in the modern age. But for all the failings of the social welfare machinery entrusted to police authorities, its introduction did mark an important shift in social policy away from a religious approach to poverty toward an approach on which the task of dealing with poverty should instead mainly fall to the secular authorities. It was the humanistic debate that set the essential building blocks for this new approach to poverty, all the while outlining the model on which to proceed in making reforms in that matter.[13] Poverty thus ceased to be perceived as a social constant—the physical incarnation of the attributes of Christ and the condition of salvation through the giving of alms—and came to be considered as rooted in causes to be addressed by careful policy. Poverty became a social phenomenon whose causes were seen to lie in the individual's weak moral fibre and in bad policy: It was soon reduced to a matter of "idleness and ill policy" (Starkey [1535] 1983, 89). As Michel Foucault put it, "misery was no longer filtered through the dialectic of humiliation and glory"; in the world of state-run charity it had become a matter of "complacency with oneself and a fault in the good running of government" (Foucault 1961, 70; my translation).

It was this approach to poverty and misery that informed the complex of regulations that, starting from the end of the 15th century, developed into the modern poor laws of the 17th century. Mitchell Dean (1992, 219ff.) refers to this thinking as the "discourse on poverty". A discourse that developed out of the reflections on good government advanced in the context of political humanism and later assembled into a coherent theory once the mercantilist politico-economic discourse grew to maturity. Together, these practices and theories enabled the socio-political structures of the time to provide for those who, for one reason or another, fell through the cracks of the economic and productive structures. In combination, pauper legislation and the discourse on poverty made it possible to deploy a police-disciplinary complex designed to make sure that individuals could be productive members of society by participating in the economic life of the country, and the method for achieving this goal consisted in compelling them to re-enter the economic and productive structure out of which they had fallen. Stated otherwise, the whole point of this complex was to root out poverty, or, in the words of a pamphlet printed to publicize the activities of the newborn *Hôpital Général* in Paris, the objective was to "eliminate mendicancy and vagrancy and

13 In investigating the causes of poverty and economic hardship, the humanists led the public debate following in the footsteps of Juan Luis Vives, who on one of his British sojourns wrote the famous treatise *De subventione pauperum* of 1526 by request of the city of Bruges. The treatise also served as a model for the reforms enacted in Tudor England (see Ferguson 1965, 228, and Geremek 1994, 196).

impede all disorder that may stem from these two sources" (Paultre [1906] 1975, 158; my translation).

Poverty was regarded as deadweight loss, a squandering of the nation's strengths. Such was the economic thinking of the period straddling the 17th and 18th centuries, according to which the strength and prosperity of the nation was primarily a function of the size and industriousness of its population. It thus became a practical imperative to put the poor to work. Social policy was entirely predicated on the mercantilist notions of how the authorities ought to proceed in supporting and stimulating industry, so much so that even at the local level the proposals put forward for establishing workhouses were driven by the aim of getting new industries to flourish across the country, and the accompanying debate supported that argument (Dean 1991, 40–41). Indeed, behind the pressing debate that developed around the question of social policy was the dream of a fully productive society (Appleby 1978, 164).

The trend toward confinement, however, did not grow only out of a strictly economic imperative. At its root there also lay broadly moral and disciplinary concerns. As Michel Foucault (1988, 46) has lucidly argued, the confinement of the poor was a "'police' matter," and as such it served as a key institutional instrument in two areas: One was the discipline historically known as *economic police*, designed to govern the social consequences of the ups and downs in the labour market; another was spiritual police, considering that the labour forced on the poor took on an educational and disciplinary significance that outweighed the economic value of the same labour. In this sense Foucault (1988, 59) has argued that on the *Hôpital Général* was conferred an "ethical status" in addition to its economic status. It was "the densest symbol of that 'police' which conceived of itself as the civil equivalent of religion for the edification of a perfect city" (Foucault 1988, 63).

Indeed, as noted, the population was regarded as a source of wealth, but it could act as such a source only so long was it was governed in such a way as to ensure that it grew in accord with a solid moral discipline. If the population was to actually enable the state to thrive, it had to be subjected to the necessary *social police* measures. "But with us in England," wrote Sir Matthew Hale, "for want of a due regulation of things, the more Populous we are the Poorer we are; so that, that wherein the strength and wealth of a kingdom consists, renders us the weaker and the poorer" (Hale [1683] 1805, 516). In this sense, the emphasis fell not so much on the productive capacity of workhouses as on their disciplinary utility:

> And were there no other Benefit to the kingdom in general, nor to the particular Places where such work-houses shall be settled but this, although the stock were wholly lost in four years, it would be an abundant recompence, by the accustoming the poor sort to a civil and industrious course of life, whereby they would soon become not only not burdensome, but profitable to the kingdom and places where they live.

> (Ibid., 527)

The persons expropriated from the land and suddenly deprived of their welfare entitlements had to learn to sell their own labour. They needed to be trained in "the discipline of their new condition" (Marx [1867] 1906, 806), primed for life in the cities and the manufacturing centres, and generally for the rhythms and discipline required to work in the context of economic structures based on the principle of intensive production. As has been underscored by a long tradition in the study of the birth of the modern prison system, in this welfare-reform process that in the modern age has brought about the great confinement of paupers and vagrants, we can certainly locate as well the seed of modern disciplinary institutions; even so, the function of the *police of the population* cannot be bounded within the circumscribed purview within which these institutions operate. Indeed, the relation between police authorities and the popular classes gives us a vantage point from which to observe the birth and development of administrative practices for identifying and categorizing the population—a complex of information-gathering-and-processing tools that would form the institutional foundation on which police knowledge would be built.

As the complex labour- and pauper-police apparatus developed, so did the technical means for gathering information and appropriately treating those who became objects of police activity. We have already considered the introduction of the release certificate as a tool enabling police authorities to exert greater control on the world of work and prevent insubordination or resistance to the work discipline. This release certificate was the forebear of the more modern *livret* (workers' passport) institutionalized in France in the late 18th century. The *livret* originated out of the practice of some guilds whose charters required them to collect all their certificates into a single register, a practice that wound up being made obligatory countrywide by a letters patent of 1781 (Kaplan 1979, 56). Workers wishing to obtain a *livret*, serving as a work permit, had to register with their guild and pay dues. The *livret* contained all the annotations that shop masters and the police made relating to the worker's moral conduct and proficiency on the job, and over time it became an identity card proper, clearly reflecting the population-control policy sought to be implemented by the police. It was, after all, this same goal of identifying and classifying the population that had previously shaped the complex of technical instruments deployed by pauper police so as to more accurately select the patrons of welfare institutions.

It was the need to accurately distinguish able-bodied workers from disabled ones—and to further distinguish the idlers and the vagrants in the former category, so as to mark them out for the harshest treatment provided under the poor laws—that prompted the 1724 introduction of a national general register of mendicants recording all arrests of beggars picked up and arrested by the police, thus making it easier to bring charges against such repeat offenders. Under this system—quite complex relative to the bureaucratic capabilities of the time (Paultre [1906] 1975, 76)—as much information as possible was to be systematically gathered about the patrons of welfare institutions, and the information was to be sent out across the realm to all authorities entrusted with governing the population.[14]

This practice of booking the poor inevitably led to the birth of a complex parallel system of police records and archives for governing the population. Indeed, from the outset the rule requiring general hospitals to gather information on paupers and vagrants also came with an obligation to report that information to police lieutenancies. And thus was created the first alphabetical register of persons arrested under the poor laws. Within a few years, however, police authorities realized the potential those records held for making more effective the activity of exercising control over the population. So in 1753 the practice was begun of collecting and annotating information on arrestees of all sorts and even on suspects. These records were kept in the infamous *livre rouge*, or red book, so named because the names of the people listed in it were printed in red. The annotations were entered in chronological and alphabetical order in records on persons arrested for theft or robbery or detained under a police law or a royal writ, or again simply on suspicion as "persons who have no means of sustenance other than trickery or who keep unsavoury company" (de Chassaigne [1906] 1975, 159).

After all, the practice of ascertaining the exact place of residence of the poor held in welfare establishments meant from the outset that police authorities had to be able to monitor the movement of the population across the territory (Paultre [1906] 1975, 76). This function of monitoring population movements became crucial with the demographic growth of big cities, when police authorities found they had to improve the technical tools at their disposal (Blanc-Chaléard et al. 2001, 15–16). This itinerant human mass thus became an object of close surveillance on accommodation establishments, meaning inns and rentals, the stomping ground of choice for the "mobile vulgus" that made up the labour force in the big cities—often the only setting where youths eradicated from traditional community ties could socialize, but one of anomie and subversive association in the eyes of the authorities. The police thus tried to extend its surveillance well beyond workplaces and welfare poorhouses, seeking to more generally monitor the movement of the popular classes across the territory by surveilling the places they frequented in their

---

14 In this regard, the provision was thus worded under Article 5: "In order to make it possible to more easily identify those who have had a prior arrest or against whom complaints have been raised or facts have been alleged that deserve investigation, we order that there shall be established at the general hospital in Paris a *bureau de correspondance* coordinating with all other hospitals across the realm, for the purpose of keeping an accurate register of all mendicants who have been arrested, recording their given name, surname, age, and city of birth [. . .], as well as all other facts that may be extracted by questioning them, and also the characteristics relating to their person; and all provincial hospitals shall keep a similar register of the mendicants admitted into their care, and a copy of such records shall be sent every week to the *Bureau Général* set up in Paris. On the basis of the information so gathered, a general register shall be compiled in Paris, listing all mendicants arrested anywhere in the realm, and recording the name of each mendicant, along with the annotations and observations gathered from their interrogations as well as from all copies of the records held at other hospitals" (Kaplan 1979, 337; my translation).

day-to-day lives. This surveillance was carried out by keeping tabs on licenses, check-in registers, and business hours, or again by requiring innkeepers and hoteliers to deny room and board to those who could not produce the appropriate papers (the worker's passport) and were thus deemed vagrants (De Frémeville 1758, 177ff., and Des Essarts 1786–91, 466ff.; see generally Milliot 2001).

Keeping a count of and surveilling a moving population became a primary police objective, an obsession proper that expressed itself in a *police vise* that gradually tightened its chokehold on the lives of the popular classes. Paupers, apprentices, domestic workers, day labourers, and the like were corralled within a surveillance system that extended to every aspect of their existence covering work, leisure, and the private sphere. In the hustle and bustle of city life, red books, police records, and the sign-in registers kept by inns and rentals offered the comforting illusion that the comings and goings of the popular classes could be frozen in time and space. Police institutions thus grappled with the task of governing an increasingly mobile society, although it is not quite accurate to rely on the notion of migrants in reference to society in the Ancien Régime. Indeed, the reference made to vagrancy encompassed more than just the idea of demographic movement over a territory. The legal categories used in the police laws of the Ancien Régime were meant to include groups such as propertyless people, dissolute women or women suspected of prostitution, and libertines; that is, they were meant to take in the whole lot of individuals who had fallen beyond the reach of the corporative structure of production or who had escaped the discipline of marital or parental authority, independently of their actual ability to move about from place to place. The attention of police surveillance in the Ancien Régime, in the effort to gather the largest possible amount of information on the life of the popular classes, was devoted not only to *spatial* mobility but also, and especially, to the *social* mobility of those who attempted to evade their duty to actively participate in the social and economic life of the realm, thus moving out of the station allotted to them within the productive and familial structures.

The police thus worked with confined surveillance institutions in establishing a discipline for the popular classes, which became a source of deep concern, especially when they left the countryside and the suburbs and headed for the cities. The job entrusted to the police was to lock the popular classes into the different socioeconomic structures, in such a way as to put a cap on the number of people making up the rambling mass that flocked to the city in search of work (unskilled manual or day labour), thus contributing to demographic growth in the urban areas. As evidence of the alarm raised by such trends, one need only consider that the terms *ouvrier* and *manouvrier*, comprising between them the whole mass of unskilled labourers, could often be used as synonyms for *vagrant*, if not in the law at least in police science treatises. Thus, under the entry for *ouvrier*, Des Essarts's *Dictionnaire universel de police* reflected the full disciplinary obsession with which the police looked on the world of the roaming popular classes:

> For a long time now, the desire has been expressed for the government to classify this mob of men beyond number who seem to have wrested themselves

from the wholesome yoke of the law, for it appears that they can too easily
escape its rule.

(Des Essarts 1786–91, 459; my translation)

Here, of course, what police authorities became apprehensive about was the
constant inflow of people streaming into the cities, especially the capital, Paris:

Enclosed within the boundaries of the capital and the large cities are many
men whose names, abodes, professions, and means of subsistence are unknown
to the city's magistrates and the public security officers. There is no doubt that
the provinces are becoming increasingly depopulated, in such a way as to
enlarge the capital; that is often the riffraff who abandon the provinces; and
the immense bowels of the city act as a safe haven for the vices of the province,
as well as for crimes that escape the proper severity of the law.

(Ibid.)

On this population was pinned responsibility, no less, for the most serious outbreaks
of unrest, rebellion, and sedition. As Des Essarts insisted,

these are still men whose names and abodes are not known to anybody: They
are individuals who seem foreign even to the city that affords them subsistence,
beings who live for the moment and vanish with the same ease with which
they materialized; they are, finally, unpropertied men who own nothing.

(Ibid., 460)

The police thus developed the complex of instruments just described to gather
information on the life of the population, and it did so expecting to expand its
watch over the spatial and social mobility of individuals—over the existence of
those who escaped their duty to have an active role in economic life and to defer
to familial authority and were thus perceived as a limitless source of disorder. Des
Essarts was very much aware of the central importance of these classifications and
surveillance instruments, so much so that he even advocated for the establishment
of a general register on which to record all information on anybody who came into
the city to work as a day labourer:

During the day these men are scattered across the city in workshops and in
squares and streets; at the slightest suggestion of discontent they retreat, immediately clustering together like hordes of savages, ready to act on cue [. . .]; since
they have no fixed place to stay in the city, their movements are as prompt as
they are shadowy. They therefore easily elude the magistrates' control.

(Ibid., 461)

The classification and obligation to register advocated by Des Essarts served
precisely the purpose of fixing this fleeting population into place, a population that

did in some way take part in the economic life of the city, but was not stably situated in the socio-professional structure of the trades. But once the situation is brought under control, he thought,

> the rule of licentiousness will give way to that of order, and instead of a mob of men unknown and undisciplined there will be citizens of known identity, and the capital will be purged of so many malicious citizens who commit so many crimes.
>
> (Ibid., 461)

We have seen that the notions of idler and vagrant were ambiguous in the language of police authorities, and indeed that they were used in reference to people who could not be distinguished from the poor as such or from unskilled workers and day labourers, and equally ambiguous were the labels "dissolute woman" and "woman suspected of prostitution" or libertinage. This broad use of some key labels shows that the essential function of police discipline was not so much to punish behaviour deemed to be objectionable as to cast the widest possible net across the universe of the popular classes—identifying the whole swath of people who fell outside the socio-professional and familial structure and thus escaped the discipline of Ancien Régime society—so as to bring these people under *police tutelage*. The aim was to fight all lifestyles that might have called into question the viability of a social order that fit each person into a proper role under the authority of a master, a husband, a paterfamilias. The *police of the population* of the time was essentially predicated on the need to replenish the productive structure with the social forces that tended to fall away from it, locking these forces into specific institutional places, be they physical places proper (such as workhouses) or ideal places constructed through the network of police surveillance and control that enveloped the lives of the popular classes.

4.4. Social disciplining

To be sure, the previously described complex apparatus set up to police the population could be understood as simply a chapter in the history of social policy. But it would be more accurate to read it as the best evidence we have of the massive and as yet unsurpassed effort put forth at the dawn of the modern age to force the kind of structural change in spirituality, morality, and psychology needed to forge the anthropological type best suited to responding to the political and economic challenges being raised by the modern capitalist society. As Gerhard Oestreich has suggested, a change on this scale could have been produced only through a vast process of *social disciplining*.[15] The disciplinary push can be

---

15 On the concept of social disciplining, see Oestreich 1980, 215ff.; Beuer 1986, 62ff.; and Schiera 1996, 28; see also Härter 1996, 636.

appreciated in all the practical manifestations of the new governmental rationality that underlay the modern administrative monarchy: "Bureaucratism; militarism and mercantilism; and civil, military, and economic service were all manifestations of the social disciplining process enacted in administration, the military system, and the economy" (Oestreich 1971, 185; my translation). And the best expression of such rationality was, of course, the Prussian garrison state (Rosenberg 1958, 42).[16] More generally, however, it was through this push toward social disciplining that a receptive environment was created, particularly in more economically advanced areas of Europe, for the spread of an institutional model for marshalling, organizing, and exploiting the forces of individuals, a model based on the triad formed by the house of confinement, the manufacture, and the garrison. At the historical time when modern warfare based on large armies came into being and the artisan workshop gave way to the factory, the three homologous institutions just mentioned marked the rise of a complex of political technologies with which to redeem the economic and military capacity of the greatest number of individuals, all the while managing the social problem of the unredeemables.

Nor was this project of individual and social disciplining limited to the establishment of *closed or confined spaces* for keeping people under control. Indeed, just as disciplinary institutions were coming into being, the question arose of how to keep *open* or *non-disciplinary spaces* under control, that is, how to enhance the system for keeping individuals in a state of generalized surveillance and constant control in such a way as to extend the reach of that system beyond the limited areas they could each separately manage. This extension of the disciplinary network across the entire social space was effected by building a centralized state apparatus coextensive with the entire body social, an apparatus based on the work of functionaries and police institutions entrusted with exercising surveillance and control over spaces that stretch between separate closed institutions. It was thus a complex function that the police carried out, for it was tasked with stretching an intermediate network between disciplinary institutions, in such a way as to act where the latter could not. In a sense, the police was tasked with "disciplining the non-disciplinary spaces" (Foucault 1977b, 215), serving as a sort of "interstitial discipline and meta-discipline" (ibid.). The police function thus extended well beyond the role that disciplinary institutions in a strict sense played in governing

16 The Prussian model was decisive in giving birth to "this new species of thoroughly disciplined man, activated by quasi-moral compulsions and chained to a large-scale apparatus and thus to the collective pursuit of objectified, utilitarian tasks. In line with the conception of the bureaucratic state as a machine, man himself was destined to become an automaton" (Rosenberg 1958, 89–90). The model of Prussian administration was that of military discipline, where any delay or negligence in discharging one's duties was deemed an act of insubordination and mutiny. According to the vivid image used by Hugh Elliot, British ambassador to Prussia in the final years of the reign of Frederick the Great, "the Prussian Monarchy reminds me of a vast prison in the centre of which appears the great keeper occupied in the care of his captives" (quoted in Gooch 1947, 104).

individuals. It encompassed the activity of disciplinary institutions in a broader project to canvass and discipline the entire social space.

The police apparatus was undoubtedly the main instrument through which the modern state managed to extinguish the ancient vestiges of the feudal political system based on independent loci of power, thus building the first institutional basis on which to rest the idea of territoriality specific to political sovereignty. It thus served as a tool enabling modern political institutions to progressively increase their ability to exercise a hegemonic control of space. Although this was very much the case, it matters little to us here. More than the emergence of political sovereignty and the structuring of its territorial counterpart, we need to investigate the way the birth of the police apparatus dramatically augmented its capacity to in effect control individuals and populations *within* the bounds of space. Indeed, the birth of a police apparatus capable of exercising a constant surveillance over every aspect of social life and to report to the top through an unbroken line of communication meant that the panoptic effect associated with the functioning of every disciplinary institution could indefinitely be multiplied across the entire territorial surface of the state.

In 1667, the first true police magistracy of the modern age was established, the general lieutenancy for the city of Paris, well expressing this need for an institution capable of casting a sovereign glance across the entire body social:

> The king, in the seclusion of his palace, will observe the most minute details of national existence from the bottom of his cabinet. Simply by exercising his will, he will be able to ensure universal order, meaning not just order in the streets, itself a feat of no small account, but also order in the souls and hearts.
> (de Chassaigne [1906] 1975, 39; my translation)

Nowhere was this disciplinary drive more vividly expressed than in the very ordinance establishing the new magistracy, therein empowered to act as "the eyes, ears, and hands of the king" (Delamare 1705, 131; my translation). Each police functionary thus moved as if he were an extension of the king; collectively they were entrusted with multiplying the effectiveness and granularity of sovereign surveillance and control. As a whole, the police apparatus built a "great pyramid of peering eyes"[17] at whose apex was sovereign power. This idea is broken down in La Maire's account of the complex structure of the Paris police:

> It is through this correspondence and immediate, unending, and easy com-munication set up between magistrates, on the one hand, and this small cadre, on the other, that the police can (i) govern a million inhabitants gathered in a boundless city; (ii) extend the reach of its relations and initiative to every

---

17 The French original: "grande pyramide de regards" (Foucault 1974, 1477).

ordinary citizen; (iii) multiply itself and, as it were, be everywhere at the same time; (iv) see and foresee everything, know everything, and make provision for everything; (v) issue the appropriate orders whenever and wherever they may be necessary; and (vi) make sure that these orders are carried out with the same speed and accuracy with which they are issued.

(La Maire 1878, 30; my translation)

So what accounts for the birth of the apparatus and the development of police legislation—with its countless areas of intervention and the details it was asked to take into account—was a clear project of social disciplining, a project whose importance should not be downplayed just because the authorities could not fully achieve their objectives. To be sure, as historians of law are aware, the constant reiteration of police provisions testifies to all the difficulties and resistance the authorities came up against in pushing their agenda forward. But that does not warrant the conclusion that police action was thereby entirely ineffective. That activity required a constant effort thwarted over and again by a spate of police provisions drafted using a legislative technique that was still too broad-brush. These provisions needed constant reiteration and clarification, in part because the system for publicizing them was ineffective. Any particular provision was bound to get lost in the morass of police legislation, making it necessary to reissue it in order for it to find any application, and that went double when the objective was to implement ambitious social reforms (Olivier-Martin 1948, 29ff.; Raeff 1983, 51ff.). At any rate, even conceding that police action was ineffective, that would not by itself diminish the historical significance of the complex police *dispositif* created in the modern age. This apparatus speaks to the effort of governors and administrators to shape their society in a given way and a given direction, to forge populations, the economy, and culture in accordance with certain norms and standards.

This disciplinary push can clearly be appreciated in the investigations that police science at the time was devoting to the nature of police provisions. The question at issue was how to draw the distinction between police and criminal justice, two areas that both relied on the use of sanctions and thus tended to often overlap. Indeed, there was a sanctionative and afflictive component to police that La Maire called judicial police, entrusted with "upholding the ordinances and regulations pertaining to general police, its task being to uphold the rules of general police, applying the punishments handed down when those rules are violated, observing the forms of procedure, and complying with rulings" (La Maire 1878, 11; my translation). So there was a judicial aspect to police whose nature crucially needed to be specified, not least because, in the context of the conflict we have looked at between *iurisdictio* and *politia*, the ordinary courts were constantly trying to expand their sphere of competence so as to bring rulings on police violations within the purview of their power.

Jurists, in particular, began to see a difference in *kind* between criminal law and police ordinances, observing how the former more often consisted of prohibitions, whereas the latter tended to be injunctive, ordering individuals to carry out or refrain from carrying out specific actions (Durand 1996, 175). It was also observed that unlike criminal laws, which are designed to protect *specific* legal goods, police ordinances tended to protect the public good as a whole, rather than the legal interest of this or that person or group in particular. Muyart de Vouglans thus pointed out that police violations "can be distinguished from other crimes in virtue of the fact that the latter are by their nature punishable as acts whose effect is to directly disrupt public order"; they are therefore artificial punishments, and as such are punishable not because they cause injury to persons in their *private* sphere, but rather because they bear on the broader public interest and involve "acts the nature of which makes them permissible, becoming illegitimate only when they turn out to be in contravention of police ordinances and regulations" (De Vouglans 1780, 362; my translation).

The fundamental criterion for distinguishing police from justice lay in the kind of sanction the two institutional compartments resorted to. Indeed, Montesquieu ([1748] 1989, 42) had already pointed out that police sanctions tend not so much to punish as to compel the offender to "live according to the rules of society." The point was reiterated by La Maire, who wrote that while police laws are all criminal, "the punishments they set forth are no more than corrections [disciplinary punishments] and, much more commonly, monetary awards, neither of which entails a note of reprimand for those against whom they are enforced"; they "rather serve as preventive measures, as warnings against recidivism, not as acts of severity" (La Maire 1878, 9–10; my translation). The point of police measures is therefore neither to repress offenders nor to bring them into disrepute. Police laws are not designed to punish but to inspire people to do good and abide by the law. Their purpose is to

> return subjects to their duties by way of warnings and soft and wholesome remedies applied through the public apparatus, which needs to make a stronger impression than the punishment itself, lest the punishment should be excessive, for that would have the effect of turning people against the law rather than getting them to learn the law and convincing them of its usefulness.
> (Ibid., 27)[18]

It is fair to say, in conclusion, that the broader aim of the police apparatus created in the modern age was, in Justi's words, to "arrange things so that all subjects have the specific capacities and qualities and the order required for the ultimate aim consisting in the happiness of the collectivity" (von Justi 1756, 290; my translation).

18 Similarly, Du Chesne (1757, 7) defined police sanctions as corrections that do not entail any reprimand: "Les amendes & autres corrections infligées en matiere de Police, n'emportent point infamie." Indeed, as a rule they need to be lenient, serving only to prevent recidivism: "Ces peines doivent être communément modérées, & servir seulement de préservatifs contre récidives" (ibid.)

In short, the first task assigned to police as a whole was to guide the socio-economic process and model the population's behaviour and lifestyles so as to favour the aims set by the public authorities. As La Maire put it, police is "the science of governing men and do good to them, in such a way as to mould them as far as possible into what they have to be in view of the general interest of society" (La Maire 1878, 28). This disciplinary program, as we have seen, was perfectly encapsulated in the ordinance that established the police lieutenancy in Paris, expressly inviting the new magistracy to act in such a way as to *have everyone live according to their condition and duty*.

The police apparatus was thus the central node of a social disciplining and regulation project involving a vast institutional complex that flanked justice while operating in a different compartment. This complex no longer relied on the *ius commune* and the classic judicial provisions as key tools but on a governmental technology proper with which to forge new forms of coexistence. Next to and beyond the image of the *king as enforcer of justice* a new image had now firmly established itself: that of the *king as guardian and tutor*, who, like a caring father, nurtures and educates the population.

Chapter 5

Public security and liberal governance

With the end of the 18th century, the era of modern police draws to a close; or, rather, we see the end of a long-drawn-out historical phase over the course of which the concept of police—encapsulating the whole complex of activities the state was taking over as its scope of intervention in socioeconomic life—became the object of a growing body of practical experiences and theoretical reflections out of which the founding principles of modern governmental rationality emerged. The thick core of *police générale* and *Wohlfahrtspolizei* (social welfare police) was breaking up into a constellation of disciplines. In fact, the very meaning of *police* was already beginning to narrow down, to the point where even on the Continent the concept came to be widely understood in its stricter sense of police as a security apparatus, the sense that we have seen taking hold early on in English-speaking political thought.

This process leading to the breakup of modern police essentially gave rise to a general "dispersion of police powers" (Chapman 1971, 34), ultimately effecting a deep transformation of the police apparatus. The police of the ancien régime was left with the single function of governing social dangerousness, meaning the increasing social risks incident to life in cities grappling with the incipient process of demographic growth and industrialization. Having shed the function of directing economic life, the police entered the 19th century as a fundamental tool with which to set and enforce social policy and govern the popular classes that were pouring into the industrial cities, where it was assumed that even the inviolable civil liberties might have been sacrificed to security, if it came to that.

The process that splintered the modern police apparatus unfolded along two parallel tracks. One was driven by the contraposition between legal and political discourse, but at the same time the police apparatus continued to taper under the weight of another force—namely, the discourse of modern economic reason. The latter—in alliance with the discourse of modern legal reason—wound up radically changing the nature of police (Foucault 2004, 266ff; 2008, 11–16, 27–26).

Indeed, for one thing, in the ongoing dialectic we have looked at, which set legal reason against modern governmental reason, the former element, legal reason, became an essential tool in the hands of liberal political philosophy in its persistent effort to limit and circumscribe the sphere of politics. Liberalism framed the ancient question of *iurisdictio* in modern terms by seizing on the idea of man's natural and inviolable rights, and in so doing it managed to put up an important barrier against the expansion of police power. We saw this with the English case and the emergence of the rule of law, and we will see the same thing happening with the liberal tradition that emerged out of the clash between the different compartments of the state in the late 18th and early 19th centuries. Indeed, the battle fought over the criteria on which basis to draw the line between justice and administration—a battle which originated out of the dialectic between *iurisdictio* and *politia* and which then intensified in the 19th century over the question of justice in administration—formed the background against which the modern science of public law came into being, but, even more importantly, it was this development that brought to maturity the juridification of political power that, as discussed, formed the basis of the liberal conception of the state.[1]

For another thing, in this process through which legal reason gained the upper hand over political reason—or through which an administrative discipline was transformed into a legal one: police science into the science of public law— liberalism was able to offer an internal criticism of political reason by working within the selfsame discourse on the governmental arts so as to lay the foundations of modern economic discourse. Indeed, it would be inaccurate to depict the liberal economic doctrine as a crudely anarchic criticism of political reason: It was, rather, an attempt to constrain that reason by a principle of self-limitation. In short, it was not the *justice* of political interventions in socioeconomic life that the liberal economic doctrine called into question but rather the *utility* of such interventions (see Foucault 2008, 22–26; see also Gordon 1991, 16; Dean 1999, 115; and Zanini 2006, 130).

What in particular acted most forcefully in revolutionizing the sphere of police from within was the concept of civil society that modern economic reason conjured into existence by transforming a strictly politico-legal concept into an economic one placed at the centre of a new governmental technology. Next to the agent *qua* legal subject who had been the focus of political and legal theory came the agent *qua* pursuer of interests who populates the sphere of civil society. It was once again in England, in the second half of the 17th century, that the first steps were taken toward this theoretical revolution, which later developed an epistemology on which basis it would extend its influence across the entire landscape of European social and economic thought. But it was in changing the governmental arts that this revolution was particularly disruptive. Indeed, authority turned away from the ambitious objective of providing for the welfare of the population and focused instead on guaranteeing security and regulating the autonomous dynamic of interests by which civil society operates. The *homo œconomicus* of the new

---

1 On the battle over justice in administration, see Mannori and Sordi 2001, 312; for a detailed analysis of the ways in which the rule of law and the *Rechtsstaat* were conceived in different philosophical and cultural traditions, see Costa and Zolo 2007.

governmental reason is not only a subject of inalienable rights but also a pursuer of specific interests, and it becomes the aim of authority to act not *against* such individuals but *through* them (Foucault 2008, 272ff.; see also Dean 1999, 98–99).

In essence, by wading into the debate then underway on the question of the dynamics between *iurisdictio* and *politia*, political economy managed over time to remove the subject of economic relations from the scope of the police disciplines into which mercantilism and cameralism had boxed it—and thus was laid the theoretical ground for the autonomy of economic discourse according to the process described by Karl Polanyi ([1944] 2001). Cameralism was thus made to follow a path that reduced it to a science of finances, but even more importantly, liberal economic thought overturned the whole premise of mercantilist *economic police*—predicated on the idea that the dynamics of socioeconomic processes could be controlled by issuing political directives—thus giving birth to modern political economy, which by contrast came to an awareness that those spontaneous dynamics are driven by their own logic and can at best be *managed*, not controlled. The advent of modern economic reason was thus brought about by working from within the ancient discourse of the public economy embraced by mercantilism. This was achieved by progressively expunging governmental reason from the discipline out of which it originated and fashioning the economy itself into a powerful principle pointing to the inherent limitation of politics.

The two principles limiting the police apparatus thus proceeded from two sets of opposite theoretical and epistemological foundations. One was the deductive logic of modern rationalism and of liberal legal science; the other was the inductive empiricism that gave birth to political economy and modern social science. Both foundations, however, would act in alliance in shaping a principle for the limitation of the political sphere. This they did by posing the question of the limits to be placed on power and the limited scope of power itself, a question they posed simultaneously through a mutual feedback between the discourse on natural rights and that of society as a natural or spontaneous order. So even though these two traditions proceeded from opposite theoretical and epistemological premises, they acted in concert, in close contact, so much so that they would often crop up as dual themes in the work of authors trained as both jurists and economists. Indeed, as Michel Foucault (2008, 38) has observed: "You could not think of political economy, that is to say, the freedom of the market, without at the same time addressing the problem of public law, namely that of limiting the power of public authorities."

Here, too, even though the process leading to the dispersion of police powers got underway at about the same time across all the territorial areas we have considered, it did not unfold everywhere in the same way or at the same pace. Indeed, whereas in England the police sciences never developed their politico-administrative knowledge to theoretical and epistemological maturity, even slowing down to a state of near atrophy in the late 18th century, on the Continent this knowledge flourished, so much so that, as we have seen, it led to the establishment of academic disciplines proper. In the second half of the 18th century, the liberal philosophy of politics and society and the new model of governmental arts it ushered in began to increasingly exert influence even on the Continent: It was now grafting itself onto original intellectual movements, like the one propounded by the French physiocrats, now merging in peculiar ways with the ancient police sciences, as in the German area, but always advancing the process that reformed political and social structures by introducing the deep changes widely thought to have marked the end of the ancien régime. Even the police apparatus would come out of the liberal revolution in an entirely different shape, ultimately settling on the paradigm of the security police that grew to full theoretical and institutional maturity in England in the early 19th century.

5.1. The emergence of administration

The first crisis of *police générale* came about as the outcome of an attack that physiocracy levelled on the *economic police* of the Ancien Régime. By *physiocracy* is commonly meant the school of economic thought that developed in France in the mid-18th century, and whose most paradigmatic expression is François Quesnay's 1758 *Tableau économique*. The name derives from the title chosen for a collection of works by Quesnay published in 1768 by Pierre-Samuel Dupont de Nemours (Quesnay 1768), and it aptly captures the sense of the theoretical challenge the economic thinkers in this current threw at the French politico-social philosophy of the time, and in particular at its pretension to exercise a *police générale* over the realm. Indeed, the physiocrats clearly asserted the principle that social and economic life is possessed of a natural physiological order of its own, according to a dynamic with which the authorities *cannot* and *ought not* to interfere through irrational and arbitrary police regulations. In this sense, according to the physiocratic conception of the governmental arts, it was not enough for administrators to be versed in what at the time were considered to be the police sciences, which, as we know, used a set of notions pertaining to law no less than to so-called *economic police*: "The study of law," Quesnay argued, "does not in itself suffice to train men of state; those who are going to work as administrators need to be made to study the natural order that is most advantageous to men in society" (Quesnay 1888, 331; my translation).

The challenge the physiocrats raised against Ancien-Régime *police* was entirely built on this idea that economic and social processes are governed by natural laws which the authorities therefore should not try to interfere with. The criticism was aimed in particular at the precautionary principle that governed the action of police agencies, and in its place a *conservative* principle of English lineage was favoured. It was argued, proceeding from a French understanding of the way English institutions worked, that government action should be confined to protecting citizens against the infringement of their rights and interests, without preventively reducing the sphere of individual autonomy. It is impossible for lawmakers to foresee and regulate everything, and any attempt to do that would risk choking and poisoning (two physiological metaphors cherished by Quesnay)

the regular course of social life. All of a sudden, the whole regulatory and disciplinary potential of ancient police seemed dangerous. The sovereign therefore
needed to be much wiser and more cautious, exercising great prudence in his
governing activity. But this was no longer the *prudentia civilis* of Aristotelian descent.
The prudence envisioned by the physiocrats ceased to be "a virtue necessary to the
conduct of politics" and became "the art of gauging the effectiveness of government, accurately measuring its limits" (Napoli 2003, 84; see also Mannori and
Sordi 2001, 187). The new art of government was grounded in a principle
of rationality aimed at limiting government interference as far as possible:

> The government of the prince does not, as is commonly thought, consist in
> the art of governing men: It rather consists in the art of guaranteeing their
> security and providing for their subsistence by observing the physical laws
> which govern the natural order of the economy, and through which the
> existence and subsistence of nations and of every individual in particular can
> be guaranteed; once this objective is guaranteed, the conduct of men is fixed,
> and everyone governs himself.
>
> (Mirabeau 1763, xlij, xliij; my translation)

These proposals for deregulation were thus informed by a marked epistemological
scepticism based on the idea that it is impossible for the authorities to foresee and
regulate all matters relating to the economy and society. But this thesis that the
dynamics of the social process by and large fall beyond the scope of sovereign
knowability went along with the principle stating the inviolability of the landed
property which formed the basis of the physiocrats' political philosophy. Indeed,
their economic theory was largely infused with the political themes of natural
law theory, and in this sense their criticism of *police économique* anticipated and supported the liberal political revolution (Tarello 1976, 356–67; Mannori and Sordi
2001, 187; Maffey 1980, 491–530). Physiocracy thus worked together a motley set
of themes, coupling economic principles with epistemological scepticism and
liberal natural law theory, in such a way that its discourse hovered between two
planes: an ontic-analytic plane relative to a sphere of social life that by nature
could not be brought under coercion, and a deontic-philosophical plane that
instead pertained to a sphere of social life that must be kept free from sovereign
intervention. But these two discursive planes did converge in seriously challenging
both the legitimacy and the efficacy of an extensive reliance on police agencies to
intervene in social life. This direct challenge to the classic paradigm of a policed
and disciplined society *(société policée)* served as a strategic tool with which to stake
out a sphere of autonomy for civil society—the domain of the natural freedoms—
in such a way that the competing interests which make up society would finally be
free to self-discipline and self-regulate without the oversight of the authorities
(Napoli 2003, 94).

The deep roots of the physiocratic criticism of the ancien régime's *economic police*
are certainly to be traced to the tangled web of complications stemming from

ancient grain police; the physiocrats certainly seized on the perplexities people had about a policy that failed to prevent speculative schemes and the stockpiling of grain and often wound up fuelling the black market (Olivier-Martin 1951, 624). On the physiocratic conception, price controls had no other effect than to prevent the economy from increasing its output by improving production, the only means through which to ensure plenitude and a thriving market *(bon marché)*. Their liberalization programme enticed the large landowners and everyone who had an economic stake in the land, and even though as early as 1763 it gave start to several efforts to reform ancient police, these reforms did not include the city of Paris, where the local authorities put up a strong resistance.[2] This push toward liberalization found a more resolute official support under the regency of Anne-Robert-Jacques Turgot, who was appointed comptroller general of finances from 1774 to 1776, in which capacity he introduced a systematic plan to reform the *economic police* of the ancien régime, in what was perhaps the first attempt to apply the economic theories advanced by the physiocrats (Border-Marcilloux et al. 1982).

Marking a key moment in Turgot's struggle to liberalize the ancient *economic police* was undoubtedly the *Arrêt du conseil sur la liberté du commerce des grains dans le royaume*, issued on September 13, 1774, whose preamble reads like a proper manifesto of physiocratic economic theory. This provision was short-lived, to be sure—for it was immediately repealed the moment the office of comptroller general was turned over to Turgot's successor, Jacques Necker, who reinstated a moderate dirigiste policy—but while it lasted it did reopen free trade in grain throughout the realm with the single exception of Paris, which was kept under a regime of partial liberalization. Whatever flaws the experiment may have had, it did engage the *parlements* in a debate that brought into focus two different conceptions of the market. One was the traditional conception that went back to the ancient understanding of the socioeconomic functions attributed to police and saw the market as a *physical place* to be kept under surveillance by the authorities so as to guarantee that it is abundantly supplied with commodities available at a fair price; the other was the emergent conception that saw the market not as a physical place to be kept under watch, but as an abstract entity to be investigated, a *principle* governing the functioning of the economy's underlying dynamics (see Foucault 2008, 30–31; Kaplan 1988, 16ff.; Napoli 2003, 78ff.).

---

2 The Parisian *parlement* and police authorities were firmly convinced that deregulation amounted to a leap in the dark. Liberalization was blamed for the rising price of bread, and this in turn provided an opportunity for a new round of challenges, but behind the vague appeal to social justice made in these challenges lay an interest in maintaining an imbalance between the country and the city, an imbalance that ran counter to the interests of the emergent agrarian bourgeoisie. These tensions flared at a general police assembly held in 1768, where the new intellectual vogue in favour of liberalization was openly denounced as a harbinger of social ills, famine, and abuse, and a call was made to reintroduce police regulation of trade in grain (Olivier-Martin 1951, 625; 1948, 345–55).

Not only ancient grain policy but also ancient *labour police* was beginning to attract criticism. This criticism was aimed in particular at guilds for their tendency to shut newcomers out of the trade, a problem compounded by the steep price that apprentices were asked to pay for the title of master tradesman. This often required them to take out a loan with the guild itself, which with equal frequency would withdraw the appointment. Throughout the ancien régime, various ordinances were issued in an attempt to break through this firewall and open the crafts and trades to outsiders (Olivier-Martin 1951, 628). Even in this area the physiocratic conceptions favoured a radical free-market approach, and in 1776 Turgot attempted to pass deregulatory measures such as the one he hazarded in the area of grain commerce. He did so with the *Édit du Roi, Portant suppression des Jurandes & Communautés de Commerce, Arts & Métiers* (Royal edict concerning the suppression of guilds and unions controlling commerce and the crafts and trades), a policy that would not be brought to completion until the French Revolution, under the Le Chapelier Law of June 14, 1791. Turgot's royal edict was aimed at bringing the regulation of commerce and production back within the scope of the *ius commune*, under the regular jurisdiction of the sovereign courts, completely doing away with the corporative system. But the policy came up against opposition from the Parisian *parlement*, which once more took a conservative stance in seeking to preserve the ancient order and proved unwilling to embrace bolder reforms. As discussed, the corporative model had long been serving a crucial function in disciplining the social classes, a function that was now being explicitly reasserted in the challenges the *parlements* were mounting against Turgot's provision.

> The police only has two instruments at its disposal: One is the use of force, which it can resort to only when necessary; the other is the terror it strikes with its vigilance, and it is in virtue of the latter that it governs without anyone taking notice. Being woven into the interstices of a city as vast as Paris, it rests on the intermediate authority of a multitude of domestic guarantors whose power is broader than the city's own, for their surveillance is direct and they command by example.
>
> (Flammermont 1888, 308–24; my translation)

The 1776 reform, by contrast, solemnly asserted every individual's right to work without restrictions, but in so doing it outlined a different model of *labour police*:

> In ensuring the full freedom and competition that commerce and industry require, we will take the measures needed to preserve the public order, in such a way that those who work in different crafts and trades have a known identity and enter those crafts and trades under police protection and discipline.
>
> (Isambert 1826, 379; my translation)

The police had been transformed into an institution entrusted with guaranteeing freedom of industry and work. Its function was now limited to one of formal oversight, a merely conservational function designed to guarantee the conditions on which rests the order resulting from the autonomous movement of social and individual forces. In physiocratic thought, the ancient *economic police* was cut down to size as a tool with which to ensure good faith in commerce, or "truth and security in the market" (Napoli 2003, 118).

However, the physiocratic attack against the apparatus entrusted with the ancient *police économique* was only a chapter, however much a major one, in a larger transformation that was overtaking the entire police function in France in the second half of the 18th century. More to the point, as mentioned, physiocracy was gaining a prominent role as an intellectual and reform movement that set the stage for the great revolutionary upheavals that would break out at the close of the century. Indeed, the process that transformed the *economic police* of the Ancien Régime ran parallel to another process that transformed the concept of administration over the course of the deregulatory efforts made over the same period in the second half of the 18th century, a process that, more generally, invented the administrative space created through the reforms undertaken in the revolutionary season (Mannori and Sordi 2001, 201).

The term *administration* had long been absent from the legal and political lexicon of modern France, but now, in the second half of the 18th century, it was making a comeback, so much so that, as has been argued by Roland Mousnier (1975, 34), the concept was beginning a long resurgence as a result of which it would ultimately replace that of *police* as the main way to designate the sphere of domestic policy and the management of the public good.[3] As much as it may be impossible to pinpoint the exact moment or the one work that marked the changeover, we can agree with Paolo Napoli (2003, 152) that this transition was unfolding by virtue of two fundamental trends: One was the development of the technico-financial knowledge pertaining to the administration of the public good; the other was the parallel development of the science of public law, which in these crucial years— revolving around concepts such as administration, bureaucracy, and police—was beginning an endeavour to progressively juridify the ancient police power. Indeed, in a sense, the shift to a more transparent technique with which to manage public finances can be seen as parallel to the shift that was taking place in legal theory with its assertion of the principle of legality and its attempt to increasingly tie government action to the exercise of legislative and judicial power.

This whole movement found an apt expression in Prost de Royer's definition of *administration*, in which Luciano Mannori and Bernardo Sordi (2001, 153) have located the first attempt ever made in France to define that term with technical rigour. Although de Royer was still working within the classic paternalistic paradigm, his definition ascribed a central role to the concept of delegation, and

---

3 Luciano Mannori and Bernardo Sordi similarly observe that, from the earliest stages of the French Revolution, the term *police* in France would yield to the freshly minted *administration générale* (Mannori and Sordi 2001, 178).

hence to the need to exercise oversight and control over administrative functions. Indeed, as defined in his *Dictionnaire de jurisprudence*, administration was "a proxy, commission, or mandate by virtue of which one is entrusted with preserving the welfare, security, and tranquillity of the individuals who make up a body, *hôpital*, city, or province or an entire state, while also expanding their rights" (de Royer 1782, 809; my translation).

In pre-revolutionary France the conflict among institutional apparatuses, and the attendant difficulties in identifying the relative spheres of competence, gave rise to a situation in which it was at best challenging to draw a distinction between *justice* and *police*. In this context, the idea of an administrative power separate from legislative and judicial power could not yet emerge except as a general idea about the existence of an executive apparatus—an apparatus consisting of offices now separate from their officeholders and therefore coinciding with the idea of a bureaucratic office, an institution that in Prost de Royer's entry for the term *administration* is broken down into three classes depending on the type of relation that holds between an office and the power from which it gets its delegation or mandate.[4] However, even considering the difficulty involved in identifying the nature of the specific function attributed to different public officials—a difficulty as a result of which the entire institutional universe of Ancien-Régime France tended to be brought under a single definition encompassing both judicial power and police officials such as intendants and lieutenants—there clearly emerged the need to bind the exercise of such administration to the law (de Royer 1782, 810). And here, as elsewhere, Prost de Royer made explicit reference to Montesquieu's conception of the separation of powers, a conception that in the following decades would lead political thought to focus on the notions of police, government, and administration.

When political thought finally brought into focus the idea that there existed an administrative power separate from the other spheres of state action, it described that power as empty, entirely subject to the law in force. In virtue of this understanding of administrative power, the sphere of the ancient *police générale* wound up being progressively limited. This can be appreciated even in Montesquieu, who reduced the police apparatus to a sort of residual power tasked with the minutiae of police management. As he wrote in *The Spirit of the Laws*, the police "is perpetually busy with details" and thus "has regulations rather than laws" (Montesquieu [1748] 1989, bk. 26, chap. 24, p. 517). By comparison with the matters addressed by statutory law, which operates at a higher level and is passed in accordance with prescribed formalities, the "business of the Police consists in affairs which arise

---

4 He thus spoke of *administration mobile*, referring to high-ranking fiduciary offices, such as those held by ministers; *administration perpetuelle*, referring to clerical offices, such as those in the ordinary administration of justice; and *administration tournante*, referring to offices filled by commission appointment *(par commission)*, like the majority of the magistracies in the autocratic administration (De Royer 1782, 820–23).

every instant, and are commonly of a trifling nature: there is then but little need of formalities" (ibid., 518). Montesquieu's attitude to police is typical of those who feared the expansion of a sphere of sovereign activity that seemed to threaten the sphere normally attributed to ordinary magistracies. It was thus to be expected that, even in outlining a theoretical conception, these authors should have tended to limit the sphere of public law encapsulated in the idea of *police*, which was perceived as posing a threat to the sphere of relations under private law, which in turn fell within the jurisdiction of the ordinary courts. But this approach to the study of police also signalled the emergence of the merely executive and instrumental conception of government activity that would later be developed by Jean-Jacques Rousseau.

In the "Discours sur l'économie politique," written in late 1754 and published in 1755 in the fifth volume of Diderot and d'Alembert's *Encyclopédie*, Rousseau ([1758] 1964, 239–78) proceeded from a definition of *economics* as the government of the state. The topic was akin to the subject matter customarily treated under the entry *police*, so much so that Rousseau himself would occasionally couple the two notions of *police* and *économie publique*, testifying to the slow transition that these two terms of Aristotelian descent were undergoing in the intellectual discourse of the time. Indeed, government activity was now beginning to be brought under the notion of *économie publique* rather than that of *police*, and for Rousseau—despite the etymology of the term *economy*, with its reference to the government of the household—it would have been a mistake to compare the government of the state to that of the family. Indeed, unlike the family, the state is an *artificial* society created by way of conventions: "In the large family, all of whose members are naturally equal, political authority, purely arbitrary as far as its establishment is conceived, can be founded only upon conventions, and the magistrate can command others only by virtue of the law" (Rousseau [1758] 2012, 23). Political Aristotelianism was thus being criticized by Rousseau as tending to conflate public power with patriarchal power, and from this preliminary criticism Rousseau distilled a definition of the essential aims of government activity. Unlike the paternal government that only follows the dictates of the heart, civil government must strictly adhere to the dictates of the law. Thus Rousseau ([1758] 2012, 125) characterized as follows the role entrusted to the magistrate: "The only rule he should follow is the public reason, which is the law." Here Rousseau introduced another capital distinction, one he would go back to in the *Social Contract*—namely, the distinction between sovereignty and government:

> I ask my readers also to distinguish carefully between the *public economy*, about which I will be speaking and that I call *government*, and the supreme authority that I call *sovereignty*. This distinction consists in the one having the right of legislation and, in certain cases, in placing an obligation on the very body of the nation, while the other has only executive power and can place an obligation only upon private individuals.
>
> (Ibid.)

The political body of the nation was represented through an elaborate organicistic metaphor where the judges and administrators—acting as organs of the selfsame body politic—were given the task of concretizing the political will expressed by the sovereign organ and crystallized in the law:

> The sovereign power represents the head; the laws and customs are the brain, source of the nerves, and seat of the understanding, the will, and the senses, of which the judges and magistrates are the organs; the commerce, industry, and agriculture are the mouth and stomach that prepare the common subsistence; the public finances are the blood that is discharged by a wise *economy*, performing the functions of the heart in order to distribute nourishment and life through the body; the citizens are the body and limbs that make the machine move, live and work.
>
> (Ibid., 125–26)

The law was further described as the will of the political body, a will that had to be closely followed in all government action: "The first and most important maxim of legitimate or popular government, that is to say, of a government that has the good of the populace for its object, is therefore [. . .] to follow the general will in all things" (ibid., 128). It is to law alone that people owe the protection of their rights and privileges; it is to the law alone that rulers and ministers are accountable in performing their functions:

> It is with this voice alone that political rulers should speak when they command; for no sooner does one man, setting aside the law, claim to subject another to his private will, than he departs from the state of civil society, and confronts him face to face in the pure state of nature, in which obedience is prescribed solely by necessity. The most pressing interest of the ruler, and even his most indispensable duty, therefore, is to watch over the observation of the laws of which he is the minister, and on which his whole authority is founded. At the same time, if he exacts the observance of them from others, he is the more strongly bound to observe them himself, since he enjoys all their favour.
>
> (Ibid., 129)

For the first time in the history of French legal and political thought, the entire activity of government was being reduced to the obligation of government officials and administrators to respect the law, understood as being at once the only source of governmental authority, the basic principle for the accountability of administrative action, and the foundation on which rests the protection of individual rights: "I conclude therefore," said Rousseau, "that just as the legislator's first duty is to conform the laws to the general will, the first rule of the public economy is that the administration should be in conformity with the laws" (ibid., 130).

The entry on political economy touched on themes that Rousseau would revisit in his main political work, the *Social Contract*. This is true of the criticism to which he subjected political Aristotelianism and the idea of the natural origin of political society, a discourse he ultimately developed into a fully fledged theory of the contractual, and hence artificial, origin of the state. But even more important, as far as we are concerned, is the basic distinction he drew between sovereignty and government (the former now treated in Book II, devoted to *législation*; the latter now forming the subject matter of the whole of Book III). The distinction is taken directly out of the organicistic metaphor he previously used in the entry on political economy to identify the general will and the law as the source and foundation of the moral force that moves the political body. Government action was now being expressly compared to a physical, executive force placed at the service of the moral force of the law:

> Every free action has two causes that come together to produce it. The one is moral, namely the will that determines the act; the other is physical, namely the power that executes it. [. . .] The body politic has the same moving causes. The same distinction can be made between force and the will; the one under the name *legislative power* and the other under the name *executive power*.
>
> (Rousseau [1762] 2012, 192)

Legislative power belongs to the people, but the same cannot be said of executive power,

> since this power consists solely of particular acts that are not within the province of the law, nor consequently of the sovereign, none of whose acts can avoid being laws. Therefore the public force must have an agent of its own that unifies it and gets it working in accordance with the directions of the general will, that serves as a means of communication between the state and the sovereign, and that accomplishes in the public person just about what the union of soul and body accomplishes in man.
>
> (Ibid., 192)

This is properly the function of government, which has too often been confused with the function specific to sovereign power:

> What then is the government? An intermediate body established between the subjects and the sovereign for their mutual communication, and charged with the execution of the laws and the preservation of liberty, both civil and political.
>
> (Ibid.)

And—further underscoring the need to dilute the ancient *police générale* into the idea of an apparatus tasked solely with mechanically carrying legislative issuances into execution—Rousseau (ibid.) emphatically states the following conclusion: "Therefore, I call *government* or supreme administration the legitimate exercise of executive power; I call prince or magistrate the man or the body charged with that administration."

In several important respects, Montesquieu's attempt to confine the scope of *police* competence to that of details and particulars, and Rousseau's parallel attempt to reduce the government to a merely executive function subject to the law, can be understood as having anticipated the liberal experience at its mature stage in law and politics, an experience through which the discipline that Le Bret still referred to as the science of government would be transformed into a science of public law in the proper sense of the term (Mestre 1985, 175). The administrative apparatus was beginning to fall under the rubric of *bureaucracy* (eliciting in its most outspoken critics the idea of the inertia of a body governed by its own independent logic), and the effort now was to construct that apparatus so as to make it fully subject to the sovereign will as expressed in the legislation. Hence the need to design a decision-making system that located administration at the outermost edge of the provisions of law, reducing it to a mechanism serving the sole purpose of carrying out the will expressed in the law (Napoli 2003, 177). It is not paradoxical that in order for this objective to be achieved, the administrative apparatus had to be reduced to a mere machine lacking any political independence, by locating power in other loci of decision-making authority. In French liberal thought, this neutral apparatus tasked solely with carrying the general will into execution is constructed as having its hands tied behind its back by the law, so much so as to almost become one with judicial power. It must let go of its meta-legal prudential toolkit that anciently enabled police magistrates to exercise the remarkable decision-making power traditionally conferred on them.

A clear testament to this transformation can already be found in that monumental feat of administrative knowledge that was achieved with the two volumes of the *Encyclopédie Méthodique* devoted to *police* and published at the end of the Ancien Régime, when the French Revolution was still raging (Cremer 1989, 11).[5] The two volumes on the subject of *police*, written by Jacques Peuchet, stand as a manifesto against despotism and paternalism and lucidly bear witness to the transformation in the ancient police apparatus that was afoot in France under the influence of the spreading political and economic liberalism. Indeed, as Peuchet wrote in his *discours préliminaire*,

> men are enemies of the constitution; slavery deteriorates them, and everything that may provoke them or incite them to action must be regarded as

5 The publisher of the last volumes of Diderot and d'Alembert's *Encyclopédie* wanted to give the project a more systematic cast and thus committed himself to the prodigious *Encyclopédie Méthodique*, published from 1789 to 1832. The contributions devoted to law were collected under the heading "Jurisprudence," containing the two aforementioned volumes on the subject of *police*. These were put out from 1789 to 1791 and were written by Jacques Peuchet, who was trained as a lawyer and held several offices as a public functionary during the revolution, the empire, and the restoration.

contrary to the first aim that society sets for itself. Freedom and security, by contrast, elevate their souls, unloose their passions, and grow in them the seeds of virtue.

> (Peuchet 1791, XCV; my translation)

Authority is thus charged with favouring that natural human disposition toward freedom, a prominent part of which is the disposition to enjoy the goods acquired by labour:

> It is in order to establish an order among rights and keep the growing volume of competing interests and passions at peace that public power has envisioned a variety of instruments and has handed the primary such instrument to the magistrates entrusted with police.
>
> (Ibid.)

Police activity thus appears to be straightforwardly confined to the function of ensuring the free dynamics of individual interests and protecting rights, and this is especially true of rights to property, which Peuchet sees as forming the basis of social sentiment:

> We have property; we have acquired it through our effort and have made it the foundation of our social rights; from it we expect the wellbeing and sweetness and light afforded by peace; without its influence and the love we bring to it, we would be unable to properly perceive the rights of others and would probably be prompted to encroach on such rights.
>
> (Ibid.)

The worst degeneration of political power derives from its historical role as a tool of social disciplining fashioned after the military apparatus. Its "conduct" and principles, Peuchet went on to say, are "modelled on those of a camp," on the same organization "that keeps a nation under the orders of a sergeant or a drum roll, runs the life of a citizen like that of a soldier, and respects only the will of a military commander in meting out punishments" (ibid., XCVI). The main source of abuse lay in the very structure of the apparatus run by sovereign commissaires, intendants, and lieutenants:

> These magistrates had combined in their person all the rights attributed to the bodies responsible for provincial and municipal administration [. . .], giving rise to abuses of authority and to mistreatments and persecutions whose roots lay in the awkwardness of an outsized administration, in the errors of a vast department, rather than in any personal flaws or in the ambition of those who staffed it.
>
> (Ibid., LVI)

Not incidentally, for the first time a dictionary devoted to *police* included an entry for *bureaucratie*. This was defined from the start as "government, administration, and command for *bureaux*" (Peuchet 1791, 457), and immediately the whole concept was framed in uncompromisingly pejorative terms as consisting in the activity of

> (i) governing, considering that by an abuse at once bizarre and incredible, offices conceived to play a subsidiary role elevate themselves to the status of magistrates, exempting this or that functionary from compliance with the law, or otherwise subjecting citizens to obligations they had no knowledge of; (ii) administering, considering that stupid or compromised commissaries elevate themselves to the status of ministers, use the public purse to engage in peculiar speculations, reform and alter the best regulations, suspend or hinder useful provisions, and the like; and (iii) commanding, considering that the agents of sovereign power are particularly likely to take orders from men incompetent to give them, in connection with both the conduct of military operations and the execution of arbitrary orders. This last kind of abuse runs rampant in the state, from the highest offices to the police offices, which are, as it were, the soul and essence of the despotic system that has governed us for so long.
>
> (Ibid.)

Proceeding from this depiction of the despotism of offices entrusted with police functions—from this vitriolic criticism of the discretionary decision-making power ascribed to these offices within the ancient administrative structure—Peuchet developed the Rousseauvian idea of an administrative apparatus strictly confined to the fulfilment of specific tasks: "As cogs in the machine of politics, bureaus cannot function as its engine. A bureau is not a council, and clerks cannot step into the shoes of administrators and legislators" (ibid.). Administration consists of "a complex of means and agents tasked with maintaining in society a certain order among things, rights, and items of property, whether private or public" (Peuchet 1791, 152, s.v. "administration"). As was previously the case in Rousseau, administration is an exclusively instrumental complex devoid of any political will and is thus kept neatly separate from sovereignty: "The first duty of all administration is to conform to the general will," and this is "the principal rule of conduct imposed on it under the obligations of its own ministry" (ibid.). More than that, administration is deprived of any room for action and any power to discretionarily interpret the law through which the general will is expressed:

> Administration will therefore never conduct itself on the basis of an accessory or expanded meaning of the laws; it will always have to comply with the letter of the law, lest it should upset the established order and act beyond its powers.
>
> (Ibid., 153)

If administration should overstep these boundaries, particularly by failing to respect public freedom, it will "degenerate into a sort of despotic bureaucracy, for everything will be bent to the whims of underlings" (ibid.). A *bureaucratie* so described amounts to no less than "an abusive form of administration, a kind of government whose existence in this form is known only to France" (ibid.); it is based on the work of officials who, on the one hand, should be formed into "passive beings" but, on the other, are free to act like "little despots within their own departments," for they control "legislative and executive power" (Peuchet 1791, 458, s.v. "bureaucratie"). And so, Peuchet asks in this regard,

> is it not disgraceful that the person the nation pays to serve as an instrument of its affairs should install himself as dispenser of favours and grace in place of the sovereign, as arbiter of the citizen's fortunes and of their liberty and honour—precisely in the manner exemplified by police bureaucracy?
>
> (Ibid.)

It was the French Revolution that definitively established the notion of administrative power, when the National Assembly, instituting the local administrative assemblies and separating administrative power from judicial power, isolated the idea of a specific power distinct from both judicial and legislative power. When this administrative power was established—becoming theoretically independent from judicial power, with which it had long been confused—it was made subject to the direct sovereignty of legislative power. At the same time, the broad notion of *police* inherited from the ancient past was brought within the sphere of administration, its function being restricted to that of ensuring and safeguarding the public order (Mannori and Sordi 2001, 213). And here, too, it is Peuchet who bears witness to this transformation in exemplary fashion. Indeed, in his dictionary, the entry for *police* reveals all the influence that the expanding politico-economic liberalism was exerting on the functions and institutions of the ancient police apparatus. And so it came to be that in the late 18th century the police could be described as that "part of the government of the state whose object is to maintain order, keep the peace, and ensure that things public can be freely used" (Peuchet 1791, 637, s.v. "police"). The era of *police générale* had definitely come to a close, and that of *security police* was about to begin.

The date that by convention marks the formal end of ancien-régime police is July 16, 1789, when the last general police lieutenant in Paris, Thiroux de Crosne, tendered his resignation. The revolution, however, did not just put an end to police as an institution: It also marked its end as a model considered to be despotic and arbitrary, by finally subjecting police authority to the rule of law, and in particular by making sure that the police cannot infringe the rights of man and citizen declared in 1789. Indeed, at the National Assembly the issue of reforming the police apparatus and building a new administrative structure was immediately put on the agenda. The debate revolved around the notion of security and the need for the new police to act as a tool with which to guarantee the individual's basic rights and the public peace. The definitive dissolution of the old police apparatus came with the administrative reform enacted in

December 1789 and with the establishment of municipal administrations, to which were attributed all local police powers, and in particular the task of protecting "property and health and the tranquility of public venues and buildings" (Article 50 of the decree issued on 14 December 1789, quoted in Arnold 1979, 19; see also Napoli 2003, 192).

The police born of revolution thus came into being as a body of local administrators elected by different constituencies, an essentially decentralized structure that would remain standing for no more than a few years, until the Reign of Terror. But the significance of the debates and reform projects of this period lies not so much in the institutional arrangements they gave rise to (still uncertain and far from finding the stable forms they would settle into under Napoleon) as in the theoretical conception they provided within which to frame the new police power, in a sense bringing to completion the process through which the ancient idea of *police générale* was taken apart, a process that had got underway with the criticism addressed to the *economic police* of the Ancien Régime. It was therefore in these crucial years that there emerged in France the idea of a *security police*, which would set the theoretical model for the century to come.

The notion of *security police* was first fleshed out in the projects introduced in 1790 at the National Assembly by Adrien Jean-François Duport (1790a, 1790b, 1790c) for the purpose of reforming police and criminal procedure. These projects clearly brought into prominence the idea that *justice* and *police* both contributed in their own way to the task of guaranteeing and protecting the natural and civil rights of the citizen: the rights to life, reputation, security, and property. From the outset, then, police was closely associated with the judicial function of persecuting any attack on these rights (a repressive function); but it was also entrusted with a more general preventive function that made it in a sense independent of judicial power, and in this way a distinctly policial sphere of action was marked out. The reformers were bringing into focus a distinction that would become crucial for modern police, the distinction between the activity of preventing crime and that of guaranteeing public order and security:

> Everything pertaining to the means by which to prevent crimes, promptly restore order, and identify and apprehend those who disrupt it belongs to police. Everything pertaining to the means by which to ascertain the facts on which basis crimes may be prosecuted and the law may be applied essentially belongs to justice.
>
> (Duport 1790a, 101; my translation)

On the conception of those who drew up the reform project, then, the security police served a preventive function that, even as it flanked the strictly repressive function fulfilled by the judiciary, needed to be distinguished from the latter. What the reformers had in mind was a system of interlocking parts. While security pertained to the action taken by society to protect itself from potential assailants and prevent any potential assault, criminal justice served as the tool with which to protect individual rights from the threat of abuses committed in the collective response to crime (Napoli 2003, 204).

At about the same time, a project to reform the organization of judicial and police power was published and presented to the National Assembly by Emmanuel Joseph Sieyès, proposing a strict determination of police functions. More to the point, Sieyès assigned three tasks to police authorities: to prevent crimes and misdemeanours as much as possible; to hunt down the authors of the crimes; and to hand them over to justice. These functions, which he characterized as *prejudicial*, constituted

> police properly so called, or *police générale*, which must not be confused with the administrative police entrusted to the municipalities and to other administrative bodies, nor must it be confused with the purely adversarial or adjudicative police [*la police purement contentieuse*], which cannot be separated from judicial activity.
>
> (Sieyès 1790, art. 6; my translation)

The projects put forward by Duport and Sieyès outlined the basic contours of security police by attempting to secure for the law and for judicial power the ability to include crime prevention among the activities under their control, for that specific activity continued to be perceived as a potential threat to individual liberties (Napoli 2003, 210). The challenge, of course, was to reconcile the need for society to protect itself against possible assaults, if need be by taking preventive measures, with the need to protect the basic rights of the individual. This was a thorny question, to be sure, but a solution might be found by taking a closer look at the perceived causes behind the spiralling crime rates of the time and the increasing threats to the citizens' personal security, and by accordingly looking to two further areas that were being carved out for police as part of its function of keeping the public peace and controlling unruly behaviour. Indeed, next to security police, two areas of police activity were coming into focus which in the debate at the National Assembly tended to be referred to as *municipal police* and *correctional police*. These two areas were clearly identified in the entry that Peuchet devoted to police, where a distinction was drawn between two types of police:

> one that might be called correctional, its object being to contain *persons* within the rules of public peace and imposing merely correctional punishments on them, meaning punishments that do not bring any infamy on them; and another one that only concerns itself with *things* and keeps careful watch over them so as to make sure that they can be freely used in full security; this latter area mainly regulates the care that must be taken to ensure the provisioning of victuals, the cleaning of streets, public illumination, poor relief, and so forth. This is properly the province of municipal police, and in it lies the main function of municipal administrators.
>
> (Peuchet 1791, 673; my translation, italics mine)

These two areas were now being extended so as to cover the extant functions of the ancient *police générale*. On the one hand, this meant undertaking responsibility for governing the territory, ensuring a stable state of affairs, and securing the general peace in the citizens' use of public spaces; on the other, it meant having responsibility over the complex of functions that the general police was anciently entrusted with in its activity of governing the population, which functions included keeping vagrants, idlers, and *gens sans aveu* (the dispossessed) under control; keeping unruly behaviour in check; and ensuring proper familial and social relations.

The creation of a new police system was completed in 1791 with the July 19 passage of the *Décret sur la police municipale et correctionnelle* and the September 16 passage of the *Loi sur la police de sûreté, la justice criminelle et l'institution des jurés*, two documents that definitively laid out the picture of police functions as refashioned by the National Assembly according to a hierarchy moving up from the *municipal police*, charged with keeping the peace, providing security, and ensuring that public venues are properly used; to *correctional police*, charged with managing unruly behaviour and the life of the popular classes and with preventing crime and disorder in general; to the *judicial police*, responsible for repressing crime. Even with all the political regimes the country went through, these would stick as the essential traits of police functions in France in the century to come.

5.2. The decline of *Polizeiwissenschaft*

A similar evolution, leading to a narrowing down of the meaning of *Polizei*, was underway in Germany as well. Thus, for example, in *Institutiones Iuris Publici Germanici*, the leading theorist of public law in the second half of the 18th century, Johann Stephan Pütter, clearly described the police as a mere security apparatus aimed at protecting the personal sphere from accident and attack, and the activity the state carries out under its police powers he described as a simple *cura advertendi mala futura*, the "art of preventing ills"[6] (Stolleis 1998a, 472; Laborier 1999, 24). But, of course, the most radical attack levelled at the notion of police and the philosophical ideal of happiness *(Glückseligkeit)* that had inspired the sciences of the state under the ancien régime came from those who were committed to carrying forward the enterprise of setting German philosophy of law on a new liberal foundation. As is known, this effort to rejuvenate legal and political thought cleared the way for the partial liberalizing trend of the 19th century, a shift that would carry deep theoretical consequences for the sciences of the state even under the ancien régime, and in particular for that *Wohlfahrtspolizei* (social welfare police) that had been the primary theoretico-practical instrument available to government agencies throughout the era of enlightened despotism (Stolleis 2001, 220).

---

6 "Ea suprema potestatis pars, quae exercetur cura advertendi mala futura in statu rei publicae interno in commune metuenda, dicitur politia. Promovendae salutis cura proprie non est politiae" (Pütter 1770, 335).

It is well known that Immanuel Kant proceeded from a different anthropological ideal, one that in certain respects was opposite to that which typified German natural law theory of Wolffian lineage and the literature on *Policey* informed by that theory. Indeed, on the Kantian conception, the strong inclination of humans to form into society did not rule out their mutual antagonism and their tendency to seek their own advantage. In this sense, it was precisely this *unsociable sociability* of individuals that drove social development and accounts for the birth of civil society. Without the egoistic sentiments that move individuals to action, "all man's excellent natural capacities would never be roused to develop" (Kant [1784] 1991, 45). It was on this realistic anthropology that the Kantian conception of law and the state rested, an anthropology which championed individual assertiveness as the engine of progress, and which bore the strong influence of the English-speaking tradition.[7] Government agencies were explicitly being called on to fulfil a coercive function constraining the interaction of individuals so that they could all coexist in civil society even while exercising their full individual discretion and freedom:

> Man, who is otherwise so enamoured with unrestrained freedom, is forced to enter this state of restriction by sheer necessity. And this is indeed the most stringent of all forms of necessity, for it is imposed by men upon themselves, in that their inclinations make it impossible for them to exist side by side for long in a state of wild freedom.
>
> (Kant [1784] 1991, 46)

Law and the state thus exist to guarantee the conditions of constrained freedom enabling individuals to each develop their full potential. The presupposition is that individuals are equipped with an innate ability to manage their lives and shape their individual destinies:

> But the whole concept of an external right is derived entirely from the concept of freedom in the mutual external relationships of human beings, and has nothing to do with the end which all men have by nature (i.e. the aim of achieving happiness) or with the recognised means of attaining this end. And thus the latter end must on no account interfere as a determinant with the laws governing external right. Right is the restriction of each individual's freedom so that it harmonises with the freedom of everyone else (in so far as this is possible within the terms of a general law).
>
> (Kant [1793] 1991, 73)

At the foundation of the Kantian state thus lay (i) the freedom accorded to each member of society as a human being; (ii) the equality of all citizens as subjects of the state; and (iii) the independence that each member of a common body

---

7 On the emergence of the notion of civil society in the German area, see Riedel 1978, 746–67.

enjoys as a citizen (ibid.). It was above all on the basis of the first principle that Kant could develop his celebrated criticism of the eudaemonistic political doctrine on which rested Prussian enlightened absolutism. Indeed, having defined freedom as the right to set the terms of one's own happiness, he could go on to famously equate paternalism with despotism:

> A government might be established on the principle of benevolence towards the people, like that of a father towards his children. Under such a paternal government (*imperium paternale*), the subjects, as immature children who cannot distinguish what is truly useful or harmful to themselves, would be obliged to behave purely passively and to rely upon the judgement of the head of state as to how they ought to be happy, and upon his kindness in willing their happiness at all. Such a government is the greatest conceivable despotism, i.e. a constitution which suspends the entire freedom of its subjects, who thenceforth have no rights whatsoever.
>
> (Kant [1793] 1991, 74)

In Kant, then, the state is reduced to a mere legal structure or legal constitution serving to guarantee individual freedoms understood as issuing from the capacity of humans to freely develop their individual potential. As Norberto Bobbio has commented, the Kantian state under the rule of law is "a state which lacks an ideology of its own—be it religious, moral, or economic—but which, through the order afforded by respect for the law, makes possible the greatest degree of expression and realization for the values and ideologies embraced by individuals themselves" (Bobbio 1957, 228; my translation; see also Stolleis 1982, 367–75). So in no uncertain terms this conception rejected the paternalistic state by offering a fully developed criticism of eudaemonistic philosophy that German thought had hitherto known, and the outcome was a state reduced to the mere function of guaranteeing a purely formal legality devoid of any substantive principle on which the legal system might base the pursuit of happiness.

At about the same time, this criticism of the Prussian police state found a parallel statement in Wilhelm von Humboldt's famous *Limits of State Action*, where the conception of the state as a purely conservational entity, serving no more than a security function, came into its own in a fully developed form:

> It has been from time to time disputed by publicists, whether the State should provide for the security only, or for the whole physical and moral well-being of the nation. Concern for the freedom of private life has in general led to the former proposition; while the idea that the State can give something more than mere security, and that the injurious limitation of liberty, although a possible, is not an essential, consequence of such a policy, has counselled the latter. And this belief has undoubtedly prevailed, not only in political theory, but in actual practice.
>
> (von Humboldt [1792] 1969, 14)

Even in Humboldt, the inevitable basis from which to proceed in mounting a criticism of political eudaemonism lay in an individualistic and liberal anthropology:

> The true end of Man, or that which is prescribed by the eternal and immutable dictates of reason, and not suggested by vague and transient desires, is the highest and most harmonious development of his powers to a complete and consistent whole. Freedom is the grand and indispensable condition which the possibility of such a development presupposes.
>
> (Ibid., 16)

This individualistic principle formed the rational foundation on which to build a theory of law and of the liberal state, and by reference to which to define the limits and scope of the activity of government agencies: "We could proceed to derive the still stricter limitation, that any State interference in private affairs, where there is no immediate reference to violence done to individual rights, should be absolutely condemned" (ibid., 22). Indeed, if the state were to take it upon itself to provide for the wellbeing of citizens, government agencies would so expand their scope of intervention as to stifle the very individual liberty to defend which individuals have formed into society to begin with. The eudaemonistic principle

> invariably produces national uniformity, and a constrained and unnatural manner of acting. Instead of men grouping themselves into communities in order to discipline and develop their powers, even though, to secure these benefits, they may have to forgo a part of their exclusive possessions and enjoyments; they actually sacrifice their powers to their possession.
>
> (Ibid., 23)

As had been the case with Kant, paternalism was here taken as a condition of moral degeneration, reducing individuals to a state of minority which it was incumbent upon them to wrest themselves from:

> The evil results of a too extensive solicitude on the part of the State, are still more strikingly shown in the suppression of all active energy, and the necessary deterioration of the moral character. This scarcely needs further argument. The man who is often led, easily becomes disposed willingly to sacrifice what remains of his capacity for spontaneous action. He fancies himself released from an anxiety which he sees transferred to other hands, and seems to himself to do enough when he looks for their leadership and follows it.
>
> (Ibid., 25).[8]

---

8 As is known, the Enlightenment was characterized by Kant as "mankind's emergence from his self-incurred immaturity," which in turn is understood by him as "the inability to use one's own understanding without the guidance of another" (Kant [1784] 1991, 14).

What followed from this whole argument was the political imperative that the function of the state be limited to a merely negative activity: "The State is to abstain from all solicitude for the positive welfare of the citizens, and not to proceed a step further than is necessary for their mutual security and protection against foreign enemies; for with no other object should it impose restrictions on freedom" (ibid., 37), where by *internal security* was meant "the assurance of legal freedom" (ibid., 84).

In short, in the compact and lucid *Limits of State Action*, Humboldt essentially outlined a conception of the state that overturns the philosophical assumptions underlying *Polizeiwissenschaft*. Perhaps nowhere is this more evident than in the tenth chapter, devoted to police laws. Indeed, Humboldt points out that he is not concerned with "those regulations which do not relate to security, but are directed to the positive welfare of the citizen" (ibid., 86). These regulations should rather be done away with, for they fail to comport with the fundamental principle under which the police should be exclusively concerned with the means for preventing violations of the rights of others and aiding the process of prosecuting such violations. The police institution was thus explicitly squeezed on two sides, for on the one hand it was made an instrument of judicial power, while on the other it was reduced to a security technology entrusted with managing danger:

> In order to provide for the security of its citizens, the State must prohibit or restrict such actions, relating directly to the agents only, as imply in their con-sequences the infringements of others' rights, or encroach on their freedom or property without their consent or against their will; and further, it must forbid or restrict these actions when the probability of such consequences is to be feared—a probability in which it must necessarily consider the extent of the injury feared, and on the other hand the consequences of the restriction on freedom implied in the law contemplated. Beyond this, every limitation of personal freedom lies outside the limits of state action.
>
> (Ibid., 91)

In the years straddling the 18th and 19th centuries, the enlightened reformist surge that in the 17th century had contributed to rejuvenating the institutions of the Prussian state was stopped in its tracks by the reactionary fears that gripped Europe when revolution seemed to be brewing. The final product of the reformist surge was certainly the 1794 *Allgemeines Landrecht für die Königlich-Preußischen Staaten* (General law of the land for the states of the Prussian kingdom), reflecting the enlightened despotism and liberal legal philosophy embraced by Carl Gottlieb Suarez. The Prussian code was meant to authentically open Prussia to the principles of liberal political and legal philosophy by redesigning the political structure around the protection of individual rights, but it would not survive intact the reactionary mood that overtook Europe in the closing years of the 18th century, for, like a Janus-faced creature, it wound up incorporating the ancient corporative or estate structure *(Ständestaat)*.[9] However, as Reinhart Koselleck has argued, for all the backward revisions that undermined the project's original intent, the code still carried historical significance as the first step on the way to institutionalizing the principles of the rule of law, in a process that could be slowed down but not altogether stopped (Koselleck 1981, 30–31). Indeed, the code gave legal recognition to the inviolability of the private sphere, and even though this was still a limited inviolability that could be trumped by the need to serve a higher public purpose, the private sphere now firmly established itself as a de facto interest over which the sovereign could no longer trample at will. The process was still lurching under the pull of opposite forces, to be sure, but for the first time in Prussian history, individuals found themselves firmly protected in legal positions that could not be sacrificed to a notion of the common good conceived independently of what individual interests themselves require.

Suarez's legacy would be picked up by the reformers who sought to modernize Prussia's institutions in the wake of Prussia's defeat to Napoleon in 1806. The reform effort was primarily administrative, to be sure, but it took place on a vast scale, enlisting a whole generation of young men of state set on giving a liberal cast to Prussian society (ibid., 153ff.). Although it was a long and gradual process that brought about this transformation, the attempt was to move Prussia from a state based on an explicitly absolutistic model to a liberal state where citizens could find the opportunities they needed to flourish as individuals. This reform movement in a sense grafted itself onto the discourse begun by Suarez, advancing toward what seemed, by all appearances, to be shaping up as a constitutional reform proper (on these reforms, see also von Unruh 1983b, 399–469). However, the reform and liberalization process did not automatically prompt government agencies to withdraw from the sphere of civil society. Quite the contrary: It was the state itself that stood behind and actively promoted the liberal transformation of the Prussian socioeconomic structure, in a process that was essentially engineered from the top down (Blackbourn and Eley 1984).

One can see here why, even in a context that was increasingly giving a liberal cast to the ancient sciences of the state, these same disciplines continued for a long time to provide technico-theoretical support for the administrative agencies entrusted with the colossal task of modernizing Prussian society (Stolleis 2001, 213–14). The notion of police had already come under the radical philosophical criticism of liberal thought. Likewise, the *Allgemeines Landrecht* seemed to narrow the meaning of police by defining it as an institution serving to "keep the public peace, guarantee order and security, and prevent threats to society in general and individuals in particular" (II, § 17, 10), signalling that police powers were now definitively reduced to a public-security function, and nothing else besides

---

9 Koselleck 1981, 23–51; Tarello 1976, 486–506. The latter source also discusses the theoretical father of Prussian codification, on which topic see also Bussi 1966.

(Lüdtke 1989, 23). At the same time, however, the notion was still being used in a broad sense by administrative authorities. Indeed, in the administrative reform enacted under the ordinance of December 26, 1808, and the *Instruktion* for district administrative organs of October 23, 1817, these organs were explicitly entrusted with the task of providing for the welfare of the citizens, and in such a way as not to confine themselves to guaranteeing public security, so much so that in the provision a series of powers were listed that covered the functions the police apparatus had historically been entrusted with since the 18th century.[10]

In essence, even though the liberal cast of the *Allgemeines Landrecht* seemed to be completely contradicted by the subsequent reforms, the reformist wave had provoked an all but irreversible crisis of the ancient *Wohlfahrtspolizei* (social welfare police). Indeed, as much as Article 7 of the 1817 *Instruktion* continued to invoke classic notions like that of public welfare, it signalled a partial shift in perspective and reflected all the influence exerted by the spread of a liberal political economy. As the provision stated in addressing administrative organs, "No constraint should be put on the ability of individuals to enjoy their property, civil rights, and liberties unless that is necessary to promote the collective good" (quoted in Lüdtke 1989, 42; my translation). What now came into the foreground were individual rights, even if their protection was still in large part contingent on the authorities' discretion in pursuing the higher interests advanced by the government itself.

The 19th century in Prussia was marked not only by its constitutional experiment and its opening to liberalism but also by the birth of its administrative state (Stolleis 2001, 207). The latter development—which ran parallel to the political transition from a state conceived on the model of enlightened absolutism to the liberal *Rechtsstaat*—was part of a broader process through which what had traditionally been the single, cohesive body of the administrative sciences splintered into a family of numerous different disciplines. As discussed, this process is evidenced by the breakup of the unitary discourse proper to the *Polizeiwissenschaft* of ancient tradition into the different discourses through which the science of public law and modern political economy developed, and this transition is reflected as well in the development of academic curricula, which over the same period tended to split into two broad areas, one pertaining to law and politics, the other to society and the economy (Lindenfeld 1989, 141–59; Stolleis 2001, 209).

Even in Germany, where economic matters were mostly addressed by academic disciplines devoted to the sciences of the state, the liberalizing currents of economic thought also resonated outside academia. Several translations were made of the physiocratic works, even if they could only be met with lukewarm reception in an environment where economic thought was still under the sway of the cameral sciences (Tribe 1988, 119–31). Similarly, Adam Smith's *Wealth of Nations*, translated into German in the very year it was published in English, was all but ignored by the German thinkers at least until the end of 1790, when the spread of liberal

---

10 An excerpt of the provision can be found in the appendix to Lüdtke 1989, 206.

political philosophy created the cultural conditions in which Smith's thought, and in particular his individualistic anthropology, could find a more welcome reception (ibid., 153–56). When interest developed in Smith's work in Germany, its effect on economic thinking was in the long run transformative, for even though German economic science remained anchored in the discourse of public economics, or *Staatswirthschaft*, it was beginning to ponder the existence of a system of natural needs proper to civil society apart from the action of government agencies, thus limiting the function of the state, at least formally, to that of securing the conditions necessary to satisfy those needs (ibid., 160–66; Steiner 1990, 1081–86). This limitation was only partial, often accompanied by a long list of public functions that in effect rebuilt the frame of the ancient *economic police*, and, by the same token, the uptake of the new epistemological models was quite eclectic—but for all that, these models did make their way into the classic discourse, and a shift away from the latter was clearly underway.

The first clear sign of this epistemological shift that would lead to the foundation of modern political economy even in Germany came with the work of Ludwig Heinrich von Jakob (von Jakob 1805), who explicitly set out to expel from the study of economics all things having to do with police and the management of finances. In his lexicon, the term *public economics* was set in contrast to *National-Ökonomie*, highlighting that the new science was concerned with the sphere of civil society, an autonomous sphere protected from the state's intervention, where the creation and distribution of wealth took place according to a natural dynamic that the new discipline undertook to investigate. The first section of his treatise was nothing short of a manifesto of politico-economic liberalism based on ten key points. As Jakob saw the matter, the main reason that individuals enter into civil society is to live happier lives in conditions of greater security. The means by which to attain happiness in life, to the extent that humans can acquire such means, lie in part in the private powers each person is possessed of, and in part in the public and in the combined powers of the state. A happy life depends in large part on the extent to which the means by which to satisfy human needs are available. These means are produced by the members of the nation, and in them lies the wealth of the nation. The first condition for acquiring and increasing such national wealth is that individuals need to be secure in their person and property, and only where they lack the resources or private powers needed to come by and increase their wealth is public power called on to intervene. It is to this end that the state is set up, and its action can never conflict with its task of protecting and growing the national wealth. Among the other tasks entrusted to the state are those of protecting and defending the citizens' legal claims, guaranteeing their security, and promoting the general welfare of the nation, and these tasks Jakob associates with *Policey* (ibid., secs. 1–9, 1–4).

Capping off this introductory discussion was a general definition of *National-Ökonomie* as the discipline devoted to investigating (i) the means through which the population, under the protections afforded by government, achieve their aims, chief among which is to acquire, increase, and enjoy property; (ii) the way in which national wealth grows and is distributed, used, reproduced, and maintained; and (iii) the influence that the different circumstances and affairs of the state can have on the forgoing (ibid., secs. 4 and 10). It was Jakob's specific intent to follow in the footsteps of Smith in laying out this definition, and in particular in distinguishing public economics as a branch of the science of government from the theory of the creation, distribution, and use of wealth in civil society. In this, he was the first German author to recognize the need to distinguish economic knowledge from the more general sciences of the state, a distinction that would progressively be formalized over the course of the 19th century. But in this early part of the century the economic science was not yet fully developed. As long as the state's intervention in civil life continued to be so extensive as to require officials and administrators to receive specific training in public economics, the only chance for the principles of *National-Ökonomie* to develop was by carving out a space for themselves in an environment shaped by the dominant influence of *Staatswirtschaft* (Tribe 1988, 176).

At the same time, the ancient police science was slowly evolving into a legal discipline devoted to the study of what was still being defined as police law, becoming part of the curriculum taught at law schools. Running parallel to this juridification process was the conceptual evolution that was giving rise to *Verwaltung*, the generic term for the idea of the state's internal administration (Bödeker 1989, 15–32). The administrative reforms and the growing juridification of the administrative apparatus was increasing the demand for functionaries with some legal training under their belt; the ancient experts in the sciences of the state were thus being turned into experts on police law or, as it was beginning to be called, administrative law. Despite a growing push to provide future functionaries with legal training, law schools were still not placing much emphasis on the study of public law. The study of the ancient imperial constitution, or *Reichpubblicistik*, no longer carried any practical relevance, and the study of the politico-legal constitutions in effect in the territorial states could seem a politically sensitive subject, especially in those states, such as Prussia, that still lacked a constitution. What began to emerge was instead the study of the law that the administrative agencies were responsible for applying every day, a study that was turning increasingly practical, for that was the nature of administration itself (Stolleis 2001, 211).

The treatment of legal questions had been rather episodic in treatises on *Polizeiwissenschaft*. The function of police laws was instrumental, in that they served as means by which to carry out *gute Policey*. When the more strictly legal aspects of administrative work needed to be addressed, this happened in works fashioned after the model of the lawbook collecting all the statutory and regulatory sources pertaining to police subject matter, often without any attempt at systematization.[11]

---

11 One example is Johann Heumann von Teutschenbrunn's *Initia iuris politiae Germanorum*, published in Nuremberg in 1757, and the treatises that followed its example, such as Von Hohenthal's *Liber de Politia*, published in Leipzig in 1764, and Friedrich Christoph Jonathan Fischer's three-volume *Lehrbegriff sämtlicher Cameral- und Policey-Rechte*, published in Halle in 1785.

These were in essence practical guides designed to aid functionaries in their administrative work, while making it possible to exercise greater control over the administrative apparatus, which had to operate under efficiency criteria framed in legal terms. The fixing of administrative procedures in a sort of police law *(Policeyrecht)* was thus essentially meant to serve the internal purpose of exercising oversight of an activity that the administrative apparatus was solely competent to judge.

As the treatment of *Policeyrecht* became more systematic, it steered toward the liberal tendencies of the period in subjecting administrative activity to a more stringent legal control. In this way police science progressively unmoored itself from the study of police law, a law that in the meantime, in line with the design of the *Allgemeines Landrecht*, was beginning to recognize a private legal sphere in which the state could interfere only in exceptional cases. One of the first contributions to attempt a systematization of police law, Günter Heinrich von Berg's (1799–1809) *Handbuch des Teutschen Policeyrechts* (Handbook of German police law), did not entirely part with the ancient idea of *Wohlfahrtspolizei* (social welfare police) but did try to confine police to the function of guaranteeing internal security (Stolleis 1998a, 588–89). Informing Berg's handbook was the moderate liberalism that would characterize Prussian reformism, holding on to the idea that public power needs to be concerned with population policy, but at the same time beginning to demand that authorities intervene much less intrusively in the nation's economic and commercial life. A typical feature of this moderate liberalism was its tendency to constrain the activity of police power within strict legal limits that took on a quasi-constitutional force (Stolleis 1998a, 590).

In the broader scheme of things, in essence, the need to protect the security of private rights was beginning to outweigh the more general need to promote the public good, even if this latter concern could not entirely disappear from the theoretical framework, considering that for a long time the authorities would continue to claim a vast scope of intervention in their effort to modernize Prussia (Stolleis 2001, 221; Maier 1966, 218). Soon, however, in the changed political landscape of the 19th century, the tendency to encase administrative activity within a legal framework naturally led to the demand that the administrative apparatus be subject to external oversight, and hence to a more clearly defined set of public legal parameters.

This growing awareness of the need to provide a legal framework for the administrative apparatus and to subject its activity to legal oversight thus pushed the ancient police sciences into decline (Stolleis 2001, 217), a decline reflected in the way the academic curriculum began to change from 1850, with the phasing out of the ancient disciplines such as cameralism and the sciences of the state so as to make room for the courses on *Verwaltungsrecht*, or administrative law (Stolleis 2001, 213; Lindenfeld 1989, 154). The foundation of a state based on the rule of law necessarily had to enact a progressive juridification of police science, turning this science into a legal discipline on a par with the science of administrative law. Only in the second half of the 19th century would this juridification be fully accomplished, with the establishment of the administrative courts in keeping with the French model and the publication of Otto Mayer's *Deutsches Verwaltungsrecht*, where administrative science had already become a science of public law (Lindenfeld 1989, 154–55).

We previously saw how this long decline of the ancient sciences of the state provided the backdrop to the debate on the nature of police and the proper scope of its meaning and hence of its activity. As can be appreciated, then, this debate carried huge political implications, for depending on how broadly or narrowly the term was defined, the powers and activity of the state in this area would have to be framed accordingly, and a corresponding constitutional model would also have to follow. As much as the ancient themes persisted, liberal political philosophy dealt a significant blow to the ancient eudaemonistic philosophy that had formed the basis of the police sciences, and as the liberal political programme moved forward, the ancient idea of public wellbeing receded into the background, yielding to the idea of security and to the accompanying assumption that the state should step into the role of protecting private rights.

Even so, the theoretical framework built around *Polizeiwissenschaft* continued to thrive. It still formed a core part of the academic curriculum, continuing to shape the training of future functionaries, while at the same time finding further philosophical backing in the idealist theoretico-political project set out by Hegel.[12] Then, too, *Polizeiwissenschaft* continued in a sense to respond to the needs of an administrative apparatus that had itself taken on the task of moulding society into a liberal cast (Lindenfeld 1989, 145). The theoretical solution adopted to reconcile the emergence of a liberal political philosophy with the model of the ancient police sciences consisted in reinterpreting the ancient concept of wellbeing as the foundation on which to legitimize the activity of the state in its effort to clear away the obstacles to the free development of individual personality. Far from being a datum for which the state had only to provide a security guarantee, freedom was still conceived as the end product of the administrative agencies' action.

The greatest interpreter of this vision was no doubt Robert von Mohl, whom Michael Stolleis describes as the Adam Smith of police science (Stolleis 2001, 229), for in his main work he articulated the original liberal motif of the *Rechtsstaat* as a state whose only purpose is to protect the individual sphere. To be sure, his systematic treatment of police science *(Polizeiwissenschaft)* is built on top of the traditional blueprint laid out by Justi, so much so that Mohl took up the ancient

---

12 Hegel, as is known, saw a close relation between police and corporative entities. Indeed, on his conception, the estates form the second basis of the state (Hegel [1821] 1991, § 201, p. 234), this for their ability to counterbalance the atomism of society, a function they can play as intermediate moments in the transition from the family to the state as a superior organic entity. In this way, Hegel provided a fresh theoretical basis on which to rest the 18th-century model of welfare police (see also Neocleous 1998a, 43–58).

idea of the need to provide for the citizens' wellbeing, which may not be the main thrust of the discussion, but the idea is still there. So, for example, Mohl argued that the state's action covers "the entire arc of a man's life," and he even theorized an active function of the state aimed at realizing the conditions that may favour a full development of individual capacities and rights. But he did this in a distinctly nonpaternalistic way, entrusting to the state the task of "arranging the collective life of the population in such a way that every single member of it can receive protection and fully realize himself by putting his overall strengths to use in the freest and broadest possible way" (von Mohl 1833, sec. 8; my translation). A statement of this kind offers a perfect synthesis whereby the themes of liberal political and philosophical thought are worked into the 18th-century tradition of the administrative sciences, which in the early decades of the new century was being asked to provide the technical support needed to carry out the programme for reforming Prussian society. This active, concretely productive function of the state was merged by Mohl with the ancient notion of police, defining the latter as

> the complex of institutions and orders whose aim is to foster the development of human capacities, to this end bringing public resources to bear so as to remove all obstacles to such development when those obstacles cannot be overcome by relying on private resources alone.
>
> (Ibid., sec. 3)

In this case, too, an overt effort is made to move away from the ancient notion of wellbeing. Indeed, as Michael Stolleis has commented, the more security was held up as the basic aim of the state, and the more the state was set in opposition to public liberties, the less it made sense to embrace happiness *(Glückseligkeit)* as the overarching aim of the state's activity. Not only did happiness become a hated symbol of absolutism among liberals, but it also began to be disavowed by conservatives themselves (Stolleis 1993, 67). Even so, Mohl sought to strike a balance between government action and private rights, framing the police as a complementary institution having the merely auxiliary role of supporting individuals when they are no longer free to enjoy the autonomy guaranteed by the rule of law. The police was thus conceived as a *security technology*, but in this role it was more than just a tool at the service of judicial power, for it was entrusted with sustaining the dynamic of individual freedoms that formed the basic condition of personal and societal development. Its job was to bring about or *produce*, as it were, that condition of freedom absent which it would be impossible for society to flourish or for individuals to bring out their full potential. It was from this conception of police and of the aims of government action that Mohl proceeded to reconstruct an organic science of the state capable of taking in the political phenomenon in its entirety—a project that in several respects went back to the ideal of the unity of the ancient police sciences, but did so setting those sciences on a renewed philosophical and political foundation.

5.3. Liberal police

In England, where political and legal liberalism got in the way of mercantilist *economic police*—stifling its theoretical and practical development, even as far back as the 17th century, by nipping in the bud a still unripe police apparatus—the meaning of the terms derived from the Greek *politeia* wound up increasingly eluding the legal and political debate. The term *police* inevitably came to be understood as closely associated with the idea of absolute power, an idea which sinisterly conjured up that of the sovereign prerogative the Glorious Revolution had sought to neutralize, a prerogative tied to the constitutional setup typical of Continental Europe that the English in the late 17th and early 18th centuries felt to be quite removed from their own tradition. So deeply rooted was that sentiment of remove that the term eventually fell into disuse, to the point where *Johnson's Dictionary*, of 1755, underscored its French derivation. Indeed, there was no longer any institutional referent in England that one could point to in illustrating the meaning of the term *police* to designate the general activity of governing a country's socioeconomic life, and so the term gradually retreated from political and legal parlance, so much so as to all but disappear from everyday parlance, too (Radzinowicz 1956, 1).

By the mid-18th century the ancient term *police* was already making its way back into the English language, and even though it was a slow resurgence, the effect would be to fundamentally alter the very nature of modern police. Indeed, when the term came back into use it found a sociopolitical context that had in the meantime been revolutionized by economic development and the Industrial Revolution, as a result of which the ancient police measures of *economic police* that typified mercantilist and manufactural proto-capitalism fell out of use, ushering in the era of modern industrial capitalism. In this socioeconomic context marked by the start of powerful urbanization and industrialization processes, it was the plight of the popular classes, and the attendant need to design social policies on which basis to govern them, that provided the seedbed on which police theory could flourish anew. The epistemological development of the budding science of economics would form the basis on which to lay out the model of government rationality that would distinguish liberal politico-social philosophy, but even more importantly it would foreground the problem of governing the popular classes in a liberal society.

Far from being entrusted with the mere task of managing the shortcomings of a socioeconomic structure based on corporative entities, as had traditionally been the case, the new liberal police was now being designed to govern the social consequences of the void left by the definitive demise of that ancient social structure. In this context, the term *police* developed along two parallel tracks, for on the one hand it was taken up critically by Adam Smith as the foundation stone of modern economic reason, and on the other it was revived by the modern reformers of the London police, who gave it a narrower sense than the one ascribable to the ancient idea of policy. Let us now trace out the trajectory that political economy and the London police reformers followed in constructing, albeit not fully consciously, the liberal police model that would firmly establish itself in 19th-century England.

5.3.1. Police and the birth of economic reason

In the phase where police powers reached their greatest expansion, policy and economics were progressively melded into each other, this by proceeding from the basic assumptions of a political and social philosophy that identified the *state of prosperity* with the *prosperity of the state*, as Mark Neocleous (2000a, 14) has aptly described the situation. When economic thought came upon the discovery of the market as the principle by which to explain the dynamic underlying the nation's socioeconomic life, ancient *economic police* slipped irreversibly into crisis and was finally put out of service when modern political economy grew to epistemological maturity, giving birth to its classic paradigm, an event that by convention is made to coincide with the 1776 publication of Adam Smith's *Wealth of Nations*.

Even more important to Adam Smith than his economic theory was his work in moral and legal philosophy, so much so that he proposed to follow up his 1759 *Theory of Moral Sentiments* by developing a system of natural jurisprudence, a proposition he would never be able to make good on, even though in the mid-1700s he devoted academic courses to the subject at the University of Glasgow. As much as these *Lectures on Jurisprudence* may have been a work in progress, however, they do suggest the overall scheme of what would have been his contribution to the philosophy of law.[13] The *Lectures*, especially those for the 1762/63 and 1763/64 academic years, mark the occasion on which the concept of *police*—after a long leave of absence—makes its first appearance in an English text on legal and political philosophy. Indeed, as mentioned, the term had practically lapsed into disuse in the learned English of the 17th century, so much so that Smith repeated the commonplace that *police* was a loanword: "*Police*, the word, has been borrowed by the English immediately from the French, tho it is originally derived from the Greek πολιτεια, signifying policy, politicks, or the regulation of a government in generall" (Smith [1763] 1982).

Police is treated by Smith as part of his discussion of jurisprudence—defined as the "theory of the rules by which civil governments ought to be directed" (ibid.)—and so as part of a broader discussion of law and the state.[14] The discussion is organized around four functions that in order of importance he ascribed to the government. The first of these functions is *justice*, whose purpose is "to prevent the members of a society from incroaching on one anothers property, or siezing what is not their own" (ibid.); stated in even more general terms, this is the function of

---

13 On Smith's Glasgow lectures, see Zanini 1997 and Haakonssen 1981.
14 On police in Adam Smith, see Porta 1988, 37–68, and Neocleous 1998b, 425–49.

ensuring the state's "internall peace," a broad heading under which Smith takes up all the classic themes of ancient *iurisdictio* as revisited by legal thought in its modern liberal form. The second function is that of *defence*, which consists in ensuring the existence of the state, considering that the latter "cannot give security unless the government can defend themselves from foreign injuries and attacks" (ibid.); indeed, external threats are no less serious than internal ones, for they undermine not only the security of private citizens but the very existence of the state (ibid.). The third function he turns to is *finance*, considering that the internal peace and external security of the state make it necessary to construct complex apparatuses, which in turn need to be managed by public finance.

The fourth function is that of *police*, under which heading the government is entrusted with "promoting the opulence of the state" (ibid.). As Smith writes: "This produces what we call police. Whatever regulations are made with respect to the trade, commerce, agriculture, manufactures of the country are considered as belonging to the police" (ibid.). At least initially, then, the definition of *police* from which Smith proceeded belongs with the classic governmental arts and the science of the state that grew out of the experience of Continental Europe under the ancien régime, so much so that in laying out his argument on police, Smith looks to the famous three-pronged summation of police functions which in the 1667 decree instituting the office of lieutenant in Paris were entrusted to this newly established position: *neteté*, *sûreté*, and *bon marché*. The first of these, *neteté*, or public cleanliness, is dismissed by Smith as "too mean to be considered in a general discourse of this kind" (ibid.). He thus turns directly to the second area of police activity, that of *sûreté*, or security, which he divides in two parts: one pertaining to the security of places, the other to protection from injuries and crimes and the punishment of those who are responsible for them. In this latter case, we are looking at police strictly construed as a preventive and repressive (prosecutorial) apparatus set up to support regular judicial activity, and indeed Smith suggests that this "may be called the justice of police" (ibid.). But even this topic struck him as not worthy of being taken up. What did appear to him as worthy of discussion was the third prong in the tripartite division of police functions, where the government was entrusted with ensuring *bon marché*:

> The third part of police is bon marché or the cheapness of provisions, and the having the market well supplied with all sorts of commodities. This must include not only the promoting a free communication betwixt the town and the country, the internall commerce as we may call it, but also on the plenty or opulence of the neighbouring country. This is the most important branch of police and is what we shall consider when we come to treat of police.
>
> (Ibid.)

Smith's *Lectures* thus seem to draw on the intellectual tradition of the Continental politico-economic sciences, which, as noted, tended to closely associate the state of prosperity with the prosperity of the state. However, in treating police he did not espouse the basic tenets of ancient mercantilist *economic police* but turned them on their head, making the prosperity of the state a condition of civil society understood as the outcome of the spontaneous interplay of social forces. Indeed, mercantilist police is explicitly characterized by him as "bad policy" (ibid.), precisely because it pretends to control the natural dynamic of economic processes that Smith is beginning to bring to light.

Smith thus proceeded from the ancient governmental arts and from the concept of police that typified the Continental experience, but even in his *Lectures on Jurisprudence* he sets out to empty them of their meaning, beginning to challenge the basic premises of ancient *economic police*, eventually turning it into the discipline that in *An Inquiry into the Nature and Causes of the Wealth of Nations* he would call *political economy*. Indeed, although in this latter work, and in particular in Book IV, titled "Of Systems of Political Economy," he reiterated almost to a tee the themes and theses that in his *Lectures* he had previously developed under the heading *police*, this latter term would now disappear from sight, and it was the concept of *political economy* that would take its place. But even the concept of political economy did not completely sever its ties with the ancient police out of which it originated. The connection it bore to its theoretical matrix can be appreciated in its very definition:

> political economy, considered as a branch of the science of a statesman or legislator, proposes two distinct objects: first, to provide a plentiful revenue or subsistence for the people, or more properly to enable them to provide such a revenue or subsistence for themselves; and secondly, to supply the state or commonwealth with a revenue sufficient for the public services. It proposes to enrich both the people and the sovereign.
>
> (Smith [1776] 1843, bk. IV, p. 173)

Political economy is thus the science of the statesman, as was the case with the ancient police science, but here the statesman or legislator is explicitly asked to give up any pretence of steering the country's social and economic life, for the job at hand is rather more limited: It is to support a system of perfect liberty by creating the conditions that will enable everyone to secure a livelihood. The notion that the political and economic process can be engineered in light of the state's policy objectives seems not only an illegitimate intrusion into the sphere of everyone's natural freedom of action, but also a vain pretence, considering that even in physiocratic thought the realization had been made that any attempt to alter the natural dynamic of economic processes would not only come to naught but would even be counterproductive. Writes Smith in this regard:

> Every man, as long as he does not violate the laws of justice, is left perfectly free to pursue his own interest his own way, and to bring both his industry and capital into competition with those of any other man, or order of men. The sovereign is completely discharged from a duty, in the attempting to perform which he must always be exposed to innumerable delusions, and

for the proper performance of which no human wisdom or knowledge could ever be sufficient; the duty of superintending the industry of private people, and of directing it towards the employments most suitable to the interest of the society.

(Smith [1776] 1843, bk. IV, chap. IX, p. 286)

At this point Smith turns to the functions of the state, essentially taking up the considerations he made in his previous *Lectures* but striking out any reference to *police*:

According to the system of natural liberty, the sovereign has only three duties to attend to; three duties of great importance, indeed, but plain and intelligible to common understandings: first, the duty of protecting the society from violence and invasion of other independent societies; secondly, the duty of protecting, as far as possible, every member of the society from the injustice or oppression of every other member of it, or the duty of establishing an exact administration of justice; and, thirdly, the duty of erecting and maintaining certain public works and certain public institutions which it can never be for the interest of any individual, or small number of individuals, to erect and maintain.

(Ibid.)

In the *Wealth of Nations*, however, Adam Smith's criticism of the ancient mercantilist *economic police* importantly introduces another novel element with respect to his *Lectures on Jurisprudence*. For in addition to expunging a concept like that of police, which in the lectures already loses much of its theoretical significance, the *Wealth of Nations* marks the moment when Smith appreciates the important role that wage work and a free labour market play in a capitalistic economy. Indeed, the *Wealth of Nations* elaborates on the basic principles of economic reason previously laid out in the Glasgow *Lectures*, which discuss the law of supply and demand on the market as the basis on which to explain the formation of the prices of commodities. In Book I, Chapter VIII, titled "Of the Wages of Labour," the same principles are applied to that peculiar commodity which is labour. Smith can thus describe the economic processes by virtue of which the price of labour is set. He does so by bringing the law of supply and demand to bear on the labour market, thus arguing that labour actually behaves like any other commodity, for it is the *demand* for labour that induces the market to up its *supply* of labour, this by accelerating demographic growth, and, vice versa, a greater supply of labour will bring down demand and adjust prices accordingly:

If this demand [for labour] is continually increasing, the reward of labour must necessarily encourage in such a manner the marriage and multiplication of labourers, as may enable them to supply that continually increasing demand by a continually increasing population. If the reward should at any time be less than what was requisite for this purpose, the deficiency of hands would soon raise it; and if it should at any time be more, their excessive multiplication would soon lower it to this necessary rate. The market would be so much understocked with labour in the one case, and so much overstocked in the other, as would soon force back its price to that proper rate which the circumstances of the society required.

(Ibid., bk. I, chap. VIII, p. 33)

On the threefold basis just sketched out—namely, the idea that (i) the labour market is governed by its own dynamics, which lie in the interplay between supply and demand; that (ii) this interplay sets the price of labour (wages); and that, therefore, (iii) a free supply of labour is needed that can adjust to those forces by virtue of the labour force either contracting at will or expanding by population growth—the powerful criticism raised by political economy would fall on *social police* as well. This criticism took its cue precisely from Adam Smith, and in particular from the stance he took against any policy requiring that the natural dynamics of the labour market be altered, by restricting access to the trades and professions or by restricting the free movement of labour. The criticism thus targeted two of the pillars of mercantilist social policy: One was the discipline that governed apprenticeships and the control the guilds exercised over access to the trades; the other was the discipline that governed the management of the poor, and in particular the principle that each community is responsible for its own poor, for on this basis the free flow of labour was choked, causing wage imbalances from place to place. Writes Smith in this regard:

The very unequal price of labour which we frequently find in England in places at no great distance from one another is probably owing to the obstruction which the law of settlements gives to a poor man who would carry his industry from one parish to another without a certificate.

(Ibid., bk. I, chap. X, p. 59)

Except for that criticism expressly aimed at the Settlement and Removal Act (also known as the Poor Relief Act 1662), the *Wealth of Nations* did not directly concern itself with questions relating to the poor laws. Its analysis of the labour market did, however, proceed from a bioeconomic principle that would become the basis of the entire subsequent debate on welfare reform (Dean 1991, 123). Indeed, having described the dynamics by which wages are set, Smith immediately made a remark, almost in passing, whose import would be nothing short of revolutionary: "It is in this manner that the demand for men, like that for any other commodity, necessarily regulates the production of men; quickens it when it goes on too slowly, and stops it when it advances too fast" (Smith [1776] 1843, bk. I, chap. VIII, p. 33). Certainly, he was calling the attention of economic and social thinkers to the central role of a freely available labour supply, but in pointing to the basic principle that governed the dynamics of the labour market and the relation between wages and the demographic process, he was at the same time laying the groundwork for the bioeconomic principle that would frame the whole discussion on social policy that would follow.

Smith essentially turned the pauper into an economic agent like any other. No longer objects of administrative action or of social policy, the poor would henceforth be holders of an asset—namely, their own labour—that could be freely bought and sold on the open market (Dean 1991, 135); without any going back, they were newly turned into wage workers, into the *labouring poor* of an ideal society that poses no hindrance to the buying and selling of labour on the market or to its free movement. This unchecked freedom further became the condition necessary to ensure the right balance among demographic trends, the cost of labour, and the available means of subsistence, a balance that in turn formed the basis for the prosperity and strength of the nation. It is therefore in Smith that we find the first suggestion of the idea of poverty as the condition common to all those persons whose livelihood depends entirely on their ability to sell their own labour on the open market, and who in virtue of that exchange activity find themselves subject to the bioeconomic laws that govern the relation between demographic trends and the development of the forces of production. This idea stood in direct contrast to that of the poor as agents in the care of administrative police bodies, and so as agents to be restored to a condition of productive activity (ibid., 137).

The *Wealth of Nations* marks the end of the *discourse of the poor*, while ushering in what Mitchell Dean (1991) has aptly defined the *constitution of poverty*. At the same time, the conception put forward in this seminal work was also the first to undermine the populationist assumption that for over two centuries had stood unchallenged as the centrepiece of the theory behind the art of government. Smith, in essence, effected nothing less than an epistemological revolution in our thinking about the population. Indeed, the governmental arts and the police sciences had historically focused all of their attention on the question of governing the population, conceiving the latter as an object to be tended to by administrative activity. In the discourse of the classic police sciences, the population was the product obtained by the exercise of political and governmental rationality (Foucault 2004, 93; Pandolfi 2006, 93ff.); the *liberal* arts of government, by contrast, advanced a new way of conceiving the population, by proceeding from the assumption that the processes by which the life of the population is governed lie beyond the scope of what can be brought under the control of administrative action (Dean 1999, 108). The population, in other words, is no longer understood as an object amenable to the direct action of government agencies but is rather approached as a complex element resulting from the interaction that takes place among a whole set of variables (environmental, climatic, social, cultural, and so forth) that filter the ability to politically govern their dynamics.

5.3.2. The principle of population

The first criticisms expressly aimed at the model of ancient social policy came as early as the beginning of the 18th century, and, as is known, the first and most influential of these criticisms was the one that Daniel Defoe ([1704] 1970) raised in his *Giving Alms No Charity, and Employing the Poor a Grievance to the Nation*.[15] To be sure, Defoe's discussion was still in certain respects based on classic populationist assumptions, so much so that he started out with a eulogy in praise of Elizabethan social policy (Dean 1991, 43). But at the same time Defoe recognized that the socioeconomic landscape he was dealing with had quite appreciably changed:

> The manufactures of England are happily settled in different corners of the kingdom, from whence they are mutually convey'd by a circulation of trade to London by wholesale, like the blood to the heart, and from thence disperse in lesser quantities to the other parts of the kingdom.
>
> (Defoe [1704] 1970, 17–18)

In this context, it would have done more harm than good to the prosperity of the nation to put up workhouses and launch public-works projects, for that would amount to rewarding a vagrant with the job that should belong to an honest worker (Dean 1991, 47; Himmelfarb 1984, 26). But rather than advocating a free labour market, his argument looked like an attempt to keep intact the manufacturing industry of the time, in such a way as not to upset the order achieved through previous policies. Defoe's argument led to the conclusion that in the English manufacturing system it made no sense to stipulate the existence of a class of able-bodied and willing workers who nonetheless, through no fault of their own, lacked the means they needed to support themselves: "Tis the men that won't work, not the men that can get no work which makes up the numbers of the poor" (Defoe [1704] 1970, 27). Poverty was still conceived as a condition ascribable to the individual's moral baseness and lack of discipline, to a temperament and cast of mind distinctive not only to vagrants proper but also to the popular classes at large, considering that they tended to give in to vice, squandering their means of livelihood even in good economic times, when the labour market seemed to offer opportunities for work (Dean 1991, 45).

Even if Defoe worked within a theoretical frame that was essentially the same as that of the discourse of poverty, he was in many respects beginning to move away from the trope of the idler or vagrant, with the attendant anxiety about the social and territorial mobility of the poor. In its place he was bringing in the image of the worker wasting his time at the inn, where he can fall prey to the moral turpitude of drinking, gambling, and other forms of entertainment, which in turn may act as a gateway to political activity, and hence to subversion. We thus have the first realization that the social disruptions brought about by the spread of the modern capitalist and manufacturing economy carry profound implications from which there was no going back, and therefore that the effort would have to go into

15 On the reform of English social policy, see Dean 1991, Himmelfarb 1984, and Poynter 1969.

adequately governing such transformations rather than trying to hold them in check. This realization, however, was filtered through a reading of the problem that was not yet thoroughly economic but was still imbued with moral concerns and policy objectives (Dean 1991, 62).

The first reformer to explicitly break with the ancient discourse of poverty, in a sense developing the theoretical outlook introduced by Adam Smith, was Joseph Townsend with his 1787 *Dissertation on the Poor Laws by a Well-Wisher to Mankind*. Indeed, according to Karl Polanyi ([1944] 2001, 116), this was the first work on social policy to have set aside the view that the state should be more actively engaged in solving the problem of poverty, arguing to this end that poverty is rooted in biological and economic causes which the administrative agencies of the state have no ability to address. Townsend essentially brought to the debate on the poor laws the naturalistic theme previously developed by the founders of modern political economy, laying the groundwork that would enable Malthus's principle of population to find a firm footing, while also paving the way for the arguments that would later be developed in anthropology by drawing on the idea of natural selection. Townsend's criticism of the welfare system proceeded from the observation that all previous attempts at reform had failed. Indeed they seemed to aggravate rather than alleviate the problem. Unlike the rich, the poor cannot draw on any sense of honour, pride, ambition, and the like as motivating forces that will drive them to work: "In general it is only hunger which can spur and goad them on to labour; yet our laws have said they shall never hunger" (Townsend [1786] 1971, 23). Therefore, welfare can only take away the main stimulus that will prompt them to work. It will take away their "natural motive to industry and labour" (ibid., 24). But even here the naturalistic argument was not expressed in its purest form, considering that Townsend's criticism of the welfare system proceeded on moral and political bases. He argued that the system "does not promote [the] cheerful compliance [of the poor] with those demands, which the community is obliged to make on the most indigent of its members" and that it will destroy the "harmony and beauty, the symmetry and order of that system, which God and nature have established in the world" (ibid., 36).

In Section VIII of the *Dissertation*, Townsend uses the rhetorical device of the fairy tale to introduce the idea that there existed a biological and economic principle which by natural selection sets a balance between the size of the population and the amount of natural resources: "It is the quantity of food which regulates the numbers of the human species" (ibid., 38). But even here the principle that selects those who are winnowed out when resources are scarce is itself based on moral assumptions, for the selection was made by looking at how enterprising an individual is rather than at biological criteria such as physical strength or endurance. And here, too, the argument was that by promoting population growth and altering the equilibrium between a region's demographic structure and its economic structure, welfare policy violated not only a bioeconomic principle but also a moral and political one, in that welfare gave a free pass to the less enterprising members of society, enabling them to artificially survive and reproduce (ibid., 38–42). The wise legislator would therefore have had to abandon such bad policy and restore the moral and bioeconomic principles that had been violated. But beyond the criticism Townsend devoted to ancient *social police*, his argument that the nation's poverty and weakness was actually attributable to the distortion injected into the system by the artificial population growth effected by social policy (ibid., 41–42) explicitly called into question the populationist assumption that underpinned all of social and economic thought up to that point. This assumption had already been weakened when Adam Smith stated the principle of the balance between population trends and economic output, but even he did not venture to challenge that assumption outright (Dean 1991, 75).

In several respects, Robert Malthus developed the considerations Townsend made on the balance that needs to be maintained between the population and the people's means of subsistence, but he did for the first time introduce the idea that demographic and economic trends moved in correlation under a natural equilibrium that could be thrown off-kilter. In the theory Malthus developed in his 1798 *Essay on the Principle of Population*, the relation between the two trend lines— one demographic, the other economic—is explained by two sets of anthropological constants: the need for food, and hence for the productive activity that will sustain humans biologically, and sexual attraction as the basis of biological reproduction (Malthus 1798, 12). But these two kinds of production develop by different kinds of growth rates. Biological reproduction develops by a *geometric* rate, while economic production follows an *arithmetic* rate (ibid., 10). According to Malthus's calculations, this difference in growth rates lies at the root of a persistent imbalance between demographic growth and means of subsistence. Ergo, if the damage this natural imbalance will increasingly provoke is to be avoided, some checks will have to be put in place that will curb the natural dynamic of population growth (ibid., 18ff.). In the different editions the *Essay* went through, these checks were classified in different ways without finding a definitive systematization, but in the last edition Malthus did alight on a classification that makes logical sense. He drew a distinction between *preventive checks*, designed to curb birth rates, and *positive checks*, which instead seem to increase mortality rates. Thus, for example,

> a foresight of the difficulties attending the rearing of a family acts as a preventive check, and the actual distresses of some of the lower classes, by which they are disabled from giving the proper food and attention to their children, act as a positive check to the natural increase of population.
>
> (Ibid., 63)

As is known, Malthus thought that the nation's wealth and happiness depended in large part on the government administrators' ability to prevent overpopulation. To this end, however, he did not advocate a purely noninterventionist policy—for on his theory the natural development of the bioeconomic principle was bound to lead to a significant imbalance where the means of subsistence would not suffice to sustain the population—but rather took a two-pronged approach. On the one hand, he took up some of the theses advanced by those who called for the abolition of poor relief, arguing in particular for a policy that would keep systemic positive checks in place simply by making it so that those who improvidently saddle society with their offspring are abandoned to their fates; on the other hand, he argued that the authorities should encourage temperance and moral restraint among the popular classes, thus making for a more effective self-regulation of demographic trends (ibid., 71ff.).

This policy was based on an unusual blend of bioeconomic principles and political and moral concerns, for on the one hand it held that society is not responsible for those who get themselves into situations where they can no longer support their family and children—and the view here was that people of that ilk should be made to bear the full weight of the natural and economic principles that condemn them to hunger, disease, and death—but on the other hand it was felt that the popular classes needed to be taught to practise sexual temperance and a careful and provident management of household finances, and in general that every able-bodied adult male who is fit to work should be educated to take a responsible attitude in fulfilling the duty incumbent on him to support himself and his family. It was this peculiar blending of theoretical and moral themes that enabled the *Essay* to resonate even among philanthropists, who in Malthus's conception saw the basis for a divine plan by which to achieve the moral and spiritual strengthening of man. They could draw on Malthus in laying out something like a *theology of scarcity*, arguing that it was God's design for the means of subsistence to be scarce and for man to be condemned to work (Dean 1991, 89).

The strength of Malthus's conception thus lay in its subjecting the welfare system to a criticism that managed to work together otherwise incompatible lines of argument: one based on theologico-moral principles, the other based on the principles of political economy; "Malthus' doctrine not only marks the point of the elaboration of a new kind of rationality towards poverty and matters of poor policy, but also the point of intellectual co-optation of Christian charity as an instrument of that rationality" (ibid., 92). This extraordinary feat earned him the praise of evangelical circles, providing his principle of population with a theological stamp of approval, so much so that his policy proposals were even endorsed by *The Observer* (Poynter 1969, 229ff.; Himmelfarb 1984, 100ff.).

Malthus's *Essay* found its setting in an intense debate on the question of welfare reform, with a spate of dedicated treatises and reform proposals. Prominent among these were Frederic Morton Eden's (1797) *The State of the Poor: A History of the Labouring Classes in England* and Jeremy Bentham's writings on the poor laws (see Bentham [1796] 2001), both occasioned by the reform proposals advanced in Parliament by William Pitt, and both essentially critical of the ancient system. Eden's work in certain respects took up Adam Smith's notion of the labouring poor, for it seemed to use the definition of poverty to single out those who were not bound by any relation of servitude or servanthood and whose only livelihood depended entirely on their ability to sell their labour. At the same time, Eden continued to attribute poverty to the impossibility of finding work:

> To the introduction of manufactures, and the consequent emancipation of those who were dismissed by masters, and those also who ran away from them with the adventurous project of trying their fortunes in the lottery of trade, I ascribe the introduction of a new class of men, henceforward described by the Legislature under the de nomination of *Poor*; by which term, I conceive, they meant to signify freemen, who, being either incapacitated by sickness, or old age, or prevented by other causes from getting work, were obliged to have recourse to the assistance of the charitable for subsistence.
>
> (Eden 1797, 57)

As we can see, Eden was concerned with the question of the "incapacitated poor," those who for one reason or another are prevented from finding any gainful employment—a question that Smith left out of the picture entirely, proceeding from the assumption that it is by virtue of the dynamics between demographic and economic trends that the ideal equilibrium can be struck in which work is always rewarded at a fair wage and there are no labouring poor unable to work.

At any rate, for the first systematic account of the idea of poverty, in which poverty gains theoretical recognition as a basic fact of modern political economy, we undoubtedly have to look to Jeremy Bentham. He, too, recognized the need to overhaul the ancient *social police* system, but in addressing the question of the poor laws in the late 18th century, he embraced a reformist outlook, taking a clear stance against the still current radical abolitionist views.[16] More to the point, even more clearly than Adam Smith he stressed the need for an open wage-labour market as central to the dynamics of the capitalist economy, and hence the need for a ready supply of people who, lacking any other means of sustenance, are forced to sell their labour in order to survive. Indeed, in his *Essays on the Subject of the Poor Laws* he worked out a concept that, as we will see, would prove to be crucial to the subsequent development of a liberal police. This was the concept of poverty understood as "the state of everyone who, in order to obtain subsistence, is forced to have recourse to labour" (Bentham [1796] 2001, 3). It is on this basis that he rested his proposal to reform social policy, the idea being that poverty was not to be eradicated from society, as the mercantilist poor

16 See generally Himmelfarb 1984, 78–85, and Campos Boralevi 1984; 1981, 287–99. Even though Bentham's work on the poor laws was well known and very influential—so much so that the reform principles he advocated are rightly considered to have substantially informed the 1834 reform and the passage of the so-called New Poor Law—the bulk of the writings he devoted to the subject were not published until much later. They are now available in Bentham [1796] 2001.

police had sought to do, but instead needed to be recognized as integral to its functioning:

> As labour is the source of wealth, so is poverty of labour. Banish poverty, you banish wealth: banish all those who, (in the words of the English law of Settlements) are liable to become chargeable, you banish all those who are either disposed or qualified to become serviceable.
>
> (Ibid., 3, 4)

The problem that social policy needed to address, Bentham argued, was not poverty per se but indigence, understood as "the state of him who, being destitute of property [. . .], is at the same time either unable to labour, or unable, even for labour, to procure the supply of which he happens thus to be in want" (ibid.).

Bentham designed some forms to be sent out to various local agencies so as to collect information about the paupers for whom they were providing welfare. There were two kinds of tables on these forms. One, called "pauper population table," was to be used to collect statistical data about the number of paupers on welfare; the other, called "table of causes calling for relief," was instead meant to collect *qualitative* data about people on poor relief. These tables were conceived by Bentham ([1796] 2001, LVII) as devices by which to gain a kind of understanding that was radically different from the kind sought through the discourse of poverty. Indeed, through this device he was able to lay the groundwork for a distinction that would become central to the socioeconomic sciences of the time: the distinction between poverty and indigence, also referred to as pauperism. The object of his inquiry lay precisely in the latter, the only social problem that on this conception was to become the focus of administrative oversight and action. Bentham proposed a definitional scheme where the poor were individually classified according to (i) their labouring capacity, (ii) the cause that prevented them from working, and (iii) the period over which they would be unable to work. This conception of poverty, carrying strong moralistic overtones, served the purpose of pointing to the tendency of the welfare system to gradually reduce the poor to a state of moral and physical degeneration. Pauperism was thought to spread by physical and moral contagion and was associated with epidemics, mental and physical disease, and rioting and crime, and more generally with the moral degeneracy of the working classes (Dean 1991, 174). The evil to be rooted out, then, was indigence and pauperism, the object to which the administrative agencies were to devote their attention.

The reform of the poor laws was conceived by Bentham as a way to govern this segment of the population that for whatever reason is incapable of supporting itself. Still, his proposal to replace the old laws based on local administrations with a centralized system capable of making welfare more efficient was certainly not dictated by a concern to ensure humane conditions for the poor, much less conditions in keeping with standards of distributive justice. His rejection of the abolitionist stance still in vogue at the time did not stem from a sense that there was anything morally objectionable about weeding out any excess population by allowing the bioeconomic principles to take effect. Rather, he was making a very deliberate utilitarian calculation:

> If compassion for the indigent themselves were not sufficient warrant for the continuing the provision made for their relief on the steady basis of public contribution, regard for the security of the affluent would of itself be sufficient to forbid the abolition of it. When a man has no other option than to rob or starve, the choice can hardly be regarded as an uncertain one: it can seldom be a matter of much doubt which side of the alternative will be embraced.
>
> (Bentham [1796] 2001, 19)

The close relation between the Benthamite project for governing indigence and the insecurity or alarm associated with indigence was a function of the central role the concept of security played in Bentham's science of legislation. That concept wound up shaping all aims that were more specific than, or otherwise subordinate to, the general principle of the greatest happiness of the greatest number. It was this concept, in other words, that shaped the imperative to provide poor relief, ensure an abundance of resources, and favour an equal distribution of them. Indeed, the essential aim of the legislator was to ensure "the happiness of the individuals, of whom a community is composed," and this happiness consisted precisely in guaranteeing "their pleasures and their security" (Bentham [1789] 1996, 34).

So, as much as it was essential to at least partly liberalize the ancient mercantilist social and pauper police if an open wage-labour market was to be created, any such project would entail social costs that needed to be governed by reforming the poor laws in the manner Bentham felt to be appropriate. His proposed liberalization required a centralized administration and a network of houses of industry in which to confine those who sought relief. It thus bore out some of the basic tenets of ancient *repressive welfare*, replicating its duality, for on the one hand the system provided a social safety net—giving sanctuary to those unable to work and supporting those who, despite their best intentions, wound up being unemployed—but at the same time it served as a disciplinary institution for idlers and vagrants, who deliberately withdrew from the labour force even though they were able bodied.

Even so, there was a marked difference in comparison with past practices and policies. Indeed, as mentioned, whereas the ancient poor laws took it as their essential aim to blot out poverty itself—providing people with jobs and forcing them back into the socioeconomic structures from which they had escaped—Bentham's project was by contrast designed to keep people in a state of poverty, striving only to avert a process of physical and moral degeneration that could cause them to slide into indigence. The idea was to favour the creation of a free labour market, while keeping the social costs of poverty under control by managing demographic trends in relation to swings in the demand for labour. The project was thus conceived to work without altering the natural dynamic by which the cost of labour was set, in such a way that the relief provided for the poor should not take away the necessary stimulus they needed to go out and seek work.

Indeed, the whole welfare mechanism was predicated on the basic principle of *less eligibility*, which acted as the cornerstone of the New Poor Law of 1834. This was a principle that Bentham extracted from modern economic reason itself:

> If the condition of individuals, maintained without property of their own, by the labour of others, were rendered more eligible than that of persons maintained by their own labour, then, in proportion as this state of things were ascertained, individuals destitute of property would be continually withdrawing themselves from the class of persons maintained by their own labour, to the class of persons maintained by the labour of others; and the sort of idleness, which at present is more or less confined to persons of independent fortune, would thus extend itself sooner or later to every individual on whose labour the perpetual reproduction of the perpetually consuming stock of subsistence depends: till at the last there would be nobody left to labour at all, for any body. The destruction of society would therefore be the inevitable consequence, if the condition of persons maintained at the public charge were *in general* rendered more eligible, upon the whole, than that of persons maintained at their own charge, those of the latter not excepted, whose condition is least eligible.
>
> (Bentham [1796] 2001, 39)

In the scheme envisioned by Bentham, it could not be that the condition afforded by poor relief was more attractive to those capable of providing for themselves than the worst condition they could find by selling their labour on the job market. Poor relief had to be doled out according to the most stringent criteria. The *deterrent workhouse* was in fact designed to provide a potent stimulus for people to work, and if anybody did not find the newly established institution to be a powerful enough deterrent, they would be shut out of the system and left to fend for themselves.

Having displaced the ancient *economic police*, modern economic reason also upturned the basic principles of ancient *social police*. Indeed, under the criticism launched by Smith and carried forward by Bentham, the construction of poverty became a key element of economic theory itself. Poverty, and more generally the upward mobility of the poor in search of better-paying jobs, was now seen as essential to the productive process, which by now had become heavily reliant on the ample and ready supply of unregulated labour that only poverty could provide. This was the new scenario in which the functions of the ancient *social police* grounded in mercantilist doctrine had been upended. It spurred the theoretical development of liberal police even further, and the transformation moved forward in large part by seizing on the idea of police as a means by which to control social danger, an idea that with increasing clarity was taking shape in the work of those who in the city of London set out to reform the tools with which to protect public order.

5.3.3. The police of the metropolis

In parallel to the definitive emptying out of the term *police* at the hands of modern political economy, another process was getting underway. In pamphlets and parliamentary debates, reformers were bringing back the use of the term in reference to the activity of managing social disorder, crime, and threats to the public peace, and this use became prevalent among them. It was in fact in the debates on the tools for keeping public order that there emerged this idea of police as no more than a *cura adverendi mala futura* (care taken to avert future ills), an idea which on the Continent was still nestled within the more general one of police broadly construed, but which ultimately wound up being predominant not only in England but also abroad. Even so, the term *police* in the stricter sense was still struggling to emerge in the work of the Fielding brothers, who preceded everyone else in launching a serious challenge against the ancient structure for the protection of public order, a function that in England still fell within the competence of judicial administration and was thus entrusted to the care of honorary functionaries—namely, the justices of peace—with the support of constables.

Henry Fielding was justice of the peace for Westminster and Middlesex from 1748 to 1754, an office that his brother, John, filled after the death of Henry, who took on an active role as a reformist magistrate and also devoted several works to the question of public order and crime. Their attention was primarily devoted to two questions. One was that of *popular disturbances* and *licentious rabble*, which would occasionally rise beyond the threshold of the daily scuffle within the city, breaking out into outright rioting; the other was that of the "dissolute indecency of customs" by which the popular classes in particular were afflicted. In Fielding's time this latter concern was shared by many philanthropic associations committed to the moral reform of the poor, but it was also part of a broader set of concerns that enjoyed much currency, especially in cities like London, with their booming population, where the problem of governing poverty and disciplining the popular classes always emerged front and centre in connection with any matter pertaining to public order. And so, in the work of the Fielding brothers, the discussion was mainly taken up with the question of reforming the customs of the popular classes and regulating and disciplining their places of entertainment (inns, taverns, and the like), and a particularly pressing issue for them in this latter connection was that of alcohol consumption (Radzinowicz 1956, 17–18; Reith 1938, 25–26). And, as Leon Radzinowicz (1956, 21) points out, Fielding took the view that this "supervision of popular diversions should be coupled with an equally strict control over that moving mass of potential criminals, the wandering poor, the beggars and the vagabonds" who in great numbers were flocking into the industrial cities, causing great anxiety among those who stood witness.

But the Fielding brothers' contribution to the rebirth of the concept of police was mostly of the practical sort. They were recognized not so much for their role in founding a new *police science* as for the innovations they introduced in their capacity as justices of peace. It was through their work that the office of justice of the peace at Westminster gained a pre-eminent legal status in comparison with other similar offices in London, so much so as to take on a significant role in shaping policy in London in matters pertaining to the protection of public order (Radzinowicz 1956, 29). Indeed, the Fielding brothers managed to reorganize the famous Bow Street Magistrates' Court, and under their tenure the protection of public order became more efficient and professionalized by comparison with the ancient system based on the activity of honorary judges and parish constables. In part, this was accomplished by instituting what John Fielding (1755, 1) called "a regular body of real thieftakers."[17]

In the Fielding brothers' vision, the office of justice of the peace was to be transformed from a typically judicial one into a strictly policial magistracy charged with preventing crime and governing what were considered to be the main sources of risk. Indeed, their project to reform the parish constables included a programme under which to systematically collect and share information on criminal offences and offenders—the kind of information that would be indispensable to crime prevention (Radzinowicz 1956, 41ff.). Thus John Fielding's (1776) *Brief Description of the Cities of London and Westminster* put out a good deal of information that public officials had collected about the places and methods of the most widespread criminal activities, providing residents with a source they could look to in protecting themselves from the most common crimes.[18] Furthermore, starting in 1759, and on the model of the Paris lieutenancy, the Bow Street Magistrates' Court kept an officer on duty whose job it was to collect and sift through all relevant information, as well as a register clerk entrusted with keeping an exact register of all robberies committed and all goods stolen, specifying as well the name of all persons brought before the same magistrate on charges or even on suspicion of fraud or felony, and also describing the house that gave them safe harbour and took the goods stolen (J. Fielding 1755, 18). This information was to be shared through a constant exchange with the offices of the other justices in London and across the kingdom. The Fielding brothers fervently championed this design, which made Bow Street "a central bureau of information" (Radzinowicz 1956, 46).

The problem of public order in the capital also attracted the attention of the central political organs, which devoted three committees of enquiry to it between 1750 and 1772, all deeply influenced by the work of the Fielding brothers. Indeed, their work was held up as a model in conclusion to each of the parliamentary debates held by the committees of enquiry, and it essentially provided the blueprint

17 On the birth of the first preventive-police unit in England and the first professionalized service providing surveillance and control of the territory—the so-called Bow Street runners—see Radzinowicz 1956, 36ff., and Reith 1938, 28ff.

18 Here John Fielding essentially followed in his brother's footsteps, making more systematic the latter's initiative of distributing fliers on which merchants, journeymen, and residents could find cautions they should take to avoid robberies, snatch thefts, fraudulent schemes, and the like (Radzinowicz 1956, 43).

for modern English police. This blueprint also served as a model for the reforms advanced by the government, which reforms introduced two sets of tools. One set was designed for crime prevention, or what Leon Radzinowicz (1956, 69) called "preventive justice"; the other was designed for exercising control over customs, and more generally for disciplining the popular classes, or what Radzinowicz (ibid.) called "social prophylaxis."

Under the first rubric, starting as early as 1757, a body of laws was enacted to provide the enhanced kind of protection against property crimes which was required for a society whose growing commercial and manufacturing activities multiplied the amount of consumer goods available on the market. Under this enhanced scheme, the standard for a finding of guilt was lowered to that of suspicion, and the range of offences was broadened to include a whole spectrum of activities that revolved around larceny and were punishable as such even if they could not be so classified in a legal sense.[19] Under the second rubric, the popular classes were constantly being required to account for the goods in their possession, and under the preventive legislation the control exercised over these classes became even more direct and inclusive, with measures designed to also target idlers and vagrants. As we know, these measures had had a long history, but in the 18th century, as urbanization picked up speed at a dramatic new rate, they were made increasingly more stringent and drew public opinion into the big debate over the previously mentioned reform of the poor laws.[20] In particular, the provisions of the ancient poor laws were complemented with new controls on the customs of the popular classes and the venues of popular entertainment, such as inns and taverns, so as to limit gambling, prostitution, and the consumption of alcohol, and keep a closer watch on the movements of the population across the territory (Radzinowicz 1956, 74ff.).

However, at the time when these measures were developed and enacted, implementing a programme of preventive justice and social prophylaxis, there was no accompanying effort to overhaul the structure of police powers, which continued to be entrusted to the traditional administration of justice. The push to set security on a more bureaucratized and professionalized foundation was

19 A vast body of rules thus came into force that were designed to prevent the pawnbrokers' activity from becoming an easy conduit through which to traffic in stolen goods. In the same period the law on the trafficking of stolen goods became harsher, when that activity was made into its own crime, separate from the larceny out of which it originated, while the authorities were endowed with broad powers to stop, search, and arrest individuals suspected of larceny or trafficking in stolen goods, a rule that indeed applied to anyone who could not account for given goods in their possession (Radzinowicz 1956, 72).

20 As early as from the 1752 Act for the Better Preventing Thefts and Robberies, which was not passed into law until 1755, it was provided that authorities could arrest and detain idlers and vagrants, or anyone who could not account for himself or herself, if they were suspected of a crime; their name and particulars could be published, and they could be held in detention until the complaints or charges against them were dropped.

confined to the Bow Street offices and the independent initiative of the Fielding brothers. Even the public unrest that swept through London in 1780 did not provoke a sense of alarm strong enough to prompt the authorities to establish a police commissioner responsible for protecting public order. English political culture resisted the idea of instituting an overtly executive office that could hold authority even over the regular justices (a traditional expression of the independence of the judiciary). As a result, the only reforms that managed to pass were those that enhanced the existing structure by appointing new justices and providing for broader search and arrest powers (Radzinowicz 1956, 91ff.; Reith 1938, 54ff.). One of these new justices for the city of London—appointed in 1792 under the Middlesex Justices Act—was Patrick Colquhoun, the authentic father of the new liberal police science.

Colquhoun was first a merchant and then Lord Provost of Glasgow, and was always putting forward new reform proposals. However, his fame is owed not so much to his practical activity as a reformer as to the theoretical works he devoted to the question of pauperism and the public order. Chief among these were his *Treatise on Indigence*, published in 1799 and then significantly revised in 1806 (Colquhoun 1806), and the famous *Treatise on the Police of the Metropolis*, first published in 1795, republished in an expanded edition in 1806 (Colquhoun [1806] 1969), having gone through several reprints, and then translated into French (Colquhoun 1807)—two works that earned him extraordinary fame among his contemporaries, in addition to becoming a publishing sensation.

Although Colquhoun is widely regarded as the true architect of modern English police (Radzinowicz 1956, 231; Neocleous 2000b, 720–21; Reith 1938, 107), this historiographical interpretation of his significance is not entirely accurate. He was certainly the first mature theorist of modern English police, but the conception he worked out was not the circumscribed one usually ascribed to him, where police is exclusively understood as a tool of crime prevention and prosecution (Neocleous 2000b, 721). Indeed, this vision had not even informed the reforms inspired by the Fielding brothers, for in their work, as we have seen, preventive justice was never conceived as a freestanding objective but was coupled with social prophylaxis. Colquhoun's *Treatise on the Police of the Metropolis* in any event proceeded from a remarkably broad definition of police which, as was the practice on the Continent, tended to lay emphasis on two different meanings of the term:

> Police in this country may be considered as a *new Science*; the properties of which consist not in the Judicial Powers which lead to *Punishment*, and which belong to magistrates alone; but in the PREVENTION and DETECTION OF CRIMES, and in those other Functions which relate to INTERNAL REGULATIONS for the well ordering and comfort of Civil Society.
>
> (Colquhoun [1806] 1969, preface; Colquhoun's italics and small caps)

The only sense in which Colquhoun's police can be considered modern is that it was no longer making any attempt to regulate commercial and productive activities, so much so that nowhere in the *Treatise* is his initial mention of "regulations for the well ordering and comfort" followed up with any discussion of mercantilist *economic police*. Colquhoun only describes a municipal police, entirely focused on "Municipal Regulations, which have been established for the comfort, accommodation, and convenience of the inhabitants" (ibid., 591), without taking up the idea of a general police or of wellbeing in the sense of broad economic and *social police* activity carried out by government agencies. Municipal police seems rather to be concerned with the general function of governing the urban space, a function whose object lies in the upkeep and cleanliness of public places and buildings, and whose meaning seems akin to that of *polite*, in the sense that something is said to be civilized or respectable, or someone well-mannered.

So what emerges from Colquhoun's work is a police conceived to address the needs of economic development in England in the second half of the 18th century, a police that can handle the risks incident to a growing urbanization, keeping threats to public order under control, and responding to the need for *social police* raised by liberal society. In this sense Colquhoun can be considered the authentic theoretical founder of modern *liberal* police, for in establishing a close association between the question of governing the social classes and that of preventing crime, he built his new police science by merging the police reform propounded by the Fielding brothers with the social policy reform propounded by modern economic thought. This can be clearly appreciated through a combined reading of his two main works, which are inextricably bound up.

Colquhoun's *Treatise on Indigence* explicitly took up the main themes of the *social police* worked out by Jeremy Bentham (with whom he was, after all, in close contact), building his entire conception on Bentham's basic distinction between poverty and indigence. And much in the same vein as Bentham, Colquhoun defined the former, *poverty*, as "that state and condition in society where the individual has no surplus labour in store, and, consequently, no property but what is derived from the constant exercise of industry in the various occupations of life; or in other words, it is the state of every one who must labour for subsistence," and the latter, *indigence*, as "the state of any one who is destitute of the means of subsistence, and is unable to labour to procure it to the extent nature requires" (Colquhoun 1806, 7–8). Here too, as in Bentham, poverty was considered an essential element of the dynamics underpinning the economic process:

> Poverty is therefore a most necessary and indispensable ingredient in society, without which nations and communities could not exist in a state of civilization. It is the lot of man—it is the source of wealth, since without poverty there would be no labour, and without labour there could be no riches, no refinement, no comfort, and no benefit.
>
> (Ibid.)

Police therefore cannot be entrusted with rooting out poverty, for its function is rather to adequately manage the poor so that they will not slide into indigence. This aim was made explicit in the *Treatise on the Police of the Metropolis*:

> Labour is absolutely requisite to the existence of all Governments; and as it is from the Poor only that labour can be expected, so far from being an evil they become, under proper regulations, an advantage to every Country, and highly deserve the fostering care of every Government. It is not Poverty therefore, that is in itself an evil, while health, strength, and inclination, afford the means of subsistence, and while work is to be had by all who seek it.
>
> (Colquhoun [1806] 1969, 365–66)

The most fundamental of the functions entrusted to the police apparatus thus became to ensure the "health, strength, and inclination" the poor need to maintain themselves, and this can be achieved by issuing the "proper regulations," through which poverty will become a factor contributing to the nation's wealth. Stated otherwise, the function of police is "to prop up poverty" (Colquhoun 1806, 8)— that is, "to establish Systems whereby the poor man, verging upon indigence, may be propped up and kept in his station" (Colquhoun [1806] 1969, 366). This system—sometimes referred to by Colquhoun as the "general internal board of police," other times as the "pauper police institution"—thus takes on a specific role in "the political œconomy of the Nation" (Colquhoun [1806] 1969, 365), for it supports and disciplines a segment of the population thought to be essential to the nation's economic prosperity, so it is not surprising that Colquhoun should see police activity as functional to political economy: "In all the branches of the Science of Political Œconomy, there is none which requires so much skill and knowledge of men and manners, as that which relates to this particular object" (ibid., 359).

The true social problem and main source of disorder, then, was seen to stem not from poverty—in fact, this was a social status that needed to be kept securely in place—but from indigence, which according to the theory expounded by Colquhoun (ibid., 352) "may be considered as the principal cause of the increase of Crimes." For this reason, the pauper police to which he assigned the job of governing the popular classes was also conceived by him as an indispensable security tool. However, by managing the boundary that separated poverty from indigence, the pauper police served not only as a criminal police tool in the strict sense but also as a tool of political economy. Unlike what is the case in the conception outlined in the *Wealth of Nations*, on Colquhoun's conception, police is not set in opposition to political economy but is rather an essential complement to it in an industrial society, contributing to the latter's existence by ensuring one of its fundamental presuppositions, namely, a free labour market (Neocleous 2000a, 57). At the same time, Colquhoun's conception enacted a certain shift in the concept of security. Indeed, in liberal political philosophy, to provide security was to protect the inalienable individual rights which make up the private sphere, but here security was also a matter of making sure that economic and commercial activity could proceed in its regular course, without the disruptions occasioned by that activity itself, which in the given context—one of constant demographic growth in the industrial cities, coupled with the birth of unhealthy factory districts—tended to aggravate the problem of pauperism by multiplying its numbers.

Indigence in particular was thought to stem from several factors, which Colquhoun, drawing on Bentham ([1796] 2001, LVII) and his classificatory tables, distinguished into three classes. The first two he called "innocent causes of irremediable indigence"—typically an illness or some other permanent physical condition that would make one partly or completely unable to work—and "innocent causes of remediable indigence," making one partly or completely unable to work, but only temporarily. And the third he called "culpable causes of indigence" (Colquhoun [1806] 1969, 239ff.). It was in this third class of factors that he located the main source of indigence, which, as the descriptor "culpable" suggests, was essentially to be ascribed to a moral fault or degeneration of the popular classes. And likewise imputable to the same fault were the crimes and disorders that go along with indigence: "Offences of every description," Colquhoun ([1806] 1969, 311) contended, "have their origin in the vicious and immoral habits of the people, and in the facilities which the state of manners and society, particularly in vulgar life, afford in generating vicious and bad habits." It was on this basis that the police was entrusted with seeing to the moral and physical health of the popular classes, a function regarded as more important than that of providing them with straight economic support: "It is not pecuniary aid that will heal this *gangrene:* this *Corruption of Morals*" (ibid., 358; Colquhoun's italics). Well before Honoré-Antoine Frégier (1840) proposed his famous definition of *classes dangereouses*, Patrick Colquhoun arrived at an entirely similar concept through his distinction between *culpable* and *innocent* indigents. As noted, it was the former class that he identified as the main source of indigence, so much so that in his *Treatise on Indigence* he offered an itemized census of such culpable indigents:

1. *Indigent persons* already stated to be objects of parochial relief [. . .].
2. *Mendicants*, comprising *indigent and distressed beggars, sturdy beggars, trampers*, persons pretending to have been *in the army and navy*, lame and maimed, travelling all over the country, and using many devices to excite compassion, estimated, including their children [. . .].
3. *Vagrants*, under which description are to be included gypsies, and another race of vagabonds who imitate their manners, although not of that community, now become pretty numerous, wandering about the country with jack-asses, sleeping in the open air under hedges, and in huts [. . .] and tents, loving idleness better than work, and stealing wherever opportunities offer [. . .].
4. *Idle and immoral persons*, who are able to work, but work only occasionally, who neglect their families, and either desert them totally, or loiter away their

time idly in alehouses, and half support them, leaving the deficiency to be scantily made up by the parishes [. . .].

5. *Lewd and immoral women*, who live wholly or partly by prostitution [. . .].

6. Persons described in the statute of 17 Geo. II as rogues and vagabonds, comprising wandering players of interludes at fairs, mountebanks, stage-dancers and tumblers exhibiting in the open air, showmen, ballad-singers, minstrels with hurdy-gurdies and hand-organs, &c. vagabonds with dancing bears and monkies, low gamblers with E O tables, wheels of fortune, and other seductive implements of gambling; duffers with waistcoat pieces and other smuggled goods, and petty chapmen and low Jews, with trinkets without licenses, alluring ignorant purchasers by apparent good bargains, and securing, notwithstanding, a large profit by giving change in bad money; pretended horse dealers without licenses, exposing stolen horses for sale. All these different classes of vagabonds visit almost every fair and horse-race in the country, and live generally by fraud and deception. Foreign vagabonds, who also wander about the country, pretending to sell pictures, but who are also dealers in obscene books and prints, which they introduce into boarding-schools, on pretence of selling prints of flowers, whereby the youth of both sexes are corrupted, while at the same time some of these wanderers are suspected of being employed by the enemy as spies. [. . .]

7. *Lottery vagrants*, or persons employed in procuring insurances during the drawing of the lotteries, or as proprietors of Little Go lotteries, confined chiefly to the metropolis [. . .].

8. Criminal offenders, comprising highway robbers, footpad robbers, burglars, house-breakers, pickpockets, horse-stealers, sheep-stealers, stealers of hogs and cattle, deer-stealers, common thieves, petty thieves, occasional thieves who cannot resist temptations, receivers of stolen goods, coiners of base money, venders and utterers of base coin, [. . .] and other offenders.

(Colquhoun 1806, 38–43; italics in the original)

This list of sundry persons who "live chiefly or wholly upon the labour of others" (ibid., 43) can be considered the first attempt ever made in Europe to lay out a systematic breakdown of the so-called dangerous classes. For all its guesstimation and anecdotalism, it made a fine impression on contemporaries and was remarkably influential.

In Colquhoun's view, police thus offered itself as the tool of choice in the effort to counteract this process of physical and moral degeneration of the popular classes, an objective to be achieved by a system of checks and restraints. Police would keep temptations in check and strengthen the moral fibre and sociality of those who were thought to populate the ranks of the army of crime, vagrancy, dissipation, and insubordination. Its political puritanism (Radzinowicz 1956, 234) thus identified police as the primary societal-security tool capable of playing in the public sphere the role that religion was meant to play in the private sphere, thus serving the function of morally disciplining people and neutralizing the irredeemables.

> The evil propensities incident to human nature appear no longer restrained by the force of religion, or the influence of the moral principle.—On these barriers powerful attacks have been made, which have hitherto operated as curbs to the unruly passions peculiar to vulgar life: they must therefore be strengthened by supports more immediately applicable to the object of preserving peace and good order.
>
> (Colquhoun [1806] 1969, 562)

More to the point, the police was entrusted with two complementary tasks, for on the one hand its job was to keep under control those who had lapsed into indigence and were thereby reckoned as part of the dangerous classes, and on the other it was the job of the police to carefully govern the labouring classes—or poverty, in Colquhoun's terminology—so that the criminal classes would as far as possible be prevented from attracting new members to their ranks.

Because Colquhoun's project for reforming police envisioned a centralized and bureaucratized apparatus, it could easily smack of absolutism in the eyes of the British,[21] and so it had to strike the most sensitive chords of the national political consciousness if it was to have any following. And so, just as Bentham justified his centralizing welfare-reform proposal by pointing to security needs, Colquhoun justified his own reform proposal by pointing to the threat of a misconstrued liberal spirit:

> To live encircled by *fears* arising from uncontrolled excesses of the human passions, either leading to turpitude or terminating in the commission of crimes, *is to live in misery.*—Police is an improved state of Society, which counteracts these excesses by giving energy and effect to the law.
>
> (Colquhoun [1806] 1969, 349; italics in the original)

On this conception, the threats originating from the segment of the population that had lapsed into a state of *culpable indigence* had to be curbed or at least kept under control, to this end implementing a *general police system* having three main objectives: The first, with regard to "the general delinquency of the Metropolis, and the country, [was] to check its progress by lessening the resources of the evil-disposed to do injuries, and to commit acts of violence on the peaceful subject" (ibid., 561); the second was "gradually to lead the *criminal, the idle,* and *the dissolute* members of the community into the paths of innocence and industry" (ibid.); and the third was to make sure that those who made up the laborious classes did not slide into indigence (ibid.).

---

21 Nor did it help, in this regard, that his *Treatise on the Police of the Metropolis* itself contained a passage praising the Paris police, however much superficially and misinformedly.

What Colquhoun offered in his police model, then, was in essence a systematization and formalization of the proposals previously sketched out by the Fielding brothers and later by Bentham. The model stood on three pillars: The first was a *preventive* or *security police* aimed at thwarting explicitly criminal activities and keeping the dangerous classes under control; the second was a more general *social* or *correctional police* aimed at disciplining the customs and mores of the popular classes and governing the boundary line separating the dangerous classes from the laborious ones; and the third was a *municipal police* aimed at managing the urban public space by ensuring the security and good upkeep of public places, as well as maintaining respectability and the health and sanitation of the environment.

5.4. The government of social danger

Within a couple of decades, the police reform introduced in 1829 moulded into shape a bureaucratized and professionalized police proper on the abhorred model of the Continental institutions.[22] This process, in combination with the parallel 1834 reform of the poor laws, was key to creating a free labour market and delineating a sphere in which individuals are responsible for themselves and in which the public authorities therefore cannot interfere except to govern the risk that individuals should fail in their responsibility, this through the use of police tools and only insofar as the risk at issue entailed a danger and a cost to society at large (Dean 1991, 168–69). The complementary nature of the relation between the two administrative sectors—police and poor relief—was perfectly clear to Edwin Chadwick, who spelled it out in an 1829 article on preventive police published in the *London Review*, an article that piqued the interest of Bentham (Neocleous 2000a, 66). As a member of the 1832 Royal Commission into the Operation of the Poor Laws, Chadwick endorsed Bentham's proposal for

---

22 The reform of English police was accomplished under the leadership of Prime Minister Robert Peel. Seizing on the mood for change that lingered in the wake of the criminal law reforms sponsored by Samuel Romilly, Peel realized that the latter reforms would be incomplete without their natural complement: the professional police that many had tried to institute since the mid-18th century (Reith 1938, 221–23). And so on April 15, 1829, a bill was introduced in Parliament which drew in large part on the legacy of the Fielding brothers and Colquhoun and would become the model for the country's future professional police. It was called the Bill for Improving the Police in and Near the Metropolis and was passed into law as the Metropolitan Police Act, establishing a new police office that reported to the Home Secretary and went into operation in Scotland Yard on September 29, 1829 (ibid., 249ff.). The reform was initially confined to the city of London, excluding the greater metropolitan area and the suburbs, but from the outset it was conceived as a first step toward the creation of a countrywide police force. This objective was achieved under the Municipal Corporations Act 1835, the Rural Constabularies Act 1839—which set up similar police forces and empowered the justices of the peace in the rural areas to appoint chief constables serving as commanding officers of the police forces in their area—and finally the Police Act 1856, requiring each county to set up its own police force subject to government oversight (see, generally, Critchley 1972).

reforming the poor laws, and in his writings of the time he took up Bentham's distinction between poverty and indigence, restating it almost to the letter and ultimately making it the cornerstone of the reformed poor relief system (Chadwick 1837, 18).

The reformers of the first half of the 19th century thus unmistakably identified the domain of the administrative agencies' activity. The target of their attack was no longer poverty, but the whole complex of circumstances which made up the environment and lifestyle of the popular classes, and which might have been conducive to transforming a pauper into an indigent. Indeed, whereas the main objective of welfare reform was to depauperize those fit to work, instilling in them an attitude of responsibility for their own economic situation, the deterrent workhouse and the reformed police acted as a system for managing the risk posed by those less willing to accept the discipline of wage labour. This was precisely the finding reported by Charles Shaw Lefevre, Charles Rowan, and the selfsame Edwin Chadwick in the First Report of the Constabulary Force Commissioners of 1839:

> Having investigated the general causes of depredation, of vagrancy, and mendicancy, as developed by examinations of the previous lives of criminals or vagrants in the gaols, we find that in scarcely any cases is it ascribable to the pressure of unavoidable want or destitution; and that in the great mass of cases it arises from the temptation of obtaining property with a less degree of labour than by regular industry, which they are enabled to do by the impunity occasioned by the absence of the proper constitutional protection to the subject.
>
> (Chadwick, Lefevre, and Rowan 1839, 345)

France had redesigned its police institutions in the Napoleonic era in keeping with a trend toward restoration that had taken hold in the revolutionary period. The decentralized administration set up during the French Revolution was extremely weak and was further undermined in the Reign of Terror by the Committee of Public Safety. So, in an effort to strengthen the administrative apparatus, the Directory submitted to the Council of Five Hundred a proposal to institute an independent Ministry of Police. This was done on January 2, 1796. The new ministry was entrusted with executing all laws pertaining to police, security, and general peace in the republic, to this end relying on the national guard and the gendarmerie, two corps that from the outbreak of the Revolution had replaced the forces that answered to the police lieutenancy and the *marechausée* (Arnold 1979, 24; Le Clere 1957, 56; Napoli 2003, 233; Carrot 1984, vol. 1, pp. 222–23). The foundation was thus set on which to re-establish a centralized and highly bureaucratized administrative structure, and the Napoleonic regime built on that foundation to complete the project. This was done by reorganizing the administrative structure. Under a law enacted on February 17, 1800, the elective offices set up in each department during the Revolution were replaced with prefects and, at the level of the municipal administration, with mayors appointed either by the central government or by the prefects themselves.[23]

The imperial era brought back an administrative structure based on single-member offices filled by government-appointed functionaries acting in place of collegiate bodies. Although in certain respects this structure closely resembled that of the ancient administrative monarchy—and to that extent the imperial era can be said to have marked a clear break with the revolutionary period—the great codifications, now firmly in place, ruled out any possibility of going back to the ancient *police générale*. The police had by now been transformed into a public-security institution, one that under the Penal Code of 1810 was tasked with protecting the popular classes. Indeed, this code of criminal procedure took in all the ancient provisions on idleness and vagrancy, all the prohibitions of association and assembly, and the rule requiring workers to carry a *livret*, or worker's passport; so, too, in keeping with the 1795 Constitution of the Year III and the 1808 *Code d'Instruction Criminelle*, it granted broad powers of arrest to the central government and the police prefects; and, finally, it set forth provisions on *surveillance spéciale* (special surveillance), *interdiction de séjour* (barring notices, i.e., orders barring convicted felons from given premises), and *emprisonnement* (imprisonment), which would become the three main institutional tools available to security police in 19th-century Continental Europe (Carrot 1984, vol. 1, p. 289; Ferrajoli 1990, 818–20).

A similar process was unfolding in Prussia. Here the police apparatus based on the classic commissarial magistracies retained its basic design all through the 19th century, and a wide-ranging debate on pauperism broke out that took a new turn. It began to embrace the discourse of the social and economic philosophy that was being advanced in the English-speaking world, for increasingly the issue was being framed in terms of the social dangers attendant on poverty, and how these dangers could be managed by a deployment of appropriate police tools (Lüdtke 1989, 45;

---

23 In the institutional framework of the Napoleonic Empire, police matters fell in the first place within the powers of the emperor, who under the Constitution of the Year III (of August 22, 1795) was entrusted with "powers pertaining to the state's internal security" and with supreme powers as commander-in-chief of all public forces, which answered to the Interior Ministry and the War Ministry and so was still institutionally divided into two compartments, one civil and the other military. Under the aforementioned law of February 17, 1800, the redesigned civil administration revolved entirely around the prefects, who were responsible for public order and security. Paris enjoyed a special status in matters of public order, for it acted under the authority of its own police prefect, the *Préfet de Police de Paris*, a sort of heir to the ancient lieutenant. This office was established under the same law of February 18, 1800, and executed the policy directives of the central government and its competent ministers. Its task was to manage the three branches of police: the judicial police, the security police, and the municipal police. Apart from a few inevitable adjustments owed to regime changes, the structure imparted to the French police under the Napoleonic reforms was kept in place throughout the period spanning from the Bourbon Restoration of 1814 to the July Monarchy of 1830–48 (see, generally, Carrot 1984, vol. 1, pp. 279ff.; Arnold 1979, 35ff.; Le Clere 1957, 63ff.; Buisson 1958).

Beck 1995, 1–29). Even in Prussia, then, police was beginning to shift its focus away from the problem of poverty per se toward that of its externalities, for in contemplating the population on the move that was replenishing the reservoir of unregulated labour, it was asking how to deal with those in this group whose disorderly lifestyle would be likely to cause problems that needed attention (Lüdtke 1989, 79–80). In this regard the police held broad powers to detain persons suspected of vagrancy or anyone who gave no evidence of having the means necessary to provide for their own sustenance, and only in the latter half of the 19th century did this power become subject to judicial oversight (ibid., 124–27). A law on vagrants and beggars was passed on January 6, 1843, making idleness and vagrancy punishable by imprisonment for a term that increased with each new arrest (according to whether the person in question was a first-time, second-time, or repeat offender), and giving the police the power to discretionarily decide whether to grant early release from prison or whether to further commit the prisoner to a workhouse (ibid., 128). Furthermore, through a circular letter of September 12, 1815, the Ministry of Police regulated the legal practice of special police surveillance *(Überwachung der Polizei)* by making the rule applicable to a class inclusive of former detainees, persons with a criminal record, and "all those who, by virtue of their life patterns or insufficient wages, seem to pose a threat to public security" (ibid., 129; my translation).

The process just outlined, straddling the 18th and 19th centuries, can be summarized as one in which, under the pressure of a liberal turn in social and political thought, the modern police apparatus was put through a radical theoretical criticism that wound up substantially restricting its practical scope. And in this way the evolution of police powers in modern Western societies can be said to have completed its arc. Borrowing the previously invoked juxtaposition that Johann Stephan Pütter put to effective use in the second half of the 18th century (see Section 5.2), we could say that police would never again be understood as the highest expression of a *ius promovendi salutem publicam*—namely, a power of the sovereign authority to promote the public welfare—and would henceforth be reduced to a *cura advertendi mala futura*, that is, an activity concerned with averting future ills. So it was in the early 19th century that this transformation took place, for, as noted, the function attributed to the police apparatus would, from that point onward, be significantly whittled down from that of *economic police* to that of a *security police*, an institutional tool devoted to the sole task of managing the risks and dangers incident to the unhindered unfolding of spontaneous socioeconomic processes. That, in short, is the about-turn that Michel Foucault (2004, 452) was describing when he remarked that "the notion of police is entirely overturned, marginalized, and takes on the purely negative meaning familiar to us."

This reversal, however, did not have the effect of reducing the police to a subservient institution merely designed to support judicial power in the legal activity of protecting the sphere of the natural liberties, an activity accordingly conceived in the negative, serving only the function of preventing and prosecuting crimes. The 19th-century police was not the embodiment of the night watchman cherished by a large swath of liberal philosophy of law. Indeed, liberal politico-economic thought favoured an economic system heavily reliant on a free labour force, and far from putting to rest the problem of governing the popular classes, this development, at once theoretical and practical, wound up amplifying it. Being based on the principle of a minimal state whose only task is to enable economic and social processes to unfold according to their natural dynamics, the economic system advocated by liberal power raised the problem of how to govern the political and social consequences of this broad freedom and limit its costs, especially the costs and consequences of liberalizing the ancient social and labour policy. This was the problem of governing a population no longer bound by the traditional constraints characteristic of the corporative and mercantile society of the Late Middle Ages. Indeed, as Joyce Oldham Appleby ([1978]1983, 295) comments, by making the case for individual liberty, the ruling class subjected the unpropertied to a new master, namely, the market, through which they sold their labour and bought their bread. The invisible market replaced the visible and personal authority of the master. Contemporaries recognized the market as having a coercive power, but its effectiveness as a means of control rested on its being a market for sellers and buyers. Hence the first inherent danger of extending the scope of economic freedoms was the danger that the shaping of manufacturing activity and the making of an industrial labour force should be left to their own devices.

The liberal turn in essence made for a general liberalization of labour, upsetting the politico-disciplinary balance on which stood the *social police* the ancien régime. The new scenario was described in not too subtle terms in a document issued during the French Revolution under the title "Procès verbaux et rapports du Comité pour l'extinction de la mendicité, de l'Assemblée Constituante" (Minutes and reports of the National Constituent Assembly's Committee for the Extinction of Beggary, discussed in Castel 1995, 186), noting that with the suppression of the corporative system and the remaking of the ancient welfare mechanism, it was inevitable that the relation of the poor vis-à-vis their employers should likewise be set on an entirely new basis. The poor would now enter that relation as holders of an asset, their labour, which they had the "right" to freely exchange on the open market. Poverty would now become the authentic source of the nation's wealth, but obviously only on condition that those in poverty were willing to work. Vagrancy and begging, for centuries the object of the police agencies' attention, were no longer regarded as the product of human refuse that, to the extent possible, needed to be placed back into the care of the socio-professional organizations from which they had escaped. They now became a social crime proper, the most direct attack on the industrial economy that was taking shape, the latent threat of a revolution in the making, the harbinger of social unrest.

Once it became apparent that it was no longer feasible to keep up the mercantilist pretence to control the productive process and confine work within the specifically designated structures of social production and reproduction, police refashioned itself into a tool for dealing with the liberalization of the economy on a grand scale by governing and managing the attendant social costs, the ones connected with the restructuring of the productive processes and the deep changes affecting the demographic structure and the distribution of the population across the territory. Police became the institutional tool with which to manage the risks and dangers incident to a productive system based on the free circulation and contracting of labour on the market. Out of this development grew the closer and closer association between police and the government of social danger that was explicitly being theorized on Colquhoun's model of police as a tool for managing the porous border between the labouring classes and the dangerous classes.

The reform of the police apparatus let loose the social and economic forces and took the reins off the industrialization process, and in so doing it engendered a pressing new need to govern and manage the social and political costs—to wit, the threat of societal insecurity and political instability—entailed by the new organization of production. At the same time as industrialization and urbanization generated wealth and prosperity at a pace hitherto unknown, they also brought the threat of a social disintegration that was looming larger and larger. This threat was personified by the spectre of pauperism and the dangerous classes, which became the central concern of social reformers, intellectuals, and police functionaries through most of the 19th century.[24] The problem of the dangerous classes that consumed the bourgeois mind of the time was one of public order. It was the problem of the daily outbreaks of disorderly conduct that were always at risk of escalating into outright revolt. But also at issue was the overall health and hygiene of the social body, which day in and day out was undermining the labouring capacity of the popular classes, threatening to devolve into the medico-biological equivalent of revolt, namely, an epidemic. The conceit of the dangerous classes, in essence, offered the lens through which to thematize the so-called social question, that is, the question of the living conditions of the popular classes in the nascent industrial cities.

Around this idea of a generic social dangerousness was built the security apparatus entrusted with managing the externalities of capitalistic socioeconomic

24 It was previously discussed how in England, through the work of Jeremy Bentham and Patrick Colquhoun, the theoretical foundations were laid for the distinction between the labouring classes and the dangerous classes. As the reader may know, this distinction gained its fame through Honoré-Antoine Frégier's (1840) book *Des classes dangereuses de la population dans les grandes villes et les moyens de les rendre meilleures* (On the dangerous classes in the population of the large cities, and the means by which to make them better), which in the same year was translated into German under the title *Ueber die gefährlichen Classen der Bevölkerung in den großen Städten und die Mittel, sie zu bessern* (Coblenz: Hergt, 1840). Like no other work, this book captures in its full spectrum the huge debate that in the early 19th century unfolded in Europe on the question of pauperism (for an overview, see Himmelfarb 1984, 371ff.; Castel 1995, 218ff.; Procacci 1993; Chevalier (1958)1973; Lüdtke 1989, 51ff.; Beck 1995; for an analysis specifically devoted to Frégier's work, see Digneffe 1995, 137–213).

development, which were expressed in terms of orderliness, environmental hygiene, and the overall health of the population. And around the problem of public security—which would become the basis of the functioning of 19th-century police—would develop the political techniques brought to bear in controlling and administering the great urban agglomerations, governing the influx of people, and managing the risks associated with the urban environment: disease, folly, disorder, unrest. Police would take the popular classes under its protection, taking on the burden of governing those who were still incapable of making a full, responsible use of the gift of liberty bestowed on them by the liberalization of the labour market. The main concern of the police in matters of security was to monitor the popular classes (vagrants, day labourers, factory workers, domestic servants) so as to keep them under strict surveillance. This problem was beginning to make itself felt in a particularly pressing way in places such as London, Berlin, and Paris— cities with booming populations that were needed to fuel their growth as engines of the industrialization process. The *liberal police* had thus morphed into an entirely different thing from the institution that in the historiography tends to be pigeonholed into a role of strict subservience to judicial authority. To be sure, this police was no longer expected to shape and steer socioeconomic life, whose independent internal dynamics had been recognized by nearly unanimous consent. Yet with increasing insistence it was being called into play to manage the social and political costs attendant on those dynamics. And these were huge costs. In fact, such was their scale that they could undercut the very economic freedom that had just been heralded.

Conclusion

The evolution of the police apparatus in 18th- and 19th-century Europe undoubtedly followed institutional traditions marked by some deep differences.[1] Even so, in surveying that evolution we have observed a fundamental convergence among models, for they all rely on police activity as key to guaranteeing security. We have seen, in particular, that police activity progressively gravitated around three areas, giving rise to a *judiciary police*, a *security police*, and a *municipal police*. In France and England alike, police was substantially reduced to these three areas of activity as early as the late 18th century. To be sure, this *liberal police* model was slower to advance in the German lands, where the ancient police science was more deeply rooted, but even here it would eventually establish itself, becoming the dominant police model in the main Western countries. A particularly effective statement of its theoretical underpinnings can be found, for example, in Italy at the dawn of the 20th century, in that monumental condensation of administrative knowledge which is the *Trattato di diritto amministrativo italiano* (Treatise of Italian administrative law), edited by Vittorio Emanuele Orlando. Contained in the fourth volume of this work is a long treatise on police in which Oreste Ranelletti (1904, 207–1265) sums up the whole of 19th-century European police science.

In making this investigation Ranelletti naturally started out by defining the concept of police, which by this time had become synonymous with the security guarantee:

> We should call *police* that public activity of internal administration which limits or regulates the activity of individuals (be they natural or artificial persons), if necessary by the use of force, for the purpose of guaranteeing that

---

1 It is indeed well known that the police models developed in England, France, and Prussia ranged widely in their degree of militarization. Thus the English model was entirely based on civil administration. The French model, which in turn exerted much influence across Latin Europe, was based on a dual system: The administration of security in the urban centres was in large part civil, while the rural areas were administered by a public force operating under the Ministry of War. And Prussia, in line with the strong military bureaucracy that underpinned its administrative apparatus, relied heavily on the military forces in performing ordinary public-security functions.

the social whole and its parts will not suffer the harm that may derive from human activity.

(Ibid., 278)[2]

This definition entailed, at least on the face of it, a close connection between police activity and the judicial activity needed to enforce the law. But in reality the function being described was that of protecting society from possible *harm*, a much broader concept than that of a *wrong*, *injury*, or *offence*, which makes the police apparatus something different from a law-enforcement technology.

This makes sense if we consider that Ranelletti, and indeed all of 19th-century police science, took care to distinguish the activity of *judicial police* from police activity *tout court*. The former he also called *polizia investigativa* (investigative police), qualifying it as *scopritrice*, from the noun *scoprire* (to discover), referring to the activity of crime detection:

> By *judicial police* is meant the activity by which the organs of state investigate and discover crimes and criminal offenders; its task is to investigate crimes of any sort, gather evidence, and provide judicial authorities with all such elements as may enable them to find the authors of crimes, along with their main agents and accomplices.

(Ibid., 284–85)

So, as much as judicial police may importantly contribute to the maintenance of order and security, its main role in the service of judicial activity consists in uncovering facts and events that have already transpired, and in this sense it looks to the past:

> The proper function of justice is to administer the law, that is, to find and state the law, protect it from violations, and apply it. Its function is thus triggered whenever a right has been denied, breached, or threatened which therefore needs to be restored, that is, whenever an injury has already taken place. It is a function fulfilled by analyzing the case at hand so as to decide its outcome in accordance with a standard procedure, and its protection of rights and the legal order is thus an activity governed by law, that is, by a judgment rendered through a decision.

(Ibid., 286)

Police activity, by contrast, looks to the present and future. As a political technology for the management of danger, it deals with *threats*, either actual or potential:

> Police does not administer the law; it does not solve legal questions; it does not state the law. It protects the order and security of the state in point of fact.

---

2 All quotations from Ranelletti 1904 are my own translation.

Its action must therefore necessarily unfold in the present and the future, not in the past: It seeks to forestall and prevent offences and quash them if they should come to pass, so as to avert as far as possible the harm that they may bring. Falling outside its purview are harmful acts that have already been carried out, unless these acts carry consequences in virtue of which they should pose a new threat, bringing new harm. It follows that much of police activity consists in directly protecting not the interests of individuals—for the latter are as yet unharmed, not having been injured by any offence—but the interests of the public at large.

(Ibid., 286)

So whereas *judicial* police serves as a complement to law enforcement, as a preparatory activity on which such enforcement relies, *administrative* police is preventive. It comes into play *before* the law is triggered, for it consists in the activity of governing and managing risk, if need be by the use of force (ibid., 287). This distinction between justice and police comes out even more explicitly if we consider the different functions served by the legal tools available to the different organs of state:

Criminal law is concerned with the breaking of those rules which have been put into place *immediately* to protect the law itself, and which therefore spring into action whenever someone's rights or legal interests are directly breached, denied, or encroached upon, either in esse or in posse, that is, whenever there is a failure to perform a given duty. Police law, by contrast, is concerned with acts that break those rules which have been put into place to *mediately* protect the law by taking the cautions necessary to prevent the possibility of injuries to the legal order.

(Ibid., 289–90; italics added)

Police law therefore punishes acts which in themselves may be entirely harmless or otherwise legally inconsequential, but which matter as sources of danger, however remotely so:

These are acts that threaten a right, even if only indeterminately. They place a legal interest in potential danger, and so are prohibited and punished for the purpose of removing such threats of individual or social harm, keeping the peace, enabling citizens to live happily in civil society, and making sure that they feel secure.

(Ibid., 290)

From the nature of police prohibitions we can therefore derive the true nature of police powers. These are inherently the powers of a security technology, for the police "operates so that no harm is done to the order and security of the state or its parts, or so that no event takes place which may perturb the public or private order" (ibid., 290–91). The state may intervene only to prosecute crimes, in response to the breaking of a law, but it should also be able to anticipate danger so as to prevent it from materializing:

> It cannot be conceded that the state should wait for evil to realize itself before one can act in self-defence or the state can protect individuals or society. That would wind up undercutting security and the public peace and enfeebling society, always under threat, with inadequate guarantees against abuses of freedom. And it shows that threats and danger itself are in themselves evils from which society must be protected.
>
> (Ibid., 291)

Police thus acts as a political technology with which to guarantee security, but in so doing it can take on either of two concrete guises depending on the object of its action. Here Ranelletti explicitly takes up the distinction between public security *(sûreté publique)*, pertaining to the ordinary care and governance of the population, and municipal police, which instead is entrusted with governing the public space and the territory. Like security police, municipal police is also competent to protect the interests of individuals and of society as a whole from threats and dangers, but it does so only *mediately*,

> that is, by safeguarding the existence, conservation, and function of a given thing, or making provision for it to exist, be preserved, and function properly. This is achieved by limiting or regulating the activity of individuals, if necessary by the use of coercion, in such a way that the thing in question will exist and function according to its purpose. In this way municipal police indirectly and mediately protects all the interests that may be harmed or undermined by a bad mode of existing or functioning of the thing itself.
>
> (Ibid., 304)

Municipal police is thus concerned with the proper *government of things and places*. Security police, by contrast, is concerned with the *government of individuals* and of the danger associated with them, a task it carries out by regulating or even preventing activities regarded as particularly risky. Security police, in other words, is directly responsible for managing the individual and social danger associated with specific individuals or classes of individuals:

> By observing the areas where security police is active, we come to see that it directly and immediately protects the various interests of the social whole and of its parts, inasmuch as they may be harmed by the activity of any one person.
>
> (Ibid., 306)

Therein lies the properly preventive activity carried out by the security police. This activity takes two objects. On the one hand, it is aimed at the *material facts* brought

into being by individuals, and it does so insofar as these facts may pose a danger
by favouring or facilitating the commission of offences or the breach of the rights
of others. On the other hand, it is aimed at the *activities* of individuals, insofar as
these activities

> by their very nature and mode of being, and not in virtue of these activities
> themselves at the present time but in virtue of their continued existence, may
> cause, provide the occasion for, or aid the commission of acts that harm the
> legal order and are thus to be deemed dangerous or a cause for concern as
> regards the integrity of the order itself.
>
> (Ibid., 341)

But police is not just concerned with the immediate prevention of perilous facts
and actions, for even more important is the task assigned to it of governing
dangerous *individuals*. And it is this activity that Ranelletti calls mediated prevention.
Police activity can be so described

> when it is aimed at persons insofar as they are to be deemed dangerous and
> worrisome with regard to the integrity of the legal order, not in virtue of what
> they may be doing at any one time, but by reason of their habitual conduct,
> and when it is performed in connection with human acts and activities that in
> virtue of their continued existence, rather than inherently or at the present
> time, may cause, provide the occasion for, or aid the commission of acts that
> harm the legal order and are thus to be deemed dangerous or a cause for
> concern as regards the integrity of the order itself.
>
> (Ibid., 341–42)

Preventive police is thus meant to manage the complex relation between security
and danger. Its objective is to materially prevent social risks from multiplying,
which it does by breaching into the personal sphere of those who make up the
object of its activity, and in particular by making idle the social danger posed by
certain classes of individuals. Indeed, this preventive activity targets

> individuals who, in virtue of their past activity and overall patterns of
> behaviour, put the integrity of the legal order presently in danger; in other
> words, these individuals give rise to the present concern that in all likelihood
> their actions will be in breach of the legal order, and they must therefore be
> put in a condition where they cannot do any harm.
>
> (Ibid., 342)

Of course, precisely in virtue of this power conferred on the police—the power to
encroach on the private sphere of individuals regardless of any offences they may
have committed—there emerges the pressing need to avoid abuses and violations

of the very liberties that police activity is supposed to protect by ensuring the security of a safe environment.

> There needs to be established what powers police administrative authority ought to be able to exercise in determining what facts are to be deemed threats of immediate harm to the legal order, as well which persons and facts are to be deemed factors conducive to the same threats, and hence which persons and activities are to be deemed worrisome and dangerous to the integrity of the legal order; and finally there needs to be established what powers the same authority ought to be able to exercise in determining the measures it can use in carrying out this preventive activity.
>
> (Ibid., 343)

The first and most natural guarantee cemented into the politico-constitutional frame of a state founded on the rule of law consisted in setting out in detail, by statutory enactment, the limits within which preventive police activity was to the carried out. Indeed, the 19th century was distinguished by the great works on public security it produced and by the strenuous effort to *juridify* police activity. Even so, this activity always escaped strict judicial oversight because, as Ranelletti emphatically stated, there are limitations that public security law simply cannot overcome in its attempt to foresee and regulate in the abstract the full range of cases in which the police is expected to intervene, for it is impossible to accurately profile all dangerous persons and circumstances in advance:

> The legal provisions put in place to protect the various freedoms of individuals, all the while keeping them within bounds, are to be understood not only as rights of the individual but also and especially as rights of the state; and in regulating the administrative agencies we have to take into account not only the interests of the individual but also those of the collectivity, which falls within the care of those agencies themselves. And harmony among these two interests cannot be achieved by statutory means alone, for it is impossible to foresee and specify all cases of conflict and the means by which to resolve them. Much of this work needs to be left to [. . .] police authorities.
>
> (Ibid., 347)

The police is thus entrusted with managing the unforeseeable, and any attempt to set out in detail the criteria on which basis to engage its concrete action in the future can only go so far. There comes a point beyond which such pretence to foresight will pervert the prudential purpose that has always been inherent in the government of social danger.

* * *

In the account just offered we have looked at the essential theoretical features of the public security apparatus that gradually solidified itself in the 19th century.

This is an apparatus that in the theory of public administration was quite explicitly being described as a political technology deployed on a daily basis to coercively counteract the dangers that may derive from an improper use of things or from the conduct or character of some persons. However, this activity of governing things and persons was based on a political technology that differed radically from classic legal technologies. Instead of being used to deal with offences, the public security apparatus was entrusted with managing dangers. Its action thus became completely independent of the interest in providing security from assaults on specific legally protected goods and finding the culprit. Security technologies, like disciplinary technologies before them, are aimed at securing the social space, but this they do not so much by enforcing prohibitions as by bringing risk factors under a sort of normative regime. And there is a different way of relating to norms when they are enforced by security technologies than when they are enforced by disciplinary technologies. As Foucault (2003, 253) underscores, a "norm is something that can be applied to both a body one wishes to discipline and a population one wishes to regularize." This means that different political technologies use the same norm according to different rationales. More to the point, whereas normalization under the older disciplinary regimes served the purpose of governing a complex of orthopaedic tools capable of modelling an individual body in accordance with a normative paradigm worked out in advance, the use of security technologies serves the purpose of dealing with a complex of serial phenomena that cannot be so easily shaped into form, for they are governed by their own norms, conferring on them an inherent dynamic that cannot be controlled but can at best be kept in check within tolerable limits (Foucault 2004, 93).

The police apparatus can identify and manage both *individual* and *social* danger. As we have seen, this apparatus has been historically construed as a political technology acting where disciplinary and security needs intersect. Indeed, police was supposed to contribute to the project of disciplining the social space and recouping every individual's productive utility—a project that, as we saw, drove the political philosophy underpinning the government of the poor in the mercantilist age. It was in this period that the first tools were developed for identifying and managing the sources of *individual* danger (these tools included police records, poorhouses, and the like), in an effort to rid the social space of poverty, regarded as a waste of human and material resources and a factor of disorder. In the liberal age, however, police gave up the ambitious project of disciplining the nation's socioeconomic life in its every aspect. Poverty became an ordinary fact. Indeed, as Colquhoun argued, it even played an essential role in fostering the economic development the police was being asked to support by governing at acceptable political and social costs. The problem of *social* danger careening out of control was precisely the problem of keeping under control the complex of risks associated with the model of economic development that had established a firm footing in Western society. These risks were in particular those that kept multiplying as an upshot of the population density and the pell-mell socioeconomic life characteristic of the modern industrial cities. In this setting, public security was brought in as a form of rationality specifically designed to govern and minimize the dangers that came with urbanism and industrialism, an objective to be achieved by the joint pressure on the *territory* and the *population* that only the police could bring to bear.

As mentioned, when it came to governing the *population*, this public security apparatus took on the task of protecting the popular classes, spreading its footprint across all the whole of their existence, seeping into aspects that might bear some relation to their productive capacity and the threats they might pose to order and security. This apparatus thus carried out a threefold function: (i) a general *health police* function, with administrative authorities setting up a tightly woven web of medical inspections, regulating demographic trends, and developing a hygienic and eugenic project; (ii) a *conduct police* function, by ensuring proper familial relations and discipline in the workplace, keeping inappropriate consumption and lifestyles under control, and disciplining sexual life; and, finally, (iii) a *security police* function strictly construed, by constantly controlling and surveilling population movements across the territory, requiring everyone to maintain a domicile and a stable residence, and incrementally building up a record by keeping files on all people deemed suspect or dangerous.

Symmetrically, when it came to governing the *territory*, the police apparatus developed a complex of mechanisms for organizing space in view of the different security needs. Here, too, the function was threefold. For there developed (i) a set of *health police* regulations establishing increasingly strict standards for keeping public spaces healthy and the environment hygienically safe; (ii) a general *police of time and place*, setting out a strict discipline governing the use of public spaces, the time that could be devoted to work and leisure, and the allocation of different social and economic activities across the territory; and (iii) a constant oversight over the *security of places and things*, involving the upkeep of the public places where the spontaneous dynamic of daily social life unfolded, and where the purpose was, of course, to make sure that things were kept in good order and spaces were designed and organized in such a way as to minimize opportunities where crimes could be committed or unrest could generally arise, while enhancing the ability to control such disruptions and protect the population.

A quick glance at the contents of any 19th-century text on public security should be enough to convey an idea of how inadequate the notion of security is that has established itself in political theory and historiography. This notion was utterly incapable of accounting for the complex functions the police apparatus fulfilled in modern liberal societies. Indeed, this notion was taken up directly from politico-legal thought, reflecting the aim of protecting and preserving the legal system and the individual rights enshrined in it. This is quite unlike the notion of liberal police, which, as discussed, has carried out functions that go well beyond security as a legal guarantee in the negative designed to protect rights from encroachment. As much as the liberal police may have been a security device, this is a role it played not as an institution in the service of the judicial apparatus but as an agency capable of *bringing about* the conditions for the existence of the modern industrial society, and of doing so without incurring unacceptable social and political costs. From the standpoint of the functioning of the modern police, security did not just involve protecting property rights, at least not directly: It also entailed the need to manage the social costs or externalities stemming from the free dynamic of the productive process, along with the attendant risks.

To be sure, liberal thought is traditionally tied to the need to protect the personal sphere from undue interference, but the link between liberty and security established by the reason of liberal government escapes a purely legal logic. Indeed, liberty is framed not as a pre-existing entity to be protected by legal instruments but as a *product* of the activities devoted to it by political institutions. Liberty so conceived is not an essential condition inherent in nature which the institutions, going back to the purely conservative logic of politico-legal technologies, confine themselves to protecting: It is rather the object of an active production by political agencies (Foucault 2008, 63). The problem of security, so essential to the liberal arts of government, arises precisely out of the need to create the conditions for such liberty to play out without incurring excessive political, economic, and social costs. Writes Foucault in this regard:

> If this liberalism is not so much the imperative of freedom as the management and organization of the conditions in which one can be free, it is clear that at the heart of this liberal practice is an always different and mobile problematic relationship between the production of freedom and that which in the production of freedom risks limiting and destroying it.
>
> (Ibid., 64)

Indeed, security technology is aimed at constantly reproducing the good of liberty by setting up a vital environment capable of securing the potential of liberty to expand and to absorb the inevitable social costs of such expansion. Security is thus "liberalism's other face and its very condition" (ibid., 65), just as the problem of danger, or risk, is in a sense the "internal psychological and cultural correlative of liberalism" (ibid., 67). The nexus between liberty, danger, and security was thus crucial to liberal society, and placed at the centre of that intersection were the modern police institutions.

The relation between liberty and security therefore cannot be framed solely in terms of the concern that informs every effort to expand the notion of security, namely, the concern about the potential threat to individual liberty. Certainly, this menace continues to stand as a key issue to this day, and as such it even vexed the authentically liberal minds of the day in the arduous task of striking the right balance between security and freedom. But that doesn't take away the fact that the relation between liberty and security was not conceived by the reformers and theorists of the modern liberal police as a zero-sum game. Rather than seeing the police as an apparatus confined to "consuming" liberty, they saw it as a fundamental tool with which to *produce* the environmental and social conditions conducive to a full development of liberty. Or, rather, they conceived the police as an apparatus that, in order to bring about greater liberty, was specifically entrusted with using up a certain amount of liberty to be sacrificed to security.

Works cited

Adams, George Burton. 1963. *Constitutional History of England*, edited by Robert L. Schuyler. London: Jonathan Cape.

Agamben, Giorgio. 1995. *Homo sacer: Il potere sovrano e la nuda vita.* Turin: Einaudi.

Anderson, Peter. 1974. *Lineages of the Absolute State.* London: Verso.

Appleby, Joyce Oldham. (1978) 1983. *Economic Thought and Ideology in Seventeenth-Century England.* Italian transl. *Pensiero economico e ideologia nell'Inghilterra del XVII secolo.* Bologna: il Mulino.

Ardant, Gabriel. 1975. "Financial Policy and Economic Infrastructure of Modern States and Nations." In *The Formation of National States in Western Europe*, edited by Charles Tilly. Princeton, NJ: Princeton University Press.

Arnold, Eric A. 1979. *Fouché, Napoleon and the General Police.* Washington, DC: University Press of America.

Aston, Trevor, ed. 1965. *Crisis in Europe, 1560–1660.* London: Routledge & Kegan Paul.

Bacon, Francis (1601) 1825. "On Judicature." In *Essays, Civil and Moral.* Vol. 1 of *Lord Bacon's Works.* London: William Pickering.

Bader, Karl Siegfried. 1972. "Idee riformatrici imperiali e ceti durante la riforma dell'Impero alla fine del secolo XV." In vol. 2 of *Lo Stato Moderno*, edited by Ettore Rotelli and Pierangelo Schiera, 257–77. Bologna: il Mulino.

Barbiche, Bernard. 2001. *Les institutions de la monarchie française à l'époque moderne, XVIIe–XVIIIe siècles.* Paris: Presses Universitaires de France.

Beaumanoir, Philippe de. 1900. *Coutumes du comté de Clermont en Beauvaisis (1279–1283)*, edited by Amédée Salmon, tome 2. Paris: Alphonse Picard et Fils.

Beck, Hermann. 1995. *The Origins of the Authoritarian Welfare State in Prussia: Conservatives, Bureaucracy, and the Social Question, 1815–70.* Ann Arbor, MI: University of Michigan Press.

Bellomo, Manlio. 1994a. *Società e istituzioni dal medioevo agli inizi dell'età moderna.* Rome: Il Cigno Galileo Galilei.

Bellomo, Manlio. 1994b. *L'Europa del diritto comune.* Rome: Il Cigno Galileo Galilei.

Benjamin, Walter. 1921. "Critique of Violence." In *Selected Writings, 1913–1926.* Cambridge, MA: Harvard University Press.

Bentham, Jeremy. (1789) 1996. *An Introduction to the Principles of Morals and Legislation*, edited by J. H. Burns and H. L. A. Hart. Oxford and New York: Oxford University Press.

Bentham, Jeremy. (1796) 2001. *Writings on the Poor Laws*, edited by Michael Quinn. Vol. 1 of *The Collected Works of Jeremy Bentham.* Oxford: Oxford University Press.

Berman, Harold J. 1983. *Law and Revolution: The Formation of the Western Legal Tradition.* Cambridge, MA, and London: Harvard University Press.

Beuer, Stefan. 1986. "Sozialdisziplinierung: Probleme und Problemverlagerungen eines Konzepts bei Max Weber, Gerard Oestreich und Michel Foucault." In *Soziale Sicherheit und Soziale Disziplinierung: Beiträge zu einer historischen Theorie der Sozialpolitik,* edited by Chistoph SachÐe and Florian Tennstedt. Frankfurt am Main: Suhrkamp.

Bielfeld, Jacob Friedrich. 1760. *Institutions Politiques, ouvrage où l'on traite de la Société Civile; des lois, de la Police, des Finances, du Commerce, des Forces d'un État; et en général de tout ce qui a rapport au gouvernement.* The Hague: Pierre Gosse Junior, Libraire de S. A. S. Monseigneur le Prince Stadhouder.

Black, Anthony. 1992. *Political Thought in Europe, 1250–1450.* Cambridge: Cambridge University Press.

Blackbourn, David, and Geoff Eley. 1984. *The Peculiarities of German History: Bourgeois Society and Politics in Nineteenth-Century Germany.* New York: Oxford University Press.

Blanc-Chaléard, Marie-Claude, Caroline Douki, Nicole Dyonnet, and Vincent Milliot. 2001. "Police et migrants en France, 1667–1939: Questions et résultats." In *Police et migrants: France 1667–1939. Actes du colloque 28 et 29 octobre 1999 à l'Université d'Orléans.* Rennes: Presses Universitaires de Rennes.

Bloch, Marc. 1948. *La société féodale.* 2 vols. Paris: Michel.

Bloch, Marc. 1961. *Les rois thaumaturges: Études sur le caractère surnaturel attribué à la puissance royale particulièrement en France et en Angleterre.* Paris: Max Leclerc et Cie.

Bobbio, Norberto. 1957. *Diritto e Stato nel pensiero di Emanuele Kant.* Turin: Giappichelli.

Bobbio, Norberto. 1980. "Il giusnaturalismo." In *L'età moderna.* Vol. 4 of *Storia delle idee politiche economiche e sociali,* edited by Luigi Firpo, 491–558. Turin: UTET.

Bobbio, Norberto. 1995. *Stato, governo, società: Frammenti di un dizionario politico.* Turin: Einaudi.

Bockenforde, Ernst-Wolfgang. 1974. "La pace di Westfalia e il diritto di alleanza dei ceti dell'Impero." In vol. 3 of *Stato Moderno,* edited by Ettore Rotelli and Pierangelo Schiera, 333–62. Bologna: il Mulino.

Bödeker, Hans Erich. 1989. "'Verwaltung,' 'Polizei' and 'Regierung' in German Dictionaries and Encyclopaedias of the 18th Century." *Jahrbuch für europäische Verwaltungsgeschichte* 1: 15–32.

Bodin, Jean (1576) 1955. *Six Books of the Commonwealth.* Abridged and translated by M. J. Tooley. Oxford: Basil Blackwell.

Bodin, Jean. (1576) 1986. *Les six livres de la République.* Paris: Libraire Arthème Fayard.

Bodin, Jean (1576) 1992. *On Sovereignty: Four Chapters from "The Six Books of the Commonwealth,"* edited and translated by Julian H. Franklin. Cambridge: Cambridge University Press.

Bondois, Paul. 1935. "Le Traité de la police de Delamare." *Revue d'Histoire Moderne et Contemporaine* X: 313–51.

Bonnet, Stéphane. 2003. "Botero machiavélien ou l'invention de la raison d'État." *Études philosophiques* 3–4, no. 66: 315–29.

Border-Marcilloux, Christian, Jean Morange, and Roberto Finzi, eds. 1982. *Turgot: Économiste et administrateur.* Paris: Presses Universitaire de France.

Borrelli, Giulio. 1995. "Aristotelismo politico e Ragion di Stato in Italia." In *Botero e la "Ragion di Stato." Atti del convegno in memoria di Luigi Firpo,* edited by Artemio Enzo Baldini, 181–99. Florence: Leo S. Olschki Editore.

Botero, Giovanni. (1589) 1956. *The Reason of State,* translated by Pamela Joan and Daniel Philip Waley, and *The Greatness of Cities,* translated by Robert Peterson. New Haven, CT: Yale University Press.

Boulet-Sautel, Marguerite. 1980. "Police et administration en France à la fin de l'Ancien régime: Observations terminologiques." In *Histoire comparée de l'administration. Actes du XIV colloque historique franco-allemand*, edited by Werner Paravicini, André Stegmann, and Karl Ferdinand Werner, 47–51. Munich and Zurich: Artemis.

Braudel, Fernand. 1979a. *Le temps du monde*. Vol. 3 of *Civilisation matérielle, économie et capitalisme, XVe–XVIIIe siècle*. Paris: Libraire Armand Colin.

Braudel, Fernand. 1979b. *Les jeux de l'échange*. Vol. 2 of *Civilisation matérielle, économie et capitalisme, XVe–XVIIIe siècle*. Paris: Libraire Armand Colin.

Braudel, Fernand. 1979c. *Les structures du quotidien: Le possible et l'impossible*. Vol. 1 of *Civilisation matérielle, économie et capitalisme, XVe–XVIIIe siècle*. Paris: Libraire Armand Colin.

Brunner, Otto. 1968. "Das 'ganze Haus' und die alteuropäische 'Ökonomik.'" In *Neue Wege der Verfassungs- und Sozialgeschichte*, 103–27. Göttingen: Vandenhoeck & Ruprecht.

Buisson, Henry. 1958. *La Police: Son histoire*. Paris: Nouvelles Editions Latines.

Bussi, Emilio. 1957. *Il diritto pubblico del Sacro Romano Impero alla fine del XVIII secolo*. Vol. 1. Milan: Giuffrè.

Bussi, Emilio. 1959. *Il diritto pubblico del Sacro Romano Impero alla fine del XVIII secolo*. Vol. 2. Milan: Giuffrè.

Bussi, Emilio. 1966. *Stato e amministrazione nel pensiero di Carl Gottlieb Svarez, precettore di Federico Guglielmo III di Prussia*. Milan: Giuffrè.

Bussi, Emilio. 1971. *Diritto e politica in Germania nel XVIII secolo*. Milan: Giuffrè.

Bussi, Emilio. 2002. *Evoluzione storica dei tipi di Stato*. Milan: Giuffrè.

Calasso, Francesco. 1951. *Introduzione al diritto comune*. Milan: Giuffrè.

Campos Boralevi, Lea. 1981. "Jeremy Bentham and the Relief of Poverty." In *Aspects of Poverty in Early Modern Europe*, edited by Thomas Riis, 287–99. Florence: Badia Fiesolana.

Campos Boralevi, Lea. 1984. *Bentham and the Oppressed*. Berlin and New York: Walter De Gruyter.

Carbasse, Jean-Marie, and Guillaume Leyte. 2004. *L'État royal, XIIe–XVIIIe siècles*. Paris: Presses Universitaires de France.

Carlyle, Robert Warrand, and Alexander James Carlyle. 1950. *Political Theory from the Tenth Century to the Thirteenth*. Vol. 3 of *A History of Mediaeval Political Theory in the West*. Edinburgh and London: William Blackwood & Sons.

Carrot, Georges. 1984. *Le maintien de l'ordre en France depuis la fin de l'ancien régime jusqu'a 1968*. Toulouse: Presses de l'Institut d'Études Politiques de Toulouse.

Carsten, Francis Ludwig. 1954. *The Origins of Prussia*. Oxford: Clarendon Press.

Castel, Robert. 1995. *Les métamorphoses de la question sociale: Une chronique du salariat*. Paris: Fayard.

Cavalletti, Andrea. 2005. *La città biopolitica: Mitologie della sicurezza*. Milan: Bruno Mondadori.

Chadwick, Edwin. 1837. *An Article on the Principles and Progress of the Poor Law Amendment Act, and also on the Nature of the Central Control and Improved Local Administration Introduced by That Statute*. London: Charles Knight & Co.

Chadwick, Edwin, Charles Shaw Lefevre, and Charles Rowan. 1839. "First Report of the Commissioners Appointed to Inquire as to the Best Means of Establishing an Efficient Constabulary Force in the Counties of England and Wales." In *Reports of Commissioners*, published by direction of Her Majesty's Principal Secretary of State for the Home Department. London: Charles Knight & Co.

Chapman, Brian. 1971. *Police State*. London: Macmillan.

Chevalier, Louis. (1958) 1973. *Laboring Classes and Dangerous Classes in Paris during the First Half of the Nineteenth Century*. London: RKP.

Chevalier, Jean-Jacques. 1979. *Histoire de la pensée politique*. Paris: Payot.

Child, Josiah. 1693. *A New Discourse of Trade*. London: John Everingham.

Cole, Charles Woosley., 1938. *Colbert and a Century of French Mercantilism*. 2 vols. New York: Thomson Learning.

Colquhoun, Patrick. 1806. *A Treatise on Indigence: Exhibiting a General View of the National Resources for Productive Labour; with Propositions for Ameliorating the Condition of the Poor, and Improving the Moral Habits and Increasing the Comforts of the Labouring People*. London: J. Hatchard.

Colquhoun, Patrick. (1806) 1969. *A Treatise on the Police of the Metropolis; Containing a Detail of the Various Crimes and Misdemeanors by Which Public and Private Property and Security Are, at Present, Injured and Endangered and Suggesting Remedies for Their Prevention*. Montclair, NJ: Patterson Smith.

Colquhoun, Patrick. 1807. *Traité sur la police de Londres, contenant le détail des crimes et délits qui se commettent dans cette capitale, et indiquant les moyens de les prévenir*. Paris: L. Collin.

Cortese, Ennio. 1962. *La norma giuridica: Spunti teorici nel diritto comune classico*. Vol. 1. Milan, Giuffrè.

Costa, Pietro. 1969. *Iurisdictio: Semantica del potere politico nella pubblicistica medievale, 1100–1433*. Milan: Giuffrè.

Costa, Pietro. 1999. *Dalla civiltà comunale al settecento*. Vol. 1 of *Civitas: Storia della cittadinanza in Europa*. Rome and Bari: Laterza.

Costa, Pietro, and Danilo Zolo, eds. 2007. *The Rule of Law History, Theory and Criticism*. Dordrecht: Springer.

Cremer, Albert. 1989. "L'administration dans les encyclopédies et dictionnaires français du 17e et du 18e siècle." *Jahrbuch für Europäische Verwaltungsgeschichte* 1: 1–13.

Critchley, Thomas Alan. 1972. *A History of Police in England and Wales*. Montclair, NJ: Patterson Smith.

Croce, Benedetto. 1994. *Etica e politica*, edited by Giuseppe Galasso. Milan: Adelphi.

Cunningham, William. 1920–22. *The Growth of English Industry and Commerce in Modern Times*. 3 vols. Cambridge: Cambridge University Press.

D'Addio, Mario. 1970. "Machiavelli e antimachiavelli." In *Machiavellismo ed antimachiavellici nel Cinquecento. Atti del convegno di Perugia, 30 settembre–1 ottobre 1969*. Florence: Leo S. Olschki Editore.

Daly, James. 1978. "The Idea of Absolute Monarchy in Seventeenth-Century England." *Historical Journal* 21, no. 2: 227–50.

Damaška, Mirjan. 1986. *The Faces of Justice and State Authority: A Comparative Approach to the Legal Process*. New Haven, CT: Yale University Press.

Daries, Joachim Georg. 1763. *Commentatione de differentiis iurisprudentiae atque politiae, quae vulgo die Policey dicitur*. Francofurti ad Viadrum: Christiani Winteri.

David, Marcel. 1954. *La souveraineté et les limites juridiques du pouvoir monarchique du IXe au XVe siècle*. Paris: Librarie Dalloz.

Dean, Mitchell. 1991. *The Constitution of Poverty: Toward a Genealogy of Liberal Governance*. London: Routledge.

Dean, Mitchell. 1992. "A Genealogy of the Government of Poverty." *Economy and Society* XXI, no. 3: 215–51.

Dean, Mitchell. 1999. *Governmentality: Power and Rule in Modern Society*. London: Sage.

De Benedictis, Angela. 2001. *Politica, governo e istituzioni nell'Europa moderna*. Bologna: il Mulino.

De Chassaigne, Marc. (1906) 1975. *La Lieutenance général de police de Paris*. Geneva: Slatkine-Megariotis Reprints.

De Curban, Gaspard de Réal. 1761–64. *La science du gouvernement*. 8 vols. Aix-la-Chapelle: Arkstee et Merkus.

Defoe, Daniel. (1704) 1970. *Giving Alms No Charity, and Employing the Poor a Grievance to the Nation*. New York: Wakefield.

De Frémeville, Edme de La Poix. 1758. *Dictionnaire ou traité de la police générale des villes, bourgs, paroisses et seigneuries de la campagne*. Paris: Gissey.

Delamare, Nicolas. 1705. *Traité de la police, où l'on trouvera l'histoire de son établissement les fonctions et les prérogatives de ses magistrats, toutes les loix et tous les règlements qui la concernent*. Paris: Jean & Pierre Cot.

Delamare, Nicolas. 1738. *Continuation du traité de la police*. Vol. 4. Paris: Jean-François Herrissant.

Della Casa, Giovanni (Mons.). 1733. "Orazione a Carlo V imperatore intorno alla restituzione della città di Piacenza." In vol. 3 of *Opere di Monsignor Giovanni della Casa*. Naples: n.p.

De Maddalena, Aldo. 1980. "Il mercantilismo." In *L'età moderna*. Vol. 4 of *Storia delle idee politiche economiche e sociali*, edited by Luigi Firpo, 637–704. Turin: UTET.

De Mattei, Rodolfo. 1970. "Distinzioni in sede di antimachiavellismo." In *Machiavellismo ed antimachiavellici nel Cinquecento. Atti del convegno di Perugia, 30 settembre–1 ottobre 1969*. Florence: Leo S. Olschki Editore.

De Mattei, Rodolfo. 1979. *Il problema della Ragion di Stato nell'età della Controriforma*. Milan: Giuffrè.

De Pisan, Christine. 1521. *The Booke Whiche Is Called the Body of Polycye*. London: John Skot.

De Royer, Antoine-François Prost. 1782. "Administration." In vol. 2 of *Dictionnaire de jurisprudence et des arrêts*. Lyon: Aimé de la Roche.

Descendre, Romain. 2003. "Puissance et économie chez Giovanni Botero." *Revue de Métaphysique et de morale* 3: 311–21.

Des Essarts, Nicolas. 1786–91. *Dictionnaire universel de police*. 8 vols. Paris: Moutard.

De Seyssel, Claude. (1515) 1961. *La monarchie de France*, edited by Jaques Puojol. Paris: Librairie d'Argences.

De Vouglans, Pierre-François Muyart de. 1780. *Les loix criminelles de France dans leur ordre naturel*. Paris: Chez Merigot le jeune, Crapart, Benoît Morin.

Dewar, Mary, ed. 1969. *A Discourse of the Commonweal of This Realm of England*, attributed to Sir Thomas Smith. Charlottesville, VA: University of Virginia Press.

Digneffe, Françoise. 1995. "Problèmes sociaux et représentations du crime et du criminel." In *Des savoirs diffus à la notion de criminel-né*, vol. 1 of *Histoire des savoirs sur le crime and la peine*, edited by Christian Debuyst, François Digneffe, Jean-Michel Labadie, and Alvaro P. Pires, 137–213. Brussels: De Boeck-Wesmael.

Dithmar, Justus Christoph. 1745. *Einleitung in die ökonomischen-, Policey- und Cameral-Wissenschaften*. Frankfurt an der Oder: Verlegts J. J. Friedel.

Dobb, Maurice. 1946. *Studies in the Development of Capitalism*. London: Routledge.

Dorwart, Reinholt August. 1953. *The Administrative Reforms of Frederick William I of Prussia*. Cambridge, MA: Harvard University Press.

Dorwart, Reinholt August. 1971. *The Prussian Welfare State before 1740*. Cambridge, MA: Harvard University Press.

Dreyfus, Hubert L., and Paul Rabinow. 1983. *Michel Foucault: Beyond Structuralism and Hermeneutics*. Chicago, IL: University of Chicago Press.

Dubber, Markus Dirk. 2004. "'The Power to Govern Men and Things': Patriarchal Origins of the Police Power in American Law." *Buffalo Law Review* 57, no. 1277 (Fall): 101–66.

Duby, Georges. 1978. *Les trois ordres ou l'imaginaire du féodalisme.* Paris: Gallimard.

Du Chesne, Nicolas. 1757. *Code de la police, ou analyse des réglements de police: Divisé en douze titres.* Paris: Prault.

Dudley, Edmund. (1509–10) 1948. *The Tree of Commonwealth*, edited by D. M. Brodie. Cambridge: Cambridge University Press.

Dunbabin. Jean. 1988. "Government." In *The Cambridge History of Medieval Political Thought, 350–1450*, edited by James Henderson Burns. Cambridge: Cambridge University Press.

Duport, Adrien Jean-François. 1790a. *Principes et plan sur l'établissement de l'ordre judiciaire, 29 mars 1790.* Paris: Imprimerie Nationale.

Duport, Adrien Jean-François. 1790b. *Projet de loi sur la police de sûreté, la justice criminelle et l'institution des jurés, présenté au nom des comités de constitution et de jurisprudence criminelle.* Paris: Imprimerie Nationale.

Duport, Adrien Jean-François. 1790c. *Rapport, fait au nom des comités de constitution et de jurisprudence criminelle, de la loi sur la police de sûreté la justice criminelle et l'institution des jurés, séance du 27 novembre 1790.* Paris: Imprimerie Nationale.

Durand, Bernard. 1996. "La notion de police en France du XVIe au XVIIIe siècle." In *Policey im Europa der Frühen Neuzeit*, edited by Michael Stolleis, 163–211. Frankfurt am Main: Vittorio Klostermann.

Dyson, Kenneth. 1980. *The State Tradition in Western Europe.* Oxford: Martin Robertson.

Eccleshall, Robert. 1978. *Order and Reason in Politics: Theories of Absolute and Limited Monarchy in Early Modern England.* Oxford: Oxford University Press.

Eden, Frederic Morton. 1797. *The State of the Poor: A History of the Labouring Classes in England.* 3 vols. London: J. Davis.

Elton, Geoffrey Rudolph. 1953. *The Tudor Revolution in Government.* Cambridge: Cambridge University Press.

Elton, Geoffrey Rudolph. 1973. *Reform and Renewal: Thomas Cromwell and the Common Weal.* Cambridge: Cambridge University Press.

Elton, Geoffrey Rudolph. 1974a. "State Planning in Early-Tudor England." In vol. 1 of *Studies in Tudor and Stuart Politics and Government: Papers and Reviews, 1946–1972*, 285–93. Cambridge: Cambridge University Press.

Elton, Geoffrey Rudolph. 1974b. "Government by Edict?" In vol. 1 of *Studies in Tudor and Stuart Politics and Government: Papers and Reviews, 1946–1972*, 300–07. Cambridge: Cambridge University Press.

Elton, Geoffrey Rudolph. 1974c. "Reform by Statute: Thomas Starkey's *Dialogue* and Thomas Cromwell's Policy." In vol. 2 of *Studies in Tudor and Stuart Politics and Government: Papers and Reviews, 1946–1972*, 236–58. Cambridge: Cambridge University Press.

Elton, Geoffrey Rudolph. 1979. "Reform and the 'Commonwealthmen' of Edward VI's Reign." In *The English Commonwealth, 1547–1640*, edited by P. Clark, A. G. R. Smith, and N. Tyacke. Reprinted in vol. 3 of *Studies in Tudor and Stuart Politics and Government: Papers and Reviews, 1946–1972*, 234–53. Cambridge: Cambridge University Press.

Elyot, Thomas. (1531) 1907. *The Boke Named the Governour.* London: J. M. Dent & Co.; New York: Dutton & Co. Everyman's Library.

Esposito, Roberto. 2004. *Bìos: Biopolitica e filosofia.* Turin: Einaudi.

Euloge, Georges André. 1985. *Histoire de la police des origines à 1940.* Paris: Plon.

Ferguson, Arthur. 1965. *The Articulate Citizen and the English Renaissance*. Durham, NC: Duke University Press.

Ferrajoli, Luigi. 1990. *Diritto e ragione: Teoria del garantismo penale*. Bari and Rome: Laterza.

Fideler, Paul A. 1998. "Poverty, Policy and Providence: The Tudors and the Poor." In *Political Thought and the Tudor Commonwealth: Deep Structure, Discourse and Disguise*, edited by Paul A. Fideler and Thomas F. Maye, 194–222. London and New York: Routledge.

Fielding, John. 1755. *A Plan for Preventing Robberies Within Twenty Miles of London, with an Account of the Rise and Establishment of the Real Thieftakers, to Which Is Added, Advice to Pawnbrokers, Stable-Keepers, and Publicans*. London: A. Millar.

Fielding, John. 1776. *A Brief Description of the Cities of London and Westminster: the public buildings, palaces, gardens, squares, &c. with an alphabetical list of all the streets, squares, courts, lanes and alleys, &c. within the bills of mortality. To which are added, Some proper cautions to the Merchants, Tradesmen, and Shop-Keepers; Journeymen, Apprentices, Porters, Errand Boys, Book-Keepers, and Inn-Keepers; also very necessary for every Person going to London either on Business or Pleasure*. London: J. Wilkie.

Filmer, Robert. (1680) 1991. *Patriarcha; or the Natural Power of Kings*, edited by Johann Sommerville. Cambridge: Cambridge University Press.

Firpo, Luigi. 1970. "Le origini dell'antimachiavellismo." In *Machiavellismo ed antimachiavellici nel Cinquecento. Atti del convegno di Perugia, 30 settembre–1 ottobre 1969*. Florence: Leo S. Olschki Editore.

Fisher, William, and Peter Lundgreen. 1975. "The Recruitment and Training of Administrative and Technical Personnel." In *The Formation of National States in Western Europe*, edited by Charles Tilly, 465–561. Princeton, NJ: Princeton University Press.

Flammermont, Jules, ed. 1888. *Remontrances du Parlement de Paris au XVIIIe siècle*. vol. 3, 1768–1788. Paris: Imprimerie Nationale.

Fleury, Claude. (1692) 1858. *Institutions du droit français*. 2 vols. Paris: Durand.

Fortescue, John. (1775) 1825. *De laudibus legum Angliæ*, edited and translated by Andrew Amos. London: Joseph Butterworth & Son.

Foucault, Michel. 1961. *Folie et déraison: Histoire de la folie à l'âge classique*. Paris: Union Générale d'Éditions.

Foucault, Michel. 1966. *Les mots et les choses: Une archéologie des sciences humaines*. Paris: Gallimard.

Foucault, Michel. (1974) 2001. "La vérité et les formes juridiques." In vol. 1 of *Dits et écrits, 1954–1975*, 1406–1514. Paris: Gallimard.

Foucault, Michel. (1977a) 2001. "Le jeu de Michel Foucault." In vol. 2 of *Dits et écrits, 1976–1988*, 298–329. Paris: Gallimard.

Foucault, Michel. 1977b. *Discipline and Punish: The Birth of the Prison*. New York: Vintage Books.

Foucault, Michel. 1980. "The Confession of the Flesh" (interview). In *Power/Knowledge: Selected Interviews and Other Writings, 1972–1977*, edited by Colin Gordon, 193–228. New York: Pantheon Books.

Foucault, Michel. (1982) 2001. "Espace, savoir et pouvoir." In vol. 2 of *Dits et écrits, 1976–1988*, 1089–1104. Paris: Gallimard.

Foucault, Michel. 1988. *Madness and Civilization: A History of Insanity in the Age of Reason*, translated from the French by Richard Howard. New York: Vintage Books.

Foucault, Michel. 2003. *Society Must Be Defended: Lectures at the Collège de France, 1975–76*. New York: Picador.

Foucault, Michel. 2004. *Security, Territory, Population: Lectures at the Collège de France 1977–1978*, edited by Michel Senellart and translated by Graham Burchell. New York: Picador.

Foucault, Michel. 2008. *The Birth of Biopolitics: Lectures at the Collège de France, 1978–79*. New York: Palgrave Macmillan.

Frégier, Honoré-Antoine. 1840. *Des classes dangereuses de la population dans les grandes villes et les moyens de les rendre meilleures*. Paris: Baillière.

Frigo, Daniela. 1985. *Il padre di famiglia: Governo della casa e governo civile nella tradizione dell'Economica tra Cinque e Seicento*. Rome: Bulzoni.

Fumagalli, Mariateresa, and Beonio Brocchieri. 2000. *Il pensiero politico medievale*. Rome and Bari: Laterza.

Ganshof, François Louis. 1947. *Qu'est-ce que la féodalité?* Brussels: Éditions de la Baconniere.

Garizzo, Giovanni. 1980. "Il pensiero inglese nell'età degli Stuart e della Rivoluzione." In *L'età moderna*. Vol. 4 of *Storia delle idee politiche, economiche e sociali*, edited by Luigi Firpo. Turin: UTET.

Garizzo, Giovanni. 1987. "Il pensiero politico dell'età dei Tudor." In *Umanesimo e rinascimento*. Vol. 3 of *Storia delle idee politiche, economiche e sociali*, edited by Luigi Firpo. Turin: UTET.

Gasser, Simon Peter. 1729. *Einleitung zu den ökonomischen, politischen und Cameral-Wissenschaften*. Halle: Waysenhaus.

Gaudemet, Jean. 1951. "Utilitas publica." *Revue Historique de Droit Français et Étranger* 29: 465–99.

Geremek, Bonislaw. 1994. *Poverty: A History*. Translated from the Polish by Agnieszka Kolakowska. Oxford: Blackwell.

Gooch, George Peabody. 1947. *Frederick the Great: The Ruler, the Writer, the Man*. London and New York: Knopf.

Gordon, Colin. 1991. "Governmental Rationality: An Introduction." In *The Foucault Effect: Studies in Governmentality*, edited by Gary Burchell, Colin Gordon, and Peter Miller, 1–52. London: Harvester Wheatsheaf.

Grossi, Paolo. 1995. *L'ordine giuridico medievale*. Bari and Rome: Laterza.

Guicciardini, Francesco. (1520) 1994. *Dialogue on the Government of Florence*. Cambridge: Cambridge University Press.

Gutting, Gary. 1989. *Michel Foucault's Archaeology of Scientific Reason*. Cambridge: Cambridge University Press.

Gutton, Jean-Pierre. 1971. *La société et les pauvres: L'exemple de la généralité de Lyon, 1524–1789*. Paris: Presses Universitaires de France.

Guy, John. 1993. "The Henrician Age." In *The Varieties of British Political Thought, 1500–1800*, edited by John Greville Agard Pocock, 13–46. Cambridge: Cambridge University Press.

Haakonssen, Kund. 1981. *The Science of a Legislator: The Natural Jurisprudence of David Hume and Adam Smith*. Cambridge: Cambridge University Press.

Hacking, Ian. 1986. "The Archaeology of Foucault." In *Foucault: A Critical Reader*, edited by David C. Hoy Couzens. Oxford: Basil Blackwell.

Hale, Matthew. (1683) 1805. *A Discourse Touching Provision for the Poor*. In vol. 1 of *The Works, Moral and Religious, of Sir Matthew Hale, Knt*. London: R. Wilks.

Harrington, Joel F. 1999. "Escape from the Great Confinement: The Genealogy of a German Workhouse." *The Journal of Modern History* LXXI: 308–45.

Härter, Karl. 1996. "Disciplinamento sociale e ordinanze di polizia nella prima età moderna." In *Disciplina dell'anima, disciplina del corpo e disciplina della società tra medioevo ed età moderna*, edited by Paolo Prodi. Bologna: il Mulino.

Hartung, Friz, and Roland Mousnier. 1955. "Quelques problèmes concernant la monarchie absolue." In vol. 4 of *Relazioni del decimo congresso internazionale di scienze storiche*, Rome, 1–55. Florence: Sansoni.

Haruel, Louis, Jean Barbey, Eric Bournazel, and Jacqueline Thibaut-Payen. 2006. *Histoire des institutions de l'époque franque a la révolution*. Paris: Presses Universitaires de France.

Heckscher, Eli J. 1955. *Mercantilism*, edited by Ernst F. Söderlund. London: George Allen and Unwin.

Hegel, Georg Wilhelm Friedrich (1821) 1991. *Elements of the Philosophy of Right*, edited by Allen W. Wood, translated by H. B. Nisbet. Cambridge: Cambridge University Press.

Heidenhamer, Arnold J. 1986. "Politics, Policy and Police as Concepts in English and Continental Languages." *The Review of Politics* 48, no. 1: 3–30.

Hespanha, António Manuel. 1999. *Introduzione alla storia del diritto europeo*. Bologna: il Mulino.

Hill, Christopher. 1965. *Intellectual Origins of the English Revolution*. Oxford: Clarendon Press.

Himmelfarb, Gertrude. 1984. *The Idea of Poverty: England and the Early Industrial Age*. London: Faber & Faber.

Hintze, Otto. (1929) 1980. "Wesen und Verbreitung der Feudalismus." Italian translation: "Essenza e diffusione del feudalesimo." In *Stato e società*, 50–76. Bologna: Zanichelli.

Holdsworth, William Searle. 1924. *A History of English Law*. London: Methuen.

Hommel, C. F. 1770. *De differentia causarum politiae et justitiae*. Leipzig: n.p.

Hubatsch, Walther. 1973. *Frederick the Great of Prussia: Absolutism and Administration*. Translated from the German by Patrick Doran. London: Thames and Hudson.

Isambert, François-André, ed. 1826. *Recueil général des anciennes lois françaises*. Vol. 23. Paris: Belin-Leprieur.

Jones, Whitney Richard David. 2000. *The Tree of Commonwealth, 1450–1793*. London: Associated University Presses.

Kant, Immanuel. (1784) 1991. "Idea for a Universal History with a Cosmopolitan Purpose." In *Kant: Political Writings*, edited by Hans Siegbert Reiss, 41–53. Cambridge: Cambridge University Press.

Kant, Immanuel. (1793) 1991. "On the Common Saying: 'This May Be True in Theory but It Does Not Apply in Practice.'" In *Kant: Political Writings*, edited by Hans Siegbert Reiss, 61–92. Cambridge: Cambridge University Press.

Kantorowicz, Ernst H. 1957. *The King's Two Bodies: A Study in Mediaeval Political Theology*. Princeton, NJ: Princeton University Press.

Kaplan, Steven. 1979. "Réflexions sur la police du monde du travail, 1700–1815." *Revue Historique* 261, no. 1 (January–March): 17–77.

Kaplan, Steven. 1988. *Les ventres de Paris: Pouvoir et approvisionnement dans la France d'Ancien Régime*. Paris: Fayard.

Kelley, Donald R. 1996. "Elizabethan Political Thought." In *The Varieties of British Political Thought, 1500–1800*, edited by John Greville Agard Pocock, 47–79. Cambridge: Cambridge University Press.

Kenyon, John Philip, ed. 1986. *The Stuart Constitution, 1603–1688: Documents and Commentary*. Cambridge: Cambridge University Press.

Knemeyer, Franz-Ludwig. 1978. "Policey." In vol. 4 of *Geschichtliche Grundbegriffe: Historisches Lexikon zur politisch-sozialen Sprache in Deutschland*, edited by Otto Brunner, Werner Conze, and Reinhart Koselleck, 875–97. Stuttgart: Klett-Cotta.

Koselleck, Reinhart. 1981. *Preußen zwischen Reform und Revolution 1791–1848*. Stuttgart: Klett-Cotta.

Laborier, Pascale. 1999. "La 'bonne police': Sciences camérales et pouvoir absolutiste dans les États allemands." *Politix* 12, no. 48: 7–35.

La Maire, Jean-Baptiste-Charles. 1878. "La police de Paris en 1770: Mémoire inédit composé par ordre de Gabriel de Sartine sur la demande de Marie-Thérèse," edited by Augustin Louis Gazier. *Mémoires de la Société de l'Histoire de Paris et de l'Isle-de-France* 5: 1–131.

Lambarde, William. 1581. *Eirenarcha, or of the Office of the Justices of Peace*. London: Newbery & Bynneman. Anastatic reprint, Amsterdam: Teatrum Orbis Terrarum, 1970.

Lazzeri, Christian, and Dominique Reynié, eds. 1992. *La raison d'état: Politique et rationalité*. Paris: Presses Universitaires de France.

Le Clere, Marcel. 1957. *Histoire de la police*. Paris: Presses Universitaires de France.

Legendre, Pierre. 1966. "Histoire de la pensée administrative française." In *Traité de science administrative*, edited by Gérard Langrod, 6–79. Paris: Mouton.

Levy Peck, Linda. 1996. "Kingship, Counsel and Law in Early Stuart Britain." In *The Varieties of British Political Thought, 1500–1800*, edited by John Greville Agard Pocock, 80–115. Cambridge: Cambridge University Press.

Lindenfeld, David. 1989. "The Decline of *Polizeiwissenschaft*: Continuity and Change in the Study of Administration in German Universities during the 19th Century." *Jahrbuch für europäische Verwaltungsgeschichte* 1: 141–59.

Lipsius, Justus. (1589) 1998. *Politicorum sive Civilis doctrinae libri sex*, edited by Wolfgang Weber. Zurich: Hildesheim; New York: Georg Olms Verlag.

Lis, Catharina, and Hugo, Soly. 1979. *Poverty and Capitalism in Pre-industrial Europe*. Atlantic Highlands, NJ: Humanities Press.

Loyseau, Charles. 1608. *Traité des seigneuries et simples dignités*. Paris: L'Angelier.

Lüdtke, Alf. 1989. *Police and State in Prussia, 1815–1850*. Cambridge: Cambridge University Press.

Lyon, Bryce. 1960. *A Constitutional and Legal History of Medieval England*. New York: Harper & Row.

MacCaffrey, William Thomas. 1965. "England: The Crown and the New Aristocracy, 1540–1600." *Past and Present* 30: 52–64.

Machiavelli, Niccolò. (1532) 1988. *The Prince*, edited by Quentin Skinner and Russell Price. Cambridge: Cambridge University Press.

Macpherson, Crawford Brough. 1962. *The Political Theory of Possessive Individualism: Hobbes to Locke*. Oxford: Clarendon Press.

McIlwain, Charles Howard. 2007. *Constitutionalism: Ancient and Modern*. Indianapolis, IN: Liberty Fund. (Orig. pub. 1940, Cornell University Press.)

Maffey, Aldo. 1980. "Il pensiero politico della fisiocrazia." In *L'età moderna*. Vol. 4 of *Storia delle idee politiche economiche e sociali*, edited by Luigi Firpo, 491–530. Turin: UTET.

Maffey, Aldo. 2004. "Mercantilismo." In *Dizionario di Politica*, edited by Gianfranco Pasquino, Nicola Matteucci, and Norberto Bobbio, 563. Turin: UTET.

Maier, Hans. 1962. "Die Ledere der Politik and en deutschen Universitäten vornehmlich vom 16. bis 18. Jahrhundert." In *Wissenschaftliche Politik: Eine Einführung in Grundfragen ihrer Tradition und Theorie*, edited by Dieter Oberndörfer, 59–116. Freiburg: Rombach.

Maier, Hans. 1966. *Die ältere deutsche Staats- und Verwaltungslehre (Polizeiwissenschaft)*. Neuwied and Berlin: Luchterhand.

Malthus, Thomas Robert. 1798. *An Essay on the Principle of Population*. London: J. Johnson.

Mannori, Luciano, and Bernardo Sordi. 2001. *Storia del diritto amministrativo*. Rome and Bari: Laterza.

Marion, Marcel. 1969. *Dictionnaire des institutions de la France au XVIIe et XVIIIe siècles.* Paris: Picard & Cie.

Marx, Karl. (1843) 1975. "On the Jewish Question." In vol. 3 of *Collected Works,* by Karl Marx and Friedrich Engels. London: Lawrence & Wishart.

Marx, Karl. (1867) 1906. *Capital. A Critique of Political Economy.* Edited by Friedrich Engels. Vol. 1. New York: The Modern Library.

Mastellone, Stefano. 1970. "Aspetti dell'antimachiavellismo in Francia." In *Machiavellismo ed antimachiavellici nel Cinquecento. Atti del convegno di Perugia, 30 settembre–1 ottobre 1969.* Florence: Leo S. Olschki Editore.

Meinecke, Friedrich. 1957. *Die Idee der Staatsräson in der neueren Geschichte.* Munich: Oldenbourg.

Melossi, Dario. 1990. *The State of Social Control: A Sociological Study of Concepts of State and Social Control in the Making of Democracy.* Cambridge: Polity Press.

Melossi, Dario, and Massimo Pavarini. 1982. *Carcere e fabbrica: Alle origini del sistema penitenziario.* Bologna: il Mulino.

Melville Lee, William L. 1901. *A History of Police in England.* London: Methuen & Co.

Mestre, Jean Louis. 1985. *Introduction historique au droit administratif français.* Paris: Presses Universitaires de France.

Miller, Samuel J. T. 1956. "The Position of the King in Bracton and Beaumanoir." *Speculum* 31, no. 2: 263–96.

Milliot, Vincent. 2001. "Migrants et 'étrangers' sous l'œil de la police: La surveillance des lieux d'accueil parisiens au Siècle des lumières." In *Police et migrants: France 1667–1939,* edited by Marie-Claude Blanc-Chaléard, Caroline Douki, Nicole Dyonet, and Vincent Milliot, 315–31. Rennes: Presses Universitaires de Rennes.

Mirabeau, Honoré Gabriel. 1763. *Philosophie rurale: Ou, Économie générale et politique de l'agriculture, réduite à l'ordre immuable des loix physiques & morales, qui assurent la prospérité des empires.* Amsterdam: Chez les Libraires Associés.

Mitteis, Heinrich. 1948. *Der Staat des Hohen Mittelalters: Grundlinien einer vergleichenden Verfassungsgeschichte des Lehnszeitalters.* Weimar: Bohlaus.

Mollat, Michel. 1978. *Les pauvres au Moyen Âge: Étude sociale.* Paris: Hachette.

Montesquieu, Charles de Secondat. (1748) 1989. *The Spirit of the Laws,* edited by Anne M. Cohler, Basia Carolyn Miller, and Harold Samuel Stone. Cambridge: Cambridge University Press.

Mousnier, Roland. 1945. *La vénalité des offices sous Henry IV et Louis XIII.* Paris: Presses Universitaires de France.

Mousnier, Roland. 1972. "Stato e commissario: Ricerche sulla creazione degli intendenti delle province, 1634–1648." In Vol. 2 of *Lo Stato Moderno,* edited by Ettore Rotelli and Pierangelo Schiera, 107–26. Bologna: il Mulino.

Mousnier, Roland. 1975. *Institutions de la France sous la monarchie absolue.* 2 vols. Paris: Presses Universitaires de France.

Mozzarelli, Carlo. 1988. "Riflessioni preliminari sul concetto di polizia." *Filosofia politica* II, no. 1: 7–14.

Näf, Werner. 1971. "Le prime forme dello Stato moderno nel basso medioevo." In vol. 1 of *Lo Stato moderno,* edited by Ettore Rotelli and Pierangelo Schiera, 51–68. Bologna: il Mulino.

Napoli, Paolo. 2003. *Naissance de la police moderne: Pouvoir, normes, société.* Paris: Éditions La Découverte.

Naudé, Gabriel. (1639) 1723. *Considérations politiques sur les coups d'État.* Suivant la copie de Rome.

Nelson, Janet. 1988. "Kingship and Empire." In *The Cambridge History of Medieval Political Thought, 350–1450*, edited by James Henderson Burns. Cambridge: Cambridge University Press.

Neocleous, Mark. 1998a. "Policing the System of Needs: Hegel, Political Economy, and the Police of the Market." *History of European Ideas* 24, no. 1: 43–58.

Neocleous, Mark. 1998b. "Policing and Pin-Making: Adam Smith, Police and the State of Prosperity." *Policing and Society* 8, no. 4: 425–49.

Neocleous, Mark. 2000a. *The Fabrication of Social Order: A Critical Theory of Police Power*. London: Pluto Press.

Neocleous, Mark. 2000b. "Social Police and the Mechanism of Prevention: Patrick Colquhoun and the Condition of Poverty." *The British Journal of Criminology* 40, no. 4: 710–26.

Nuzzo, Ettore. 1995. "Crisi dell'aristotelismo politico e ragion di Stato: Alcune preliminari considerazioni metodologiche e storiografiche." In *Aristotelismo politico e Ragion di Stato. Atti del convegno internazionale di Torino, 11–13 febbraio 1993*, edited by Artemio Enzo Baldini, 11–52. Florence: Leo S. Olschki Editore.

Oestreich, Gerhard. 1971. "Problemi di struttura dell'assolutismo europeo." In vol. 1 of *Lo Stato moderno*, edited by Ettore Rotelli and Pierangelo Schiera, 173–91. Bologna: il Mulino.

Oestreich, Gerhard. 1972. "Il governo personale dei principi tedeschi all'inizio dell'età moderna." In vol. 2 of *Lo Stato Moderno*, edited by Ettore Rotelli and Pierangelo Schiera, 125–60. Bologna: il Mulino.

Oestreich, Gerhard. (1980) 1989. "Policey und Prudentia civilis in der barocken Gesellschaft von Stadt und Staat." Italian translation: "Polizia (Policey) e prudentia civilis nella società barocca della città e dello stato." In *Filosofia e costituzione dello Stato moderno*, 213–31. Edited by Pierangelo Schiera. Naples: Bibliopolis.

Oestreich, Gerhard. 1982. *Neostoicism and the Early Modern State*. Cambridge: Cambridge University Press.

Oldendorp, Johannes. 1530. *Van radtslagende/wo men gude Politie und ordenunge/ynn Steden und Landen erholden möghe*. Rostock: n.p.

Olivier-Martin, François. 1948. *La police économique de l'Ancien Régime. Cours de doctorat, 1944–1945*. Paris: Loysel.

Olivier-Martin, François. 1949. *Les lois du Roi: Cours de doctorat, 1945–1946*. Paris: Loysel.

Olivier-Martin, François. 1951. *Histoire du droit français des origines à la Révolution*. Paris: Editions Domat Montchrestien.

Ortu, Gian Giacomo. 2001. *Lo Stato moderno: Profili storici*. Rome and Bari: Laterza.

Pagés, Gary. 1972. "La venalità degli uffici nell'antica Francia." In vol. 2 of *Lo Stato Moderno*, edited by Ettore Rotelli and Pierangelo Schiera, 227–44. Bologna: il Mulino.

Pandolfi, Adriano. 2006. "La 'natura' della popolazione." In *Governare la vita*, edited by Sandro Chignola, 91–116. Verona: Ombre Corte.

Paultre, Charles. (1906) 1975. *De la répression de la mendicité et du vagabondage en France sous l'Ancien Régime*. Geneva: Slatkine.

Pennington, Kenneth. 1988. "Law, Legislative Authority, and Theories of Government, 1150–1300." In *The Cambridge History of Medieval Political Thought, 350–1450*, edited by James Henderson Burns. Cambridge: Cambridge University Press.

Pennington, Kenneth. 1993. *The Prince and the Law, 1200–1600: Sovereignty and Rights in the Western Legal Tradition*. Berkeley, CA: University of California Press.

Perrot, Jean-Claude. 1992. "Les économistes, les philosophes et la population." In *Une histoire intellectuelle de l'économie politique, XVIIe–XVIIIe siècles*, 143–92. Paris: Éditions de l'École des Hautes Études en Sciences Sociales.

Petracchi, Adriana. 1971. *L'intendente provinciale nella Francia d'antico regime: Intendenti e prefetti*. Milan: Giuffrè.

Peuchet, Jacques. 1791. "Discours préliminaire." In *La Police et les Municipalités*. Vol. 9 of *Encyclopédie méthodique par ordre des matières*. Paris: Panckoucke.

Plucknett, Theodore F. T. 1956. *A Concise History of the Common Law*. London: Butterworth.

Plucknett, Theodore F. T. 1958. *Early English Legal Literature*. Cambridge: Cambridge University Press.

Pocock, John Greville Agard. 1987. *The Ancient Constitution and the Feudal Law: A Study of English Historical Thought in the Seventeenth Century*. Cambridge: Cambridge University Press.

Poggi, Gianfranco. 1999. *Lo Stato moderno: Un profilo sociologico*. Bologna: il Mulino.

Polanyi, Karl. (1944) 2001. *The Great Transformation. The Political and Economic Origins of Our Time*. Boston, MA: Beacon Press.

Polito, Mary. 2005. *Governmental Arts in Early Tudor England*. Aldershot: Ashgate.

Pollard, Albert Frederick. 1900. *England under the Protector Somerset*. London: Kegan & Paul.

Pollock, Frederick, and Frederic William Maitland. 1898. *The History of English Law before the Time of Edward I*. Cambridge: Cambridge University Press.

Porta, Pier Luigi. 1988. "I fondamenti del pensiero economico: Policy, police e politeness nel pensiero scozzese." *Filosofia Politica* 1: 37–68.

Post, Gaines. 1964. *Studies in Medieval Legal Thought: Public Law and the State, 1100–1322*. Princeton, NJ: Princeton University Press.

Pound, John. 1971. *Poverty and Vagrancy in Tudor England*. London: Harlow Longman.

Poynter, John Riddoch. 1969. *Society and Pauperism: English Ideas on Poor Relief 1775–1834*. London: Routledge.

Procacci, Giovanna. 1993. *Gouverner la misère: La question sociale en France, 1789–1848*. Paris: Editions du Seuil.

Procacci, Giuliano. 1995. *Machiavelli nella cultura europea dell'età moderna*. Rome and Bari: Laterza.

Pütter, Johann Stephan. 1770. *Institutiones Iuris Publici Germanici*. Göttingen: Vandenhoeck.

Quesnay, François. 1768. *Physiocratie, ou Constitution naturelle du gouvernement le plus avantageux au genre humain*, edited by Pierre-Samuel Dupont de Nemours. Leiden: Merlin.

Quesnay, François. 1888. "Maximes générales du gouvernement économique d'un royaume agricole." In *Œuvres économiques et philosophiques*. Frankfurt am Main: Baer.

Radzinowicz, Leon. 1956. *The Reform of the Police*. Vol. 3 of *History of English Criminal Law*. London: Stevens & Sons Limited.

Raeff, Mark. 1983. *The Well-Ordered Police State: Social and Institutional Change through Law in the Germanies and Russia, 1600–1800*. New Haven, CT, and London: Yale University Press.

Ranelletti, Oreste. 1904. "La polizia di sicurezza." In vol. 4 of *Trattato di diritto amministrativo italiano*, edited by Vittorio Emanuele Orlando, 205–1265. Milan: Società Editrice Libraria.

Rechemberg, C. O. 1739. *De politiae et jurisdictione terminis accuratius definiendis*. Leipzig: n.p.

Reith, Charles. 1938. *The Police Idea: Its History and Evolution in England in the Eighteenth Century and After*. London, New York, Toronto: Oxford University Press.

Revel, Judit. 2002. *Le vocabulaire de Foucault*. Paris: Ellipses.

Riedel, Manfred. 1975. *Metaphysik und Metapolitik: Studien zu Aristoteles und zur politischen Sprache der neuzeitlichen Philosophie*. Frankfurt am Main: Suhrkamp.

Riedel, Manfred. 1978. "Gesellschaft (bürgerliche)." In *Geschichtliche Grundbegriffe: Historisches Lexikon zur politisch-sozialen Sprache in Deutschland*, edited by Otto Brunner, Werner Conze, and Reinhart Koselleck. Stuttgart: Klett-Cotta.

Rigaudière, Albert. 1996. "Les ordonnances de police en France à la fin du Moyen Âge." In *Policey im Europa der Frühen Neuzeit*, edited by Michael Stolleis, 97–161. Frankfurt am Main: Vittorio Klostermann.

Ritter, Gerhard A. 1974. "Diritto divino e prerogativa dei re inglesi." In vol. 3 of *Lo Stato Moderno*, edited by Ettore Rotelli and Pierangelo Schiera, 69–106. Bologna: il Mulino.

Rosenberg, Hans. 1958. *Bureaucracy, Aristocracy and Autocracy: The Prussian Experience, 1660–1815*. Cambridge, MA: Harvard University Press.

Rousseau, Jean-Jacques. (1758) 1964. "Discours sur l'économie politique." In *Du contrat social: Écrits politiques*. Vol. 3 of *Œuvres complètes*, edited by Bernard Gagnebin and Marcel Raymond, 239–78. Paris: Gallimard.

Rousseau, Jean-Jacques. (1758) 2012. "A Discourse on Political Economy." In *The Basic Political Writings*, edited by Donald A. Cress and David Wootton, 121–52. Indianapolis, IN: Hackett Publishing Company.

Rousseau, Jean-Jacques. (1762) 2012. "On the Social Contract." In *The Basic Political Writings*, edited by Donald A. Cress and David Wootton, 153–252. Indianapolis, IN: Hackett Publishing Company.

Sachsse, Christoph, and Florian Tennstedt. 1980. *Geschichte der Armenfürsorge in Deutschland: vom Spatmittelalter bis zum Estern Weltkrieg*. 2 vols. Stuttgart: Kohlhammer.

Saint-Bonnet, François. 2001. *L'état d'exception*. Paris: Presses Universitaires de France.

Santoro, Emilio. 1999. *Common law e costituzione nell'Inghilterra moderna: Introduzione al pensiero di Albert Venn Dicey*. Turin: Giappichelli.

Sbriccoli, Mario. 1986. "Polizia (diritto intermedio)." In *Enciclopedia del diritto*, 111–20. Milan: Giuffrè.

Schiera, Pierangelo. 1968. *Dall'arte di governo alle scienze dello stato: Il Cameralismo e l'assolutismo tedesco*. Milan: Giuffrè.

Schiera, Pierangelo. 1996. "Disciplina, stato moderno, disciplinamento: Considerazioni a cavallo fra la sociologia del potere e la storia costituzionale." In *Disciplina dell'anima, disciplina del corpo e disciplina della società tra medioevo ed età moderna*, edited by Paolo Prodi, 21–46. Bologna: il Mulino.

Schiera, Pierangelo. 2003. "Concetto di polizia e statualità nell'assolutismo illuminato: Il ruolo della scienza nella trasformazione della protezione statale." In *Aufklärung*, VII, 2 (1994), 85–100. Now in *Lo stato moderno: Origini e degenerazioni*, 180ff. Bologna: CLUEB.

Schiera, Pierangelo. 2004a. "Stato di polizia." In *Dizionario di Politica*, edited by Gianfranco Pasquino, Nicola Matteucci, and Norberto Bobbio, 947–50. Turin: UTET.

Schiera, Pierangelo. 2004b. "Società per ceti." In *Dizionario di Politica*, edited by Gianfranco Pasquino, Nicola Matteucci, and Norberto Bobbio, 899ff. Turin: UTET.

Schiera, Pierangelo. 2004c. "Assolutismo." In *Dizionario di Politica*, edited by Gianfranco Pasquino, Nicola Matteucci, and Norberto Bobbio, 45–49. Turin: UTET.

Schmitt, Carl. 1922. *Politische Theologie: Vier Kapitel zur Lehre der Souveränität*. Munich and Leipzig: Duncker & Humblot.

Schmitt, Carl. 1932. *Begriff des Politischen*. Munich and Leipzig: Duncker & Humblot.

Schmitt, Charles. B. 1983. *Aristotle and the Renaissance*. Cambridge, MA: Harvard University Press.

Schochet, Gordon Joel. 1975. *Patriarchalism in Political Thought.* Oxford: Oxford University Press.

Schreber, Daniel Gottfried. 1764. *Zwo Schriften von der Geschichte und Notwendigkeit der Cameralwissenschaften.* Leipzig: n.p.

Schreiber, G. C. 1739. *Dissertatio causarum politiae et earum quae iustitiae dicuntur conflictu et differentia.* Göttingen: n.p.

Schulz, Fritz. 1945. "Bracton on Kingship." *English Historical Review* LX: 136–76.

Schulze, Reiner. 1988. "La *Policey* in Germania." *Filosofia politica* II, no. 1: 69–104.

Schumpeter, Joseph Alois. (1954) 1986. *History of Economic Analysis,* edited from manuscript by Elizabeth Boody Schumpeter. London: Routledge.

Senellart, Michel. 1992. "La raison d'État antimachiavélienne." In *La raison d'état: Politique et rationalité,* edited by Christian Lazzeri and Dominique Reynié, 15–42. Paris: Presses Universitaires de France.

Senellart, Michel. 1994. "Le stoïcisme dans la constitution de la pensée politique: Les politiques de Juste Lipse (1589)." *Cahiers de Philosophie Politique et Juridique* XXV: 109–30.

Senellart, Michel. 2003. "Critique de la raison gouvernementale." In *Foucault au Collège de France: Un itinéraire,* edited by Guillaume le Blanc and Jean Terrel. Pessac: Presses Universitaires de Bordeaux.

Senellart, Michel. 2005. *Les arts de gouverner: Du regimen médiéval au concept de gouvernement.* Seuil: Des Travaux.

Shennan, Joseph Hugh. 1974. *The Origins of the Modern European State, 1450–1725.* London: Hutchinson.

Sieyès, Emmanuel-Joseph. 1790. *Aperçu d'une nouvelle organisation de la justice et de la police en France.* Paris: Imprimerie Nationale.

Skinner, Quentin. 1978. *The Foundations of Modern Political Thought.* Vol. 1, *The Renaissance.* Cambridge: Cambridge University Press.

Slack, Paul. 1980. "Books of Orders: The Making of English Social Policy, 1577–1631." *Transactions of the Royal Historical Society* XXX, no. 5: 1–22.

Slack, Paul. 1988. *Poverty and Policy in Tudor and Stuart England.* London and New York: Longman.

Small, Albion Woodbury. 1909. *The Cameralists: The Pioneers of German Social Policy.* New York: Burt Franklin.

Smith, Adam. (1763) 1982. *Lectures on Jurisprudence,* edited by R. L. Meek, D. D. Raphael, and P. G. Stein. Vol. 5 of *The Glasgow Edition of the Works and Correspondence of Adam Smith.* Indianapolis, IN: Liberty Fund.

Smith, Adam. (1776) 1843. *An Enquiry into the Nature and Causes of the Wealth of Nations.* Edinburgh: Thomas Nelson.

Sommerville, Johann. 1994. "Absolutism and Royalism." In *The Cambridge History of Political Thought, 1450–1700,* edited by James Henderson Burns, 347–73. Cambridge: Cambridge University Press.

Spector, Céline. 2003. "Le concept de mercantilisme." *Revue de Métaphysique et de morale* 3: 289–310.

Starkey, Thomas. (1535) 1878. *England in the Reign of Henry the Eighth, a Dialogue between Cardinal Pole and Thomas Lupset.* London: N. Trübner & Co., for the Early English Text Society.

Starkey, Thomas. (1535) 1983. *A Dialogue between Pole and Lupset,* edited by Thomas F. Mayer. London: Royal Historical Society.

Stein, Peter. 1984. *Legal Institutions: The Development of Dispute Settlement.* London: Butterworths.

Steiner, Philippe. 1990. "Cameralisme et économie politique en Allemagne." *Revue économique* 41, no. 6: 1081–86.

Stolleis, Michael. 1982. "Rechtsstaat." In vol. 4 of *Handwörterbuch zur deutschen Rechtsgeschichte*, edited by Adalbert Erler, Ekkehard Kaufmann, and Dieter Werkmüller, 367–75. Berlin: Schmidt.

Stolleis, Michael. 1993. "Droit naturel et théorie générale de l'État dans l'Allemagne du XIXe siècle." *Le Débat* 74, no. 2: 63–73.

Stolleis, Michael. 1994. "L'idée de la raison d'État de Friedrich Meinecke et la recherche actuelle." In *Raison et déraison d'État: Théoriciens et théories de la raison d'État aux 16. et 17. siècles*, edited by Yves Charles Zarka, 11–39. Paris: Presses Universitaires de France.

Stolleis, Michael. 1998a. *La théorie du droit public impérial et la science de la police, 1600–1800.* Vol. 1 of *Histoire du droit public en Allemagne.* Translated from the German by Michel Senellart. Paris: Presses Universitaires de France.

Stolleis, Michael. 1998b. "'Arcana imperii' e 'ratio status': Osservazioni sulla teoria politica del primo Seicento." In *Stato e ragion di stato nella prima età moderna*, 31–68. Bologna: il Mulino.

Stolleis, Michael. 1998c. "Il leone e la volpe: Una massima politica del primo assolutismo." In *Stato e ragion di stato nella prima età moderna.* Bologna: il Mulino.

Stolleis, Michael. 1998d. "La ricezione di Lipsius nella letteratura giuridco-politica del Seicento in Germania." In *Stato e ragion di stato nella prima età moderna.* Bologna: il Mulino.

Stolleis, Michael. 2001. *Public Law in Germany, 1800–1914.* Vol. 2. New York and Oxford: Bergham Books.

Stuardi, Donatella Marocco. 1988. "*Police* e pubblica amministrazione nella *République* di Jean Bodin." *Filosofia politica* II, no. 1: 15–35.

Sueur, Philippe. 2001a. *La constitution monarchique.* Vol. 1 of *Histoire du droit public français XVe–XVIIIe siècle: La genèse de l'État contemporain.* Paris: Presses Universitaires de France.

Sueur, Philippe. 2001b. *Affirmation et crise de l'État sous l'Ancien régime.* Vol. 2 of *Histoire du droit public français XVe–XVIIIe siècle: La genèse de l'État contemporain.* Paris: Presses Universitaires de France.

Suppa, Silvio. 1992. "Ragione politica e ragione di Stato: Rileggendo Machiavelli e Botero." In *Botero e la Ragion di Stato. Atti del convegno in memoria di Luigi Firpo*, edited by Artemio Enzo Baldini. Florence: Leo S. Olschki Editore.

Tabacco, Giovanni. 2000. *Le ideologie politiche del medioevo.* Turin: Einaudi.

Tanner, Joseph Robson, ed. 1951. *Tudor Constitutional Documents, 1485–1603.* Cambridge: Cambridge University Press.

Tarello, Giovanni. 1976. *Storia della cultura giuridica moderna: Assolutismo e codificazione del diritto.* Bologna: il Mulino.

Taswell-Langmead, Thomas Pitt. 1960. *English Constitutional History from the Teutonic Conquest to the Present Time.* Boston and London: Sweet & Maxwell.

Tawney, Richard Henry. 1923. *Religion and the Rise of Capitalism.* West Drayton: Pelican Books.

Tenenti, Aldo. 1992. "Dalla Ragion di Stato di Machiavelli a quella di Botero." In *Botero e la Ragion di Stato. Atti del convegno in memoria di Luigi Firpo*, edited by Artemio Enzo Baldini. Florence: Leo S. Olschki Editore.

Tierney, Brian. 1963. "Bracton on Government." *Speculum* 38, no. 2: 295–317.

Townsend, Joseph. (1786) 1971. *A Dissertation on the Poor Laws by a Well-Wisher to Mankind.* Berkeley, CA: University of California Press.

Tribe, Keith. 1988. *Governing Economy: The Reformation of German Economic Discourse 1750–1840*. Cambridge: Cambridge University Press.

Tuck, Richard. 1993. *Philosophy and Government, 1572–1651*. Cambridge, London, and New York: Cambridge University Press.

Ullmann, Walter. 1975. *Medieval Political Thought*. Harmondsworth: Penguin Books.

Van Caenegem, Raul C. 1973. *The Birth of the English Common Law*. Cambridge: Cambridge University Press.

Van Caenegem, Raul C. 1987. *Judges, Legislators, and Professors: Chapters in European Legal History*. Cambridge: Cambridge University Press.

Van Caenegem, Raul C. 1988. "Government, Law and Society." *The Cambridge History of Medieval Political Thought, 350–1450*, edited by James Henderson Burns. Cambridge: Cambridge University Press.

Vasoli, Cesare. 1992. "Il carattere naturale dello Stato e la sua patologia nella tradizione politica aristotelica." In *Aristotelismo politico e ragion di Stato. Atti del convegno internazionale di Torino 11–13 febbraio 1993*, edited by Artemio Enzo Baldini. Florence: Leo S. Olschki Editore.

Vasoli, Cesare. 1994. "Machiavel inventeur de la raison d'Etat? " In *Raison et déraison d'état: Théoriciens et théories de la raison d'état aux XVIe et XVIIe siècles*, edited by Yves Charles Zarka, 43–66. Paris: Presses Universitaires de France.

Viroli, Maurizio. 1992. "Il significato storico della nascita del concetto di ragion di Stato." In *Aristotelismo politico e ragion di Stato. Atti del convegno internazionale di Torino, 11–13 febbraio 1993*, edited by Artemio Enzo Baldini, 67–82. Florence: Leo S. Olschki Editore.

Vives, Juan Vincens. 1971. "La struttura amministrativa statale nei secoli XVI–XVII." In vol. 1 of *Lo Stato moderno*, edited by Ettore Rotelli and Pierangelo Schiera, 221–46. Bologna: il Mulino.

Von Berg, Günther Heinrich. 1799–1809. *Handbuch des Teutschen Policeyrechts*. Hannover: Hahn.

Von Friedeburg, Robert. 1996. "Die Ordnungsgesetzgebung Englands in der frühen Neuzeit." In *Policey im Europa der frühen Neuzeit*, edited by Michael Stolleis. Frankfurt am Main: Vittorio Klosterman.

Von Hohenthal, P. C. W. 1774. *Dissertatio de ambitu politiae eiusque a justitia discrimine*. Leipzig: n.p.

Von Humboldt, Wilhelm. (1792) 1969. *The Limits of State Action*. Cambridge: Cambridge University Press.

Von Jakob, Ludwig Heinrich. 1805. *Grundsätze der National-Ökonomie oder National-Wirtschaftslehre*. Halle: Russischen Verlagsbuchhandlung.

Von Justi, Joachim Heinrich Gottlob. (1755) 1963. *Staatswirtschaft oder Systematische Abhandlung aller ökonomischen und Kameralwissenschaften die zur Regierung eines Landes erfordert werden*. 2 vols. Aalen: Scientia.

Von Justi, Joachim Heinrich Gottlob. 1756. *Grundsätze der Policey-Wissenschaft*. Göttingen: Im Verlag der Wittwe Vandenhoeck.

Von Justi, Joachim Heinrich Gottlob. 1758–61. *Vollständige Abhandlung von den Manufakturen und Fabriken*. Copenhagen: n.p.

Von Justi, Joachim Heinrich Gottlob. 1760. *Die Natur und das Wesen der Staaten*. Berlin, Settin, and Leipzig: n.p.

Von Justi, Joachim Heinrich Gottlob. (1761–64) 1970. *Gesammelte Politische und Finanz-Schriften über wichtige Gegenstände der Staatskunst, der Kriegswissenschaften und des Kameral- und Finanzwesens*. 3 vols. Aalen: Scientia.

Von Justi, Joachim Heinrich Gottlob. 1766. *System des Finanzwesens.* Halle: n.p.

Von Mohl, Robert. 1833. *Die deutsche Polizeiwissenschaft nach den Grundsätzen des Rechtsstaats.* Tübingen: H. Laupp.

Von Schmoller, Gustav, et al., eds. 1894–1935. *Acta Borussica: Die Behördenorganisation und die allgemeine Staatsverwaltung Preußens im 18. Jahrhundert.* 15 vols. Berlin: n.p.

Von Unruh, Georg Christoph. 1983a. "Polizei, Polizeiwissenschaft und Kameralistik." In *Vom Spatmittelalter bis zum Ende des Reiches.* Vol. 1 of *Deutsche Verwaltungsgeschichte,* edited by Kurt Jeserich, Hans Pohl, and Georg Christoph von Unruh, 388–427. Stuttgart: Deutsche Verlags-Anstalt.

Von Unruh, Georg Christoph. 1983b. "Die Veränderungen der preußischen Staatsverfassung durch sozial- und Verwaltungsreformen." In *Vom Reichsdeputations-Hauptschluss bis zur Auflösung des deutschen Bundes.* Vol. 2 of *Deutsche Verwaltungsgeschichte,* edited by Kurt Jeserich, Hans Pohl, and Georg Christoph von Unruh, 399–469. Stuttgart: Deutsche Verlags-Anstalt.

Wagner, Donald. 1935. "Coke and the Rise of Economic Liberalism." *The Economic Historic Review* VI, no. 1: 30–44.

Weber, Max. (1922) 1978. *Economy and Society: An Outline of Interpretative Sociology,* edited by Guenther Roth and Claus Wittich. Berkeley, Los Angeles, London: University of California Press.

Weston, Corrine. 1995. "England: Ancient Constitution and Common Law." In *The Cambridge History of Political Thought, 1450–1700,* edited by James Henderson Burns, 374–411. Cambridge: Cambridge University Press.

Wolff, Christian. 1764. *Ius naturae methodo scientifica pertractatum.* Frankfurt and Leipzig: Ære Societatis Venetæ.

Wood, Neal. 1998. "Foundations of Political Economy: The New Moral Philosophy of Sir Thomas Smith." In *Political Thought and the Tudor Commonwealth: Deep Structure, Discourse and Disguise,* edited by Paul A. Fideler and Thomas F. Mayer, 140–68. London and New York: Routledge.

Zanini, Adelino. 1997. *Adam Smith: Economia, morale, diritto.* Milan: Bruno Mondadori.

Zanini, Adelino. 2006. "Invarianza neoliberale: Foucault e l'economia politica." In *Governare la vita,* edited by Sandro Chignola, 117–52. Verona: Ombre Corte.

Zarka, Yves Charles. 1994a. "Raison d'État et figure du prince chez Botero." In *Raison et déraison d'état: Théoriciens et théories de la raison d'état aux XVIè et XVIIè siècles,* edited by Yves Charles Zarka, 101–20. Paris: Presses Universitaires de France.

Zarka, Yves Charles. 1994b. "Raison d'État, maximes d'État et coups d'État chez Gabriel Naudé." In *Raison et déraison d'état: Théoriciens et théories de la raison d'état aux XVIè et XVIIè siècles,* edited by Yves Charles Zarka, 151–69. Paris: Presses Universitaires de France.

Zeeveld, Gordon W. 1948. *Foundations of Tudor Policy.* Cambridge, MA: Harvard University Press.

Zincke, Georg Heinrich. 1742. *Grundriss einer Einleitung zu den Cameral-Wissenschaften.* Leipzig: n.p.

Zincke, Georg Heinrich. 1751–52. *Cameralisten Bibliothek.* 4 vols. Leipzig: C. L. Jacobi.

Index

62–4; Machiavellian break 58–62; *prudentia civilis* 63, 64–8
governmentality 4–5
Grossi, P. 11, 13, 16, 17, 18, 20, 21, 47
Guicciardini, Francesco 57, 58
Gutting, G. 7
Gutton, J.-P. 132
Guy, J. 74, 75, 76, 78

Haakonssen, K. 177
Hacking, I. 7
Hale, Sir Matthew 135
Harrington, J.F. 132
Härter, K. 4, 140
Hartung, F. 21
Haruel, L. 36
health 127–8, 129, 214
Heath, Sir Robert 84
Heckscher, E.J. 23
Hegel, G.W.F. 174
Heidenhamer, A.J. 23, 87
Henry IV 35
Hespanha, A.M. 11, 20
Hill, C. 85
Himmelfarb, G. 183, 186, 187, 205
Hintze, O. 13, 14, 25
Hobbes, T. 48, 86
Holdsworth, W.S. 26, 27, 28, 29, 30, 31, 32, 78, 79, 81, 84, 87, 116, 123, 130, 133
Hommel, C.F. 112
Hostiensis 50
Hubatsch, W. 41, 44, 45

idleness 129, 164, 183, 193, 199, 202, 203; ambiguity 140; Bentham 189, 190; cities of Late Middle Ages 132; Colquhoun 197–8; demoralization 129; information gathering 136; poverty: ill policy and 134; public-works system 133; welfare system 133; Wolff 102
indigence 184, 188–9, 194, 195–7, 199, 201
information gathering on the population 136–40
information sharing: London justices of the peace 192
Isambert, François-André 152
Isidore of Seville 17
Italy 207

iurisdictio 8, 10–11, 16–21, 23, 25, 38, 39, 44, 47, 53, 72, 78, 97, 112, 143, 148; centralization and institutionalization of judicial organs 19–21; liberalism 146–7; polity of estates (*Ständestaat*) 11–16; power to state what the law is and to enact justice 18

James I 81, 82
Jones, W.R.D. 74, 75, 76, 77, 78, 79, 80, 81, 85, 86, 87
Justi, Johann Heinrich Gottlob von 107–12, 115, 117–19, 120, 121, 122, 124, 125, 126, 127, 128, 129, 144, 174
Justinian 21, 51

Kant, I. 165–6, 167
Kantorowicz, E.H. 22
Kaplan, S. 130, 131, 136, 137, 151
Kelley, D.R. 80
Kenyon, J.P. 81, 82–3
Knemeyer, F.-L. 98
Koselleck, R. 169

La Maire, Jean-Baptiste-Charles 97, 117, 142–3, 144, 145
Laborier, P. 164
Lambarde, W. 30, 116
land 150, 151
Lazzeri, C. 58
Le Clere, Marcel 201, 202
Lee, Melville 72–3
Lefevre, Charles Shaw 201
Legendre, P. 93
Levy Peck, L. 81, 82
lex mercatoria 20, 22
liberal governance and public security 146–9, 214; decline of *Polizeiwissenschaft* 164–75; emergence of administration 149–64; government of social danger 200–6; liberal police 176–200, 214–15
liberal police 176–200, 214–15; birth of economic reason and police 177–82; police of the metropolis 191–200; principle of population 182–90
limited monarchy 26, 31, 34, 35, 39, 73–4, 76, 78, 102
Lindenfeld, D. 170, 173, 174
Lipsius, Justus 63–4, 67, 68, 114–15
Lis, C. 132
Locke, John 86
Louis XIII 35